The Complete Journals of

L.M. Montgomery

The PEI Years, 1901–1911

Mary Henley Rubio
Elizabeth Hillman Waterston

OXFORD
UNIVERSITY PRESS

OXFORD
UNIVERSITY PRESS

Oxford University Press is a department of the University of Oxford.
It furthers the University's objective of excellence in research, scholarship,
and education by publishing worldwide. Oxford is a registered trade mark of
Oxford University Press in the UK and in certain other countries.

Published in Canada by
Oxford University Press
8 Sampson Mews, Suite 204,
Don Mills, Ontario M3C 0H5 Canada

www.oupcanada.com

Database right Oxford University Press (maker)

First Edition published in 1985/1987.

Library and Archives Canada Cataloguing in Publication
Montgomery, L. M. (Lucy Maud), 1874–1942
The complete journals of L.M. Montgomery : the PEI years, 1901–1911 /
edited by Mary Henley Rubio and Elizabeth Hillman Waterston.

Includes index.
ISBN 978-0-19-900211-5

1. Montgomery, L. M. (Lucy Maud), 1874–1942—Diaries.
2. Montgomery, L. M. (Lucy Maud), 1874–1942—Sources.
3. Novelists, Canadian (English)—20th century—Diaries.
4. Prince Edward Island—Intellectual life—20th century.
I. Rubio, Mary, 1939– II. Waterston, Elizabeth, 1922– III. Title.

PS8526.O55Z53 2013   C813'.52   C2012-905701-0

Cover image: Photograph of L.M. Montgomery, used by permission of the
L. M. Montgomery Collection, Archives and Special Collections, University of Guelph Library.

Printed and bound in the United States of America

1 2 3 4 — 16 15 14 13

Contents

The Complete Journals of L.M. Montgomery

The PEI Years, 1901–1911

Acknowledgements

We happily acknowledge that many helped create this unabridged edition of L.M. Montgomery's Prince Edward Island journals (1889 to 1911). People keenly interested in both Prince Edward Island and the writings of Montgomery acted as tireless aids in our research and as eagle-eyed scrutinizers of our notes: Beth Cavert, Carolyn Collins, Betsy Epperly, Judith Fingard, Benjamin Lefebvre, Jennifer Litster, Jennie Macneill, Sandy Wagner, Christy Woster, and Emily Woster. Proofreaders who helped read this entire text against the original handwritten journals included Cadence Cook, Ciara Corbeil, and Tess Hudson. Writers in London, Ontario, and Sarasota, Florida, improved the wording of our introduction, and Theresa Lemieux bravely took on the job of scanning the images, among other work. Librarians at the University of Guelph and the University of Prince Edward Island stood by, including Kathryn Harvey, Bernard Katz, Simon Lloyd, Michael Ridley, Helen Salmon, and Darlene Wiltsie. Supportive members of the administration at these universities include Donald Bruce, Dean of Arts at Guelph, who came to our aid in funding some of the development costs, including the production of the Index. We again thank all those persons and agencies who contributed to the research and production of our 1985 publication, *The Selected Journals of L.M. Montgomery, Volume I.*

At Oxford University Press, Sherill Chapman created the elegant new format for these fully illustrated journals, and Ariel Bourbonnais stepped up to the big and challenging job of production editor, as did editor Katie Scott. Indefatigable Jennie Rubio has done double duty as our totally involved and perceptive in-house editor, and as one of the family members (including Jennie's daughter Ruby) who helped us meet our deadlines. The encouragement of Doug Waterston and Doug Killam has carried us through the joys and sorrows that beset us, as we once again relived those that beset L.M. Montgomery when she recorded her exuberant, troubled, inspiring, and fascinating life.

Mary Henley Rubio
Elizabeth Hillman Waterston

Publisher's Note

These journals were written over a century ago. This facsimile edition is an attempt to reproduce the original text in its entirety. In the decades since it was written, society's attitudes toward Canada's First Nations peoples and indeed the very terms used to denote those societies have changed greatly. These journals are, like any creative work, an artifact of their time, and it is only fair to say that the twenty-first century reader may stumble across the occasional expression no longer in common use.

Introduction

As the world moved toward the twentieth century, Maud Montgomery's moods swung between elation and despondency. Elation, because she had now established herself as a dependable, productive author of short stories and poems, and could look forward to making a living as a rare professional writer. Within a year, the Charlottetown *Patriot* would name her as one of Prince Edward Island's promising authors. Despondency, however, because of the deaths of her beloved father and of the young man who had aroused her passion, and the muddle of her feelings over the broken engagement with Ed Simpson. Her home life was still sadly limited by the dependency of her now-widowed, querulous grandmother. As the Victorian century ended, L.M. Montgomery could still dance with the daffodils, and rage like the sea.

A reader of the earlier journals could never imagine, any more than Montgomery herself could, the changes that were to come. New intense friendships, a new and unusual romance; astonishing success as a writer. Nor could such a reader guess at the changes in depth and flexibility that would develop in the journals themselves. They had taken on a life of their own. Montgomery increasingly used them as an artist's workshop, trying out themes and reworking memories. Each successive year both increased the pace of the life story and deepened the power of the autobiographical prose.

As an adolescent, Maud Montgomery had travelled across the Canadian continent to spend a year in a western prairie town, less settled and orderly than Cavendish. In the more mature years covered in this next part of the journals she would venture beyond her Island home again, first to the bustling workplace of a Halifax newspaper, and later to the complex Boston of her sophisticated publisher.

Matching this expansion of her physical world, she would voyage more daringly into an inner life of memory and ideas, reading and thinking. She wrote clearly of experiences of clinical depression. She expanded poignantly on her sense of isolation and loneliness—strange, in the face of the gossipy life buzzing around her in the Macneill home, which served as the busy local post office. She lingered briefly over the fun she had when her friend Nora Lefurgey boarded with the Macneills, but left the exuberant record of a happy shared season aside when creating the full-length copy of the journals, carefully written out between 1918 and 1922.

The handwritten volumes are also strangely reticent about the secretive courtship developing at the very time she was writing *Anne of Green Gables*—a major time of creativity, also strangely by-passed in the record. This reticence is fascinating. One would think she would have recounted some enthusiasm about the coming of Ewan Macdonald into her life, or revealed some of the afflatus of the time when red-headed Anne stood at her elbow as she wrote. Readers will be lured into sleuthing, wanting to read between the lines of this otherwise so expansive diary.

In her accomplishments as a prose writer, this was the most successful period of Montgomery's life. The verve and the sweetness of *Anne of Green Gables* (1908), *Anne of Avonlea* (1909), *Kilmeny of the Orchard* (1910), and *The Story Girl* (1911) are balanced and matched by the meditative rhythms of the darker passages and the bite of judgmental observations in the journals. Grateful for this double glory of gifts, readers will rejoice that at the end of her Prince Edward Island years, in spite of woeful interludes L.M. Montgomery experienced a time of authorial pride and a hope of personal happiness.

JOURNAL
Volume II[1]

L.M. Montgomery

January 5, 1901–February 7, 1910

---

1. This is the continuation of the second handwritten journal by L.M. Montgomery. Her journal entries from April 25, 1897, to December 22, 1900, are covered in the first book, *The Complete Journals of L.M. Montgomery: The P.E.I. Years, 1889–1900*.

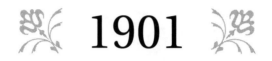# 1901

Saturday, Jan. 5, 1901
Cavendish, P.E.I.

This is the twentieth century! There has been a great deal said and written about it, so I shall not contribute any platitudes. After all, the distinction is only an arbitrary and sentimental one. I'm too cold to romance about it anyway, for I've just come in from a walk and am tingling all over, but my hands are numb. It was glorious out tonight, even though the mercury was near zero. It was calm and clear and there was such splendid colour and light, from which all the sensuous element had been eliminated leaving nothing but the pure spirit. It gave me the delicious sensation of being *all* soul, with no wretched, hampering body at all. But there *was* a body and it got very cold, and has been shivering ever since, poor thing.

I have been sitting at the window for the last ten minutes, looking out on the orchard, white and still under the moon, all ebony of shadow and silver of crusted snow, in the centre level and lustrous as a pavement of pearl, but around the fences carved by the chisel of the last northeaster into quaint cornices and curves. Over it all the delicate tracery of shadows where the trees stand up leafless, in seeming death and sorrow. But it is only seeming. The life-blood is at their hearts and by and by it will stir and they will clothe themselves in bridal garments of young green leaves and pink blossoms, and long lush grasses will wave where the snow lies now, and golden buttercups and white daisies will gleam among it. And, over where the biggest drift of all lies deep my garden plot will have its wealth of pansies and poppies and mignonette. But *now*—oh, the waiting is dreary!

Monday, Jan. 14, 1901
Cavendish, P.E.I.

Tonight a Mr. Mellish[1] lectured in the hall. Mr. M. is a harmless looking fellow whose Shakespearean brow is probably due to premature baldness, as he is certainly not overburdened with intellect. Nevertheless there is a certain aura of romance and interest surrounding him from the fact that he is one of the "First Contingent."[2] He lectured on the war and stuttered most abominably. I do hate listening to a man who stutters—I always want madly to get up and help him out. But in spite of this drawback and several others the lecture was passably interesting—couldn't help being so, considering the subject.

---

1. Perhaps Isaac Mellish of Halifax, Methodist schoolmaster.
2. Veterans of the first group of Canadian artillerymen in the Boer War arrived back in Halifax on December 23, 1900.

Wednesday, Jan. 23, 1901

Today when the mail came I pounced on the *Daily Patriot*—published yesterday—and the first thing I saw, blazoned in great black letters across the page, was "The Queen died today."[1]

The news was expected for she had been very ill and little hope was held of her recovery. Still, it was a very decided shock. One felt as if the foundations of all existing things were crumbling and every trustworthy landmark swept away. Who ever thought that Queen Victoria *could* die? "The queen" seemed a fact as enduring and unchangeable as the everlasting hills. The sense of loss seems almost personal.

Feb. 10, 1901
Bideford, P.E.I.

Here I am in Bideford—have been here for nine days, every one of which save yesterday has been stormy—snowing or raining, sometimes both, and always blowing night and day. The weather clerk seems to have turned on all the taps at once in a fit of absentmindedness or malice prepense. However, for the one fine day, let us be thankful.

I left home Friday, Feb. 1. Henry McLure drove me over to Park Corner which when we reached it we found deserted by all save Uncle John, the rest having gone to a concert in Irishtown, leaving instructions for us to follow. So I rushed up to Stell's room and prinked, Uncle John coming to my aid by bringing me a pair of curling tongs—something no other man I know would ever have thought of. We then went on to the concert and had a very hilarious time.

The next morning we went to Kensington where I took the train and left poor H. looking blue and cold—at least I suppose it was the cold!—on the platform.

I have not been possessed with any burning desire to revisit Bideford, as might be imagined from my rushing away up here in the dead of winter. But Edith England's father died last fall and her mother and she are all alone and very lonely. They implored me to come up and see them and so I came. I reached the old Ellerslie station about

Ellerslie Station

---

1. Victoria ascended the throne in 1837.

three P.M. Shall I ever forget the first time I saw it? It is the same old place grimy and grubby as of yore, with the same unwashed crowd hanging about it.

Edith met me, I found her very much changed—so thin and pale. Her trouble has aged her, poor baby. She is really nothing more than a baby in many respects. Just now she is a bundle of nerves and whims, some of which latter I cannot, in spite of my sympathy for her, call anything but arrant nonsense. Edith has been so petted and spoiled all her life that misfortune and trouble tell more heavily on her than on one better inured to "the slings and arrows of outrageous fortune."[1]

Last Sunday it stormed and I could not get to church, much to my disappointment, so I decided to stay over for another Sunday, although I had meant to go yesterday. But today is worse than ever so all hope of being benefitted by the pungent exhortations of the Rev. Mr. Pepper[2] is gone!

Monday—Tuesday—Wednesday—storm. I read novels, did fancy work, gossipped, yawned, slept—but must confess the time went slowly. To make matters worse there was no mail this week, owing to the ice blockade in the strait. Here, surrounded by huge drifts, we seem almost buried.

Thursday afternoon we were invited down to Mr. Williams to tea and got down in spite of the storm. We had a very pleasant time. The big drifts over in the parsonage yard looked very familiar. How I would have liked to revisit the dear old parsonage. But it is overrun with little Peppers now who know not Joseph[3]—that is to say myself—and I did not dare venture in among them.

Shrieve Millar was there too that evening—the same old Shrieve. He is about the only one left out of all the Bideford boys I knew. The rest are married or gone. Lou Dystant is away in the States. I wonder if he has quite forgotten the naughty little "schoolmarm" who used to have so many drives behind "Miss Flo."

Yesterday was our one fine day and I went down and spent it with the Millars. I had a very nice time, too. Nettie is married and away; Alice is quite a big girl and has improved considerably since her tomboy period.

I leave tomorrow—if I can get, that is. The roads are all but impassable. I feel sorry to go, since I hardly ever expect to be here again and Bideford is a place I always liked. But there is no use wearing out one's gray matter harbouring regrets of this nature so I will resolutely become cheerful at once. Watch me grinning!

---

1. Third line in the soliloquy "To be or not to be" in Shakespeare's *Hamlet* III.i.
2. Probably Rev. John R. Pepper, a Maritimer who attended Ecumenical Methodist conference in Toronto, 1901.
3. A favourite saying of LMM and her family. Pharaoh in Egypt "knew not Joseph." Exodus 1:8.

Feb. 22, 1901
Seaview, P.E. Island.[1]

I left Bideford the morning, after my last entry—left it in a snowstorm, somewhat dubious as to where my next camping ground might be for the trains were running very irregularly on account of the snow blockades. However, one did come along, well bearded with snow, and I climbed on it.

Uncle Robert's

I reached Kensington about three and found nobody to meet me. I was booked to spend a week at Uncle Robert Sutherland's at Seaview and had written them to meet me but the storm and bad roads had evidently been too much for them. I went to Alvin Glovers[2] and stayed there until Thursday night; and every minute of the time it snowed and drifted. Finally my cousin Leigh[3] turned up and I reached Seaview in due time.

I have had a lovely time here and only wish I could stay longer. For one thing, I've revelled in book—stacks of novels which Jack and Will have brought home in vacations. The best of them was *The Cardinal's Snuff box.*[4] It was froth—but such delicious froth.

Marian and I have done a lot of driving around, visiting relatives and friends. But what I have enjoyed most was the sense of being "at home"—in a congenial atmosphere where nothing occurred to set the teeth of my spirit on edge. Say what you will, our external surroundings have a great deal to do with our moods.

Marian

---

1. PEI village near Malpeque Bay, home of LMM's Uncle Robert and Aunt Margaret Montgomery Sutherland, parents of Jack, Will, Marian, and three other young people.

2. Alvin Glover (1869–1925). The Glovers owned property a few blocks south of Kensington Station. Perhaps LMM knew the family through Margaret MacLeod of French River (1871–1963), who had married Alvin two years previously.

3. Herbert Leigh Donald (1875–1963), a distant cousin through his mother, Christy Ann Simpson Donald, a Montgomery descendant.

4. A witty Catholic novel (1898) by prolific Henry Harland (1861–1905), an American writer who moved to London, joined the Aesthetic movement, and converted to Roman Catholicism.

March 2, 1901
Park Corner, P.E.I.

As I am going home tomorrow I might as well bring this journal up to date—that is if George and Stella will leave me in peace long enough. However, George has gone to bed, Frede has gone down to entertain a beau, and Stella and I are here in our room.

Stella's room

I came down here last Saturday evening and a few minutes later Henry McLure arrived on his way home from Malpeque. He was stormstaid here over Sunday and so also was Jack Whitehead,[1] and we had no end of fun.

Freak snap of Stella with "Maggie" in her lap. Henry McLure, George Campbell and Jack Whitehead with girls' hat on.

This is certainly the greatest house in the world for fun. We have had so many jolly rackets here that the very walls seem to be permeated with the essence of "good times." From my earliest recollection a visit to Park Corner was the greatest treat in the world. Each room has its memories—the kitchen where we toasted our toes at the glowing old "Waterloo," the front rooms where we spent so many jolly evenings, the big bedrooms upstairs where we slept and talked; and best of all, that famous old pantry, stored with good things, into which it was our habit to crowd at bedtime and gnaw bones, crunch fruitcake and scream with laughter. That pantry is historical.

The pantry

There is a certain old screw[2] sticking out from the wall on the first stair landing which always

---

1. LMM's photo of Henry McLure, George and Stella Campbell, and "Jack Whitfield" is now at University of Guelph. The journal perhaps names "Jack Whitehead" in error.

2. This is still shown to tourists at the Park Corner home of the Campbell family.

makes me realize clearly that I am grown up. When I used to visit Park Corner in the dawn of memory that screw was just on a level with my nose. *Now*, it comes to my knees! I used to measure myself with it every time I went over.

I miss Clara very much. There is a sympathy between her and me that does not and cannot exist between Stella and me. Stella is the girl for fun and jollity and *surface* things but I could never confide in her as I can in Cade. The dear old days are gone and can never return. There are times when I would give much to be as care-free and *blind* as I was then. Only at times though. Generally I am sane enough to prefer clear-sightedness to a fool's paradise.

Speaking of Henry I have disposed of him as kindly as possible. He had begun to grow foolish in spite of my strictly friendly attitude. I certainly never gave him any encouragement. He admitted that himself but said he had always loved me, long before he began to drive me about. I have often thought of telling him plainly that we must stop going around together because of gossip. But he was always talking of going west in a short time and I hoped he would, and so bring the affair to an easy and natural termination. But he never went and last summer when we were up here he told me he loved me. I told him he was very foolish and talked to him after a sensible fashion—as if that ever did any good. But then, one had to say something. Last Saturday evening I told him flatly that we must not drive about together any longer. We had a painful but—I hope—a conclusive interview.

Monday, March 4, 1901
Cavendish, P.E.I.

Came home yesterday. Found a mountain of mail awaiting me and I have been answering business letters all day—too busy to be lonely.

Two of my letters were quite nice. One was from a certain Alfred Mason,[1] who, it seems is an organist of Pittsfield, Mass., and who says he has taken a great fancy to those verses of mine "A Pair of Slippers" and wants my permission to publish them as a song with the music he had written for them. Oddly, enough, the other letter was similar in kind, being from a Miss Chadkins[2] of Boston who wants to set "When the Fishing Boats Come In" to music. Of course I am pleasantly tickled.

---

1. Alfred Mason (1866–1955), born in Ohio, active in the development of the Association for Publication of American Music, and a founder of the Music Educators National Council in 1907. LMM's scrapbook contains a program from the premiere at a musical in Pittsfield of his setting of her poem.

2. No references found to this musician.

Wednesday, Mar. 6, 1901

Today when I picked up the *Daily Patriot* the first thing I saw was a long editorial in which somebody had laid himself out to write up all the "poets" of this tight little island. Half way down this outburst I came upon my own name written out in cold-blooded fullness—"Lucy Maud Montgomery"—which I detest! I was catalogued as "the foremost of the younger school of writers," and then followed several paragraphs of compliments and quotations.

I laid the paper down with a little smile and a little heartache. Long ago, in old schooldays, this would have seemed to me a very lofty height of ambition. Olive Schreiner says, "When all the sweetness is taken out of the things we long for—they come."[1] Perhaps not *all* the sweetness was taken out of this little morsel of fame. It *did* please me, not because of its praise but because it was the visible testimony of a place won for myself by hard toil. But the pleasure was mingled with a pain still keener—for *who was there to care?* Since father died—no one. How proud and delighted he would have been. But now what does it matter? My success can please no one but myself. I am alone.

Life has never seemed the same to me since father died. Something is *gone* and in its place is a pain and loneliness and longing that is sometimes dulled but is always there. I do not mean to say I am unhappy. I am not. But my existence is a sort of *negative* affair. I enjoy life on the whole and have beautiful moments. I have success in a growing measure and a keen appreciation of all the world and the times offer for delight and interest. But underneath it all is the haunting sense of *emptiness*.

Friday, March 21, 1901
Cavendish, P.E.I.

"Munsey's" came today with my poem "Comparisons," in it, illustrated. It really *looked* nice. I've been quite in luck of late for several new magazines have taken my work.

I *know* that I am improving in regard to my verses. I suppose it would be odd if I did not, considering how hard I study and work. Moreover, I feel that I am developing. Every now and then I write a poem that serves as a sort of landmark to emphasize this fact. I know looking back, that I could not have written it six months or a year ago, any more than I could have then worn a garment the material of which was then unwoven. I have

---

1. Misquoted from Schreiner's *The Story of an African Farm*, chapter 2, XIV.

written two poems this week. A year ago I *could not* have written them, but now they came easily and naturally. This encourages me. Perhaps in the future I can achieve something worthwhile. I never expect to be famous—I don't want to be, really, often as I've dreamed of it. But I *do* want to have a recognized place among good workers in my chosen profession. That, I honestly believe, is happiness and the harder to win the sweeter and more lasting when won.

I really think that I must possess the saving grace of perseverance. What failures and discouragements I used to meet at first when, in my teens, I sent out my wretched wretched little manuscripts—for they *were* wretched, although I thought them quite fine—with an audacity that I actually wonder at now. I cannot remember the time when I did not mean to be a writer "when I grew up." It has always been my central purpose around which every hope and effort and ambition of my life has grouped itself.

I remember—who could ever forget it?—the very first commendation my writing ever received. I was about twelve years old and I had a stack of "poems" written out and hidden jealously from all eyes—for I was very sensitive about my scribblings and could not bear the thought of having them seen by those who would probably laugh at them. Even then I felt strongly, though inarticulately, that there was no one about me who understood or sympathized with my aspirations. I was not like the other children around and I imagine that the older people of my small world thought there was something uncanny about me. I would have died rather than show to them those foolish, precious little rhymes of mine.

Nevertheless, I wanted to know what others would think of them—not from vanity but from a strong desire to find out if an impartial judge could see any merit in them. So I employed a pardonable little ruse to find out. It all seems very funny and a little pitiful to me now; but then it seemed to me that I was at the bar of judgement for all time. It would be too much to say that, had the verdict been unfavourable, I would have forever surrendered my dreams. But they would certainly have been frosted for a time.

A school-teacher was boarding here then—Izzie Robinson. I liked her not and she liked not me. Had I shown her a "poem" and asked her opinion of it I would certainly have received no encouragement. But she was something of a singer and one evening I timidly asked her if she had ever heard a song called "*Evening Dreams.*" She certainly had not, for the said *Evening Dreams* was a composition of my own which I then considered my finest effort. It is not now extant and I can remember the first two verses only. I suppose they were indelibly impressed on my memory by the fact that Miss R. asked me if I knew any words of the "song." Whereupon I, in a trembling voice, repeated the first two verses.

When the evening sun is setting
Quietly in the west,
In a halo of rainbow glory,
I sit me down to rest.

I forget the present and future,
I live over the past once more
As I see before me crowding
The beautiful days of yore.

Strikingly original! Also, a child of twelve would have a long "past" to live over!

I finished up with a positive gasp, but Miss R. was busy sewing and did not notice my pallor and general shakiness. For I *was* pale—it was a moment of awful import to me. She placidly said that she had never heard the song but that *the words were very pretty.*

Under the birches

The fact that she was quite sincere must certainly detract from her reputation for literary discrimination. But to me it was the sweetest morsel of commendation that had every fallen to my lot—or that *has* fallen since. Nothing has ever surpassed that delicious moment. I went out of the old kitchen as if I trod on the amber air of the summer evening and danced down the lane under the birches in a frenzy of delight, hugging to my heart the remembrance of those words.

It was a little bit ironical, was it not? that my first literary encouragement should have come from a person who was certainly not my friend and who would have bitten her tongue out before she would knowingly have praised me or my works.

Perhaps it was her dictum that encouraged me, sometime during the following winter, to essay my first step on the slippery path of literature. I wrote out my *Evening Dreams* very painstakingly—on both sides of the paper, alas—wrote them over many times before I got a copy to please me, and sent them to the editor of *The Household*,[1] an American family magazine which grandmother took. The idea of being *paid* for them never entered my head. Indeed, I am not at all sure that I knew at that time that people ever were paid for writing. At least my early dreams of future fame were untarnished by any mercenary speculations!

Alas! The editor of *The Household* was less complimentary but more discriminating than Miss R. He—or she—sent the verses back, although I had

---

1. This cheap home paper had developed into an excellent magazine.

not "enclosed a stamp" for the purpose, being in blissful ignorance of such a requirement.

By the way, I may state that the other day that same magazine took a poem of mine for the first time. But I don't think it has the same editor. There is quite a gap in time between that first rejection and this first acceptance—as wide a gap I daresay as that between the different poems—or between the writers thereof, for that matter.

My aspirations were nipped in the bud for a time. It was a year before I recovered from the blow. Then I essayed a more modest flight. I took my *Evening Dreams*, in which I still had some faith despite the cruel editor, copied them out afresh and sent them to the Charlottetown *Examiner* of weekly

Myself at the time of my first venture

appearance. I felt quite sure *it* would print them for it often printed verses which I thought and, for that matter, still think, were no better than mine.

For a week I dreamed delicious dreams of seeing my verses in the Poet's Corner, with my name appended thereto. I saw myself the wonder of my schoolmates—a little local celebrity. When the *Examiner* came I opened it with tremulous eagerness. Alas, there was not a sign of an evening dream about it.

Still, I did not quite despair. I thought it might appear in the next issue. But it did not. Then I gave up and drained the cup of failure to the very dregs. It seems all very amusing to me now but it was horribly real and tragic to me then. I was crushed in the very dust of humiliation and I had no hope of ever rising again. I burned my *Evening Dreams* and though I continued to write because I couldn't help it I sent no more to the cold and cruel editors.

I may say that all these doings were conducted in profound secrecy—a secrecy made possible by the fact of our having the post office. I smuggled my editorial correspondence into the letter packet myself, and so not a soul but myself knew of my *Evening Dreams* peregrinations. Thus, if I suffered over the loss of anticipated success I was spared the mortification of having anyone else know of my failure. I shut my pitiful little hopes and my still more pitiful little despairs up in my own soul and dreed my weird alone.

After this mortifying experience three years passed. Then I went out west. I still perpetrated things I called poems. They were pretty bad but they really were an improvement on *Evening Dreams*. By this time my long paralyzed ambition was beginning to recover and lift its head again. I wrote up the old Cape Leforce legend in rhyme—most of it was written at my desk in the old High School under Mr. Mustard's suspicious eye and in agonies of homesickness—and sent it down home to the *Patriot*. No more of the *Examiner* for me!

Four weeks passed. One Sunday afternoon, just as I was starting for Sunday School, father came in with the Saturday night's mail—the *Patriot* among it. I snatched it up, tore off the wrapper and saw my verses!

The first thing I did, before I ever read them myself, was to thrust the paper into father's hand in a tumult of joy and pride and then I rushed off to Sunday School in a whirl of excitement. It was the first sweet bubble on the cup of success and of course it intoxicated me. When I got home from Sunday School I took the paper and stole off by myself to gloat over it. There were some fearful printer's errors in it which made the flesh creep on my bones, but it was *my* poem and in a real newspaper. The moment we see our first darling brain child arrayed in black type is never to be forgotten. It must have in it, I think, some of the wonderful awe and delight that comes to a mother when she looks for the first time on the face of her first born.

During that winter and the following summer I had other verses and some prose articles printed. My little *Marco Polo* story appeared in the Montreal *Witness* and my article on Saskatchewan came out in the *Times* and was copied and commented on favourably by several metropolitan papers. Also, several effusions on "June" and kindred subjects were published in that long-suffering *Patriot*. I was beginning to plume myself on being quite a literary person.

But the demon of filthy lucre was creeping into my heart. I wrote a story and sent it to the New York *Sun*. I didn't know one thing about said *Sun*; I had never even seen a copy of it; but I had been told it paid for articles. The New York *Sun* sent my story back to me. I flinched, as from a slap in the face—but I kept on writing. I had, even then, learned the first, last, and middle lesson "Never Give Up."

I may remark just here that one day last fall I took the plot of that identical story, wrote it up, sent it off, and took first prize[1] in a story competition. But needless to say it was entirely unlike its former incarnation.

I went on sending things away and getting them back. But one day, during my P.W.C., year, I went to the Ch'town post office and got a thin letter with the address of a third-rate magazine in the corner. In it was a brief note accepting a poem "Only a Violet," which I had sent to *The Ladies' World* and offering in payment two subscriptions to the magazine. I kept one myself and gave the other to grandma; and those magazines, with their vapid little stories, were the first tangible recompense my pen brought me. However, the price was as good as the verses. They were trash. But I copy them here, because they were the first I ever had accepted *and* paid for.

---

1. "Pennington's Girl" won a prize in *Ladies' Journal* in 1900; "A Homesick Heart" earlier won $25 in the *Family Herald and Weekly Star*.

The Violet's Spell

Only a violet in the trodden street,
Breathing its purple life out 'neath the tread,
Of hundreds restless, eager, hurrying feet,
Ere set of sun the frail thing will be dead,
"Only a violet," so its loser said.

As in a dream the dusty street passed then,
Unheeded on my ear its tumult fell,
I saw a vision from the past again,
That wove across my heart a nameless spell,
Fond memories of a spot I once loved well.

A woodland lane where ferns grew green and tall,
And beeches wove their branches overhead.
All silence save some wild bird's passing call,
Or the swift echoing of a rabbit's tread;
'Neath those green arches fear and strife were dead.

Blue smiled the sky where through the fir trees green,
The summer sunshine fell in golden sheaves,
And shyly from beneath their mossy screen,
With half-averted face as one who grieves,
Blue violets peeped through last year's withered leaves.

And one was there with me whose voice and smile,
In keeping seemed with those fair joyous hours,
A face where Nature set her every wile,
And laughing eyes blue as the sweet spring flowers,
When wet with tear-drops of the Maytime showers.

Dear friends were we and hand in hand we went,
Down the green lane where sunshine thickly lay,
The soft, low voices of the woods were blent,
A drowsy cow-bell tinkled far away—
Heart spoke to heart that far, fair, sunny day.

For us the sunshine laughed, the wild birds sang,
The purple darlings of the spring were fair,
For us each vagrant note of music rang,
And every passing breeze was like a prayer,
Heart-whisperings of Nature everywhere.

The year I taught in Bideford I wrote a good deal and learned a good deal—but still my stuff came back, except from two magazines whose editors evidently thought that literature was its own reward, and quite independent of monetary considerations. I often wonder that I did not give up in utter discouragement. At first I used to feel dreadfully bad when a poem or story over which I had agonized and laboured came back with one of those icy little rejection slips. Tears of disappointment *would* come in spite of myself, as I crept away to hide the poor crumpled manuscript in the depths of my trunk. But after awhile I got hardened to it and did not mind. I only set my teeth and said "I *will* succeed." And never, at any time had I any *real* doubt that I would succeed at last. I cannot account for this abiding faith—this confidence in my star—but it was there. I believed in myself and I struggled on alone—always alone—in secrecy and silence. I never told my ambitions and efforts and failures to anyone. I listened unmoved to the sneers and ridicule of various relatives who thought my scribbling rank folly and waste of time. *That* never disturbed me at all. Down, deep down, under all discouragement and rebuff I knew I would "arrive" some day.

That day came at last in Halifax when I received a five dollar cheque from *Golden Days* for a story. It was the first money my pen had earned—it was not much in itself, but it stood for a vast deal to me. It was the first of the letters that spell success; and since that day I have gone on and on, meeting with failures in plenty still, but with enough successes to out balance them. Today I have a foothold. I *have* succeeded.

Sunday, April 14, 1901
Cavendish, P.E.I.

I went through a "scene" tonight that has left a very bad taste in my mouth. Am feeling too disturbed to sleep so will try if an entry in this long-suffering journal will compose my gray matter at all.

I thought that I had effectually disposed of Henry and would have no further trouble with him. I certainly made matters plain enough at our last interview. And I certainly thought he understood me for he said he did. That was a month ago. Since I came home I have not seen him until this evening, when he turned up at

Henry   Under the cherry trees

service in the Baptist Church. Coming home he came up to me. The others fell back, leaving us alone. I was very much annoyed that he should do this after my express dismissal but I would not humiliate him before "the crowd" by refusing to let him walk home with me. Well, we had our "scene"—all the way home and for a very bad quarter of an hour under the cherry trees. Henry was utterly unreasonable and though I tried to be patient with him it was rather up hill work. One would really suppose from the way he went on that he had totally forgotten everything I had said to him at Park Corner. He had the same old plea—he was going away in the fall and why couldn't we go about together for the summer.

I re-explained all my reasons patiently but poor Henry did not seem able to see their evident logic. He seemed to feel very badly and I felt sorry for him, bored as I was. But at last I had to tell him shortly to go. I also told him flatly that I would accept no more attentions from him. Surely he will realize that I mean it.

Sunday Morning
May 12, 1901
Cavendish, P.E.I.

I have just come in from a walk in the school woods—a walk surcharged with a pleasure so keen and elusive as to be almost pain. And before its evanescent aroma altogether fades I wish to imprison a little of it here, if possible, for future delectation.

It is an ideal day for a woodland ramble—a dreamy, balmy spring day when a south wind is purring through the trees and the very air throbs with pulses of reawakening life—a day when it is "bliss to be alive" in such a beautiful world.

In the woods it was as if one was in a temple. Overhead, in the resinous fir boughs, the wind was harping ever so softly. The aroma drifting under the mossy arches from old sunny hollows and lurking nooks was as the incense of worship. And the thoughts that came out of the great silence were as a prayer.

I went down the path to the brook—the path worn long ago by school children's feet. It has changed little. The ferns and leaves were poking greenly up in the shadow just as they used to do in other springs. The little wood-folk were watching me from their coverts and the call of the brook came up from the valley below with all its old allurement. After a time I came to it and followed its windings. It prattles and croons to itself. The venerable firs stretch their protecting arms over it, the mosses grow green on its banks;

the red-budded maples throw delicate etchings on its deep, placid pools. In its ripple and murmur the voices of dead days sounded—all the long unheard notes were there, blended with the sorrow inseparable from the by-gones. Every trill of laughter that ever echoed over it the brook caught and held—and now gives it out again to such as have ears to hear. Old dreams— one may see them reflected in its mirror, smiling back at the beholder with deceptive allurement. Old vows—old whispers—the brook keeps them all and murmurs of them—but there is none to listen save the wise spruces that have been listening so long.

But the woods are so full of life and golden promise and deep primal gladness that even the brook's song fails to hold us. It is sad—it is of the past—and we turn from it to listen to the voice of the woods—of that great calm eternal Nature with whom there is no past or present or future but only the wonderful prescience of immortal-ity. With her is "the fullness of joy."

So I left the brook crooning to itself and wandered to the upland again coming finally to a little glade where the sunshine came sifted in as soft as thistle down; and there in the grasses white violets were growing— tiny white blossoms with purple pencillings in their little urns that were filled with the most rarely distilled perfume. I brought

A little glade

some home with me and put them in a vase on my table—they are all that are left of this perfect hour—they and this record. But this record is a fail-ure. I have not succeeded in imprisoning the glamor that attended every step. It is of heaven and eternity and spirit and so can never be expressed in symbols of earth.

August 23, 1901
Cavendish, P.E.I.

Well, this is worse than usual! It is a matter of surprise to myself that I have really got so far as getting out this journal tonight. And now that I have got it out and put in a new pen to honour the occasion, I have nothing worth writing about. That is a rather satisfying epitome of a summer, is it not?

It is a divine harvest evening. I use the word "divine" advisedly and not as an outcropping of submerged schoolgirl gush. It *is* divine and one feels the divinity in its perfect beauty. There is a hazy sky—amethyst and rose and ethereal blue, with the white paper lantern of a half moon drifting downward to the gulf of sunset. There is a wind that plays a duet with the crickets, there are golden, sheaf-dotted harvest fields already bathed in the tranquillity of dew-fall, and there is over all the glamor and the dream that is August's dower. I'm going for a walk by and by, when the sunset has faded out and the moonlight has it all its own way. I've been lazy and idle this evening for I am tired. This has been a busy summer—busy and pleasant but rather monotonous.

Just then I had to lay down my pen and go out into the garden and pick beans. But then one can pick beans and think wonderful things at the same time, glory be! It is one of the blessings that we don't always have to put our souls into what our hands may be doing—praise the gods for otherwise who would have any soul left?

So I picked the beans and roamed the milky way in imagination, and afterwards went for a walk down the old shore lane—a lane so remote and lonely that one can think out loud in it without being mistaken for a lunatic.

I have been industrious and respectable all summer. Have written stories and letters, read novels, histories and encyclopedias, and gone to church painstakingly. I have picked berries, dabbled in fancy work and photography, made cakes, pies and puddings, called and received calls! I have piped and danced to other people's piping. I have laughed and wept, exulted and groaned, and I am tired, tired, tired, of it all. I wish I could go to sleep "for an eon or two." But, after all, that is extravagant. Eight hours sleep will do just as well and I will get up in the morning, rejoicing as a strong man to run a race.

Well, about these occupations of mine? Writing letters? Oh, I do it. I can't very well help it although, as regards a great many of them, I might prefer not to—for what is the use of writing letters when you can't put any soul into them? Or reading them, under the same disadvantage?

Some letters I love to write. I have plenty to say and my pen glides smoothly along the track of my thoughts until an epistle is produced to which I am not ashamed to sign my name. But there are other letters that I never sign for very shame of such silly inanities. These are the letters I hate to write and which I grind out mechanically to correspondents with whom I have ceased to have much in common, yet whose acquaintanceship I do not wish to lose altogether.

Then, church? I sometimes ask myself why, after all, I go to church so regularly. Well, I go for a jumble of reasons, some of which are very good, and others very flimsy and ashamed of themselves. It's the respectable thing to do—this is one of the flimsy ones—and I would be branded black sheep if I didn't go. Then, in this quiet, uneventful land, church is really a social function and the only regular one we have. We get out, see our friends and are seen of them, and air our best clothes which otherwise would be left for the most part to the tender mercies of moth and rust.

Oh, you miserable reasons! Now for a few better ones!

I go to church because I think it well to shut the world out from my soul now and then and look my spiritual self squarely in the face. I go because I think it well to search for truth everywhere, even if we never find it in its entirety; and finally I go because all the associations of the church and service make for good and bring the best that is in me to the surface—the memories of old days, old friends, and childish aspirations for the beautiful and sacred. All these come back, like the dew of some spiritual benediction—and so I go to church.

Then I have read—oh, my faithful old key to the gates of fairyland! Novels—some delightful ones, so delightful that I could not sleep until I had finished them but pulled my table to the bed, bolstered myself up with pillows, and read until the hero had reached the end of his adventures and I came back with a mental jolt to the real world, to discover that my oil had almost burned out, that my back and eyes were aching and that I was very sleepy.

However, I have not confined my reading exclusively or even mainly to fiction. History and biography I have revelled in, and in *encyclopedias*, too, having lugged two or three huge volumes home from the hall every month and browsed through them for miscellaneous information. When I get book hungry, even the whole of an encyclopedia is better than no loaf!

The window of my den

As for my pen scratchings, I have toiled away industriously this summer and ground out stories and verses on days so hot that I feared my very marrow would melt and my gray matter be hopelessly sizzled up. But oh, I love my work! I love spinning stories and I love to sit by the window of my den and shape some airy fancy into verse. I have got on well this summer and added several new journals to my list. They are a varied assortment and their separate tastes all have to be catered to. I write a lot of juvenile yarns. I like doing these but would like it better if I didn't have to lug a moral into most of them. They won't sell without it. The kind of juvenile story I like to write—and read, too, for the matter of that—is a rattling good jolly one—"art for art's sake"—or rather "fun for fun's sake"—with no insidious moral hidden away in it like a spoonful of jam. But the editors who cater to the "young person" take themselves too seriously for that and so in the moral must go, broad or narrow, as suits the fibre of the particular journal in view.

I intend going down to Halifax next month to attend the Exhibition. I feel that I must have a short outing to brace me up for the winter.

Cavendish, P.E.I.
Aug. 28, 1901

There is nothing in the world so sweet as a real, "old-timey" garden. I have always known this but it came home to me with fresh force yesterday afternoon when I was down at "old Mrs. George Macneills" taking some photos for Bessie. The photo part was a bore but the garden more than made up for it.

There are certain essentials to an old-fashioned garden. Without them it would not be itself. Like the poet it must be born not made—the outgrowth and flowering of long years of dedication and care. The least savor of newness or modernity spoils it.

For one thing, it *must* be secluded and shut away from the world—a "garden enclosed"—preferably by willows—or apple trees—or firs. It must have some trim walks bordered by clam-shells, or edged with "ribbon grass," and there must be in it the flowers that belong to old-fashioned gardens and are seldom found in the catalogues of today—perennials planted there by

The old garden

grandmotherly hands when the century was young. There should be poppies, like fine ladies in full-skirted silken gowns, "cabbage" roses, heavy and pink and luscious, tiger-lilies like gorgeously bedight sentinels, "Sweet-William" in striped attire, bleeding heart, that favourite of my childhood, southernwood, feathery and pungent, butter-and-eggs—that is now known as "narcissus"—"bride's bouquet," as white as a bride's bouquet should be, holly hocks like flaunting overbold maiden's, purple spikes of "Adam and Eve," pink and white "musk," "Sweet Balm" and "Sweet May," "Bouncing Bess" in her ruffled, lilac-tinted skirts, pure white "June lilies," crimson peonies—"pinies"—velvety-eyed "Irish Primroses," which were neither primroses nor Irish, scarlet lightning and Prince's feather—all growing in orderly confusion.

Dear old gardens! The very breath of them is a benediction.

Sunday Evening, Sept. 1, 1901
Cavendish, P.E.I.

I'm really having an extraordinary fit of virtue this week, as regards journal writing. But there has been no service in C. today and it has seemed

long. I have written letters galore and now to further beguile away the time I am writing in this journal.

I have just come in from my garden. Such comfort as I get out of it! To be sure, I've worked for it. Twice every day the whole summer have I faithfully toddled out and watered it when the continued drouth seems to parch the very souls out of my poor flowers—for flowers *have* souls! Don't tell me!! I've known roses I expect to meet in heaven.

The emerald green arch

My garden is rather far away and blushes unseen. One must go through the little gate, along the path under the emerald-green arch of the big sweet apple trees through clover and caraway to one's waist and finally away over in a little hollow of sunshine find my garden plot, full of splendid pink and white an crimson poppies, big white double pinks, crimson phlox, purple and yellow pansies, and daisies galore. And now the gladioli are coming out, regal and lovely and white and pink asters—that is the few asters that are left to come out. Most of them got eaten up with rust, poor things! I hope heaven is *all* flowers. One could be good easily if one lived in a lily!

Monday, Sept. 9, 1901
Cavendish, P.E.I.

This past week has been one of those of which people say—in perfect sincerity and yet not meaning a word of it—"I wouldn't live it over again for *anything* you could offer me." I have said it myself, although I know quite well that there are a good many things for which I would willingly live it over. But really, the inducement would have to be no trifling one.

Since last Monday evening I have been too busy to think straight. I've been getting ready to

New Church

Interior of new Church

go to Halifax, helping clean and decorate the new church for dedication services, finishing up a lot of photos and MS and cleaning house and baking for expected guests. Yesterday—Sunday—was a fine cool day and our "opening" was a success. It was the climax of the week's hard work although we did nothing but go to church and prepare meals. We had three services, morning, afternoon and evening, with just enough time between to scrape a bite together and "red up."

Wednesday, Nov. 13, 1901
The Echo Office
Halifax, N.S.

Yes, I think I can write it all up now. I have got over my first agony of loneliness and homesickness, I have become accustomed to my daily routine, and I have made a little niche for myself which is snug enough although somewhat narrow. So I think I have sufficient "sand"[1] to take up the thread of this journal where I dropped it two months ago.

The Echo Office

I am here alone in the office of "The Morning Chronicle" and "Daily Echo."[2] The paper has gone to press and the extra proofs have not yet begun to come down. Overhead they are rolling machines and making a diabolical noise which jars the shades on the Auer lights[3] wildly. Outside of my window the engine exhaust is puffing furiously. In the inner office the news-editor and the "Beach-comber" are having a friendly wrangle. And here sit I—*Echo* proof-reader and general handyman. Quite a "presto change" from last entry. I am a newspaper woman!

Myself at the date of my going to Halifax

---

1. Scottish dialect: strength, determination.

2. The Halifax Chronicle Company put out the *Echo* as an afternoon paper.

3. A beam directed across the presses to check the paper as it is printed.

Sounds nice? Yes, and the reality is very nice, too. Being of the earth, it is earthy and has its drawbacks. Life in a newspaper office isn't "all beer and skittles" any more than anywhere else. But on the whole it is not a bad life at all.

I left home on September 11. Just before I left I received a telegram from the *Echo* news-editor offering me the position of proof-reader for the winter. Lottie Shatford, who does a good deal of work for this concern, had recommended me to him.

I could not decide on the spot—I was dressed to go with the mailman to the train. However, I supposed that if I did take the place I'd have time to return home and pack my trunk at least. So I started gaily off—and haven't seen Cavendish since.

I stayed in Charlottetown from Wednesday to Friday and then came down to Halifax. Had a pleasant trip but reached Halifax at eight o'clock in a pouring rain. I took a cab and went to the W.C.A.[1] where I understood Bertha Clark had, according to promise, engaged a room for me. When, however, I rang the bell and so brought the secretary to the door I was posed by her information that no such room had been reserved.

I was fagged out after my day of travel and felt just like sitting down on my valise and crying, under the cabby's eye and all. However, I didn't. Perhaps it was out of consideration for cabman's feelings. More likely it was because the secretary hastened to add that they would take me in for the night anyhow.

So I limply paid my cabby and tugged my valise upstairs to a big barn-like apartment which, with its three cot beds, looked as much like a hospital ward as anything you can imagine. I gave myself a bit of a grooming and then went down to supper. But I was too tired to eat. After supper I went to bed. My roommates were a Miss Brag, who was a business college girl, and a Miss Messenger,[2] a Dalhousie college student. Just then however, I didn't know who they were and didn't care. I slept poorly, owing to the unaccustomed clang and clatter of the cars, and next morning I felt stiff and grumpy. It was pouring rain still and I toddled down to the *Echo* office in no very jubilant mood.

Eventually I found my way to the lair of the news-editor, Mr. Taunton,[3] and by him was referred to Mr. Dunn,[4] the business manager, with whom I had a confab. At first I hardly knew whether to take the place or not. The salary was only five dollars a week. But it was not so much money I was after

---

1. Women's Christian Association.

2. Stella Messinger, second-year medical student at Dalhousie University.

3. Mr. William D. Taunton, editor of *The Echo*.

4. Mr. John Dunn, director of both Halifax papers, the *Chronicle* and the *Echo*.

as experience and a *start* in journalism. So I finally agreed. I knew grandma could get Prescott to stay with her for the winter. He probably wouldn't like it, but he would be ashamed to refuse; and he and his have got enough—and *taken* enough, too—to pay him for it. Grandmother was willing for me to stay, also.

The worst of the business, however, was that I had to go right to work. There was no returning to Cavendish.

After leaving Mr. Dunn's sanctum with instructions to report myself for duty on Monday morning, I returned to the W.C.A. and went to bed, because, by this time, I felt really ill. That evening two more girls arrived and were deposited in our room. The secretary had agreed to keep me until I found a boarding house, if I "did not mind" sharing a room with as many others as could be stowed into it. I *did* mind; but as it seemed Hobson's choice I assented as cheerfully as possible.

As the next day was Sunday I spent the morning in bed and the afternoon in writing a letter home with instructions about the sending of my trunk. Then I resigned myself to spending a fortnight on the contents of a valise which had been packed with an eye single to visiting and carousing and not to working in an office. However, "needs must go when the devil drives."

After tea Sunday evening I went to see Bertha Clark. She is housekeeper at the Halifax Hotel[1] and is quite unchanged. What a comfort it is to find our friends unchanged. She is as jolly and friendly as in the days of yore when we were such chums at H.L.C.

At first I used to inflict myself on her every other night to exorcise my demon of nostalgia. Several times I have been down to dine with her—green oases in the desert of boarding house life. *I do like a good dinner*! I feel much more *Christianic* afterwards—just as good as gold and as if I could smile at anybody and any fate. I'm sure most of the crimes in the world must be committed by hungry people. I always feel "fit for treasons, stratagems and spoils" when I'm hungry. That is why I am cross and grumpy at the present moment. There is a fearful "goneness" in my inner girl.

Echo Office, Halifax, N.S.
Thursday, Nov. 14, 1901

I am still cross and hungry and grumpy—but fortunately haven't been so continually ever since my last entry. I was interrupted then and this is the

---

1.   Historic site at the corner of Halifax Common on Robbie Street where members of the Legislative Assembly lived while in town.

first chance I've had to resume. It is now five o'clock and quite dark in the office. Must climb up and light the gas before I proceed.

There, thank goodness that is accomplished with safety to life and limb and—"what's more"—no mail man coming in while I was up in mid-air.

Well, where was I at?

On Monday morning, September 16th I solemnly waddled down to the Echo office and was initiated into the mysteries of proof-reading. I encountered nothing very formidable and got on all right.

I come down at nine in the morning. My first duty is to skim through the *Chronicle*—the morning edition—clip out and mail such editorials as I think will make their recipients either beam or squirm. That done, I dive—on my own account—into the reading room and skim with an avid eye over the *Island* dailies. By the time I have finished with them the proof rolls are beginning to come down in a queer little box through a queer little slide from the composing room, so I go to my desk, dragging thereto the most comfortable chair I can find and "hoe into" proof reading. This is not hard but somewhat tedious. The headlines and editorials are my worst thorns in the flesh. Headlines have a natural tendency towards depravity, anyhow, and the editor-in-chief has a nasty habit of making puns over which I am apt to come to grief. In spite of all my care "errors will creep in" and then there is the mischief to pay. When I have nightmares now they are of headlines wildly askew and editorials hopelessly hocussed which an infuriated chief is flourishing under my nose.

Proofs come down pretty steadily all the forenoon and between them I employ my spare time as I see fit. At noon I have an hour off when I go around to Woolnough's restaurant[1] and get my dinner and then take a prowl around town. After dinner proofs come down fast and furious until about 2.30 when the paper goes to press and there is a sudden lull. But I have to stay until five and sometimes six to answer the telephone, sign for wires, read extra proofs of ads etc. This is always a rather poky time but release comes at last.

The foregoing is the regular daily routine. On Saturday the *Echo* has a lot of extra matter, a page of "society letters" among the rest. It mostly falls to my lot to edit these. Can't say I fancy the job very much, but the only thing I positively abhor is "faking" a society letter. This is one of the tricks of newspaperdom. When a society letter fails to turn up from a certain place—say Windsor[2]—in due time, Mr. Taunton slaps a Windsor weekly down before me and says blandly, "Fake us up a society letter from that, Miss Montgomery."

---

1. At 153 Hollis Street.

2. A small town 40 miles (64 km) from Halifax.

So poor "Miss M." goes meekly to work and concocts an introductory paragraph or so about "autumn leaves" and "mellow days" and "October frosts," or any old stuff like that to suit the season. Then I go carefully over the columns of the weekly, clip out all the available personals and news items about weddings and engagements and teas etc., hash them up in epistolary style, forge the Windsor correspondent's nom-de-plume—and there's your society letter! I used to include funerals too, until I found that the news-editor in variably blue-pencilled them. Evidently funerals have no place in society.

Then I write a column or so of giddy stuff for Monday's *Echo*. I call it "Around The Tea Table"[1] and sign it *Cynthia*. I think it rather goes. Mr. Simpson, the staff artist, has made a heading for it in which four or five rather melancholy and spinsterish maidens sit around a table, presumably talking gossip. As for the stuff itself, everything is fish that comes to *Cynthia's* net—fun, fashions, fads, fancies.

The *Chronicle* Building is of red brick and is situated on Prince St.[2] The editorial offices are on the second floor. My office is a back room looking out on a back yard in the middle of the block. I don't know if *all* the Haligonian[3] washerwomen live around it or not but certainly a goodly percentage of them must, for the yard is a network of lines from which sundry and div-

Minnie Macdonald

ers garments are always streaming gaily to the breezes. On the ground and over the roofs cats are prowling continually and when they fight the walls resound with their melancholy howls. Most of them are lank, starved-looking beasties enough but there is one lovely fellow who basks on a window sill across the corner and on whom I long to get my hands. He is so sleek and plump and gray that he makes me think of my old pussy "Bobs" at home. (Here I could really squeeze out a homesick tear if I were not afraid that it would wash a clean streak on my grimy face. This office is really the worst place for getting dusty I ever was in.)

I enjoy the distinction of being the only girl on the staff, but there are two below in the business office—Miss Kensley, with whom I have merely

---

1. For this column LMM produced items on fashion, love letters, hair styles, diet, handwriting, hymns, streetcars, slang, and photography.

2. Runs from Citadel Hill to the wharves.

3. A native of Halifax.

a speaking acquaintance—and Minnie Macdonald who is a chum of mine and a lovely girl. But there are men galore. I had a shocking time getting them all placed when I came first, for introductions seem to be unknown in newspaper offices. For the first two weeks, whenever anyone was rung up on the phone I had to rush wildly about the office demanding of all and sundry. "Your name or your life?" But I've got them all sorted out now.

Mr. Dunn is at the head of the procession—that is to say, he is business manager of both papers and seems to be cordially detested by all who are under his thumb. He has always been very civil to me but I have little to do with him or he would probably comb me down too. He is a fine looking man of a certain type, with an aggressive chin and when anything goes wrong he is heard from in no uncertain tones.

Mr. Taunton, the news-editor, is a man for whom I have a "Doctor Fell"[1] aversion. I ought not to dislike him for he has been very kind to me and always takes my part in a ruction over proof errors, but I do and I can't help it. I am uncomfortable in his atmosphere and never feel at ease.

Mr. Baxter, the marine editor, shares my office and is my favourite of the staff.[2] He is really on the night staff but drops in frequently during the day to write out shipping notes and fire off puns, more or less ghastly, at the handiest victim, generally myself. He is tall and raw-boned and red-headed, very jolly and off-handed and kind.

"Jimmy" Gowan, the policeman, also inhabits this office. He is one of those people who believe silence to be golden. At first I thought him a grumpy old fossil but he is really a good soul and his silence is his misfortune not his fault.

There is also an office boy who haunts the place.

Mr. McLellan is the editor in chief, a polished elderly gentlemen, very affable and courteous except when good editorials go wrong. I have no fault to find with him except his aforesaid propensity for punning, but punning seems to be in the air here. I must have swallowed a germ—probably Baxter gives them off by hundreds—for I found myself making a pun the other day—a thing I never did in my life before. I must try to discover an antidote before the disease makes headway.

---

1. Negative reaction, as in Thomas Brown's famous quatrain based on a Latin epigram on inexplicable instinctive dislike: "I do not like thee, Doctor Fell! / The reason why I cannot tell."

2. Other *Echo* workers listed in the Halifax City Directory, 1901, include John M. Baxter, journalist; William E. McLellan, most distinguished of the *Echo* staff, a law graduate of Dalhousie, editor-in-chief (1900–1905), writer and educator, former editor of the *Winnipeg Free Press*; Tommy Fraser, columnist; and James L. Hickey (1869–1954), reporter at *The Chronicle*; Hamilton (perhaps Havelock L. Hammond, printer at *The Chronicle*); A.F. MacDonald, news editor at the *Morning Chronicle*; John H. Jost, accountant at *The Chronicle*; James Kelleher, clerk at *The Chronicle*.

Mr. Fraser runs the "Beach-comber" column and generally writes the *Echo* editorials. He has a shallow cleverness and thinks Tommy Fraser is about the only thing of any importance that ever happened. He is passably good-looking and very snobbish.

Mr. Simpson is the staff artist. I rather like him but he doesn't seem to be popular. I think he is a bit of a saphead. Messrs. Hickey, Hamilton and MacDonald are all night folk who drop in occasionally and seem quite nice. Messrs. Jost and Kellaher are in the business offices; the latter is quite likeable.

I have been gluttonizing on papers ever since I came here. We get lots of exchanges and I browse among them in my spare moments—generally with an eye cocked for ideas that can be worked up by "Cynthia," that young person having an amiable habit of taking her own wherever she finds it.

Saturday, Nov. 16, 1901
Echo Office,
Halifax

I have to write up this journal as I do everything else nowadays—by fits and starts. I forget what interrupted my last entry. Probably I got so hungry I had to stop. Anyway, this is Saturday afternoon with the slave still chained to her oar. No nice, delightful, "Saturday off" in newspaperdom! Saturday is my busiest day here because the Sat. *Echo* is the biggest of the week. However, it has gone to press and I have nothing much to do. I am going to dine at the Halifax and spend the evening with Bertha, so I feel good-humoured, and here goes to pick up the dropped threads.

Lottie Shatford ran in to the office one day in Exhibition week and I have seen her several times since. She has changed very little. One evening she and her brother called on me, the latter having been very anxious to meet me. No, don't imagine you scent a romance. He is not only married but twice married and his interest in me is purely intellectual. He admires my scribblings.

I was disappointed in him. He is not as I had pictured him from Lottie's letters—seems a rather common and opinionated sort of person, anxious to air his "liberal" views, especially on the matters of religion, in season and out of season.

Lottie's sister Edna[1] was married from another brother's house here in Halifax last week. I was invited to the wedding, got half a day off, and took it in. Didn't enjoy it at all. Except Lottie and two or three members of her family circle I didn't know a soul and naturally they were too busy with their many duties to have any time for me. There is no loneliness like the loneliness of a crowd. I was bored to death and glad when I could decently get away. But oh, oh, oh! Lonely? Homesick? Don't mention it! For the first ten days I was here I thought I should die and hoped I would. I can laugh at myself now but while it lasted it was no laughing matter. I have had such a bad attack only twice before—out west and when I first went to Bideford. I wasn't feeling very well physically and, not being settled down, had nothing to do out of office hours and this all helped things the wrong way.

It wasn't so bad all day; but when I left the office and, after walking through half a mile of streets without seeing a face I knew, found myself alone in a strange narrow little hall bedroom, with not one of my own household gods around me, loneliness seized on me body and soul, and I cast myself down on the bed and refused to be comforted. But it is all over now and I am acclimated. The only time I feel rather blue now is when I leave the office and walk home through the chill gray autumn dusk. Then I do long bitterly for my own dear "den" at home and the old red road over the hill.

It was just when my homesickness was at its very worst that I visited the Exhibition.[2] I remember that as the nadir of my woes—I sounded the deeps of ghastly, soul-sickening loneliness that day and was never quite so bad again. Having got as low as possible I began to ascend.

To began with it was a dull day. I got off at 3.30, rushed to the W.C.A., dressed, and got on a street car. It was crowded and everybody in it knew somebody else—everybody but me! When I got off at the grounds I left my raincoat on the car—didn't miss it until the car was gone and rain began to fall. I recovered the coat later on but just then it was the last straw. For one cent I would have turned then and there and gone back, not caring whether I ever saw that Exhibition or any other.

But nobody offered me the one cent so I wandered on, shelled out my quarter, and went in. I would not like to be called on to describe that Exhibition for much I fear me I should brand myself as one of those "who having eyes see not." I wandered forlornly around among throngs of people and looked idiotic. I know I looked it for I felt it.

---

1. Edna Shatford (1879–1960) from Hubbard's Point; married to Edwin Fraser. The twice-married brother was probably Sidney Smith Shatford (1864–1956).

2. The Halifax Exhibition Building and Grounds were on Windsor Street at the site of the present-day Halifax Forum.

If I had been just here for a visit, as I had expected to be when I came, I would not have cared if I had been alone in a million. But the thought that I had to *stay* here among all those strangers spoiled everything. I just felt out at the elbows and was glad when I could decide that I had stayed long enough for the money and might decamp.

I sallied out in a pouring rain, waited ten minutes until a crowded street car came along, scrambled recklessly on with a score of others, and stood on the outer edge all the way home, hanging to a strap and wedged in between two brutes of men—I'm sure they were brutes—in long wet rubber coats, one of whom smoked a bad cigar all the way.

So my trip to the Exhibition wasn't an emphatic success. Never mind, it's fun to look back on it now.

Monday, Nov. 18, 1901
Echo Office
Halifax, N.S.

This has been one of the days when things reveal their naked, natural *cussedness*. I didn't sleep well last night and felt grumpy all day, and so did everyone else apparently. Then one of those wretched editorial jokes got off its trolley again this afternoon; and altogether life has seemed like a howling wilderness.

However, the cloud is lifting now. The paper has gone to press and somebody below in the business office has just sent me up a big molasses "kiss"[1] in the copy box. This delicate attention has smoothed my ruffled plumage.

Well, "to resoom and to proceed";—after a week at the W.C.A. I removed to my present domicile at 23 Church St. I like it only fairly well.

My landlady is a Mrs. Clarke. She is a widow, her husband having departed to the realms of the just—let us hope—sometime ago. Poor man, I can't help thinking it was a happy release for him. It did not surprise me in the least to learn that he died of nervous prostration.

Mrs. Clarke has a talent, amounting to positive genius, for meddling with what doesn't in the least concern her. I have tried delicately to impress her with the fact that I prefer to manage my own affairs; but Mrs. C. like most self-elected reformers—i.e. meddlers—is decidedly obtuse and I expect I shall have to snub her very pointedly some of these days. She is, short, an impertinent, disagreeable woman.

---

1. According to a 1903 recipe, a candy made by boiling molasses, sugar, butter, and vinegar for twenty minutes, cooling, and then pulling until porous and light coloured.

Her two daughters are fairly nice. I don't dislike them, as I do their mother, but we have nothing in common and we bore each other.

Church St. is nice and quiet. I am not exactly a boarder—more like a lodger. I get my breakfast and Sunday meals there—and my dinner at a downtown restaurant. My supper consists of a snack in my own room.

I have had a hard time trying to arrange for enough spare minutes to do some writing. As my salary only suffices for board and bed and as it is against the law, not to mention the climate to go about naked, I have to make enough money to clothe myself in other ways.

My first idea was to write in the evenings. Well, I tried it. I couldn't string two marketable ideas together. Besides, I had to keep my stockings darned and my buttons sewed on!

Then I determined to get up at six every morning to write before going to work! I did that twice—or maybe it was three times. Then I concluded that was impossible. I could not do good work in a chilly room on an empty stomach, especially if, as was often the case, I had been up late the night before. So I said to myself, very solemnly,

"Now, Maud, what are you going to do? Leaving the tenets of the Plymouth Brethren[1] out of the question, you have to choose between two courses. You must either decamp back to the tight little Island or you must hit upon some plan to make possible the production of pot boilers."

So Maud thought hard.

Now, it used to be at home, that I thought undisturbed solitude was necessary that the fire of genius might burn. I must be alone and the room must be quiet. It would have been the last thing to enter into my imagination to suppose that I could ever write anything at all, much less anything of value, in a newspaper office, with rolls of proof shooting down every few minutes, people coming and going and conversing, telephones ringing and machines thumping and dragging overhead. I would have laughed at the idea—yea, I would have laughed it to scorn. But the impossible has happened. I am of one opinion with the Irishman who said you could get used to anything, even to being hanged!

Every morning here I write and not bad stuff either. I have grown accustomed to stopping in the midst of a paragraph to interview a prowling caller and to pausing in full career after an elusive rhyme to read a batch of proof and snarled-up copy. It's all in the day's work—but I don't like it over and above. It's trying. However, it has to be done and I won't grumble, no, not one little bit!

---

1. A fundamentalist Biblical Christian sect established *c.*1828 in Dublin and 1830 in Plymouth, England.

I have got into some first class magazines lately, so you may pat me on the back. Among others, the *Delineator*,[1] *Smart Set*[2] and *Ainslies'*[3] have opened their fold to this poor wandering sheepkin of thorny literary ways.

Friday, Nov. 22, 1901
Echo Office, Halifax

I'm so woefully tired tonight that I don't know if I can spin this out a bit longer or not. I've been extra busy today, even for Friday. It is now 5 o'clock and I must stay here another hour to read those wretched society letters.

Jean Lyall[4] has just been in for a chat. She was introduced to me by Lottie on the birds-of-a-feather principle, because she is a writer. I wonder why people so commonly suppose that if two persons are writers they must of necessity be hugely congenial. Nobody would expect two blacksmiths to be violently attracted to each other simply because they *were*, blacksmiths!

But Jean is a nice, clever girl who does some original work. She is indolent, however, and doesn't "push the business." If she gets an article back she doesn't send it out again. Alackaday, where would I be if I had succumbed as easily as that?

Jean is nice, as aforesaid, but not especially "my style" at all. To be honest, she bores me. She is very intellectual; but just now I'm tired of being on the mental stretch and would like, just half an hour of commonplace *gossip* with one of my old girl friends. And I'd like to be curled up in my own dear den at home—I can see it so plainly, this minute when I shut my eyes. But I open them and this is what I see—a red brick wall, a line of flapping clothes, and several chimneys vomiting black smoke. An inspiring outlook, truly! But above it there is a glimpse of silvery blue—and—saffron sky, like a promise of better things. And I shall sleep well tonight and waken in the morning full of spirit and zest again.

But just now I'd like to cry!

---

1. New York monthly fashion magazine (1873–1937).
2. Another New York monthly (1890–1930), founded by W.D. Mann as a society journal; a witty literary journal, it published prominent writers of the day.
3. London semi-monthly developed from the *Yellow Book* in 1898, publishing most popular writers of England and America.
4. A nursing sister who later served in the Canadian Red Cross Special Hospital in England during WWI.

Saturday, Nov. 23, 1901
Echo Office
Halifax

I didn't cry: and just now I'm feeling tickled to death.

There was a fearful hue and cry this morning over a mistake I made in a bargain sale ad yesterday, and later on another depraved editorial joke went the downward way and was sternly pointed out to me by an irate chief. Besides, I have a sore finger which causes me exquisite agony every time I have to pull the copy box up.

It is not because of these things I am tickled. It is in spite of them.

I have just received a cheque for $25 from the *Delineator* for a story. *Watch me smile!*

Another week has come to an end. Tomorrow is Sunday, glory be! I have been indulging in a sort of religious dissipation every since coming to Halifax—that is, I've been making the rounds of all the churches. Last Sunday evening I went up to the North End to the Universalist Church.[1] I found it quite interesting but certainly would not care for it as a steady thing. It is much like a lecture and a concert combined. The pastor gave a very logical and painfully truthful talk on "What Do Men Really Believe Concerning Immortality?" The music was charming and I enjoyed the whole service but couldn't exactly see where the religion came in. I couldn't help smiling as I imagined what some of the dear orthodox bodies in Cavendish would think of the whole performance. To be sure, they wouldn't understand half of it and the other half would probably fill them with horror.

The service was very simple. I was at the other extreme the Sunday I went to St. Luke's.[2] It is very "high" and religious observance there has become positive mummery without pith or meaning. The kernel of Christianity is so shrouded in the husks of ritual that it is almost lost altogether.

I don't know what they are doing overhead in the composing room but they seem to be celebrating a very carnival of thumping and rolling and dragging. I expect every minute to see the ceiling come crashing in.

That composing room is a curious place. I ventured up one day and found myself in a big grimy room, with a lot of grimy figures bending over grimy galleys of type, and a grimy row of linotype machines along one side. It looked like a dingy workshop of gnomes. As for the linotype, I believe it

---

1. Universalist Church of America, founded in Gloucester, MA, in 1779, emphasized salvation through God's divine grace revealed in Jesus Christ.

2. Anglican Church on Morris Street, near the corner of Church.

is magic! It seems fairly to possess a brain of its own, so wonderful are the things it can do.

My next visit was to the basement—"Hell's Kitchen" as it is poetically termed here—where the big press takes a huge roll of white paper in at one end and drops it out of the other, cut and folded *Echoes*. Truly the epic of human genius in this century is its colossal mechanical contrivances. Two and three thousand years ago men wrote immortal poems. Today they create marvellous inventions and bend the erstwhile undreamed-of forces of nature to their will. Which is the better, oh, ye gods of the Golden Age? After all, have we not lost as much as we have gained? The beautiful childhood of the world is gone forever. I believe its happiest days were in the dead-and-gone centuries of its song-singing, love-making, war-waging youth!

Bless me, I have forgotten that I am in a newspaper office.

The great Haligonian event of the season was the Royal Visit[1] in October. Halifax fairly stood on its head, tricked out in bunting[2] which might be gay and gorgeous and patriotic enough but was certainly not beautiful. Our office was adorned with yellow-and-green and looked as if it had jaundice.

The Duke and Duchess arrived here on Saturday afternoon, Oct. 19. Everybody had a holiday except us newspaper fags. However, we rushed things to get off by two o'clock. About eleven I slipped out and ran over to the Provincial building where I stood freezing for half an hour before the gates while some corner stone was being laid. At last I had my reward and when the carriage containing the Duke and Duchess left the gates I had a good, unhindered look at them.

Our future king is an insignificant man with a red nose. The duchess looks to be the best man of the two. She was a big, rather fine-looking woman dressed rather dowdily in black.

I got off at 2 o'clock but I did not go to the review on the common[3] although I suppose everybody else in Halifax went. I had nobody to go with and I knew I wouldn't be able to see anything if I did go so I just stayed home and celebrated my quarter-holiday by reading a new magazine and eating candy.

In the evening I went out with Minnie MacDonald and her sister Kate to see the illuminations. They were all good and the warships were magnificent—"like one's childish dreams of fairyland," as Cynthia took good care to remark in her next "copy." There were twelve warships in port and

---

1. King Edward VII's second son and daughter-in-law (later King George V and Queen Mary) were on a global tour to celebrate the establishment of the new British Commonwealth.

2. Brightly coloured fabric used for flags and for decorating public buildings.

3. A large recreational area in the centre of Halifax.

all, hulls, spars and funnels, were picked out with electric lights. The effect against the inky blackness of the harbour was magical.

In due time it began to rain and as I did not have my umbrella with me, I got well drenched and went home in a very disgruntled mood, vowing that I have had enough of

1. Minnie. 2. Kate

royal visits. I caught a fearful cold and my best hat has had a cowed, apologetic appearance ever since.

Well, I have at last brought this journal up to date and written, I doubt not, a vast deal of nonsense. But then, one must have a little nonsense somewhere to give zest to existence and there certainly isn't much elsewhere in my life. It is so deadly serious that it is no wonder my account of it is frivolous. So let it be!

Thanksgiving!!!
Nov. 28, 1901
23 Church Street

What a beastly day this has been! Thanksgiving, indeed! At the present moment there is but one thing I am thankful for and that is that it is nearly over! I simply *must* have a good fierce grumble in this journal by way of relief! I have grinned and looked happy all day when I was just plain, unadulterated miserable, and I *must* have this "went" for my feelings. Anyone reading this journal would, I suppose, think I was a very discontented young person. But I'm not! I *never* complain or grumble to other people. But now and then I take a fierce spasm of disgust with things in general and I work it off in this harmless fashion.

Last night I was out at a "thimble party" at Jean Lyall's. It bored me horribly; and I had to tell so many fibs about it, too, such as assuring my hostess that I had a lovely time etc. No wonder my conscience is stiff and sore today!

So I didn't get much sleep last night and that, with other things, has made me grumpy and glum today. The only thing I can find pleasure in at present is in picturing myself as the forlorn heroine of a terribly sad life story. If I pile the agony up high enough I can get a good deal of solid comfort out of this.

I had to go to work as usual this morning. Something terrible would happen to Halifax if the *Echo* didn't come out you know. It was cold and snowy and I felt lonesome. I was so blue I couldn't even laugh at Baxter's puns, although he got off some good new ones, Thanksgiving brand. I wrote out the *Cynthia* stuff for Monday and made it very sparkling—I can always write brilliantly when I'm in the dismals.

At noon I ate a cold lunch. The restaurants were all closed, so I made my Thanksgiving dinner on cold toast and a quarter of a pound of figs! Nourishing, I daresay, but not exhilarating!

I got off at 1.30, hurried home and dressed to go to a matinee. Had to go alone but determined not to mind that and took a novel to read between the acts. The play was pretty good—very melodramatic, which suited my mood to a T, and I cried in the teary places to my entire satisfaction.

I came home, had a good cry, then rose up and sewed two long, ugly black seams in a skirt I'm making. It will soon be bedtime and I'm glad—I'm so tired and lonesome.

Friday, Nov. 29, 1901
23 Church St., Halifax

I had my Thanksgiving dinner tonight and I suppose it had a mellowing effect for I feel quite fit and all my blues have turned rosy-pink. I was down at the Halifax with Bertha and demolished some turkey etc.—mostly "etc."—and then we went into the balcony off of the main dining room and watched the St. Andrew's banquet[1] in progress below.

The "HALIFAX"

After I came home, though, I got lonesome again and couldn't keep from thinking over a lot of long-dead things, until I exorcised my ghostly remembrances by reading a novel. I'm all right again now. I suppose the ghosts were the logical consequences of the "etc.." Now that it is digested they vanish—pale, phantom-like things, the fleshless, tormenting simulacra of once pulsing joys!

---

1. Annual celebration of the patron saint of Scotland.

Saturday, Dec. 8, 1901
Echo Office, Halifax

Have been busy of late—as if that were news indeedy! But I have been Busy
with a capital B. Tending to office work, writing pot-boilers, making Xmas
presents—or buying them, which is just as harrowing—etc., etc., etc.,—
mostly as in the case of my Thanksgiving dinner, "etc."

One of the "etcs" is a job I heartily detest. It makes my soul cringe. It is
bad enough to have your flesh cringe but when it strikes into your soul it
gets on your spiritual nerves terribly. We are giving all the firms who adver-
tise with us a free "write up" of their holiday goods, and I have to visit all
the stores, interview the proprietors, and crystallize my information into
"two sticks" of copy. From three to five every afternoon I potter around the
business blocks until my nose is purple with the cold and my fingers numb
from scribbling down notes. So "no more until next time." Perhaps I shall
have got back my self-respect by then. It has quite wilted under the haughty
patronage of the Halifax clerks.

Wednesday, Dec. 12, 1901
Echo Office, Halifax

If I have not got back my self-respect I *have* got a new hat! It's an ill wind
that blows no good and my disagreeable assignment has brought me some.
The other evening I went in to write up the *Bon Marche*,[1] which sets up to
be *the* millinery establishment of Halifax. I found the proprietor very genial. He said he was delighted that the *Echo* had sent a lady and by way of
encouraging it not to weary in well-doing he would send me up one of the
new walking hats if I gave them a good write-up. I rather thought he was
joking—but sure enough when the write-up came out yesterday up came
the hat and a very pretty one it is, too. Thanks, *Bon Marche*.

Monday, Dec. 17, 1901
Echo Office, Halifax

It is snowing. The big white flakes are floating down over the dingy, hideous
back yard upon which I gaze daily. Really, I think it is the ugliest place in
the world. It actually hurts me to look at it. Come, I will shut my eyes and

---

1. A shop on Pleasant Street, near the corner of Prince.

imagine I am at my little gable window at home. Outside, over the long, gentle slope of pasture and upland, russet and gray in their dreamless sleep, the white flakes are falling. The far rim of fir woods that crown the distant hills, is dim and wraith-like through its misty scarfing. Down below me the orchards are still coated with brown leafage that is catching the snow as it falls. A tiny swallow clings for a moment to the window sill, like a wind-blown wanderer resting for a space in some friendly haven. Then, at a movement of mine off it goes—

A wretched little telegraph boy pounced in just then and spoiled my vision. I signed for him and he went off with a grin, little guessing the enormity of his offence. But I have no business to be imagining such things. I have made myself homesick and that is poor policy.

What I started out to say about today's doings was that Mr. Dunn has kindly condescended to give me a rise in salary. I am to get a whole dollar more a week! So I presume I'm "giving sahtisfaction."

That reminds me of Oliver Wendell Holmes. I'm reading him just now— for the hundredth time or so. He has a trick of saying things in a half dozen words that go straight and clean to your heart, giving you either a thrill of such exquisite pleasure that the moment compensates for many long dreary hours, or else a pang of agony so keen and terrible that for a second you think you know what hell might be like. I fancy that nobody but a perfectly happy person could read Holmes with nothing but pleasure.

Thursday, Dec. 20, 1901
Echo Office, Halifax

All the odd jobs that go a-begging in this establishment are handed over to the present scribe. The very queerest one up to date came yesterday.

The compositors were setting up a story called "A Royal Betrothal," taken from an English paper, and when about half through they lost the copy. Whereupon Mr. Taunton requested me to write an "end" for the story. I gasped, not seeing how I could. I had never seen the story and what was set up was not enough to give me any insight into the final development. Moreover, my knowledge of royal love affairs is limited and I have not been accustomed to write with flippant levity of kings and queens.

However, I went home last night and fell to work. I got it done somehow or other. So today out came "The Royal Betrothal" bravely and as yet nobody has guessed where the "seam" comes in. If the original author ever sees it I wonder what he—or she will think.

Friday, Dec. 21, 1901
Echo Office, Halifax

I am horribly tired for it is nearly five and I've been typewriting most of the afternoon—for I have a typewriter of my own now, be it known unto thee. It is already well-known to the long suffering folks of this office who endure its clatter with an amiability and a resignation to the inevitable not to be found anywhere on earth save in a newspaper office.

Well, I saw a ghost last night!

I went with Jean Lyall to the Dalhousie break-up. In the middle of the performance I looked around and whom should I see in the crowd of boys at the door but Nate Lockhart!! I was very much amazed for I had no idea that he was in Halifax. I thought he had graduated from the law school here last year and was now in the States. He caught sight of me at the same moment and looked as surprised as possible—the self-same, half-whimsical look of puzzlement that I remember in—in another world, let us say. It really seems like that now.

This is a famous chance for some sentimental reminiscences! But I shall refrain! I'm too tired—and there's nothing worth saying—and it *was* all in another world. And Nate was a ghost out of it. All that was wanting was to summon up the ghost of my own old self out of that other world—the light-hearted schoolgirl with the untasted cup of life held to her lips.

But I did not summon her up. I never think of her now if I can help it. It is too bitter.

Thursday, Dec. 27, 1901
Echo Office, Halifax

Christmas is over. I had been rather dreading it for I had expected to feel very much the stranger in a strange land. But, as usual, anticipation was discounted by realization. I had a very pleasant time although not of course so wildly exhilarating as to endanger life or limb or nerves—which was no doubt just as well.

I had a whole holiday—the first since coming here, so was haunted all day by the impression that it was Sunday. I had dinner at the Halifax with Bertha and spent the afternoon in her cozy room.

B. Clark

In the evening Worth Clark[1] and I went to the opera to see "The Little Minister."[2] It was good but not nearly so good as the book. I don't care for dramatized novels. They jar too harshly on my preconceptions of the characters.

This morning I came back to work. Christmas seems to have got on everybody's nerves. We have all been cranks together today—even the genial Baxter.

Bertha's room

---

1. Bertha Clark's brother.

2. Play (1897) produced by Charles Frohman, based on the Scottish novel (1891) by J.M. Barrie (1860–1937).

 1902

Monday, Jan. 20, 1902
Echo Office, Halifax

Last night Myrtie Clark inveigled me down into the Fort Massey school hall to teach a Chinaman. I went meekly, avid for "experience." They had about thirty of them, and—on the principle of "greens to the green" I suppose—they assigned one to me—or me to one—who was just out from China. He didn't know a word of English and I sat to work to teach him to read it!!

He had a well-developed pig-tail and oh, how horribly he *did* smell! But some of the small Chinese boys are so cute-looking as they can be. Well, my pupil can't be much harder to teach than "Amos" of Bideford school, and I taught *him* to read.

Goodness! I've just thought of the time I had tea at old Archie's!

Tuesday, Jan. 21, 1902
Echo Office, Halifax

Today after lunch I wandered up to the Citizen's library[1] to get a book. Thanks to it, I've just been revelling in books of late. Today I got "Little Lord Fauntleroy"[2] and have been reading it all my spare time this afternoon. Years ago, when I was about ten, this story was published as a serial in the *Montreal Witness*. Never shall I forget the charm of it or those magical Saturdays when each successive instalment came. I have never read it since until today when I re-perused it in very different surroundings—in a dusty, very much littered newspaper office, with a sloppy rain blowing on my window and streaming off the eve troughs of that most unholy back yard. Yet the charm of the story was potent enough to make me oblivious to all this and I enjoyed it as much as I did in lang-syne days when a new story was something to be dated from in my small life.

Monday, Jan. 27, 1902
Echo Office, Halifax

I wonder what I would do if it were not for Sundays. When I was a child I didn't like Sunday—nay, I positively hated it. It seemed as long as all the

---

1. Founded 1864; situated since 1890 on the second floor of City Hall, on the Grand Parade; closed 1949.
2. The novel (1886) by Frances Hodgson Burnett (1849–1924) that set a fashion in children's books about the power of goodness in children and also set a taste for pretty suits for little boys.

rest of the week put together. The thought of a heaven which would be "one endless Sabbath day" made me feel exactly like the little girl in "Gates Ajar" who wanted to know if she were *very* good all the week in heaven wouldn't they let her go to play a little while in hell on Saturday afternoons!!

But now Sunday is the one white ewe lamb among all the black sheep of working days. I always used to have Saturday off before but now Saturday is the busiest day of all. I have just my dear blessed Sunday. By Saturday night I am always very tired and fagged but Sunday fixes me up as good as new. I always take things easy and make it as far as possible a real day of rest— as it was intended to be. I sleep—deliciously, lazily, unheedingly—until ten o'clock. After breakfast I roll myself up in a shawl, and myself up on my bed with a book and a bag of butterscotch. The Halifax butterscotch is the most delicious confection I have sampled up to date. I invariably run up to the "Kandy Kitchen" when I leave the office on Saturday night and buy a bag of it.

After dinner I either go to bed again or attend a lecture at Dalhousie. Then in the evening I go to church and after the service I teach my Chinaman.

It is pouring "cats and dogs" today. One dog has evidently rained down into the hall and is there making a noise dismal enough for the lost spirit of a dog to make, poor beastie. I wish his owner would retrieve him for he makes me feel dismal too. I am going home presently and between whiles I will employ my gray matter designing a doily pattern for a fancy work journal for which I expect to get a dollar where with I mean to buy myself a new watch chain.

But the question is:—who in all Halifax would care if I adorned myself with new watch chains from head to heels?

Later On, My Room
23 Church St., Halifax

Is there anything in the world sadder and weirder than the wail of the wind around the eaves and past the window on a stormy night? I am sitting here now in my little hall bedroom and it sounds as if all the broken-hearted cries of fair, unhappy women who died and were forgotten ages ago were being re-echoed in the wailing wind of tonight. All my own past pain finds a voice in it as if it were moaning a plea for re-entrance into the soul which has cast it out. There are strange sounds in that night wind that is clamoring at my casement. I heard the cries of old sorrows in it—and the laughter of old joys that are sadder than old sorrows—and the moans of old despairs—and the phantom songs of dead hopes. The night wind is the wandering soul of the past. It has no share in the future—and so it is sorrowful.

Saturday, Feb. 1, 1902
Echo Office
Halifax

The "cold snap" which has been snapping all the week is abating somewhat. I have been in such a state of "freezation" ever since it began that now when I find myself gradually thawing and revivifying, the sensation has all the charm of novelty.

I have just finished writing up weekly yard of "Cynthia" and in spare moments have been re-reading the "Scarlet Letter." I've read the book often since that first time years ago when I read it behind that old brown desk at school, where so many delicious "forbidden fruits" from green apples to novels were devoured.

Lottie Shatford was in to see me one day this week. Dear me, I *must* confess! There is really *nothing* in our so-called friendship!

There, *that's* a relief!

Lottie Shatford

I always felt it—even years ago at Dalhousie. There was a certain intellectual comradeship between us but I never felt really at home in her company. Bright and clever a she is, I can never shake off a feeling of restraint. There is something in my nature that shuts up instinctively when she approaches, and refused to expand again until she is gone. Lottie is up-to-date, vivacious and merry. I would not like to forfeit her good opinion. But the all-important element of mutual sympathy—that mysterious thing we call affinity—is wholly lacking and nothing can compensate for it. It may exist between two people who may seem to have very little in common. And, as in this case, it may be lacking between two whose opinions, tastes and pursuits are so very much alike that it seems almost incredible that no real communion of spirit can exist.

One may as well be honest. I have tried for a long time to pretend to myself that the nebulous tie between Lottie and me was really that of a high-plane friendship. But it is not. She really counts for nothing at any facet of my life. There is nothing in either of us that belongs to the other and so neither of us can find and claim our own in that other. Lottie, admirable as she is in many ways, is not for me and henceforth I will accept our relationship for what it is worth and no longer try to find any greater value in it and, failing, taste the bitterness of repeated disappointment. Affection cannot be generated by any intellectual rule of thumb. I will give up the vain attempt.

Saturday, Feb. 8, 1902
Echo Office, Halifax, N.S.

How can anybody believe that hell is reserved for a future life? We get it right along in this world on the instalment plan and I have had a good stiff dose of mine this past week in the shape of a wretched, persistent little ailment—nothing serious enough to justify laying up but a half-and-half sickness that left me able to do what I had to do but poisoned the doing of it until I could have cried—and *did* cry—for sheer discouragement. This week has seemed as long as three. I'm a little better today but far from well yet and have to crawl around with misery just sticking out of my eyes.

Saturday, Feb. 15, 1902
Echo Office, Halifax

Another week has dragged by. It has been a most wearisome one to me. I have not felt well—I get tired easily and feel lifeless and uninterested. I think the close confinement in the office is rather trying. The air here is generally bad—thanks to the men's cigars. But there is no use in grumbling. So I begin to grin straightway!

It is mid-afternoon. The *Echo* has just gone to press and the building is throbbing with the motion of the great machines. The office is deserted save for myself. The punning Baxter, the sphinx-like Gowan, and the sleepy office boy have disappeared. Mr. Taunton is curled up in the inner office, his legs on his desk, reading a novel.

This week has been busy—as all my weeks are. By way of future reference I'll sketch the details of the routine of my existence since last Saturday afternoon—168 hours of living in a world where we must toil *and* spin in order that we may be decently arrayed and have some butterscotch to satisfy our inner cravings.

When I left the office last Saturday the day was fine and cold. I first went up to the library to get some books. I did not feel well and my feet seemed weighted with lead. People hurried and scurried by me, not one of whom I knew. After leaving the library with "The Witch of Prague" I went to the "Kandy Kitchen" and exchanged a battered dime for half a pound of butterscotch. Then I went home to my lodging house on Church St. where the gilded cross on the spire of St. Luke's was smitten to a dazzling flame by the setting sun.

I found the house deserted as usual, Mrs. C. and the girls being away at some society function. I let myself in by my latch key and crawled upstairs where I proceeded to make myself comfortable. A bath and a change of dress brightened me up wonderfully and then I got my own tea. I made cocoa over my oil stove and filled the vacuum in my inner girl with sandwiches and doughnuts, sitting on my bed while I munched them and staring at myself in my glass through the dusk until my big eyes seemed to grow ten times bigger.

"You poor little sinner," I said, "how lonesome you do look, all alone in this dull old house! Never mind, chummy! It's all in the day's work!"

Tea over, I lighted a lamp and sewed on some more buttons. Then I climbed into bed, fished out my bag of butterscotch and started in with "The Witch of Prague." At ten the witch was finished and I went to bed sleepily.

Sunday morning I slept late and read the rest of the forenoon. After dinner I went to a lecture at Dalhousie with Jean Lyall. When I got home again I went to bed, being sick, and stayed there until Monday morning.

I got up at 7.30 and at 8.45 was at my desk. My mail was lying on it— several papers and a letter from an editor, accepting a poem. Monday passed uneventfully. In the evening Bertha Clark and I went to the Academy of Music[1] and saw "Nancy & Co." The play was excessively silly but undeniably amusing and as I wanted something to laugh at it served my turn very well. I stayed all night with Bertha. In the gray, morning I sneaked out and scuttled up to Church St. for my breakfast which as usual I ate in solitary state.

Tuesday evening I took Jean Lyall to a Symphony concert in the Orpheus Hall.[2] Very good of its kind—but I'm deadly tired of the kind. I've been to so many of those Symphony concerts this winter, having to report them. I feel as if I were so saturated with music that it must be oozing out of my pores. Perhaps that is what is the matter with me—a case of *musicitis*!

After the concert Jean and I went to the Halifax Hotel with some friends of hers, ate butterscotch, and gossipped over the concert—at least, they did.

Item:—I was much bored.

Item:—Did not get to bed until one.

Item:—Felt like the dickens next morning.

Wednesday—office all day and nothing else. Baxter got off a new joke and will never forgive me because I refused to laugh at it. In the evening I resolved to bide home. After tea I worked for an hour at a Battenburg bolero![3] Following this heroic spurt of work I read "What Maisie Knew"[4] but

---

1. Auditorium opened 1877, capacity of 1250; demolished 1929.

2. Opened 1886 on Granville Street, capacity 600; closed 1947.

3. Short sleeveless jacket made of "Battenberg" crocheted tape lace.

4. Novel (1897) by Henry James (1843–1916) about a child's maturing in a decadent, dysfunctional family.

couldn't discover just what grisly knowledge Maisie *did* possess. Did not like the book and went to bed with a dark brown taste in my mouth. On Thursday two acceptances of poems were all that broke the monotony and "Mrs. Halliburton's Troubles"[1] instead of my own filled up the evening.

Friday I wrote a story, also my *Cynthia* stuff and did an extra stint of type-writing MSS. On the way home from the office I met *Nate*. He turned and walked home with me.

We gossipped inconsequentially and talked about old friends, keeping careful to the surface of things of course. I might write several pages of reflection about this, of course. But I won't. I'll only think them. Thinking is my specialty just now. I'm so much alone that I'm getting addicted to it.

Last evening I spent at Mr. McLellan's and had a very nice time. I like Mrs. M.

Today I felt rather worse. Worked hard. Am very tired. You, poor old journal, you! What a good friend you are! I can tell all my troubles to you. I never tell them to anyone else. To others I'm as gay and blithe as you please. Lots of people envy me! Let them—I like it! If my life is a hollow show I don't want it generally known.

Saturday, Feb. 22, 1902
23 Church St, Halifax

If I don't soon get better whatever is going to become of poor little me? This week I have gone crawling about like a sick dog whipped to its harness. My physical ills have reacted mentally and at times I feel morbid and unstrung. I have doggedly done all my work but nobody knows what a grind it has been. For a wonder I am not writing this at the office having left it at four on account of feeling so ill.

The one bright spot in this dismal week was the evening I spent with Minnie Macdonald at her home. I had a lovely time, as it was one of the days I felt a little better. If I only lived near them I would not take the blues so often. I begin to fear that my chronic state of internal azureness will soon be exuding through my skin and I will turn veritably blue.

This is such a lonesome boarding house. From Monday morning to Saturday night I never eat a meal with a living soul. There is solitude for you with a vengeance.

---

1. Virtue is rewarded in spite of the opposition of snobbish antagonists in this novel (1862) about working families by Mrs. Henry Ward (1814–87).

Friday, Feb. 28, 1902
Echo Office, Halifax

If I am as miserable next week as I have been this I shall simply have to give up. I ought to have done so this week for I am not fit to be about. It has only been sheer force of will that drove me to my desk and kept me there.

I've been in hell all this week! Profane? Very well. After suffering as I have done one has privileges. If I am no better tomorrow I *cannot* go to work. I would not live this day over for all the gold of Ophir.[1]

I have had an accumulation of woes. In the first place the worrisome little ailment I have had off and on all the month has been much worse. Monday and Tuesday I suffered continually with a virulent sick headache. Yesterday and today I have had a terrible cold. I've been choking half the time and coughing my head off the other half. It doesn't seem to me as if I *could* endure much more. I have not had one day free from suffering in a whole month.

I am writing this at my desk simply and solely to see if I can take my mind off my wretched condition. I can do nothing else, except what I have to do. I only wish I could crawl away into some dark hole to writhe unseen. The office is full of men and I have to sit up straight and keep up appearances. I dread the long walk home. My nerves seem to be in such a terrible condition that I feel as if I must scream if anybody looked at me. I must stay here late tonight, too, for the society letters have to be proof-read.

I am in such abject depths that I can't even say anything funny about my predicament!

To increase the aggravation it is the most beautiful day outside—a real spring day, sunny and balmy. If I were well I should be enjoying it hugely. As it is, it is an insult to my misery. I am a blot on it and want to crawl out of it.

It is a sort of relief to write this out. Heavens! If they would only stop rolling and thumping things overhead! There goes the telephone bell! And the copy bell! G-r-r-r!!!

If I could only stand out in the middle of the office and shriek at the top of my voice it would do me good. I feel as if I were on the point of flying into little pieces.

I haven't flown into pieces but something else has. Jimmy Gowan started to pull up one of the blinds and knocked the glass shade off the Auer light. It fell on the table and shivered into fragments with a sickening crash.

It was the last straw. I sprang to my feet and shrieked involuntarily. Poor Mr. G. looked as if he had been caught breaking all the commandments at once and I felt so ashamed. But I could not help it.

---

1. The best gold: Psalms 45:9, Isaiah 13:12; Sought by Solomon, I Kings 10.

Saturday, Mar. 1, 1902
Echo Office, Halifax

I am better today. To be sure, at any other time I'd think I was pretty sick but after the unutterable wretchedness of yesterday I seem almost well by contrast. I had to give up and go home at five last night, society letters to the contrary notwithstanding. Shall I ever forget that nightmare walk home through the streets? For that matter the last 48 hours have been like a nightmare.

Saturday, March 15, 1902
Echo Office, Halifax

I am *not* dead, as might perhaps be inferred from my somewhat long silence and the general tone of glumness that pervaded my last entry. On the contrary, I am well and flourishing. But I look back yet with a cringe to that terrible time.

I got well almost as suddenly as I got sick. And how jolly it was! I feel as if I'd been made over new and I've been enjoying life ever since—except when Golding's bad tobacco shrivels up my soul within me. Golding is a sub. doing duty in Mr. Taunton's absence and some day, just for curiosity's sake I'm going to ask him what brand of tobacco he uses and where he gets it!

Baxter has just made a joke. I must stop and laugh. Excuse me for a moment.

There, that duty is done!

Yes, I'm all right again, glory be! But I've nothing to write. I've been doing and seeing nothing of late worth recording.

This is Saturday night. Tomorrow I am going to have a walk in the park— if the weather permits, that is, and the forecast *says* it is going to be fine.

Sunday, Mar. 16, 1902
23 Church St, Halifax

I had my walk—but—and—well!

The first part was Abominable, the second part pleasant and the third part again Abominable! I mean those capitals!

The day was fine and sunny and I was, oh, so lonesome! There doesn't seem to be any connection between the two ideas in that sentence and there isn't. It just came so. There were hundreds of people in the park and I didn't know one of them. For awhile I hated life!

A wilderness of pines

Then I desperately left the shore road and fled up into a wilderness of pines and along the Serpentine[1] until at last I found myself alone—and *then* I was no longer lonesome!

It *was* delicious there. The fresh, chill spring air was faintly charged with the aroma of pine balsam and the sky over me was clear and blue—a great inverted cup of blessing. How glorious it was to see the sky once more, undarkened by rows of grimy houses! (Halifax is the grimiest city in Canada—I know it is!!)

Pine trees hold the traditions of the golden age. They strike their roots deep into the romance of the world's youth. Oh, how I love trees! I have always loved trees. And I love the pine trees above all others and next to it the fir. There is something in these trees— some indefinable charm—that is not found in deciduous trees, beautiful and lovable as these are, too.

The shore road

By and by I had to leave my pine solitude where the wood-nymphs whispered to me in fancy I heard Pan piping, and go back to the shore road and the crowds I hated. Then I sneaked objectly home and buried myself in my little hall bedroom.

Saturday, March 29, 1902
Echo Office, Halifax

This week has been miserable. It has rained and "fogged" continually—the damp has crept not only into my bones and marrow but into my soul as well and is smothering it.

However, I've lived on in spite of it. I've read proofs and dissected headlines and fought with compositors and bandied jokes with Baxter. I have ground out several Sunday schooly rhymes for a consideration of filthy lucre and I have written one *real* poem out of my heart.

---

1.   Perimeter path in Point Pleasant Park, Halifax.

I hate my "pot-boiling" stuff.[1] But it gives me the keenest pleasure to write something that *is* good—a fit and proper incarnation of the art I worship. After all, the malevolent gods can't embitter everything. There is one thing at least they cannot touch.

Monday, Mar. 31, 1902
Echo Office, Halifax

Yesterday was Easter Sunday—a sorry Easter truly, all mist and rain. Spring costumes and new hats blushed unseen and Simpsons',[2] "Easter Parade" prepared so painstakingly last week will not adorn the columns of our great family journal today. Myself, not having a new hat, I did not mind. I went to dinner with the Laurences—Catholic friends of mine—and went with them to the vesper service in St. Mary's Cathedral.[3] The music was very fine and also the decorations.

Tuesday, April 8, 1902
Echo Office, Halifax

Last night I dreamed about Pensie. I dreamed we were children together again, wandering along the shore. It has brought the past back to me in the vivid fashion such dreams do—as no mere retrospection of waking hours can do.

What chums Pensie and I were in those long ago days! And what fun we did have! It was always a great treat for me to be allowed to "go and stay all night" with Pensie in that little old house under the huge willows, with that most delightful, unworldly old garden behind it, ablow with roses and musk.

We went berrying in the back fields, or camped in the barn lofts, or coasted on the hill. Or, often than any, we went to the shore, and gathered mussels on the rocks or picked gum in the woods or brought the cows home at night to be milked in the shadowy land under the poplars and willows. What simple, happy little outings they were!

Pensie and I grew apart as we grew up. It was the fault of neither. Childhood and its bond of fun once past we had no interests in common. But nothing can rob us of that sweet old past.

---

1. At least thirty stories by LMM accepted for publication during this Halifax year are listed by Rea Wilmshurst in *LMM: A Preliminary Bibliography*.

2. Major department store, based in Toronto, sponsor of Easter and Santa Claus Parades.

3.. Founded 1820, consecrated in final form 1899, on Spring Garden Road near Barrington.

Pensie is a wife and mother now. And I am so different from the child of those old frolics that she seems to me a different creature altogether—poor little lass, so often misunderstood, with her wayward fancies and her strange, inner dream life that nobody guessed at. She was a quaint little Maud—that Maud of the old days, with plenty of faults and shortcomings but at heart very loving and warm. I *had* such a warm, loving, hungry, tempestuous little heart in those days! I wonder if the embers are all burned out. I think not. They flame sometimes still in a smouldering way and then my soul aches. Poor soul! And poor heart! You have always struggled together in an unequal companionship. But in those days I had *no* soul—very little, anyway—just in an embryo state perhaps—and so I was happy and didn't know it. When the process of soul evolution began then came suffering. Still, it must be good to have a soul and perhaps some day its growing pains will cease and all will be well and worth while.

Saturday, April 12, 1902
Echo Office, Halifax

It is pouring rain now in that gruesome back yard upon which I have looked every day since I came here. I know it by heart—every kink and corner of its griminess—I could sketch it with my eyes shut—the black, dripping roofs, the dead brick walls and the flapping clothes lines across it.

The paper has gone to press and I am having a breathing spell. That fiend of a Golding has just been out to give me an assignment for tomorrow, bad 'cess[1] to him. I have to "write up" the "parade" down Pleasant St. after church tomorrow to watch Simpsons' long deferred cut on Monday.

Mr. Taunton returned today from his cruise to the West Indies, glory be! Golding and I cannot get on together at all. He worries the life out of me and I heartily and wholesomely detest him, the little beast!

Thursday, May 1, 1902
25 Morris St., Halifax

I have "flitted." The Macdonalds gave up housekeeping this spring and went boarding for the summer, so I gave warning and moved, too. I am in a much nicer place now and my congealed soul is beginning to thaw out.

---

1. Irish idiom: "bad luck"; "'cess" is short for "success."

Twenty-five Morris[1] is a big, gray, stone house and is kept by a Mrs. Andrews and her daughter. I was at first under the impression that Mrs. A. was a widow but I have since found out that Mr. A. is still in the flesh, although he appears to have been suppressed.

I have a little third-floor room looking out on a few acres of back yards. Back yards seem to be my fate.

Kate M. and Mrs. M. have a large room next to mine and Minnie has the front hall bedroom on the same floor. Needless to say, we have hilarious times. Three other boarders are on our "flat." One is a Mr. MacAfee who is a clerk in a dry-goods store. He is short and bald but very good fun. Mr. Colbourne is another dry-goods man. "Colly" is a good soul, with big "cowey" eyes. He would have made a nice girl but—well, "God made him and therefore let him pass for a man."

"Andy" his roommate is a druggist and no fun at all.

A Mrs. Pearson, with three children has the big room on the second floor. She is a nice, good, uninteresting soul. Then the last of our circle is Mr. Grant, a youthful bachelor of 84, who works in a wholesale liquor store all day and plays whist with Kate, MacAfee and myself in the evening. Besides, he serves as a peg on which we girls hang any number of jokes, good, bad, and indifferent. One can be useful, you see, even at 84.

Sunday, May 4, 1902
25 Morris St, Halifax

I am writing this in my room. Everybody else, except Father Grant, is away to church. I stayed home to "expurgate" a novel for Mr. Taunton's use and behoof. When Mr. T. was away Mr. Golding started to run a serial in the *Echo* called "Under the Shadow." Instead of setting some A.P.A.[2] stuff as he should have done he simply bought a sensational novel at a bookstore and started it. It was very long and was only half done when Mr. T. returned. So, as it would run all summer in its present form, I was bidden to take it and cut out mercilessly all unnecessary stuff. I have followed instructions, cutting out most of the kisses and embraces, two third of the love making and all the descriptions, with the happy result that I have reduced it to about a third of its normal length—and all I can say is "Lord have mercy on the soul of the compositor who has had to set it up in its mutilated condition."

---

1. This central street becomes University Street and leads to Dalhousie University.

2. American Press Association, a wire service carrying international stories.

I shall be going home the last of this month. I shall be sorry to leave the office but not to leave Halifax. I like the office extremely but I *don't* like Halifax.

Monday, May 12, 1902
Echo Office, Halifax

Today I've laughed more than I've done for a month together. I've been re-reading "A Bad Boy's Diry."

That book is responsible for *you*, my journal. 'Twas from it I first got the idea of keeping a "diry." When I was about nine years old Mr. Fraser, the Cavendish school teacher, who boarded at our place, had the book. I think I regarded it as a classic then. I read it and re-read it and promptly began a "diry." I folded and cut and sewed four sheets of foolscap into a book and covered it with red paper. On the cover I wrote "Maud Montgomery's Diry."

Years ago I burned it in one of my iconoclastic fits. It was a pity, for it really should have been preserved as one of the curiosities of literature.

The "bad boy" was, of course, my model. He spelled almost every word wrong; therefore so did I of malice prepense. He was always in mischief and wrote accounts of it in his diary. Although not very mischievous by nature, being bookish and dreamy, nevertheless I schemed and planned many naughty tricks for no other reason than that I might have them to write in my "dere diry."

But I had never seen the book since then and had forgotten it so completely that it was new to me. I just howled over it today for it was absurdly funny still—even funnier than I used to think it, I imagine, for I took it quite seriously in those days, when I made a hero and model out of "little Gorgie."

Friday, May 20, 1902
25 Morris St, Halifax

I had a good internal laugh today. Miss Russell, a Dartmouth girl, who was recently added to our staff and who is rather nice, said to me: "That story *Under The Shadow* is the strangest one I ever read. It wandered on, chapter after chapter, for weeks and never seemed to get anywhere; and then it just finished up in eight chapters, *lickety split*. I can't understand it."

I could have solved the mystery for her but I didn't!

Miss Russell

Saturday, May 31, 1902
Echo Office, Halifax

My last day in the office! Well, I'm sorry.

I am perched here at my desk. The day is fine and bright and everything is jogging on as usual. Pshaw! I believe I have a heartache.

Anyway, I have the comfort of knowing I have got along all right here. Even the redoubtable Mr. Dunn assured me of that. Mr. McClelland told me I could have the place back again in the fall if I'd like to come. I would like to; but I don't think I shall. I feel badly over giving up the chance, for I may never get another one. But I feel that I ought to stay home with grandmother. She is not happy or contented with Prescott. He has behaved very nastily to her. He always was a cad and a cad he will be to the end.

Monday Night. June 2, 1902
25 Morris St., Halifax, N.S.

I am tired and my ribs ache from laughing. I really didn't know there were so many different ways people could make fools of themselves. But as Josiah Allen's wife[1] says, "I must not anticipate." *Is* it Josiah Allen's wife? Well, if not she some other celebrity.

Yesterday morning Kate Macdonald and I "looped the loop." That is to say, we got on a street car at our door and rode on and on, until we came back to our door again. It was a five mile jaunt and we saw all of Halifax that is worth seeing. Even Halifax is pretty now. The trees are respectably leafy and every grass plot is gay with dandelions.

In the afternoon I went to tea with Mr. and Mrs. McClellan. Annie Fraser of Charlottetown was there and I had a very nice time. Annie and I went to Fort Massey in the evening. I was not sorry that it was my last Sunday at Fort Massey for as a church I have no use for it. Church, indeed! I should call it cold storage! I have been going to it regularly ever since last fall and not one living soul in it, not even the minister has ever once spoken to me. I have taught in the Chinese school every Sunday evening and not one of the teachers has ever spoken to me. When Myrtie Clark introduced me to the Superintendent and told him I would take a class he said he was very glad. When I went to him last Sunday and told him I would have to give up the work as I was going away he said he was sorry. He did not even thank me for what I had done. That was the extent of my intercourse with anyone in the school!

---

1. Pseudonym of Marietta Holley (1832–1926), author of comic dialect books including *Samantha* and *Samantha on the Race Problem* (1892).

After the service Mr. Falconer read a telegram to the effect that at 12 o'clock that day Lord Kitchener[1] had signed a treaty of peace with the Boer generals. This meant that the long dragged-out war was at an end at last. Everybody in church drew a long breath. The moment was quite dramatic.

I shall never forget the excitement of the first stages of that war. It was worth while to be alive then. But of late it has been a tedious bush-whacking affair.

Being Sunday night all they could do by way of celebration was to ring the bells. This they did with might and main. After I came home Miss Andrews and I went for a walk in the Park which was full of the servant girl and her solder, as usual.

After I got home for keeps I read a perfectly harrowing ghost story. It was the most gruesome thing. I read it in bed and after I had finished it do you suppose I could get out of bed to put the light out? No!! And if Kate M. had not fortunately come in late that lamp would have burned good and bright until morning. When I heard Kate's airy footfall on the stairs I called her in, explained my predicament, and got her to put out the light. If I had got out myself to do it I was sure something would grab me by the feet when I was getting in again.

The story was Lytton's "The Haunters and the Haunted" and I can conscientiously recommend it.

Well, tonight Halifax turned to and stood on its head—raised Cain by way of celebrating the peace. Everybody who could stand on his legs was out, Min, Kate and I among the rest. It was all too funny for words. I fear I shall never get my face straightened out again. It will wear a spectacular grin for the rest of my days.

Saturday, June 14, 1902
Cavendish, P.E.I.

I have been home for a week and have done nothing but poke out old corners. They needed it.

I left Halifax Tuesday morning after the peace celebration. Min and Kate saw me off at the station. It was very cold crossing from Pictou.[2] We got over about eight and

Home again

---

1. Herbert Horatio, Lord Kitchener of Khartoum (1850–1916), after his victory in Sudan, 1898, became commander-in-chief of British forces during the Boer War.

2. Ferry from Nova Scotia to Wood Islands, north of Charlottetown.

Bertie MacIntyre and Fanny Wise were down to the wharf to meet me. It was *good* to see 'em again. I stayed in town until Saturday and then came out to Hunter River and down with the mailman.

It's good to be home again, after all. The peace and quiet of this dear old spot is very sweet to me. There is no place on earth I love or ever will love as I do it, in spite of all the drawbacks that the recent years have brought to it.

Monday, June 30, 1902
Cavendish, P.E.I.

What would it be like to live in a world where it is always June? Would we get tired of it? I daresay we would, but just now I feel that I could stand a good deal of it if it were as charming as today.

But that is the *outside* world. Inwardly I have been as a ravening wolf!

I had a "white night" last night. I don't often have them. I generally have a firm enough grip on myself to choke back all premonitory symptoms and go to sleep like a philosopher. But last night—somehow—the floods overwhelmed me. Gods, how I felt!

I couldn't sleep—did not sleep until dawn. Every trouble I ever had came surging up with all its old bitterness—and all my little present day worries enlarged themselves to tenfold proportions and flew at my throat. Life seemed a horrible, cruel, starving thing and I hated it and wished I were dead. I cried bitterly in sheer heart sickness and loneliness. Anything like that wrings the stamina out of me. I never can stop half way in an emotion. I must sound the deeps every time and sometimes they are like to drown me. I am a hundred years older than I was yesterday. And there was not a soul in the wide world to whom I could go for understanding and comfort.

Much of this misery had a physical basis I know. It has passed and I am normal again. I shall not likely have another "white night" for a long time.

This evening I went for a walk in Lover's Lane to exorcise my evil spirit. It was efficacious as usual. Somewhere in me the soul of me rose up and said, "No matter for those troubles and problems that looked so big and black in the night. They are mortal and will pass. I am immortal and will remain."

Lover's Lane

This is true—and a great comfort and stay. But the flesh must have its little howl and make its protest now and again. This world is all *it* has and when it doesn't get its share or gets the wrong share it will rebel. Down, you vagabond of a heart! Haven't you been schooled into placidity by this time? You have no business to rise up and make a to-do because you are aching. We've all got to ache. It is part and parcel of this puzzle we call living. But there's no use moaning because we ache. The only thing to do is to laugh— outwardly, at least.

Thursday, July 31, 1902
Cavendish, P.E.I.

July has burned itself out. It has been a pleasant month. Uncle Leander, Aunt May and Kennedy have been here all the month. They leave tomorrow. Aunt May and I have amused ourselves bathing and walking. Our bathing trips were our best fun. They were really jolly. Away up the

Aunt Mary
[Also called May]

Uncle Leander

sandshore is our "dressing room"—a big basin scoops out of the heart of the sand hills and warm with the sunlight it cups all day. Here we don our water togs, scramble up the steep sides, screaming with delight as the warm sand slides under our bare feet, then pick our steps gingerly down the outer side where the sharp sand-grass will cut to the bone if it gets a chance, then

The sandy hills, x our dressing room

a race over the beach and a plunge with flesh-cringing shrieks into the water that seems so bitterly cold at first until we have been in it long enough to get "habituated to our environment." Later on, when we have waded and ducked and swum to our heart's content, there is a wet scamper back to our dressing room, a vigorous rubbing down with towels, and a wriggling into clothes again. It's all a charming little bit of daffing the world aside. Outside of the purple hills it may be waiting—that greedy old world—to pounce on us and crunch our bones. But here, by this charming blue ocean we can laugh at it.

Amanda was in for the mail this evening and as usual I walked part of the way back with her. I still keep up the old schoolgirl habit, although there is never any enjoyment for me in it now. Poor Amanda's life is a rather sombre thing for her, I fear, and she cannot, or does not, try to hide its sombreness. She lets it spread into other people's lives. Tonight she was so dull and gloomy that it reacted on me and I became dull, too, and felt as if an incubus were weighing on my mind and heart. Yet Amanda used to be a jolly girl once upon a time and we used to laugh almost constantly when together.

I felt miserable and constrained all the time I was with her and relieved when I left her. She is a foolish girl to let the world see her bitterness—the world which only mocks. It never pities anyone—and even if it did the world's pity is a very stinging thing. I'll none of it—whatever my troubles are I'll mask them with a smile as long as I possibly can.

Tomorrow I go to O'Leary to visit Mary Beaton and from there to Park Corner. I shall take my worries and problems, my ambitions and strivings, my white nights and pale days, and lock them away in a deep place in my soul. And I shall put on light-heartedness and frivolity as a garment. I mean to have a good time.

Saturday, Aug. 31, 1902
Cavendish, P.E.I.

I had it—although more at Park Corner than O'Leary. Still, I had some fun there, too, although most of the time I was furiously bored. Mary lives on a lonely, ugly, road. She doesn't appear to have *any* nice neighbours and somehow I don't think she is very happy. As for Archie, he is stupid and crude.

Stella's room at P.C.

Mary has a baby! It is the funniest thing in the world to think of Mary with a baby! Roland Beaton is a pretty, blue-eyed little fellow.

The best fun I had while there was an excursion Phemy Beaton and I had to Tignish[1] to attend a Forrester's concert.[2] We stayed all night and had a gay time.

After leaving O'Leary I spent a fortnight at Park Corner. It goes without saying that I had a jolly time there.

Now I'm home again and I must unlock the secret chamber of my "Ego"— or Fate unlocks it for me, for of my own choice the key might rust there— and take out my problems again.

Sunday, Sept. 21, 1902
Cavendish

Nora Lefurgey   Myself in 1902

I have made a new friend recently. This, in Cavendish, has a flavour of the miraculous. The person in question is Nora Lefurgey,[3] who is the school teacher here and boards at John Laird's. We "took" to each other from the start and have been enjoying our congeniality every since. Nora suits me exactly. We never bore each other and we have no end of fun together. She is a positive God-send to me for I have no other close friend in Cavendish. Amanda and I have grown so far apart that our friendship is merely a hollow show. Lucy and I used to be intimate in a superficial way. But a year or so ago I discovered deceit and treachery in her, such as I had always known her to be guilty of in regard to other people but which I had been foolish enough to believe she did not practise towards me. This utterly destroyed my old affection for her. As I am situated I could not openly break with her; but I shut her out of my intimacy wholly ever since. So Nora fills a "long-felt want."

---

1. A village near the North end of Prince Edward Island.

2. The Independent Order of Foresters, operating in Canada since 1875 as a fraternal benevolent and insurance group.

3. Nora Lefurgey (1880–1977), teacher at the Cavendish school (1902–3), boarding with the John Laird family until after the Christmas holidays.

Monday, Sept. 29, 1902
Cavendish, P.E.I.

I am just home from the exhibition in town and am feeling
miserable with a bad cold. But
I had a good time in town and I
daresay I shall survive the cold.
If I don't—well, it won't really
be much difference, you know.
Nobody would mind much.

The Exhibition didn't interest me particularly but I had a
good deal of pleasure meeting

Exhibition grounds

old friends at it. Among others I met Lou Dystant. I hadn't seen him for four
years. We met on the Ex. grounds one bitterly cold day and had a long chat.
Lou hasn't changed at all in appearance. Poor Lou! Those days when he was
so tragic seem very far away indeed now. He did refer to them once—"we
were two children then," he said; somebody blundered into us and nothing
more was said along that line. *I* didn't wish to discuss it.

Monday, Oct. 27, 1902
Cavendish, P.E.I.

Yesterday the new Baptist church was opened. That means another change
in Cavendish. The old church was just "in over the hill" from here. It was a
pleasant walk down the spruce-fringed school hill, up the long "Laird's hill"
and in along the road to the woods of maple and spruces among which a
very plain little white church was nestled. It was a beautiful site for a church.

The new Baptist Church   The old Baptist Church

The new one is away up on the other road close to the hall. It is a very nice church but it seems strange and crude yet. Time hasn't mellowed it; everything is starkly, staringly, insultingly brand-new and shoppy!

"Lairds' Hill"

Sunday, Nov. 30, 1902
Cavendish, P.E.I.

I'm extremely sleepy. Instead of scribbling here I ought to be in bed—and thither shall I go, "immediately and to onct," as soon as this journal is brought up to date.

November has really been quite an exciting month. Early in it the Baptists started up a series of revival meetings. They got an "evangelist" to help them called MacDougall—Christian name, Sam.

Really, he *was* delicious! He was good-looking—if you happened to fancy his style—and had *such* melting dark eyes. The fifteen-year-olds went down before those eyes like ninepins. *And* he could groan so heart-rendingly! Also he could sing! For the rest, he was illiterate, sensational and so vulgar that he

x Frede

set the teeth of my spirit on edge. But I went—bless you, yes. It was fine fun. I was sorry when I had to miss a night!

This went on for about three weeks—and then came the *exposé*. Cavendish hasn't enjoyed such a scandal for a decade. The Rev. Sam turned out to be, not only a fake—that night have been endured—but a *Presbyterian*—or, as he pronounced it, *Presbytarian*. The Baptist blood curdled with horror. Poor Sammy was hustled out of the place and since then peace and dullness have resumed their reign.

Nora was here all Friday night and we talked until the tiny hours. Then last night Frede Campbell and her cousin Jim Campbell[1] arrived and Frede and I conferred on sundry subjects very near to our hearts. Hence I have two nights' lost sleep to make up—and I'm off to do it.

---

1.   In 1919 LMM commented that Frede might have married Jim if he had not been her first cousin.

Wednesday, Dec. 10, 1902
Cavendish, P.E.I.

Buried alive! Last Friday afternoon it began to snow and likewise to blow. It is still at it. We have had no mail in all this time and I am ready to tear my hair out by handfuls.

Saturday morning we were "snowed up." When dug out I took my camera and waded around for an hour in snow to my neck trying to get some "snow scenes." I almost froze my hands and caught a fiendish cold. This however would not have mattered if the scenes had turned out well. But, they were all flat failures! I was too provoked for anything.

Saturday, Dec. 27, 1902
Cavendish

Since then we have had thaws—just a few dozen or so. There is no snow left.

This evening, suffering from the effects of being cooped up all day in the house, I went for a walk at sunset. It did me good, even if underfoot was all slush and mud. The air was pungent with the aroma exhaled from broken-hearted firs who have been so beaten and buffeted this stormy December that they are yielding up their very souls. I drank the pungent balsam in avidly. There is magic in the breath of the firs. It gets into my blood like wine and thrills me with unutterable sweetness, as with recollections of some other fairer life lived in some happier star.

Garden corner in winter

There is kin to me in those dark stately trees. I love them as I love no other. They carry me back to the childhood of the race when men lived under the open sky.

1903

Tuesday, Jan. 13, 1903
Cavendish, P.E.I.

I am in a state of collapse—good for nothing! Hence I shall scribble something in this journal. Last night we had a concert and tea in aid of our church debt. Therefore, my collapse. "All in a good cause." Well, was it really? I sometimes think I might find some better use for energy and gray matter than in helping get up "sociables"[1] to pay the debt on a church whose members are perfectly well able to put their hands in their pockets and pay it out of hand.

For the past ten days we have been in a perfect fury of work. Mrs. John Laird and I canvassed our road in a snowstorm. Then the programme was left to me and I had to make my soul sick hunting and begging for recitations and speeches, not to mention rushing around at nights to half a dozen choir practices, for—"those whom the gods destroy they first make mad"—I am church organist here now. Besides all this, I had to bake cake, make sandwiches, and help make candy. To be sure, we had some fun out of the affair and it was a success of its kind.

Monday, Feb. 2, 1903
Cavendish, P.E.I.

Nora came here to board[2] soon after my last entry—quite a difference in our quiet life. I like it. We room together, which I do *not* exactly like, for I prefer a solitary cubiculum. I like to have one place where I can be alone and turn over the pages of my soul. But in other respects it is jolly and companionable. We have had, are having, and expect to have a lot of fun— just undiluted fun. It is a good thing—

My downstairs room which Nora and I shared

although it doesn't satisfy me now. But it keeps me from getting mouldy.

Aunt Annie has been down for a fortnight—so our household has been quite festive.

---

1. Parties put on to raise money for the church.

2. Following common practice of providing room and board for the local teacher, the Macneills invited Nora Lefurgey to stay in their farm house, sharing in winter a room and a bed with LMM. During this period they worked together on a joint diary of the fun they enjoyed together. At intervals, LMM also continued to write in her private journal.

Monday, Feb. 9, 1903
Cavendish, P.E.I.

Once, in writing in this journal of a visit to Amanda's home I said it was a place where no changes ever came. That is true no longer for a very, great and sad change has come there at last. Mrs. Macneill died last Thursday night

and was buried today. She has been ill for some months. I spent Saturday afternoon there and last night I went there from the missionary concert in the Baptist Church and remained with the girls until after the funeral today. It seemed so strange and lonely without Mrs. Macneill. I was always very fond of her. She was a gentle, delicate woman who went out very little. It seemed impossible to think of the house with-

Amanda's home

out her. Today I went into the long dim parlour and looked for the last time on my old friend who was always so kind to me. I had been in to see her a few days before she died and she told the next comer that "little Maudie" had been to see her, going back to the old days when she used to call me that.

She looked calm and peaceful, as the dead nearly always look. How difficult it is to realize that one we have always known can really be dead. We see the dead lying before us, and we know that those closed eyes will never again open. But still it seems to us that they must be somewhere about. I wonder if this instinct be not a true one—if indeed the soul may not still be hovering near us, looking on at all our sorrow, and going with us hand in hand.

Today was cold and stormy—an ill day to lay any loved-body away in that cold bleak hill burying ground.

Saturday, Feb. 21, 1903
Cavendish, P.E.I.

Of late I seem to pick out for journal writing days when I am "played out." My present state of fag is owing to the party at Alec Macneill's last night.

For the past fortnight Cavendish has been almost gay. Everything came on at once. Last Friday night John C.

Alec Macneill's house

Clark's gave a party and Nora and I were invited. We had a fairly nice time. Of course there was no dancing in *that* house.[1]

Last night the party at Alec's came off. I had to attend the Literary first and read a paper before that august fraternity. But when that was over Nora and I betook ourselves to Alec's where we danced until five o'clock and had a really jolly time.

Friday, Mar. 20, 1903

Tonight wound up the Literary for the winter. Nora read a paper on Byron. It was very fair but the ensuing debate was deadly flat—tasted insipid. Or perhaps it was simply that *I* felt insipid. I did—and do. I feel inane and dragged out this spring. I have worked hard at my writing all winter and have had besides a good deal to worry me. In some respects life here this winter has been very hard for me. Well—well—well—it will be all the same in a hundred years!

Will it, I wonder!

Tuesday, Apr. 12, 1903

And a snowstorm! But *that* is no novelty. We have had several the past fort-night, with cold rainstorms sandwiched in between. It has been a very dis-agreeable spring—cold and dull. The weather has had a bad effect on me and I have been dull and depressed—sick of life and of myself. My only guard against absolute misanthropy this past week has been the re-reading of four old favourite books. Today I read "The House of Seven Gables"[2]—a rather unfortunate choice for such a day in such a month, for it is a weird, melancholy creation, and every few paragraphs I would stumble over a sen-tence that brought stinging, painful tears to my eyes. Such tears always hurt me now. Once, tears over a book-woe were something sweetly, sadly pleas-ant—tears over imaginary pain always are. But now—oh, they are bitter—bitter! Still, I love the book and found pleasure in reading it. I have by this time become accustomed to taking my pleasure diluted with pain. Once I protested against it fiercely, but have grown reconciled to it of necessity and feel thankful that there *is* pleasure mixed with the pain. The "Seven Gables"

---

1. As Baptists, the John Clark family considered dancing a sin.
2. Novel (1851) by Nathaniel Hawthorne in which a young girl, accepted by an elderly brother and sister into a strange, gabled mansion, becomes their joy.

has the indefinable charm of all Hawthorne's books—that airy, fantastic, elusive fancy of his permeates every line of it.

But one of my books did not hurt me—Irving's "Alhambra."[1] It was a volume of pure delight and I burned the heart out of a dismal day with it. For a time I forgot everything and wandered happily in the deserted halls and courts of the old Moorish palace with Irving, seeing with his eyes, hearing with his ears, and drinking in with him the romance and charm of a civilization long dead and an empire long passed away. The book seemed to me the gateway of an enchanted world. I stepped in and lo, I walked with happiness and youth and pangless pleasure again. Washington Irving, take my thanks. Dead and in your grave, your charm is still potent enough to wave a tissue of sunshine over the darkness of the day. I thank you for your "Alhambra."

Then I read George Eliot's "Adam Bede"[2]—another cup of mingled pain and pleasure, bitter and sweet. It is a powerful book, with an inartistic ending. Her delineation of character is a thing before which a poor scribbler might well throw down her pen in despair.

Last of the four came "The Rubaiyat"[3]—a string of pearls threaded on the blood-red cord of an oriental fancy. How very modern was that old Persian poet who lived nearly a thousand years ago—modern in his scepticism, his epicureanism, his philosophy. He was probably an unhappy man in spite of his "let, us, eat, drink, and be merry for tomorrow we die" dictum. People who have come to that stage always are unhappy. They have only a gloomy future to look forward to and so they give themselves over with a fierce intentness to getting all they can out of today. "Tomorrow!" exclaims old Omar scornfully,

> Tomorrow I may be
> Myself with yesterday's seven thousand years.

So he means to have a good time of it today, the frank old sinner. But does he have it? Do we, any of us, ever have a good time simply by flinging ourselves after it. Oh, no! Happiness is an elusive thing. We may not lay violent hands on it or cajole it into our hearts by "the cup of wine"—or whatever equivalent we may take to coax it to us.

---

1. Sketches (1832) by Washington Irving, who had lived in the ancient Moorish palace in Granada, Spain, in 1829.

2. Novel (1859) by George Eliot: a dramatic story of seduction and child murder, told in naturalist style and set in a pleasant rural community. LMM criticizes the "happy ending" of marriage between Adam and the preacher, Dinah.

3. The Rubaiyat of Omar Khayyam (1859), a translation by Edward Fitzgerald of the philosophical quatrains of the twelfth-century Persian poet.

I wish spring would come. I'm tired of existence. Life has been a sorry, business for me these past five years. I don't think anybody suspects this. To those around me, even my most intimate friends, I am known as a "very jolly girl," seemingly always light-hearted "good company" and "always in good spirits." It makes me laugh rather bitterly to hear people say this. If they could only see below the mask! I am thankful they cannot. I don't want to be pitied. And pain would not be any the less because it were known—nay, it would be—for me, at least—far greater.

The worst of it is, I don't think things will ever be much better. Life will just go on getting a little harder for me every year. I am practically alone in the world. Soon youth will be gone and I shall have to face a drab, solitary, struggling middle age. It is not a pleasant prospect.

I think the weather is largely responsible for my blues. When the sunshine comes again I shall find life quite tolerable—yea even pleasant. Not an ecstatic, rapturous affair at all but something one can jog along very comfortably with. In sunlight the soul of me shines out and conquers the flesh.

What a comfort this old journal is to me! It is my one outlet for my dark moods. Into it I pour the bitterness which might otherwise overflow and poison other lives. My greatest fear is that eventually the bitterness will grow so deep that I will not be able to write it out. That will be my darkest

The old Homestead

day. It will probably come when I leave this old home. The mere thought of it makes me sick at heart. I am not very happy here but I should be wretchedly miserable, I fear, anywhere else. I consider it is a misfortune to love any place as I love this old homestead—the agony of parting from it is so intolerable. I shall never forget what I suffered in Halifax last fall. And when I must go, knowing that there will be no return will it not be tenfold worse?

When Nora came here we started for sport's sake a sort of co-operative diary,[1] she writing it one day and I the next. It was to be of the burlesque order, giving humorous sketches of all our larks, jokes, etc. and illustrated with cartoons of our own drawing. In short we set out to make it just as laughable as possible. I think we have succeeded. Nothing could be more ridiculous than its pages—yes there could be and is! And that one more

---

1. LMM included a copy of this joint diary in a shortened version of the journals that she typed near the end of her life (she planned to give each son a copy, one handwritten and one typed). The joint diary has been published, with comments by Beth Cavert and Jenny Litster, in *The Intimate Life of L.M. Montgomery*, ed. Irene Gammel, and will be available online at lmmrc.ca.

ridiculous thing is that *I* should have helped to write them. If a stranger were to read that record he would be sure to think that it was written by a couple of harum-scarum girls in their frivolous teens who had not yet attained to the remotest conception of real life and had never felt or known a sorrow. Yet it was written—at least half of it—by *me*!

Thursday, Apr. 30, 1903
Cavendish, P.E.I.

The shadows have gone and we have had sunshine. With the shadows went my dark moods and I have been a cheerful being ever since. After all, it's not

View no. 2 of my room

a bad old world—and the folks in it are not half bad either. Oh, dear sunshine, what a potent medicine you are!

I've been having a busy, wholesome time of late with not much chance to brood. We have been housecleaning and I am moved upstairs to my own dear, dear, dear little room again. I could sing a paean of joy over it. It's the home of my heart this little room—the spot I love, for here I am happiest. You dear pictures, you dear books, you dear little window where I love to sit! Oh, I am glad to be back in you, little room.

I've been sitting here and dreaming tonight, in the soft, odorous spring twilight, while the robins are calling to each other in the dark spruces at the foot of the garden—dreaming over old days and hopes and raptures, and thinking of all the changes that have come since I first put my lips to life's goblet—and oh, how intoxicatingly sweet and new and wonderful the draught was!

I want to have a nice summer if I can. I have had a rather hard winter; but things are better now and will remain so for awhile I hope. Now I'm tired and I'm going to bed in my old white bed with the moonlight falling over me. And I shall sleep—and perhaps I'll dream that I am a carefree little child again. Sometimes I am tempted to wish that

The foot of the garden

I might just lie down on that same white bed and, with the moonlight on me and the great deep pitiful silence of the night about me, fall asleep to wake no more. I wonder if that is wicked—no, I don't think it is. It is just a symptom of heartache. And it is only at times I feel so. Most of the time I'm content enough to wake. After all, although life is not very sweet for me, still, I find it interesting—and I want to go on and find out what is in it for me, whether bitter or otherwise. Somehow, I can't see any chance of its being otherwise than bitter. But you can never tell—and even so, one has the feeling that it is better to get all that pertains to you, even if it be bitter. One wants to "dree one's weird" be it for good or ill. So after all, Life, I front you unquailingly as a general thing. You can't treat me much worse than you have—there is not much left for you to take from me. So I will smile at you and take all you offer. Here's to a good summer, Life, and our boon companionship! Stop scowling at me for the space of five golden months and let's be friends!

Sunday, May 2, 1903
Cavendish, P.E.I.

Dear Spring, you are the year's good angel! The hope of you and the memory of you keep our hearts alive through all the other seasons.

Yesterday I went Mayflowering and spent the whole afternoon in the barrens that overflowed with pools of sunshine and those wild sweet odors that are only found in waste places. And the Mayflowers—how sweet they were; hidden away under dusty, unpromising leaves like sweet thoughts blooming under a homely exterior. May flowers must be the souls of flowers that died last autumn. They have been buried under the snow all winter and this is their resurrection.

This morning I had a walk back to "the Devil's punch-bowl"[1] for ferns. This spot is a new discovery Nora and I made this spring. It is back in the woods beyond Lover's Lane and it is a queer enough freak—a great deep gash cut right down in the heart of the woods, with steep banks fringed with ferns an birches, and an amber-tinted brook brawling along the bottom. It looks like a bit out of one of Walter Scott's poems.

Oh, the dear woods and flowers! What perfect companions they are!

---

1. Named for a natural amphitheatre in Surrey, England. LMM later commented on how many places in the UK were named after the Devil.

May 29, 1903
Cavendish, P.E.I.

Something very nice happened today. I feel pleasantly exhilarated. I've got into *MacClure's* Magazine!!!![1] Yes, it deserves some explanation points after it to a certainty. It is very hard to get in there. Don't I know! Haven't I tried it repeatedly? And at last it has opened its doors to me. I sent it a short story, written along quietly humorous lines and today had a letter from the editor accepting it. The dear man was kind enough to remark that it was "a very charming little story."

There now, Maudie, sit up and pat yourself on the back! That, and the $60 cheque which accompanied it, is a bouquet not to be disdainfully sniffed at.

I'm pleased—oh, yes I'm pleased. But, as always, on the heels of the pleasure, follows the little chill of the question, "What is the use? There is nobody to care."—nobody but yourself to be pleased and pleasure loses half its flavour when it can't be shared. Pat yourself on the back if you like, poor childie, but it's an awkward process and not worth somebody else's hearty thump.

There, there, don't be pessimistic. After all, you've done your best and your reward is sweet in itself.

Saturday, June 6, 1903
Cavendish, P.E.I.

Am just home from a week in town. Did not have as good a time as usual, somehow—felt rather bored. So many things bore me now. I stand rather appalled at the changes I see in my inner self. Where or in what will they end? But this self-analyzing is foolish; misleading, too, for just as soon as I have settled that I am bored and blasé something happens—a chance word, a pungent thought, a passing emotion—and something stirs in me that makes me half believe that away down under it all I'm the very same passionate mortal I used to be, and that very little might make it flame out again into stormy conflagration.

But just now I'm tired! I don't care vividly about anything. I know quite well that most of this boredom and morbidness is the outcome of over-strained nerves. I'm not at all well just now and hence the general flatness and staleness of life.

---

1. The major American illustrated magazine *McClure's* was founded 1893, but failed in the 1920s. Contributors included Kipling, Conan Doyle, and Jack London.

Tonight I went to Lover's Lane. I wonder what I shall do without that lane in heaven! I love it idolatrously. I am never anything but happy there. There is charm about it that bars out all earthly pain and lets only peace and gladness through. How beautiful it was tonight! The wild cherry trees arched it with feathery bloom and the sunset flooded it with glory through the wood gaps, the ferns breathed spicery out of the purple air and over the tall white-misted wild plums shone a slender new moon burnished silver. Oh, the shadows that lurked under the low-

Lover's Lane

growing firs—the dear, companionable, elfin shadows. Oh, the call of the brook down in the hollow! Oh, the amazing miracle and glory, and wonder of the spring tide. Yes, yes, yes, it is good to be alive after all I am going to try to have a happy summer. I will fill my heart up with the wine of life and sip it drop by drop. Then, when it is drained, let come autumn and dreariness again—I shall have had my summer.

I am earnestly trying to teach myself to live in the present and stop med-dling with the future. It is a hard lesson for one of my temperament to learn but it is my only hope of making life endurable. I have never been a dull pupil—let us see if I cannot learn this old lesson "Sufficient unto the day is the evil thereof"[1]—likewise the good thereof. It's a simple, easy, hard old les-son—very very old, but always to be learned anew.

Well, it is star-time and good night time. Over in Lover's Lane it is dark under the cherry bloom. Out in the dim orchard the apple trees are breathing their souls out in bridal sweetness. It's the sweet of the year—her wedding month. Dear life, you are very beautiful and wonderful and sad and joyous!

Tuesday, June 30, 1903
Cavendish, P.E.I.

I have decided that June has been a delightful month—a sheaf of happy days. I have enjoyed it. The world has been bright and beautiful. One cannot fall into gloomy moods in June. That must be left for the drear November days.

---

1. Matthew 6:34.

Nora went away a few days ago.[1] She has given up the school. I miss her terribly; and yet her going was a real relief to me. For this reason: grandmother, never at any time of her life, very tolerant of the tastes and ways of other women, has become so childish in this respect that she is not now fit to have any stranger in the house. The way she has acted towards Nora this winter would have been positively ludicrous if it had not been so bitterly unpleasant for all concerned—and especially for me, as I was between the hammer and the anvil. What with trying to make things decent for Nora and trying to screen grandmother's absurd behaviour I was worried to distraction nearly all the time. I wouldn't live some of the days of last winter over again for the most congenial companionship in the world.

Nora and I celebrated our last days together as royally as possible. The night before she went away we came up to my den and wrote the last chapters in those two absurd "diaries" of ours. We have bound them in covers of fancy paper, with adornments of gold paint and ribbon, and have illustrated them with "home-made" pen-and-ink sketches which are so ridiculous that I howl every time I glance over them.

Uncle Leander came the day Nora left. He is a physical wreck with *paralysis agitans* and is, it must be admitted, extremely *cranky*. I don't wonder at this for *paralysis agitans*[2] is, I think, the most horrible disease that can attack anyone. It is so hopeless and remorseless and continual—the very last disease that a man of Uncle Leander's temperament could endure patiently.

We are getting up a "Strawberry Festival"[3] in aid of the church debt and are busy preparing a programme. Is the game worth the worry? I—don't—know—but it's easier to march with the crowd. I haven't much surplus energy these days to expend in striking out a path of my own in all matters.

Saturday, July 4, 1903
Cavendish, P.E.I.

There is no use in thinking that you are done with your "past." When a woman possesses that unenviable thing she must just make up her mind to reckon with it occasionally. She may bury it and imagine it is going to stay buried. Then, just when she is fondly supposing that the turf is growing free

---

1. Nora Lefurgey left at the end of the school year. She later married Edmund Campbell and led an adventurous life in western Canada and the United States. In 1928 she and her family relocated to Toronto and she was reunited with LMM; *Magic for Marigold* (1929) is dedicated to her.

2. Possibly Parkinson's Disease (which was identified in 1817) or another neuro-muscular degenerative disorder.

3. A tea party on the church grounds featuring the season's strawberries was the major social event of the Cavendish summer.

Baptist Church

on its grave, she hears something—and there is that wretched "past," mewing and gibbering at her very elbow.

The Baptist Association began to meet in Cavendish yesterday. Everybody goes to the evening meeting. Tonight I was late and as the church was full the usher showed me into a side pew by the pulpit where seeing anything was out of the question. It was not until the meeting was over that I got my blow between the eyes, delivered squarely and vindictively by malicious old fate. Had it been a physical blow it could hardly have had a more effectual physical effect.

We stood up to go out. I turned around indifferently and found myself looking into the face of—Edwin Simpson, not three feet away. The surprise and shock rattled me completely. Whether he saw me or not I cannot tell, for the next moment a wave of people rushed between us. I hurried through the vestry, out of the door, and started home at once.

This is really dreadful. Ed will probably remain in Cavendish for some time. He will be in church tomorrow and I shall have to go, for I have no excuse for staying home. Nay, I would not stay home if I had a dozen excuses for people would be sure to say I stayed away on his account. Well, this would certainly be true enough but I would not enjoy thinking that people knew it. So go I will—but shrink from the thought.

Interior of Baptist Church

I did not even know Ed was on the Island or expected to be, so to turn around and meet him like that was a very disagreeable shock. He has been at Chicago University for the past three years. I have seen and heard nothing of him. I feel all the old shame and humiliation revive at the sight of him. It flicks me on the raw to think that there is a man in the world whom I cannot meet squarely and unflinchingly because of the fool I once made of myself where he was concerned and the way I treated him.

There is really no valid reason why I should shrink so much from meeting Ed. It was all long ago and he must have forgotten completely. But it is just that I cannot overcome the feeling of constraint and distaste that comes over me at the thought of meeting him.

Well, we must pay the price of our mistakes!

Sunday, July 5, 1903
Cavendish, P.E.I.

Today is over and so far I have avoided the dreaded meeting. I don't know that I have done wisely in avoiding it. I have a presentiment that it must come yet. But at least I shall have more time to get used to the thought of it.

This morning I went up to the Baptist Church. It was crowded. Ed came late and went into the vestry. When church came out I hurried away before he got out. In the afternoon there was another service. When it was over Lizzie Stewart asked me to go over there to tea. While I was standing at the side door talking nervously to Fred Clark, Ed appeared and stood talking to someone a short distance away, directly in front of me. Of course I knew quite well I *ought* to speak to him. Common courtesy required that much. But I simply could not go and speak to him before all that crowd, where his cousins who have gossiped about me so much were all looking on, eager enough, no doubt, to see what they could see. I dared not even look at him lest I should catch his eye. Then I would have *had* to bow and he would probably have come over and spoken to me. I wonder what he thought—likely that I have lost any manners I ever did possess. I don't care what he thought—it is my own uncomfortable situation I'm taken up with!

I dreaded going to Stewarts for I feared someone would ask me if I'd seen him etc. If he stays in Cavendish long I foresee unpleasantness along this line. But nothing very bad occurred today. Lizzie did say, "Did you see Ed Simpson, Maud?" but we were alone. I said "Yes." I think I said it very well. No, dear Lizzie, I am not going to spread my feelings out for *your* inspection at all!

At the evening service the church was also crowded. When we came out into the night moonlight I had another bad ten minutes. Ed came out and walked around chatting to various people. I think he wanted to speak to me. He appeared to follow me about in the crowd and kept talking to people who stood just behind me. I know I was behaving foolishly. The dim light would have been a good opportunity for speaking to him. But I couldn't! I tried once—he was standing just behind me and I honestly tried to hold out my hand and say, "How do you do?," as I might have said to any old friend. But to my morbid sensitiveness it seemed to me that the whole world would stand still and look mockingly on at our meeting.

Of course this is ridiculous. My musty love affairs are not of such interest to other people!

Saturday, July 11, 1903
Cavendish, P.E.I.

This has been a pleasant week. I have seen and heard nothing of Ed. He has probably gone home.

Fred Clark

Laura and Bertie McIntyre spent Wednesday here and it was a good Wednesday. There was a prayer meeting Thursday night and Fred Clark walked home with me from it. Fred goes around with me a little this summer. He is nothing but a friend, but he is good company. We went into the garden and sat for an hour or so under the apple tree having a merry gossipy chat. It was a lovely night, the air mild, misty and fragrant, the moonlight falling in a rain of silver through the apple boughs on the white waves of blossoming caraway that broke into foam all around us.

The rest of the week has been filled up with "festival" business. It is a worry, but there is a little fun in it too.

Later On, Bedtime

Coming home from choir practice tonight Fred said that Ed is to preach in the Baptist church tomorrow night. I shall *have* to go for if I stayed away everybody would guess why. But it will be an ordeal to sit there and listen to Ed preaching—there is no mistake about that.

Sunday, July 19, 1903

My little protecting gods have not altogether forsaken me. A thunderstorm came up last Sunday evening just before church time and lasted until it was too late to go. It's an ill wind that blows nobody good.

Aunt Mary and Kennedy came over on Wednesday. Our strawberry festival came off on Friday night and was a financial success at least, but a very dull affair—at least I found it so. I stewed and puttered all day Wednesday making candy for it and all day Friday making ice-cream. Now that it is over I can call my soul my own again and I celebrated my emancipation by a good bout of reading all yesterday and today for I've not had time to glance at a book for a fortnight. I read "The Virginian,"[1] "Darrell of The Blessed Isles"[2] and "The Pit." *The Virginian* was very good and had an ending so idyllic that it hurt. The perfect happiness of *Mollie* and her *Virginian* was really insulting. *Darrell* rather bored me. *The Pit*[3] was strong and exciting, but brutal and rather crude of thought. But it is rank waste of time to be criticizing the books of the day. They amuse and pass time pleasantly and that is all that is really expected of them. They are not under any obligation of immortality.

Sunday, July 26, 1903
Cavendish, P.E.I.

Yes, certainly my little tin gods[4] are looking after me. Ed preached in the Baptist Church this morning again. It was our regular Sunday for evening service but Uncle L. who was to preach today wished to have the service in the morning. So in the morning it was, glory be!

I've been having a good time this past week—plenty of pleasant drives and walks and a book or two; all outdoors to prowl about in—yes, life and I are on excellent terms of truce.

Today I've been reading "A Daughter of Heth"[5]—a dear little story with an ending that made me want to take the author by the ears and bang some sense into his head.

Monday, Aug. 10, 1903

My little gods have protected their own again—really. I am almost ready to believe seriously in some such protection. If destiny had not worked in a side-slap in this very protection I should almost be tempted to suppose that she had grown tired of persecuting me and want to leave me disdainfully alone.

Last Friday evening Bob McKenzie came up and suggested that we make

---

1. *The Virginian: A Horseman of the Plains* (1902), set in Wyoming, first among serious novels in the Western genre. Owen Wister wrote this novel in a vigorous style reminiscent of LMM's favourite Kipling novel.

2. Irving Bacheller's novel (1903) sentimentalizes the life of an old "clock–tinker" who dwells in his imagination.

3. Frank Norris's bitter exposé (1903) of Chicago financial finagling, very different from LMM's usual fare.

4. The powers that ironically govern her fate. The quotation is from Kipling's "Public Waste" (1886), referring to self-important authorities who unwittingly reward someone they despise.

5. A sentimental old-fashioned tragedy (1871) by William Black climaxing in an evocative Scottish setting.

a long planned excursion to St. Eleanor's to see Nora on Saturday. As this would mean my absence from Sunday evening service in our church I had to get someone to take my place at the organ. It was not known certainly who was going to preach but Mr. Archibald was expected. So I wrote to Mabel Simpson asking her to be organist for Sunday evening and then I went to St. Eleanor's with a conscience void of offence towards all men—except Ed—and most women. We had a lovely time in St. Eleanor's and Nora and I enjoyed ourselves hugely. Sunday evening we came home and arrived here about ten. My first question was "Who preached in our church tonight?" The answer was "Ed Simpson."

At first I was amazed—then relieved—then *vexed*—vexed *because I was not there!*

This is where the aforesaid slap of destiny comes in. It was all very well to be glad I had escaped being there—and I *was* glad. To sit on that choir platform and face that congregation while Ed preached would have been an ordeal very trying to the soul of me. *But*—would people think that I *knew* Ed was to preach and decamped because of that? Would Ed himself think so? My pride was up in arms at the idea. Of course they would—of course he would! I would have endured a great deal rather than have anyone suppose that.

However I shall likely have a chance to redeem myself, as I understand Ed has been asked to speak at our missionary concert Thursday evening.

Fred was down today to say good-bye as he is going to Boston. I shall miss him considerably—although of course it is only a surface miss. My companions in C. of either sex are growing few, so that the loss of one makes a serious gap.

Tonight while on my way home from a choir practice at Laird's Bob McKenzie overtook me and we went for a drive.

"I hear we missed a fine sermon last Sunday night," said he.

"So I understand," said I.

"Greatest preacher ever was in Cavendish, so they say," said Bob. "Pretty *Simpsony* though, I guess."

This is the sort of thing I have to expect every time I venture out these days. It is more than aggravating.

Wednesday, Aug. 12, 1903
Cavendish, P.E.I.

Oh, oh, my little gods have deserted me! I felt sure all along that they would—I felt in my bones that all these respites were merely by way of enhancing the torture. I remember a schoolmaster who had a habit of making several feints with a ruler before he really brought it down on my tingling outstretched palm. The experiences of life seem to repeat themselves.

I wasn't expecting anything to happen today. I knew that Ed had gone over to French River. Well, comes the mail! Old Santa Clausy Mr. Crewe, with his bushy gray head and his limp, was fate's incongruous messenger. I got a letter. No need to look at it twice—I knew that handwriting only too well.

And I knew before I opened it just what the letter was about. My absence from church on Sunday night caused it. Of course, just as I had feared, Ed had jumped to the conclusion that I had stayed away because he had preached.

Old Santa-Clausy Mr. Crewe

Then he reproached me with not having spoken to him on Association Sunday. He said he had wished to meet me and had been much disappointed. Then he went on to say that he found our present relations intolerable. "If, *as one at least may wish*," he wrote, "surely we can at least be friends." He then went on to say that he had been asked to speak at the concert Thursday night but if his presence meant my absence he would certainly decline. He would await my answer and if I did not reply he would take it to mean that I would not go if he were to be there.

I was in an awkward predicament. I must write, of course.

But this was Wednesday and the mail had gone. A letter could not leave until the next day and hence would not reach Bay View—where he had asked me to address him—before Friday, which would be too late. But I was resolved that my reply should reach him in time if I had to walk all the way to Bay View myself with it.

In my letter I explained why I was absent Sunday evening and apologized for not speaking on Association Sunday. I added that I felt friendly to him and that, although I did not think in view of the past that future meetings would be a source of pleasure to either of us, if he wished at any time to call I would be pleased to see him—a conventional phrase which masked a distortion of truth—for I would *not* be pleased.

There were two ways in which I might get the letter to Bay View post office in time. At first I thought of walking up to Bay View this evening at dusk and mailing it there. But I decided this would not do except as a last resort. Mrs. Jim Stewart, the Bay View postmistress, is one of the most inveterate gossips alive. If I walked up there to mail a letter to Ed Simpson she would publish the news far and wide. No, it would never do. So I am driven to asking Bob McKenzie to mail it for me in the morning when he takes the milk to the Stanley cheese factory. I dislike the idea of stooping to ask him very much but it is a choice of two evils. Bother Ed Simpson. Will I never have done with getting into disagreeable situations on his account?

I am certainly in for meeting him tomorrow night. But I knew it had to come. I have somehow felt that all along. I could not go on dodging Ed all summer and so it is better to have it over and done with. But I wish tomorrow night were over.

Saturday, Aug. 15, 1903
Cavendish, P.E.I.

Bob

I got up at five on Thursday morning for Bob generally gets along by six. It was a foggy, drizzly morning. I took the letter and tied it intricately up in two wrappers with sewing silk. If Bob would stop on a wet morning to untie two knots of sewing silk he would, I thought, be pretty curious. I hated to have him know who the letter was to and I also feared he would kerflummery everything by telling Mrs. Jim who had sent it—which of course would be just as bad as if I had gone myself. But those were risks that had to be taken. So I sallied out, took up my post behind the barn and waited. I *had* to wait, too. Of course on this particular morning Bob had to be late—it was nearly seven when he came. I huddled there in the drizzle and grew chilled to the bone and thought things not lawful to be uttered. But at last Bob did come. He cheerfully agreed to mail the letter and I came in with a huge sigh of relief.

Was busy all day decorating the church for the concert. At dark I dressed and went over to the church. Presently Ed came in and soon after was asked to a seat on the pulpit platform. I crouched down behind the organ and tried to be as inconspicuous as possible.

Interior of the Presbyterian Church pulpit

The programme began and went speedily on. Ed's address was the last number. Just as the choir was singing the hymn preceding it Mabel Simpson came in and up to the choir. When the hymn ended she coolly sat down in the only vacant chair—mine. It was really the last straw. For a moment I wondered whether to bolt out of the church or hurl the organ stool at Mabel's head. Of course, I did neither. Instead, I did the only thing I could do—walked quietly down and took my seat in one of the pews. Ed had risen and was standing by the pulpit. I was directly before him but you need not suppose I looked at him. I glued my eyes to the pulpit lamp and there I kept them unblinkingly.

"The steps"

Ed's address was very good but far too long—a fault he has. When he finished the meeting closed and we went out. I went down one aisle, Ed down the other. I knew we must meet at the door but I determined that it should be outside in the darkness. We met on the steps. *I* said "How do you do?" *He* said, "How do you do?" and we shook hands. Then I plunged off the steps into the crowd, dragged Aunt Mary away and came home. What a relief it is to have that hateful, necessary meeting over!

Sunday, Aug. 16, 1903
Cavendish, P.E. Island

Aunt May and I went up to the B. Church this morning. Lizzie Stewart showed me into a pew and when I sat down I discovered that Edwin Simpson was sitting right behind me teaching a Sunday School class! When he dismissed the Sunday School with prayer he was bending right over my head. I wonder if anyone would have supposed from the expression of my face that I was enjoying myself hugely!

Ed's sermon was very good, though it was nearly an hour long. I have always been willing to do perfect justice to his intellectual gifts. Just at the last he said,

"To some of us, standing here this morning and recalling memories of past happiness as contrasted with our present hopelessness"—then he looked straight at *me*. What application he went on to make I shall never know for I did not recover my power of attention until he was away on in something else.

We went again to the evening service. When we came out we met Ed on the platform and this time I managed to hold myself still and talk to him in platitudes for a few moments. It was *beastly*—with all John Clark's and Arthur Simpsons[1] staring covertly at us.

Monday, Aug. 18, 1903
Cavendish, P.E.I.

I've had a decidedly nerve-racking day!

Fannie Wise came out to Uncle John's today for a week's visit and I went over to see her. Aunt Margaret and Tillie Houston were there and Tillie lost no time in beginning.

It seems—this didn't come out at first, nor all at once, but dribbled out in the course of the ordeal—that last week George Montgomery and his wife visited at Will Houston's. He told them that I was engaged to Edwin Simpson and that we were to be married this fall!!!

He further clinched the "fact" by stating that some of Ed's own people up in Sixteen had told him so! This must surely have been sheer embroidery on George M's part.

Will and Tillie Houston are great friends of mine and this amazing news set them by the ears. Tillie gave me no peace either at Uncle John's or in her call here later on. In fact, she pushed her remark to the very limit of good taste. I writhed inwardly but outwardly I laughed and bluffed all her insinuations off. My soul feels raw all over, however.

Sunday, Aug. 23, 1903

Lu, Fannie and I have been "on a jag" of visiting this week and were out every afternoon. We had fun and are tired to death. And of course *I* had my own private and particular *pleasure* out of it. Take this as an example.

Scene:—Mrs. Alec Macneill's parlour.

Mrs. A. Macneill, crocheting in foreground. Maud, in centre of stage,

Alec Macneill's house

---

1. LMM is inconsistent in her manner of referring to families collectively. The manuscript has "John Clarks'" and "Arthur Simpsons" but the typescript has "John Clark's and Arthur Simpsons." Compare the references to "Uncle Johns," implying reference to a whole family.

netting. Lu to right, Fannie to left, slightly in background, embroidering pillow shams.

Mrs. Alec:—"Were you up to hear Mr. Simpson preach last Sunday evening, Maud?"

Maud:—"Oh, yes." (Misses a loop in her netting)

Mrs. Alec:—"Isn't he just a splendid preacher?"

Maud:—"Very good." (Feels Lu and Fannie exchanging significant smiles behind her back)

Mrs. Alec:—"And I think he's very fine looking, don't you?"

Maud:—"Oh, yes." (Nets furiously and says "Darn" under her breath)

That is just about the way it has been right along. I really don't know which were the worst—the people who knew that there was once something between Ed and me, or the people who have no such suspicion. Those who do know say mean things and watch me to see how I take them. That is bad enough, but there *is* a limit to the things they dare to say. On the other hand, those who don't know blunder into some speeches and questions that are positively dreadful to me.

Thursday, Sept. 10, 1903, Cavendish, P.E.I.

Lately I've been having a fairly nice and peaceful time. Today I spent a merry hour reading a bit of a book—"The Real Diary of a Real Boy."[1] It certainly was very real although in one or two places it was impossible to avoid the suspicion that some parts have been doctored up by a more mature hand. What amused me most was his faithful record of each day's weather—so like my own first "diry." "Today was cold with wind north-east"—"Very mild and showery"—and so on.

Monday, Sept. 14, 1903

Last night Ed preached again in the B. church. Soon after I arrived there Sophy Simpson walked in. Oh, that dear Sophy! How I *do* love her!! When we went out I went and spoke to her. She at once asked me in a voice loud enough to be heard all over, "Have you seen Ed?"

I responded that I had but perhaps Sophy thought I was prevaricating, for, as Ed passed by at that moment, she clutched him and said loudly,

"Ed, here's Maud!"

---

1. Henry Shute's novel (1902) revives the popular appeal of a mischievous child's story, set by LMM's early favourite, *A Bad Boy's Diary* by Metta Fuller Victor.

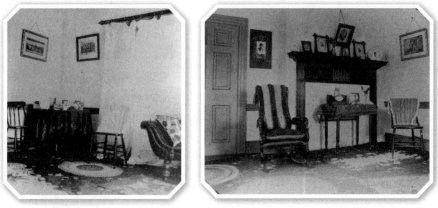

In the parlor   In the parlor

If Ed were blessing Sophy as devoutly at that minute as I was she would be beatified forever!

This evening Sophy and Ed called. We all sat in the parlour and talked for about an hour. I don't know what *I* said, or much of what *he* said. Everything seemed very unreal. As for Sophy, she was as impossible as ever but her gaucheries served a good purpose since they gave me something to think about. I don't think I made a fool of myself outwardly. Ed did pretty well also. Goodness only knows, though, what we were all thinking about—for I suppose even Sophy does occasionally think. That girl makes the flesh creep on my bones. She seems to radiate a repulsive force.

I never heard one living soul say they liked her, (Grammar? Grammar!) so the poor soul is to be pitied. And I *do* pity her—but I like to do it from a distance.

I was thankful when their call was over. As they rose to go Ed picked up my *Omar* which was lying on the little table under the mantel and said that he had admired the Rubaiyat—very much ever since he had heard a college professor quote a quatrain from it. Then *he* quoted it, looking straight into my eyes.

> A book of verses underneath the bough,
> A loaf of bread—a flask of wine—and *thou*
> Beside me singing in the wilderness,
> Oh, wilderness were Paradise enow.

It was not in especial good taste to quote it under the circumstances. But then good taste is not Ed's long suit.

He leaves for Chicago next Thursday so there will be no further danger of meeting him everytime I stir abroad.

Tuesday, Oct. 20, 1903
Cavendish, P.E.I.

George Campbell was married to Ella Johnson[1] on the seventh. I went over and stayed for several days. Clara was home for the event. I had not seen her for three years and found her very much changed both interiorly and exteriorly—and not for the better in either case. I really felt far more at home with Frede.

We had a big reception and dance at Uncle John's the night after the wedding and I had quite a nice time but two nights of late hours almost played me out. As I had still a little life left in me

George and Ella

on Friday however I tried to get rid of it by going to the woods with Frede in the afternoon where we sat on a damp moss bank for three hours and talked our souls out. As a result I had to stay in bed all day Saturday with a bad cold.

I found Clara half a stranger. We used to be on very confidential terms in the old days but this time there seemed to be a constraint between us. At the last, however, Cade thawed out and told me her troubles as of yore. Poor girl, she has had a hard enough time. But I'm afraid it has been largely her own fault. Clara always had poor judgment and false views as to the real values in life and it has cost her much.

Parlor at Park Corner

I left Park Corner sadly enough. George's wife is a nice little thing—in many ways far too good for *him*—but still I fear Park Corner will never seem quite the same again. It has always seemed a second home to me. Certainly, from a social point of view, I had always much better times there than in Cavendish and I love the place. But things will probably be much changed after this.

Saturday, Oct. 31, 1903

Summer is over and gone! How very short it has seemed! But I have enjoyed it in the main. Last spring I made a truce with life and we both kept the pact

---

1. From Long River, a friend from Park Corner days.

faithfully. Now the winter approaches and I shrink from it. Situated as I am, all alone here with poor old grandma, with no one to do anything for me or take me anywhere it can't be pleasant. However, I'll set my teeth and face it as courageously as may be. At least there is a spring beyond.

Saturday, Nov. 14, 1903
Cavendish, P.E.I.

Half of November is gone, glory be. It is the most dismal month of the year.

On the fourth Lucy was married to Ben Simpson[1] and has gone to live at St. Peter's, about 60 miles from here. Poor girl, she has made a poor match of it, both from the point of view of man and prospects, and has gone to a very poor home. It is surprising how little I miss her, considering our long association. But of late years it has been a surface association merely. When I lost confidence in her, affection and pleasure in her companionship went too. Her going seems to have made absolutely no difference to me.

Today I started in the morning to walk down to Will Houstons! I went across the fields by way of "Montana" and "Sam Wyand's field." I haven't been through the former for years and found it grown over with scrub maples out of all recollection. Our old paths were not even to be seen and I had quite a difficult time finding my way through the woods to the Rustico side. And as for the barbed wire fences—but I have resolved to forget about them!

My visit atoned for fences and everything else. I had a delightful day and enjoyed every minute of it.

W. Houston's house

Thursday, Nov. 19, 1903

I wonder if this is to be a sample of the days all winter! No, of course not. No doubt there will be plenty of fine and sparkling days. But on a day like this the grayness and dampness creeps into one's very soul and one believes that "all the tomorrows will be as today"—and life becomes very stale and flat.

---

1. Two men named Benjamin Franklin Simpson, each roughly the same age as LMM, lived in Bayview at this time: one (1871–1952) the son of Walter Simpson, the other (1878–1946) the son of William Simpson.

It was raining heavily when I woke. I was loth to get up to another dull lifeless day. But I finally did so, ate breakfast, did up some chores, wrote for an hour, did a "stint" of type writing, and then worked point lace until dinner time. After dinner—I worked point lace till tea-time. It rained steadily. The world, so fair and brave in her springtime, was a drenched, bedraggled old hag weeping and gibbering to herself. No mail came—the last straw of dismalness. Life is tolerable when the mail comes every day; when it doesn't come it isn't tolerable. After tea I worked point lace until bed-time! I was dreadfully weary of it but there was nothing else to do— not even anything to read. My face ached dully with neuralgia all day. I have seen nobody and could not stir outside the door. It is still raining and I am going to bed. I feel gray and nerveless to the very core of my soul. Satan will come along some of these days and tempt me to mischief and he will find me all ready to listen to him. I don't see what good at all my getting up today did.

I haven't done a solitary thing worthwhile—for even my story proved obstinate and wooden. What a dull, unsatisfying life mine is at present.

But softly—softly! There are far worse lives! Oh, yes, yes! You may tell a starving man truly that there are more painful deaths than starvation but he will die for all that!

Pshaw! I am ashamed of myself for this grumbling. It is the outcome of this weather and the unwholesomely lonely and analytical life I lead at present. I am never morbid in the sunshine.

Friday, Nov. 20, 1903
Cavendish, P.E.I.

Tonight while rummaging in an old trunk upstairs I found an old "Third Royal Reader" and for fun took it down and looked it over. I found my childhood in its musty, flower-stained leaves; those faraway days behind the brown desk in the old school drifted back into my consciousness again. The old reader seemed very small. I can remember that it once seemed to me a large and important volume. Almost every page recalled some long forgotten memory. I had my favourite selections of course—and some others that took just as strong a hold on me because they hurt me. Among the latter were "Little Jim," "The Sale of The Pet Lamb," "The Child's first grief," and above all, "The Dog at his Master's Grave." That last in especial affected me very deeply. I cried every time I read it—and I could not help reading it repeatedly. I remember distinctly waking up in the night once and thinking of that poor dog and crying.

"The Ant and the Cricket" used to vex me. I was always so sorry for that poor gay improvident little cricket and I used to solace myself by picturing out various appropriate vengeances on that miserly ant. "Lucy Gray" also vexed me because it puzzled me. I could never understand just what happened to the heroine. The awful vagueness of the line, "And further there were none," haunted and worried me.

I enjoyed looking through that old book.

Wednesday, Dec. 3, 1903

Got a cheque for another serial[1] today—the second I've sold. This has been a pretty good year for me in regard to literary work. I have attained a pretty firm foothold and have made $500 also. Editors often *ask* me for stories now; my name has been listed in several periodicals as one of the "well-known and popular" contributors for the coming year, and the Editor of the Pres. Board of Publication in Philadelphia[2] wrote recently to ask for my autographed photo.

Yes, I *am* beginning to realize my dreams. And the dreams were sweeter than the realities? Yes, but the realities are quite decent, too. I enjoy my success for I've worked and fought hard for it. I have the satisfaction, too, of knowing that I've fought my own battles. I have never had any assistance and very little encouragement from anyone. My ambitions were laughed at or sneered at. The sneerers are very quiet now. The *dollars* have silenced them. But I have not forgotten their sneers. My own perseverance has won the fight for me in the face of all discouragements and I'm glad of it now.

Sunday, Dec. 27, 1903
Cavendish, P.E.I.

Christmas is over. It was even duller than usual for we did not have the mail. My Christmas treat consisted of a walk through Lover's Lane in the afternoon. It was very delightful for the day was as mild and fresh as spring and the woods were full of a great friendliness.

Among my Xmas remembrances was a calendar of the University of Chicago!!! As my acquaintance with the students of that university is limited

---

1. "The Running Away of Chester" ran in *Boys' World* weekly from November 14, 1903, to December 26, 1903; "The Bitterness in the Cup" ran in *American Home*, December 1903 and January 1904.

2. The Presbyterian Board of Publications was one of a group of church-related presses that had developed a number of popular authors including Ralph Connor and Marian Keith.

to one, it would not have been hard to guess who sent it, even if Edwin Simpson's card had not accompanied it. The calendar is quite an artistic and interesting one but if Ed had picked out an embarrassing gift of malice prepense he could hardly have made a worse selection. Almost everything else could have been comfortably disposed of somewhere out of sight. But a calender is only good to hang up somewhere *in* sight. However, I will hang it in the parlour where I seldom go. Besides, nobody else will see it there. The wayfaring man though a fool

Lover's Lane

could hardly miss understanding the significance of the legend "University of Chicago" emblazoned across it face. Therefore, to avoid giving Cavendish gossip a very toothsome tidbit I will *not* display the Calendar when I show my Xmas presents to my friends.

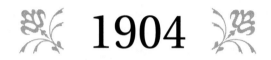

1904

Sunday, Jan. 3, 1904

What a day! One huge snowstorm from end to end and the thermometer at zero. I feel smothered. Even the windows are so thickly covered with snow and frost that the sensation is of being literally imprisoned. This has seemed as long as three days.

The other day I came across this sentence in a magazine.

"It is the unhappy people who keep diaries. Happy people are too busy to keep diaries."

At the time it rather impressed me as clever, but after thinking it over I have decided that it may be epigrammatic but it is not true. To be sure, I am not exactly a happy person; but I kept a diary and enjoyed doing so when I was quite happy. Besides, if being busy made people happy I ought to be a very happy mortal. No, the epigram should have read "It is the *lonely* people who keep diaries"—people who are living solitary lives and have no other outlets for their moods and tenses. When I have anybody to "talk it over with" I don't feel the need of a diary so strongly. When I haven't I *must* have a journal to overflow in. It is a companion—and a relief.

Today I was reading over the Prince Albert part of my diary. It brought back those days and sensations with almost startling vividness. That is what I like best in diary keeping—its power to reproduce past scenes and feelings and emotions.

I certainly would not wish to live that P.A. year over again in all its entirety for my stepmother made it very unhappy for me as far as her power went. But if I could live the part of it segregated from her atmosphere again I would gladly do so. What "larks" Will and Laura and I had! My heart ached a bit when I was reading about them.

Twilight of a stormy day

I don't know what to do with myself tonight. I feel like a caged creature. Sitting round all day with the storm howling outside, reading and reading *and* reading but with nothing new to read has induced a condition of brain-fag and restlessness which I seem to have no power to control. I honestly feel that it would be a relief to stand up and *swear hard* for ten minutes on end. That accurately expresses my state of mind.

However, I feel better for writing it out. It is almost as efficacious as swearing would be and much more respectable.

Sunday, Feb. 6, 1904

It is storming and bitterly cold. As this is just the sort of weather we were enduring when I wrote last it may be asked if it has been storming ever since. The answer would be "In the Main, yes." It has simply been one storm after another and zero right along. I cannot remember such a winter. We are surrounded by huge drifts.

Since my last entry my cousin Kate Macneill[1] died of broncho-pneumonia. She was Uncle John's second daughter and a rather bright girl. She was ill three weeks and I was over there waiting constantly on her night and day. Since then I have been feeling the effects of the strain and long vigils. Besides, it has been so bitterly cold and stormy and generally dismal that I feel worn out.

Saturday, Feb. 20, 1904

As usual, it is storming and freezing the very mercury. I really don't know where any more snow is to be put. Roads, mails and boats are blocked two thirds of the time.

I am lonely enough but not exactly in the blues. I have got rested and am feeling better physically. Besides, Aunt Annie has been down for a week and that was quite cheery. Still, life is very flat and dull. I do a hundred little tasks in which I feel no great interests. Oh, if it were not for my dreams I would go crazy! In them I can be as adventurous and happy and triumphant as I wish, while the world around me is a prison to the body.

Nevertheless, sometimes even dreams pall, and one longs for a little bit of decent *livable* life!

Snow—such snow—mountains of it! The orchard, where last summer buttercups danced and the pink blossom petals fluttered down on gold and green, is heaped almost to the tree tops with drifts. Drifts everywhere, as high as the house. Yesterday I went upstairs and peered wistfully from the frosted window of my dear den. I saw nothing but heaps and wastes of snow—enough to chill heart and hope in anyone.

Today I've had life kept in me by a couple of new books from the library. We have got a lot of new books this winter and so I think I'll weather it through till spring. Spring? What a dear, delightful word, heard long ago. Can it be that spring is really lurking ahead in April and May and that we will eventually emerge from drifts and find her? It seems beautiful but impossible—something to be dreamed of but never attained.

---

1. First cousin (1884–1904), sister of Lucy, Annie ("Tot"), Prescott, Frank, and Ernest, children of Uncle John.

Sunday, Feb. 28, 1904
Cavendish, P.E.I.

Storming? Of course! That is the normal state of the weather this year. Cold? Equally of course. Ten and fifteen degrees below zero doesn't precisely suggest a thaw. But I have used up all my weather vocabulary long ago so I shall henceforth have to treat it with silent contempt.

I have nothing to write about—which is mainly why I am writing. If I were doing or seeing or enjoying things I wouldn't have time to write. As it is, it is my only resort to while away this dull evening. Aunt Annie went home on Friday and I have been trying to get used to the loneliness again. I have succeeded tolerably well, aided thereto by a couple of new books and several magazines.

Last night I dreamed of Herman Leard! I don't know why. I seldom think of him now. And even in the early days of that unhappy time I hardly ever dreamed of him—and that was a great bitterness to me because I wanted to.

And it was very sweet, that pale dream! We were together again—I was in his arms—his lips were on mine—and the old rapturous thrill coursed through my veins as of yore. I hated to wake, and the dull wintry morning seemed doubly dull and chill and drear beside the loveliness of that vision of the night.

I sometimes ask myself this question. If Herman Leard were still alive and circumstances were to throw us together once more would I love him again? Would he have the same power over me as of yore? I like to smile proudly at this question and say, "No, I have outgrown such folly and the capacity for such folly; he could not move me now."

But, under all, I know that he could—that if he were to come into my life again I would make just precisely the same fool of myself over him that I did then. Such a dream as I had last night would convince me of this—so real and so vivid was the pleasure I felt in his dream presence.

Monday, March 11, 1904
Cavendish, P.E. Island

Life has become *livable* once more. That is, the weather has been fine, the cold has moderated, and the walking has got good. That last is, for me, the greatest item. I am no longer a prisoner—I can get out to the dear comradeship of woods and field again. I went across the snowy fields to Lover's Lane I love that place idolatrously. I am happier there than anywhere else. What is the power of that silent shadowy wood lane, even in its white winter solitude? Why can it always steal away the sting of life and pour the oil of gladness into my heart? I do not know why or how—but it always does

and so I love it with an intensity that sometimes makes me ask miserably how I'm ever going to live without it, when the day comes for me to leave Cavendish; it certainly will come in near or far and the thought is always unspeakably bitter to me.

Tonight it was perfectly beautiful back there. The air was very clear and still and silent. In the west there was a clear saffron sky against which the tracery of the bare maples and birches on the hill came out clearly. Under the firs it was dim and shadowy and white. The woods were all asleep.

Snowy scene

The fir branches snow powdered, were dreaming dreams of a spring to come and a joy to be. I tramped along over the snow and my spirit sang a song of delight. The evening was a cup of glamour, the purest vintage of the winter's wine, held to my lips. I drained it gladly—there was life on it that would help me live through many a dull tomorrow.

Jack Laird is home now. He went out west six years ago and this is his first visit home. He spent Thursday evening here and we laughed and chatted over old days and reminiscences. Jack has not changed at all in any respect. As far as appearance and manner go, he might have been away for

six weeks instead of years. I was glad to see Jack again. We were always good friends in the old schooldays. There was never very much depth to Jack—but he was companionable. There were ways in which I really liked him much better than Nate though Nate was incontestably the cleverer. Of course, Nate and I had much more in common intel-

Dreaming of spring to come

lectually. But at times, doubtless because of our very likeness to each other, Nate irritated and vexed me. Jack never did.

There is still "not much in him." The years have not enriched his nature any—they could not do so. But I did not tell Jack that I was analyzing him thus. Instead, I told him—what was the truth and what he took as a compliment in that he had not changed a particle. We had a jolly evening and a famous good chat over old times—the old times that *were* very jolly and bright, and yet were far from perfect after all. Looking back through the mellowing mists of the years and contrasting their bright hues with my dull and subdued present I am often tempted to think that they were better than they really were to overrate them. But in sober truth, there were often, very often, times even then when I was very unhappy. And I do not think that if the choice were offered me I would go back. I am not so *happy* as I was then but, paradoxical as it may seem, I am more *contented*. Life is richer and I get more out of it in many ways. No, dear early girlhood, you were a good and beautiful thing, and I enjoyed you; but, in this present mood of calm clear-sightedness, I do not hold you as the best or most desirable. And I would not go back to you if I had to go back to your limitations also.

Wednesday, Mar. 16, 1904
Cavendish, P.E.I.

I did a crazy thing this evening—and now I'm suffering from it.

Today was a furious snowstorm. I did not feel well all day—not well enough to be able to throw myself absorbingly enough into work to help me fight off the "blues." For oh, I *do* try to fight them off and not give way to morbid broodings. And I have pretty good success all things considered; but today I hadn't enough spirit to try. This evening I had nothing to read and wasn't well enough to work—my only safeguards against the "horrors." In an evil moment I unlocked my little trunk, saw there a packet of Will Pritchard's letters, took them out and read them. I knew it was a foolish thing to do—I knew they would make me blue and restless—but I did not anticipate the effect they did have! I don't know what has got into me. As I read on and on it seemed as if a cruel hand were tightening its clutch on my throat. Yet I dreaded to come to the end of them and stop reading. It was awful—horrible. When I had read the last I fled to my room and thought for a few minutes that I would surely go *mad* if I couldn't scream out loud until I had exhausted all the feelings that were in me. I couldn't do that so I cried madly instead—horrible crying it was and hurt me cruelly instead of relieving me.

I am sitting up in bed writing this and I am half frozen but I *must* write it out. Oh, how am I ever going to put out the light and lie down here alone in the dark? I *can't*!!

I don't know why Will's letters should have such an effect on me. He was never anything to me but a good comrade. And while his letters were pleas-ant and friendly they were not such as would be expected to stir up such a riot of feeling in me. But I've been lonely and sick at heart all day, and I just long wildly for his bright *friendliness* again. He *was* such a good friend—and we had such good times together. And he is *dead*!!

I cannot understand my mood at all. And I have no one to help me out of it. I am so horribly *alone*. Poor grandmother is old and deaf and in some respects very childish. She is no companion to me in any way. I have no *real* friend near me and when I am pent up here for a week at a time without even seeing an acquaintance to speak to I can't help my soul getting sick within me!

This old journal is a regular grumble book but that is all it is good for. I work it off here and don't let it flow in any other direction. In reality I am not discontented. I love this old home deeply, although grandfather's more than foolish will has made it no home to me—and I love Cavendish. I would be perfectly contented here if I had just a little companionship and the average freedom to come and go. And when I read those letters I wanted to get back to the days I received them and answered them with jest and chat and delightful foolishness.

I'll be all right again when the sunshine comes back and I'm able to work. But that doesn't make it any easier now. Oh, I'm so alone—alone—and just now I can't endure it—I can't indeed. I feel like a sick, frightened baby with no hope or strength or courage or—anything! I'm afraid of the dark and the wail of the wind. Oh, such feelings as are in my heart! If I could drag them out and put them into words it would help me. But I can't—I can't describe or define them.

I said in my last entry here that I would not change back to the old days and I thought I meant it. I felt so then—but now I would—I would! Those letters of Will's showed me what I was then—brought back the old life for just one maddening space. And then it went and the present by contrast seemed intolerable—the present with which I was almost satisfied the other night—and with which I will be almost satisfied again, I suppose, when this wears off.

But I know one thing—I won't read old letters again under such conditions as today's—no, no, no—I don't want the past made alive any more to show how dead the present is. The present may be dead—but so long as I don't realize it I can get along.

Oh, Will, Will, if you could only come back and be my friend again! I'm not thinking of *love* at all—that has nothing to do with *this* mood—indeed, I feel just now rather a distaste for the thought of love. But I just long bitterly for the old good comradeship—the sense that Will was *there* to turn to when I would. Oh, Will, where are you? Are you anywhere?

I just wish I could die! I hate the thought of living—of the miserable night before me—of getting up tomorrow to another dull lonely day. I know when

I put out the light I'm going to cry wildly. That's why I'm writing on and on—all this foolish stuff. It reads like drivel but I don't care.

It's strange—but if I had my choice tonight of calling *Will* or *Herman* out of that black outer void I'd call *Will*. I never cared for him in the way I cared for Herman—but it is he I want tonight. I want to see him—to laugh with him—to look into his gray eyes and bring the smile to his crooked pleasant mouth—I want to talk nonsense to him—to have him talk nonsense to me—about dances and picnics and flirtations, just as he talked in his letters. I want to be saucy and frivolous with him. I want him to say nice things to me and pay me boyish compliments.

But he's dead—he's dead. And if he is living somewhere he doesn't care for these things now—nothing like that matters to him. Oh, I don't *want* to believe in another life just now. There is something oppressive in the thought. It can't be like *this* life—everything would be different! No, no, I don't want to believe in it.

This is getting crazier. I will stop writing. But I won't put my light out yet for awhile. Oh, I am so tired of living!

March 17, 1904. Morning
Cavendish, P.E.I.

I've been reading over what I wrote last night. It is pretty bad but no worse than I felt, so I'll let it stand. After I managed to put out the light I cried myself to sleep. This morning when I woke I didn't want to get up—it didn't seem worth while. But now that I am up things are better. It is a fine bright day and I'm well enough to work. If I could only get out for a run I'd be all right again. But we are worse drifted in than any morning all winter. It is dreadful. Here it is mid March and ought to be spring-like. Instead we have a January landscape and temperature. Winter is jolly enough under some circumstances but under my present ones it is just dismal and I long madly for summer and freedom.

April 9, 1904

Well, that "bad spell" I had when I wrote last didn't prove fatal. I am all over it now. But that curious obsession lasted a week or so and fight it as I would I couldn't shake it off. It seemed to me that I wanted Will in everything. When anything nice happened—which was seldom—I wanted to tell him about it and talk it over with him; and when something nasty happened—which was often—or when nothing at all happened—which was really worst of all—I wanted to tell him about it, too, and get him to sympathize with me. Wasn't it all silly—and strange? If I were superstitious I could really believe that Will's spirit was near me in that strange mood.

But the mood is gone, thank heaven, and since then life has been livable in spots. I have learned—so meek have I become in my demands on fate—to be abjectly thankful for that. There have been so many times of late when it has *not* been even livable.

My "blues" are mostly due to brain-fag and the irritation of countless, ceaseless little worries. I write and study the greater part of the day. Then I'm tired of it and want something wholly different for a change—a cheerful chat, a drive, or any little diversion like that, and in winter especially it is very rarely forthcoming. Consequently, thrown back on myself, on my wearied brain and tense nerves, I get limp and flabby and blue.

If I could ask my friends here occasionally my life and my outlook on life would be much more normal and wholesome. But that I cannot do. My friends, even those of my own sex, have never been welcome here. Grandmother is in many respects a peculiar woman. She has never at any time, since I was old enough to remember at any rate, seemed to want *anyone* to come here, except her own children. My visitors have always been made to feel distinctly that they were unwelcome. Naturally they did not care to come again. This unfortunate failing or lack of hers has increased with age and finally I have ceased to ask anyone to come here. I have been compelled to do this. Of course it places me in a very embarrassing situation in regard to my acceptance of invitations elsewhere but it cannot be helped. I have tried at times to talk the matter over with grandma. But she has always been a very difficult woman to hold any such discussion with. She is up in arms at the slightest hint that there is anything I can be dissatisfied with in her conduct and takes refuge in blank denial of anything I may ask the reason of. "I never did this"—"I never did that." These incidents have been so unpleasant and futile that I have decided that it is wisest to submit and say nothing. She is old and has a good deal to contend with. Grandpa's absurd will placed her in a very disagreeable position and Uncle John and his boys treat her very badly. I make allowances for her in all this and for my own part have resolved to let all attempt at social life go.

But it is unwholesome for me—it is the main reason for most of my morbid moods. Things will be better in summer—they always are. And I know they can't be mended by complaining. I never do complain anywhere but in this journal. I daresay it has saved me from some alarming outbreaks elsewhere.

It is really beginning to look a little like spring. There have been some thaws and there are a few bare spots. I have been cheering myself up by planning out and ordering some new spring toggery and in getting ready to think of a garden by and by. Both are quite pleasant occupations for I am very fond of pretty clothes and I love flowers. To be sure, my garden plot has three feet of snow on it yet but "there will come a time"—to quote the slang phrase most in vogue just now. I have got some bulbs planted for it in the house and I watch them every day for the beginning of the miracle—for the growth and development of little crinkly brown seeds and ugly bumpy bulbs into rainbows and perfumes *is* a miracle and keeps alive my belief in God.

Then as for the clothes—that's just another form of *flowers love*. I want to put on bright hues and pretty garments, just as the flowers do. God intended people for his human flowers but left their choice of raiment to themselves. And a very poor choice some of them do make, it must be confessed! One is almost tempted to think it would have been better if he had let them *grow* their clothes like the roses and the tulips.

April 19, 1904
Cavendish, P.E. Island

"What can minister to a mind diseased?"[1] Why, sunshine. The sun has been shining for a week, the snow is almost gone and lo, life is a friend once more—not the shrewish old hag who has been scolding and rating me all winter but a young laughing comrade ready to run hand in hand with me in pursuit of the worthwhiles.

Besides, I've been gardening a bit and nobody can do *that* and be morbid. To potter with green growing things watching each day to see the dear new sprouts come up, is to take a hand in creation. How we all love to create! It is a little bit of the divine in us.

April 20, 1904

Who spoke of *spring*! Why, it is November or surly December. A northeast storm is abroad in the world. But I've kept it out of my soul so far—I *won't* let it in. I really ought to be pessimistic *now*. I've every warrant for it—for it's mud and gloom and rawness out of doors and I have a wretched, unromantic cold in the head. But I'm not, somehow.

---

1. *Macbeth* V.iii. In *AGG*, Anne says plum puffs cannot perform this ministry.

I've been re-reading "Tommy and Grizel"[1] this afternoon and delighting in it. When I first read it two years ago in Halifax I didn't like it. Thought it was horrid all the way through and damnably horrid at the end. I was then still young enough to demand a happy ending at any price. I've grown wiser now and I love the book because it presents so wonderfully the irony of life and is so incomparable in its subtle analysis of character and motive—at least in "Tommy's" case. *Grizel* isn't quite so well done, it seems to me. But *Tommy* lives and is lovable in spite of—or is it because of—his faults. I hate people, in books or out of them, who haven't any faults!!

Saturday, April 30, 1904

Of course I must sing my little paean of delight because I have got back to my own room again! It's silly how I love this room—but it's the Mecca of my heart, so consecrated by happy old dreams and bitter old sorrows that no place on earth can ever be to me just what this little room is. In winter I have to sleep in a downstairs room because it is too cold here. I hate that room venomously. It's dark and dull

My own room

and I can't even fix it up as I want to because it was "newly papered" *ten* years ago and poor grandmother would have a convulsion if so much as a tack were driven into that "new" paper. So I have no pictures and feel as if I had no eyes. But up here everything is different. Here I am a woman, not a child, and order my ways as suits me.

Thursday, May 5, 1904
Cavendish, P.E.I.

Oh, dear spring, you are so beautiful! I seem to be drinking in your loveliness. Every sense absorbs your delight for me, and eye and ear and touch make me glad I am alive in this dear old world where there are springs.

Today had some bitter sweetness in it for me. While housecleaning I came upon a box of old yellow letters and looked them over before burning them. Three or four I did not burn—I carried them reverently upstairs and locked

---

1. In J.M. Barrie's sequel (1900) to *Sentimental Tommy* (1896), Tommy's sentimental attachment to Grizel, child of a tragic "painted lady," is childlike and deleterious.

them away with my dearest belongings. But I read them first and cried over them. They were written years ago to grandfather Macneill by my dear father before I was old enough to write him, and they were full of references to his "dear little Maud." Oh, how the tenderness of it hurt me! There is no one to call me or think of me as "dear little Maud" now. Father's "little Maud" has grown up a lonely woman, missing his love and pride and tenderness heart breakingly. Oh, my dear father, if you were still living everything would be worthwhile. But I am very tired of striving and struggling—yea, even of attaining when there is nobody to care for my success.

All my life I have longed for a brother—a big brother just a year or two older than myself. How delightful it would have been! I never wanted a sister half so much—my many girls friends supplied that lack. But a brother—to love me and stand up for me and be proud of me! I *know* my brother would have been a dear for he would probably have been like father. I like to dream about this imaginary brother. A tall fellow, looking a little bit like me, perhaps, with dark hair and dark blue eyes and a merry tender smile. I like to dream of walking in the twilights with him and talking of our futures and our places for them. Oh, such dreams are pleasant! But to waken from them and realize that there is nobody—neither father nor mother nor sister nor brother—oh, how it hurts!

Still, in spite of all life is an interesting thing just now and I am enjoying it. There is a bunch of mayflowers on my table that tells me "God's in His Heaven, all's right with the world."[1] He *must* be—else such lovely things could not exist as those stars of rose and snow with their pure, spiritual haunting fragrance, as of something know and loved in another life ages upon ages ago. Oh, if I had nothing else to thank God for I would thank Him for flowers. There is more of His inspiration and revelation in them than in all the writings of Jew or Greek, bond or free. The Great Teacher knew that, when he told his disciples to consider the lilies. But his disciples, then as now, would rather be disputing over place and power and their own interpretations of his words and works.

Friday, May 20, 1904
Cavendish, P.E.I.

How delightful it is to watch things *grow*—things that you have planted. It seems almost as if you had given them life. I make little pilgrimages to

---

1.   A faith-filled song by Robert Browning, placed ironically in the sinister drama *Pippa Passes* (1841).

my garden every hour of the day and discover something new each time—
another leaf out on my pet rosebush, buds far down in my white narcissus
bed, green spikes pushing up through the brown earth from bulbs hidden
away therein, tiny folded shoots pushing aside the clods, or a new purple
and gold pansy unfolding its wings. Oh, flowers must be the souls of beautiful things that happened long ago! The poppies, aflame with gold and crimson, were the passionate kisses of lovers in olden days, the pansies were the
rainbow dreams of the world in its youth, the lilies star white and star cold,
were the prayers of sinless hearts, the twinkling daisies were the laughter of
children who lived a hundred springs ago, the mignonette is the essence of
faithful friendship, the white narcissus was the delight of a maiden's song, the
honeysuckle was the sorrow of all crushed noble souls grown wondrously
fine and sweet through pain. And the rose was a thought of perfect, enraptured love. Dear garden, no wonder God walked in you when the world was
young. The traces of His footsteps have him in you ever since.

This has been a good day after all. I write "after all," because when I woke
this morning I almost felt as if it were not worth while to get up and go
forth to another day just like so many of the yesterdays—pleasant enough,
perhaps, but somehow hardly worthwhile. So I turned my face into the pillow and thought what a pity it was that one need ever waken when fallen
on happy dreams. Of course I knew that I had to get up but I didn't want to.

The day was just as pleasant and harmless as I had expected it to be. I
worked hard and thought hard and so put something into it that made it
worthwhile "after all." And now at dusk I am glad I got up and lived it—but
all the same I am not sure that I want to get up and live tomorrow. Oh, these
tomorrows! It is they that are hard! I can always cope with "today" but it
wearies me to think of "tomorrow."

The day is done and I am tired. I want somebody to pat me on the shoulder and say cheerily "Fagged out, little girl? Never mind! Stop thinking over
things and let us have a little jamboree to clear out the cobwebs."

But there is nobody to say it and I haven't the spirit to say it to myself, as
I sometimes do. When my *ego* goes back on me I'm lonely indeed.

Today I was reading Jean Ingelow's "Dead Year."[1] What a beautiful thing
it is! She wrote it for me, I think. There was once a wilful royal year of mine
that queened it over my whole life and heart and soul. And when it was
dead, I too, hewed it a tomb and put it away in "beaten gold and glorious
red"—"wrought upon with colours fine, stolen from this life of mine"—and

---

1. Jean Ingelow (1820–97), Victorian poet and creator of fanciful stories for children. Ingelow's tightly
    rhymed "A Dead Year" (1876) strikes a darker note on the persistence of unhappy memories: "The
    dead year, stiff and stark / Drew me down to her in the dark."

told my heart I would forget when it was laid. But oh, I could not! And so after awhile "I took the year back to my life and my story" again for I had grown wiser, and learned that, to it, even in its tomb, belonged all that made life yet worth living. Strange, dead tyrannous old year! Will I ever be free from you? Perhaps I don't really want to be free. Perhaps I cherish a secret hope that I shall meet you again—or the soul of you—in eternity, and that you will then give back to me all you ravished from me.

I wonder if Jean Ingelow wrote that poem out of her own experience. She doesn't look like it. Her frontespiece photograph shows a respectable, commonplace old lady, very stout, in a striped, much passamenteried silk dress and *lace mitts*. *How* could a woman who would have her photograph taken in lace mitts live "A Dead Year"? Will *I* ever be stout and commonplace, wearing a striped silk dress and lace—but no, no, I shall *never* wear lace mitts! I shall be spared that at least. But then—I shall never be able to write such a poem. *Would* I be willing to wear lace mitts if I could thereby write "A Dead Year"? No, I don't believe I would.

L.M. Montgomery

But I do wish there was a law against putting the photographs of authors into their books when they don't "look the part." I know what the face of a woman who has lived "A Dead Year" ought to be—but of course never is! My own isn't. People tell me I have a "mischievous face"! Horrors! Think of a girl with a "mischievous" face living "A Dead Year." Why, it is almost as immoral as the lace mitts!!

Sunday, May 29, 1904
Cavendish, P.E.I.

On Wednesday I went over to New Glasgow and didn't get back until last night! I came home in love with loneliness!

I was over at Maggie Bulman's getting a coat made. There is a houseful of people there but I was bored to death. They exist to make money and—apparently—for nothing else. There wasn't a book in the house. They can talk of nothing but gossip and crops—and they *do* talk of them *ad nauseam*. I felt as if my soul were being smothered. Granville Bulman,[1] one of the lank

---

1. Granville Bulman (1878–1924), cousin of Penzie's husband, William Bulman.

sons of the house, used to take me out driving every evening. Goodness knows why he did it—by way of amusing me I suppose. He couldn't have enjoyed my company in the least; and I was so horribly bored that I was always devoutly thankful when we had driven far enough to turn back!

Last night I came home and when I had got upstairs, here in my dear room with my books and pictures I just bubbled over with joy. I flew about and kissed everything!! I would rather live my whole life utterly alone, seeing not even a fellow creature, than live with such people or in such sapless surroundings.

My dear garden, too, how glad I was to get back to it! Everything had grown surprisingly while I was away. Oh yes, yes there are things a hundred-fold worse than loneliness!

Sunday, July 3, 1904
Cavendish, P.E.I.

Here is a gap! I have been too busy to write and I have had no blue spells to be worked off. It is dear midsummer and I can always keep wholesome in summer.

It is Sunday evening. I am up here in my room and although I have lighted my lamp to see to write it is not yet dark outside. There is an emerald light all over the hills and trees; the fields are green and dewy and placid— "haunts of ancient peace."[1]—and the sky is a silvery starless arch. Some birds are whistling to each other among the firs. Oh, how I love summer twilights!

"Haunt of Ancient Peace"

Uncle Leander, Aunt Mary, and Kennedy are here—have been here since early in June. They are not pleasant guests. Kennedy is by way of being a spoiled cub. Uncle L. is a complete nervous wreck and is a very unpleasant person to have about. Grandmother has a most unreasonable and childish dislike of Aunt May, who on her side is not tactful or politic, and I am worn out trying to keep the peace between them. If it were not for this little den of mine up here where I can flee for refuge and find peace and solace of soul I think I would fly into little bits!

---

1. An English country home appears as one of the pictures decorating Tennyson's "Palace of Art" (1832).

Well, well, never mind. Apart from the Macneill infliction I'm enjoying my garden and the summer and my rambles. After all, I suppose, as *David Harum* says, "A reasonable amount of fleas is good for a dog—keeps him from brooding on being a dog."[1]

True—but then we all think we have an *un*reasonable amount of fleas.

Tuesday, July 5, 1904
Cavendish, P.E.I.

This evening I was looking over the part of my journal written ten years ago. It brought home to me very vivid the difference between my old self of ten years ago and my present self. In many ways, of course, the difference is not altogether pleasant. And yet, in many other ways, I am very glad of the difference. I am, I believe, a much better and wiser woman for it, and if I am not as happy as I was then the lack of happiness does not arise from the change in me but from the changes about me. I would be much more unhappy still *if* I were the same girl mentally and emotionally, that I was then. Indeed, it is only the changes in me that render my life tolerable.

Yes, I have changed very much. Let us see in what respects, both for better and worse, I differ from the girl of ten years ago.

I have not a definite aim in life. Ten years ago I was a schoolgirl without any such aim, for the expectation of getting through P.W.C. and teaching could not be called a real aim. Beyond that, I had no definite plans for future attainment, although I always hoped I would be able to do something in literature some day. I did not need such plans, having enough girlish interests and pleasures to occupy me; but if I did not have an aim now I should be in a sorry plight, therefore I consider it to be of the greatest advantage that I have attained one.

Again, I do not now suffer over *small* things as I did then. When things went wrong in those days I gave myself up to despair. I never yield in such fashion now. Evil spirits of depression, fits of the "blues" still come, but for the most part I have learned to fight them off. Once or twice a year, mostly in winter, I have a "white night" and go down into the deeps—but not over the trifles that once drove me to a sleepless pillow. Moreover, I have learned well the lesson,

> Laugh and the world laughs with you,
> Weep and you weep alone,[2]

---

1. E.N. Westcott (1846–98) uses American dialect in his novel (1899) to present the small town philosophy of a canny horse trader.
2. From Ella Wheeler Wilcox's "Solitude" (1883).

and I confine tears to my pillow and keep a most choice assortment of smiles for the world.

I have learned to be tolerant of other people's whimsies, failings, and even lapses from morality for I have discovered how much of our own vaunted virtue lies in not being tempted. I have learned to take life as it comes, not being too wildly slated over its joys, nor too much cast down over its sorrows. These things pass and nothing concerns me vitally but to hold fast to my soul—though by "soul" I do not mean what the theologians do. I can now smile at, and speedily recover from disappointments which would once have crushed me to the very dust. I do not now believe—alas!—that happiness is mine by birthright, and I do not rebel struggle because it is no longer mine. I appropriate all the bits of it that lie in my daily path and am thankful for them. I am beginning to understand the great law of compensation—how everything in life balances—how much less difference there is in reality than in appearance between lives outwardly diverse.

And in what is the change for the worse? Principally, I fear, in the lowering of my ideals. They are not half as high, either for myself or others, as they were ten years ago. I have lost faith in a great many things I believed in then. I couldn't—or wouldn't—now sacrifice a strong desire or taste to an abstract idea of right as I could then. It wouldn't seem to matter enough. In short, I have rather drifted into the state of philosophy expressed in the saying "It will all be the same in a hundred years." Such an attitude has, to be sure, made me more tolerant. But it has its dangers.

Wednesday, July 6, 1904
Cavendish, P.E.I.

I think that Cavendish just now is really one of the prettiest spots on earth. I thought so this evening when I was out for a walk. Everything is so green and fresh, the ripe but not over ripe luxuriance of midsummer without as yet a hint of decay. And beyond the green fields and slopes was the blue girdle of the gulf, forever moaning on its shining shore. Cavendish would suit me perfectly as a place to live in if I had a home here and a little social life. There are so few young people in Cavendish now and the most of them are shallow, commonplace souls.

Wednesday, Aug. 3, 1904

I've had a *good* fortnight. Nora has been down. She stayed at John Laird's for of course I could not have her, since Uncle L.'s were here. But we spent most of our spare time together and I just lived with all my might. Several afternoons we spent at the shore, going down with our cameras and lunch baskets, donning bathing suits as soon as we got down and living a sort of amphibious life, wading and diving and snap shotting. One day we had a never-to-be-forgotten surf dip. It was glorious.

Nora   Nora

Nora went home today and I shall miss her terribly. But I'll live on the memory of these two weeks for many moons.

Wednesday, October 5, 1904
Cavendish, P.E.I.

The summer is over. I realize it bitterly and shrink from the coming winter.

Tomorrow I leave for a fortnight's junketing. I go to St. Eleanor's first to stay over Sunday with Nora. Then I proceed to O'Leary to waste a week on Mary Beaton. That infinitive is just the word to use. I do not want to go in the least. But Mary has urged me so repeatedly that I could no longer excuse myself out of it, so go I mean to, but most reluctantly. After that I shall spend a week in town. Let me prophesy a bit. I shall have a very good time in St. Eleanor's, I shall be bored to death in O'Leary and I shall have a fair, all-round time in town. When I return I shall see what sort of a prophet I am.

Monday, Oct. 24, 1904

I am a very good prophet. My predictions were fulfilled to the letter.

I went up to St. Eleanor's on the Thursday morning after my last entry and stayed with Nora until Monday morning. I enjoyed every minute of

the time and just *lived* to my fullest capacity.
It makes me feel blue now to think of those
delightful, companionable days.

Nora's room

I went up to O'Leary by train on Monday
morning, remained with Mary until the next
Monday morning, and left. That is really all
there is to say about it. I put in a dreary week
with not even the pleasure of pen and book to
wile it away. The weather, too, was bad.

Mary and I have little in common now, save
old memories. She seems to have degenerated
since her marriage.

Secrets

She lives on a lonely "road," among impossible
people. She is such a poor housekeeper that even
physical comfort is lacking in her household. She
has two children. The baby is named for me.

The time really seemed endless. I was
thoroughly glad when the day of my departure
came and I went down to town.

I had a very nice time in town. I stayed a week
and came home yesterday. Am doing penance for
my pleasures now by all the work that is waiting
for me.

Sunday, Oct. 30, 1904
Cavendish, P.E.I.

It is so fall-like that my heart aches. My poor garden—its glory is all departed.
Yesterday I covered the plants with leaves and boughs and tried to hope for
the spring. But spring seems very far away.

Yesterday I decanted my pot-pourri into a couple of rose jars I picked up
in town. It is delicious. The souls of all the roses that bloomed last summer
seem to be prisoned there as in a sort of flower purgatory. Perhaps I ought
to have left them free to go to heaven. But I was selfish—I wanted to have
them to cheer me in the dull winter days when a passing whiff will beguile
me into thinking it is still June.

Monday, Oct. 31, 1904

This evening I went for a walk—all alone but not lonely. I am sometimes lonely in the house or in uncongenial company, but I have never known

a moment's loneliness in the woods and fields. I have ripe, rich, rare good company, on these twilight rambles. Tonight in spite of the world's sadness, I was not sad. I felt a conscious inner gladness, as if there were in my soul something buoyant and immortal that rose above the decay and death of the year.

A corner of the woods

The air was very clear and frosty. There were some wonderful sunset lakes of crimson and gold among the dark western hills. the fields were gray and quiescent, as if brooding over old joys and folding their arms about baby possibilities that must be kept safe for another spring.

The woods were very silent. The birches and maples were bare and gray, but the firs were greener than ever and the frost had nipped them until the air about them was all resinous with their balsam. There is no sweeter odor than fir balsam on a frosty autumn night.

I went up through Lover's Lane—not the Lover's Lane of June, lovely with the loveliness of spring and maidenhood, but the Lover's Lane of autumn, beautiful with beauty of a woman who has lived deeply and wept bitter tears and now wears her sorrow like a garment of praise.

A brook laughed to itself down in the hollow. Brooks are always in good spirits. They are

Lover's Lane

always laughing. It is infectious to hear them—those gay vagabond's for valleys and wildernesses.

When I left the lane I came home across the fields and down the hill. There was one star out. The sea was calling afar and the autumn dusk was coming down. I had a good walk and was glad for it. I will say a prayer of Thanksgiving for it tonight.

Across the fields

Today I did my last bit of garden work for the year—making ready for next spring. The mail brought me a box of roots and bulbs from a florist's—an unsightly little tangle of rainbow possibilities. I took them out and buried them in the garden mould. Then I heaped their grave over with dead leaves and spruce boughs. They will have their resurrection next spring I hope.

Today, too, I got into *Lippincott's*[1] with a poem. *Lippincott's* is one of the "big ones" and never took me into its fold before. Another step upward—paid for with the usual price of toil and gray matter—ay, and of tears. I shed few tears now because I will not let myself. But often they flow inwardly and scorch my heart with their pent-up bitterness.

And yet—and yet—after all, I wouldn't be anybody but myself not even a happier anybody. How dear our personality is to us! And life is a good thing—yes, I can say in perfect sincerity that, in spite of everything, life is a good thing and I enjoy it more keenly every day.

Monday, Nov. 14, 1904
Cavendish, P.E.I.

What a fit of bad temper the world has indulged in! Day before yesterday she was not unbeautiful—a dignified old dame in fitting garb of brown and ermine. Yesterday she tried to ape juvenility, putting on all the airs and graces of spring, with warm sunshine and blue hazes—and what a bedraggled, uncomely old hag she was, all tatters and wrinkles! She grew angry then at her own ugliness and has raged all night and all day. I wakened up in the wee hours and heard the wind shrieking in the trees and tears of rage and spite sleeting against the panes. I like to hear a storm at night. It is so cosy to snuggle down among the blankets and feel that it can't get at you.

Today was outwardly wild and dismal and so is tonight. It is difficult to believe it is the same world it was a few weeks ago.

This evening I spent in my dark room developing some photos. One mild gray day last week I took my camera and went to the woods. I wanted some pictures of the year asleep and I got them—still, pasture corners, a brook under the spruces, birches all leafless and white limbed. They came out well and I already

"Birches all leafless and white limbed"

---

1. A monthly magazine (1868–1915) based in Philadelphia that published respectable literary material.

foresee them finished and mounted on some spandy new mounts I got in town. What a boon all my little hobbies are to me!

After I finished with my negatives I sat me down and wrote a letter or two to people whom I have never seen and hardly even expect to see. If they are the right sort of people such letters, both on writing and receiving, are among the greatest pleasures of my existence.

Miss Zieber

Four years ago a personage, styling himself a writer, yclept Frank Monroe Beverley of Virginia— his name was the best thing about him, poor soul—wrote to me, saying he had read a poem of mine—"Rain In The Woods"—in a magazine and asking me to correspond for mutual advantage in our literary career. I assented quite eagerly for I had no such friends or any chance of making any. But I soon found that although F.M.B. might call himself a writer nobody else would. He couldn't write *at all*, desperately as he tried. His letters were nonentities—neither helpful, interesting or amusing. This correspondence dragged on for three years and then I simply dropped it. Before this, however, Mr. B. had "introduced" me to another "literary" correspondent of his a Miss Miriam Zieber of Philadelphia. The name seemed formidable but I entered into the correspondence with vim and interest. Alas! Again I was disappointed. Miss Zieber could certainly be of no help to me in any way. Still, *her* letters were hugely amusing and I enjoyed the correspondence after a fashion. Miriam Zieber was a curious character, as unconsciously depicted in her letters. As a *personal* friend I fear she would be a nerve racking failure, so unbalanced in temperament, so exacting in emotional phases, was she. As an *impersonal* correspondent however, she lent considerable spice to life and I rather regret that our correspondence has ceased. Miriam got married last June. What effect it had on her I can only surmise for I have never heard from her since.

Before this, however, she had in her turn, introduced me to two of her correspondents, one, Ephraim Weber,[1] of Didsbury, Alta. and the other Geo. B. MacMillan[2] of Alloa, Scotland.

I began my correspondence with Mr. Weber with but little enthusiasm, for my experiences with Mr. Beverley and the eccentric Miriam had sobered my

---

1. LMM's early letters to Ephraim Weber (1870–1956) have been published as *The Green Gables Letters*, edited by Wilfrid Eggleston (1960). In 2006 Paul and Hildi Tiessen published *After Green Gables: L.M. Montgomery's Letters to Ephraim Weber, 1916–1941*.

2. Letters to this correspondent, discovered by Mollie Gillen, appear in *My Dear Mr. M.: Letters to G.B. Macmillan from L.M. Montgomery*, edited by Francis Bolger and Elizabeth Epperly (1980).

young dreams. Moreover, I did not expect much from anyone who was so congenial to Miriam as she affirmed Mr. Weber to be—although she had never met him personally. From this can-any-good-thing-come-out-of-Nazareth attitude I was pleasantly aroused. Mr. Weber turned out to be an ideal correspondent. His letters are capital. The man himself I rather think is a dreamy, impractical somewhat *shiftless* person, hampered also by delicacy of health. But his intellect is unquestionable. His letters are cultured, thoughtful, stimulating epistles to which I look eagerly forward. They are written from a lonely Alberta ranch but they sparkle from beginning to end.

E. Weber

My other correspondent, Mr. MacMillan, a Scottish journalist, is also a success. He is not so academically clever as Mr. Weber but he makes a good second, and I think that, as a man, he is superior to the former. His land, too, lends him an added interest.

If I lived where I could meet with intellectually congenial friends I suppose these correspondences would not mean so much to me. But under my present limitations these unseen friends are of vital interest to me. In my letters to them I "let myself go,"—writing freely from my soul, with no fear of being misunderstood or condemned—or, worst of all, meeting with a blank wall of non-comprehension. Between these letters and my journal I manage to keep my intellectual life tolerably wholesome. If I could not "write out" freely certain words, opinions and fancies they would remain bottled up in my soul and would probably ferment and sour and cause some acute disturbance.

George Boyd MacMillan

Tuesday, Dec. 20, 1904
Cavendish, P.E.I.

It is a most exquisite night out—a white poem, a frosty starry lyric of light! Last night it snowed a little; today was sunny and mild as spring; there was a creamy, misty sunset and then moonlight—such moonlight! I have just been to the door—and realized afresh that I had a soul. As long as I stood there I did not remember that I had a body. It is such a night as one might fall asleep on and dream happy dreams of youth and gardens and songs, feeling all the while through one's sleep the soft splendor and radiance of the white moon-world outside, as one hears soft faraway music sounding through the thoughts and words that are born of it.

I know what I would like to do—what I would do if I could. I would slip away and walk by myself through that fairy world of glamor. I would go through the orchard where the black shadows of the trees fall over the snow. I would go up to those far gleaming white hills with the stars over them. I would lurk along fir copses dim with mystery, I would journey adown the still wood aisles where the night has hidden from the moonshine, I would linger in level, dazzling fields—and every breath of me would be a prayer and every thought a lyric, and I would come back with a soul washed pure and white in the great crystal bath of the night.

But I cannot do this without grandma knowing it. And poor grandma! She never felt such a vagrant impulse in her life and would understand it less than she would Greek; and if I were to follow it up she would immediately conclude that I was up to mischief and was probably stealing out to "see some fellow" as she would choicely phrase it. She would therefore make herself unpleasant and I would feel as if my soul were shrinking within me. So I cannot wander out to tryst with the night and the silvery silence.

I have been re-reading "Trilby"[1] this evening—it matches the night somehow—that dear delightful book where three of my very dearest friends live—"Taffy" and "The Laird," and "Little Billee." It has made me quite happy for the time being. And the verses that end it were, with one exception, written for me.

> A little work—a little play
> To keep us going—and so good-day.
> A little warmth, a little light
> Of love's bestowing—and so good-night.
> A little fun to watch the sorrow
> Of each day's growing—and so good-morrow.
> A little trust that when we die
> We reap our sowing—and so good-bye.[2]

---

1. George du Maurier's vastly popular book (1894), set in Paris, presents a young woman who is tone deaf. The hypnotist Svengali releases her voice.

2. Quotation from *Trilby:* "A little work, a little play / To keep us going—and so good-day! . . . A little warmth, a little light / Of love's bestowing—and so, good-night."

The exception is in the second verse. It should be cut out for me. There is no love in my life—nor ever will be, I suppose.

Well, I must stop writing. I feel in a mood to sit up till twelve and write a little and dream a little and look out into the wonderful white night and think about "Taffy" and the others. But it is nine o'clock; and grandma, who always goes to bed at nine o'clock, is beginning to fidget. For nobody must sit up for a minute after grandma goes to bed, and woe be unto anyone who attempts it. So I must go to bed, too, because it is too cold to sit up in my room, and toss restlessly for a couple of hours in the darkness before I shall sleep.

1905

Monday, Jan. 2, 1905
Cavendish, P.E.I.

This evening, reading over a packet of old letters, I came across a very old one written to my mother in her girlhood by a girl friend. I found it a few years ago in a box of old letters and have kept it among my treasures ever since. It gives me such a delightful *realization* of my mother—that girlish letter full of old jests and allusions at whose meaning I can only guess.

It is a dreadful thing to lose one's mother in childhood! I know that from bitter experience. How often, when smarting under some injustice or writhing under some misunderstanding, have I sobbed to myself, "Oh, if mother had *only* lived!"

But quick on the heels of that wish always came the instinctive thought. "But oh, if she were like Aunt Emily, or even like Aunt Annie, that would only make it worse." Even in childhood I realized that *that* would have been for me a worse tragedy than her death.

Aunt Annie   Aunt Emily

Aunt Annie is a woman I have always loved. She is kind, jolly, and good hearted. But she is otherwise merely a practical soul—grandmother without grandmother's narrowness of mind and intolerance. She is a capital *aunt*; but as my *mother* she would have been a failure.

As for Aunt Emily, I have never cared for her. She jars on me in every fibre; she has no intellectual qualities; she is unsympathetic, fault-finding, nagging and "touchy." I can never forgive her for the sneer and slurs she used to call upon my childish ambitions and my childish faults.

This fall in town I spent an evening with a Mrs. Campbell *nee* Eliza Macneill, a second cousin and girlhood friend of my mother's. She told me that my mother did not resemble Aunt Annie or Aunt Emily in the slightest respect physically, mentally, or emotionally. She assured me that if mother had lived I would have found in her all that I could wish in a mother—she spoke of her as a beautiful, spiritual, poetical girl full of fine emotions and noble impulses. I cannot express how glad I was to hear this. It seemed to me that Mrs. Campbell had given me a talisman to make life beautiful. There was now no hindrance to the wish that went out from my heart for my mother. *She* would have understood—*she* would have sympathized.

The older I grow the more I realize what a starved childhood mine was *emotionally*.[1] I was brought up by two old people, neither of whom at their best were ever very sympathetic and who had already grown into set, intoler-

ant ways. They seemed to cherish and act upon the contradictory opinions that a child of ten or a girl of fifteen was as old as themselves and as young as a baby—that is, she should have no wish or taste that they did not have, and yet she should have no more right to an independent existence than an infant.

Grandfather Macneill, in all the years I knew him, was a stern, domineering, irritable man. I was always afraid of him. He bruised my childish feelings in every possible way and inflicted on my girlish pride humiliations whose scars are branded

Grandfather

into my very soul and which were not at all atoned for by his rare and spasmodic freaks of arbitrary and often embarrassing kindness—embarrassing because it nearly always conflicted with and over turned little derangements which I, never expecting him to concern himself about me, had already made.

I seemed to myself in those years to be alone, with all the world—*my* world against me. My childish faults and short comings—of which I had plenty—were all detailed to the Macneill uncles and aunts whenever they came to the house. I resented this more bitterly than anything else. All children's faults were not exploited by their parents in family conclave. Why then should mine be? Again, these aforesaid uncles and aunts arrogated the right to reprove and scold me at their own will and pleasure, as they would never have dared to do had I had parents to resent it. I had a remarkably keen sense of justice even then. I acknowledged the right of grandfather and grandmother to correct me but I felt no such right in the others and my revolt against it did not highten me in their good opinion at all. I thought then—and I think still, for that matter—

Grandmother

that they would better have devoted their reforming energies to their own children. Judging by the way some of them have turned out they must have needed it quite as much as I did.

1. Memories reinforced while LMM was writing *AGG* by reading three recent bestsellers about unloved orphan children: Alice Hegan Rice's *Lovey Mary* (1903), Kate Douglas Wiggin's *Rebecca of Sunnybrook Farm* (1903), and Gene Stratton Porter's *Freckles* (1904).

As for grandmother she was very kind to me in a material way. I was well-cared for, well-fed, and well-dressed—and I may also add that these benefits were unfailingly cast up to me whenever I showed any rebellion. But nature never made two people more dissimilar in every respect essential to mutual comfort. I was impulsive, warm-hearted, emotional; grandmother was cold and reserved, narrow in her affections and sensibilities. When two such people are compelled to live under one roof one of them must invariably be uncomfortable and that one is the dependent one. Grandmother was kind to me "in her own way." Her "way" was very often torture to me and I was constantly reproached with ingratitude and wickedness because in childhood, before I had learned any self-control or understanding of my position, I sometimes rebelled against "her" ways.

I would not, however, convey the impression that my childhood was actually unhappy. It was never as happy as childhood should be and as it easily might have been; and there *were* times when it was fiercely unhappy. But between these times I got on very well. It has always seemed to me, ever since I can remember, that, amid all the commonplaces of life, I was very near to a kingdom of ideal beauty. Between it and me hung only a thin veil. I could never draw it quite aside but sometimes a wind fluttered it and I seemed to catch a glimpse of the enchanting realm beyond—only a glimpse—but those glimpses have always made life worthwhile.

I had besides, then as now, two great refuges and consolations—the world of nature and the world of books. They kept life in my soul; they made me love my home because of my dreams and rambles and the deep joy and delight they gave me— because of the halo they threw over what was otherwise bare and savorless. To be sure, I never had an unhampered indulgence in them. I was always nagged about "reading too much" and scolded because I preferred stores to the "Peep of Day" series.[1] Also, if I crept away for a solitary ramble in the woods or along a country lane, poor unwise grandmother, who never could understand in the slightest degree how anyone could find pleasure in what gave no pleasure to her, would conclude that I had sneaked off for some improper motive and would greet me on my return with remarks that made me hate living.

All this was not because she did not love me. She did and does; but her love has never had the slightest saving grace of understanding in it and so had no power to draw us together. Looking back now, calmly and reflectively, I unhesitatingly state that grandmother's method of dealing with my nature and temperament was the most unwise she could possibly have adopted.

---

1. Evangelical instruction for children, inculcating religious terror, by Mrs. Favell Lee Bevan Mortimer (1802–78).

Of late years I have learned, under the bitter compulsion of necessity, to be sufficient unto myself. I stay here with grandmother, because if I did not do so she could not remain in her old home and it would break her heart to leave it. I try to bear patiently with her in all things because I acknowledge the debt of care and shelter she bestowed upon me in childhood. But she makes my life hard in a score of petty ways and is quite incapable of understanding that she does so.

I well remember the *first* sorrow that came into my life. I could never forget its bitterness. I was nine years old. I had a little gray kitten, a playful, winsome little creature, which I loved with passionate intensity. It died one day of poison. I can never forget the agony I endured. At first I could *not* believe that my little pet was dead. When I realized it I almost went mad. I was beside myself with grief. It was my baptism of sorrow and I was submerged beneath the waters of Marah. I have never since laughed at my passionate sorrow over that little death. It was too real—and too symbolical. I had *learned what pain was*; my poor little heart was almost broken. If I had had a mother—a wise, tender mother—to take me in her arms and comfort me understandingly, not underrating the suffering through contempt of the cause, it would have been well for me. Instead, grandmother only said, sneeringly, "You'll have something to cry for some day," and left me to sob my soul out in loneliness over the poor gray body of my little pet. I grieved stormily all that day and more quietly for weeks afterwards. Sorrow found me a hard pupil, determinedly light-hearted and joyous, so she made her first lesson a severe one. It was the Alpha of life's pain and it was branded deep into my consciousness. I think I have spelled the alphabet nearly through since then. Oh, Sorrow, will I not soon have learned all your dreary primer? I have lost many dear things since that little gray kitten died; I have taken each successive loss a little more quietly, a little more restrainedly, until now the tears and cries are all inwardly at my heart. Will not the discipline soon be accomplished? Ah, perhaps sorrow knows that the self-control *is* only outward—that underneath it the capacity for passionate feeling is as strong and vivid and greedy as ever. And so the end is not yet.

Probably when grandfather and grandmother were young they were not as I have known them. But their children left them early in life and they remained alone together with no influence to prevent them from growing narrow and set and warped. Emotionally they grew old before their time, getting into a rut of feeling and living which suited them but was utterly unfitted to anyone who was yet growing in soul or body. It is a great misfortune for a child to be brought up by old people. The gap between youth and age is too wide to be bridged, save by those exceptional natures that do not grow old in heart.

Tuesday, Jan. 17, 1905
Cavendish, P.E.I.

We are just in the throes of a cold snap. So far this winter has been very cold but it has been fine. I have got on pretty well—have had no bad "blue spells." But there are two months of winter before us yet—and "call no man happy until he is dead."

Tonight, coming home from prayer meeting, I halted a moment in spite of the cold to look over the orchard fence at my flower bed. Not that I could see much of it—it is heaped over with a snowdrift six feet deep, gleaming in the moonlight like a mausoleum of marble build over buried hopes. What are my tulips and daffodils doing down under it, the dear things? I dreamed of them last night. How I love that bit of a garden! What with it and my books and pen and my life o'dreams existence is a pretty good thing after all.

Friday, Jan. 27, 1905
Cavendish, P.E.I.

We have had a terrible two days' storm—I would say the worst storm we ever had if I didn't know that every bad storm seems the worst by reason of

[Snowy scene]

the contrast its present badness offers to the badness of past ones grown dim. But I am quite within the mark in saying that the drifts *are* the worst we have ever had. They are as high as the house, hemming us in on all sides— "Alp on Alp."[1] The rooms on the ground floor are as dark as twilight. The drifts are certainly very beautiful; but one does not care greatly for architectural beauty in a prison. We have had no mail for two days. When I look out on those huge white barriers I feel like screaming.

It is well I am used to dullness or the unutterable dreariness of these past two days would have mildewed my very soul. As it was I kept myself sane by working; a story was finished, a

Our front orchard

---

1.   Misquoted from "Alps on Alps arise "in Alexander Pope, "An Essay on Criticism" (1771).

lot of typewriting done, a fancy collar made, and a book re-read that took me away from my snowy prison into a wonderful world.

Our front orchard is worth looking at—the very trees are coated with snow until it is like some fairy court of marble seen in a splendid dream. Tonight the weather cleared and there was a wonderful sunset of fiery rose and gold. When its light fell down through that orchard I forgave the storm. Nothing more lovely could be imagined.

Tuesday, Feb. 7, 1905
Cavendish, P.E.I.

Another storm! No mail! Abominably dismal!

Query:—where is any more snow to be put? Our yard is full now. The windows are all snowed up and the house is as dark as a tomb.

My only consolation today, when I had finally given up hope of the mail, was to get out a flower catalogue and plan out my garden for next summer. With six feet of snow over the entire orchard it was very satisfying to arrange a clump of dahlias here, a bed of lilies there, a plot of asters somewhere else. Really, it almost cheered me up; at anyrate it certainly rescued me from the deeps of doleful dumps where into I should otherwise have fallen. The storm is raging worse than ever now and sleeting viciously at the west window. I shall have to get up in the morning and shovel snow. Ugh!! However, it's not morning yet and sufficient unto the day is the evil thereof. I'm going to lose myself in a book presently and thereby escape from my prison of drifts. What a blessing that the soul can always be free if it chooses!

Wednesday. (Is it Wednesday? Yes, it is)
Feb. 8, 1905

I did not have to sally out and shovel snow this morning after all—for the excellent reason that I could not get out. This morning the door and every window on the east side of the house was completely snowed over. I do not think the like of this storm has ever been seen on P.E. Island in the memory of living man. The storm has raged all day.

After breakfast I forced myself to finish writing an Easter story[1] which a Sunday School paper lately ordered. (Item:—I *hate* writing stores to order!) Then I type-wrote until dinner time. After dinner more typewriting; then

---

1. LMM published at least thirty-two stories in 1905.

2. A doily made with a needle and fine thread, following a complex pattern.

worked half an hour at a point lace centrepiece.[2] Then, there being nothing more that had to be done I amused myself jotting down in a note book all the detachable epigrams in my books. They are easily discoverable as I have them all marked. I've always had the habit of marking my books. I do it now with a pencil. I was not so wise in my teens and used ink. Consequently, I cannot now erase the marks of passages and opinions I no longer agree with, and they stare me in the face as reminders of my sentimental "salad days."[1]

After dark I wrote a letter, did fancy work and read. I am steeped in dullness. We can have no mail tomorrow. All this accumulation of ills beggars complaint. As the old Scotch emigrant said when he came home, found his house burned, and his entire family butchered by Indians, "This is perfectly ridiculous."

Thursday, Mar. 3, 1905
Cavendish, P.E.I.

It is no use—I *must* growl out my growl in this poor journal again tonight. I've just been having a bitter cry in the twilight and now I must work off the rest of my dark mood with my pen. This life is simply terrible!

The day after my last entry word came that George Campbell's baby had died of pneumonia. I went over to Park Corner the next day and remained for a fortnight. I am thankful I did for I think if I had been here I should have lost my reason. It was storm after storm. The trains were completely blocked. For *ten* days there was no mail. Then they began to *drive* the mail from the boats and from town and they are still doing this as no train can yet get through. Nothing like it has ever been known on the Island.

As I was at Park Corner I did not mind it so much. Stella and I kept ourselves amused. We got around and had a good time in spite of the storms. I came home last Sunday and have worried along so far in this dismal week without slumping. But all strength and courage seem to have gone out of me tonight. There has been no mail since Monday. I cannot even get out for a walk and the lack of all exercise and companionship makes me feel positively wretched, mentally and physically. I can't work *all* the time. I have nothing to read; and the long and short of

Park Corner

---

1. The mature Cleopatra's phrase for her youth, in Shakespeare's *Antony and Cleopatra* I.v.

it is I hate to wake up to another day every morning. I haven't the spirit of *anything*—even work is a drag.

I've been trying to get up a paper on Mrs. Browning[1] to read before the Literary tomorrow night. My heart isn't in it—I don't care a hoot for Mrs. Browning—and it has dragged horribly. I hate the thought of going up there tomorrow night to read it. My whole being seems out of tune—nothing but jangling discords. This is only "nerves" of course; if ever this fearful blockade lifts I shall soon recover my normal poise. But just now I seem eaten up by an internal fire of restlessness and loneliness.

I have nothing to write about and yet I fear to stop. It seems to me I can only preserve an outward calm by writing, and that if I stop a choking fit of tears and sobs will come in. If I could only get away by myself and "cry it out" I would feel better but that I cannot do because the rooms are all too cold. I must not let grandma see me crying—it always seems to anger her. Grandmother is a curious woman. She always seems to resent bitterly anyone else not being perfectly happy in a life that suits her. Moreover, she also resents bitterly any independence in thought, taste, or wishes of those she lived with. In summer I can escape up to my own room and enjoy enough of freedom there to reconcile me to other evils but in winter I cannot do this.

I suppose grandmother cannot help it and I have resigned myself to it as to any other unavoidable ill. It is my duty to stay here and I do it willingly, but she makes it very hard for me in a hundred petty ways.

Just for example:—grandmother goes to bed at nine o'clock; everyone else must go at nine o'clock, too, whether they want to or not. Grandmother *never* takes a bath; it seems to drive her into a perfect frenzy of childish rage because, in winter when my room is too cold, I insist on staying up *once a fortnight* after she goes to bed, to take a bath in the warm kitchen. Grandmother is angry if I use any lamp but my own small and insufficient one to curl my hair and shows it in pitiful petulance. She will not permit me to have a fire in the room on the rare occasion when a friend comes to spend the afternoon—I must entertain her in the kitchen. Grandmother will not allow me to bake a cake if the smallest, stalest piece of an old one remains in the house. She resents it if I venture to sweep my bedroom oftener than she sweeps hers—and so on and so on in every detail of my life. I do try to bear this patiently but I am sick at heart.

Another thing, too, is grievous to me. I fear that this life I am living is unfitting me for any other life. I am being compelled to shape myself into habits that will—or may—hold me prisoner when the necessity for them is

---

1. Poet of love songs such as *Sonnets from the Portuguese* (1850) and also of feminist sagas such as *Aurora Leigh* (1857).

removed, I shall, I fear, be unable to adapt myself then to any other exist-ence. I know, too, that although my present life is anything but a happy or satisfactory one, it is likely to be still less so when changes come. This thought often rebukes me when I feel discontented with my present condi-tions. Yet the fact that a pain is going to be worse in its later stages than in its earlier does not much help one to bear the earlier—rather makes it harder indeed. Even so, I could bear all the hard things in my life now if I could look for something better beyond. But it is all dark and uncertain.

Oh, you poor pessimist, writing in this strain because you can't write in any other just now and yet afraid to stop lest this pain that is gripping your soul break out in tears! Cheer up—do! Spring will come and then you will be cheery and hopeful again and life will seem pleasant enough to be quite worthwhile in spite of all its pin-pricks.

Saturday, Mar. 11, 1905
Cavendish, P.E.I.

No, I'm not going to grumble tonight—even though it is stormy and we have had no mail. In spite of this I feel quite contented and cheerful. The blue fit has passed and I am interested in things once more.

The next night after my dismal entry I went to the Literary and read my paper. The thought of it bored me all day; nevertheless when evening came I put on a cream silk blouse, did my hair elaborately, and betook myself to the hall. In the end I rather enjoyed the affair although the whole business was really time and gray matter wasted. That Literary is a very dull affair nowa-days. I only hold to it for the sake of the new books we get. We have about thirty new ones coming if *ever* the ice blockade lifts in the Strait.[1] When they do come I'm going on a jamboree.

Thursday, Mar. 16, 1905

If it's not an impertinent question, pleas'm, when is it going to be spring? Here it is mid March and not even the weeniest, teeniest sign of spring yet. Yesterday morning it was 16 below zero!

I have just come in from a walk. The walking was poor but my soul was pining for freedom, so I went out to slip its leash for a little while after sun-set. The evening was mild and wrapped in a great white brooding stillness a

---

1.   Strait of Northumberland; ferries to the mainland were blocked.

silence which was yet threaded through with many little silvery sounds which you could hear if you harkened as much with your soul as with your ears.

I couldn't get to Lover's Lane—I would have had to wade through two fields of deep snow to reach it. So I choose the old hill road for its soli-

A great brooding stillness

tude and wandered happily along, pausing every few moments or so to think out fully some rare thought or fancy that came to me like a winged spirit. Later on I began simply to dream. One can *dream into* one's life everything that isn't in it, so fully and vividly that for the moment the dream seems real—at least, I can, and I thank God for the power, even though the price is the bitterness of awakening.

I hated to come back in and mew my soul up again. I can't dream in here. I could dream in my dear den upstairs if I could get to it—but it's too cold.

Thursday, Mar. 23, 1905
Cavendish, P.E.I.

We have had a thaw—a really, truly thaw. Oh, the joy of it! I think even the hearts half century dead over there in the graveyard must have throbbed in unison with the beating of the great heart of spring. There are bare spots in the fields—they are not so beautiful as the white drifts but oh, so dear to see for their promise. I feel like a prisoner released. There are mountains of snow yet—but spring is coming. I could clap my hands for joy—I *did* clap them tonight up on the hill and laughed aloud for shear gladness of heart. All at once life seemed beautiful again. I felt as if I could run, dance, sing with delight, like a child.

Sunday, Mar. 26, 1905
Cavendish, P.E.I.

This has certainly been a rather dreary day—rain and fog, and no service. But I did not really mind its dullness because it means spring. I could put up with anything that means that. I ventured out tonight in defiance of fog and slush for a walk around the square. The old mill-bridge hollow is a sight— the water over the tops of the fences. This means no mail tomorrow—but never mind, it also means spring.

I've read all day. One story in a magazine brought vividly back an odd fancy of my early childhood. The story was of a lonely little girl who lived with two grim aunts; having no real companion she evolved one from fancy. This companion, whom she called *Elizabeth* "lived" in a grove on the hill, and the child shocked her unimaginative aunts by persistently retailing "lies" to them concerning her talks and adventures with *Elizabeth*. In our sitting room there has always been a big bookcase used as a china cabinet. In each door is a large, oval glass, dimly reflecting the room.

When I was very small each of my reflections in these glass doors were "real folks" to my imagination. The one in the left-hand door was *Katie Maurice*, the one in the right-hand *Lucy Gray*. Why I named them thus I cannot say. Wordsworth's ballad had no connection with the latter, because at that time I had never read it or heard of it. Indeed, I have no recollection of deliberately naming them at all. As far back as consciousness runs *Katie Maurice* and *Lucy Gray*, lived in the fairy room behind the bookcase. *Katie* was a little girl like myself and I loved her dearly. I would stand before that door and prattle to her for hours, giving and receiving confidences. In especial, I liked to do this at

Sitting room with bookcase

twilight when the fire had been lighted for the evening, and the room and its reflections were a glamor of light and shadow.

Lucy Gray was grown-up—and a *widow*! I did not like her as well as Katie. She was always sad and always had dismal stories of her troubles to relate to me; nevertheless, I always visited her scrupulously in turn, lest her feelings should be hurt, because she was jealous of *Katie*, who also disliked her. All this sounds like the veriest nonsense, but I cannot describe how real it was to me. I never passed through the room without a wave of my hand to *Kate* in the glass door at the other end.

Friday, April 14, 1905
Cavendish, P.E.I.

Why do I get this journal out tonight? I've nothing to write. But I'm very lonely and must have some sort of companion. These past three weeks have been the worst since Christmas; had it not been for the saving fact that they are the forerunners of spring they would have been unendurable. I have been nowhere—seen nobody. Slush and mud forbid even a solitary walk at sundown.

Today was cold, gray, dreary. I've felt depressed and discouraged without any special reason—which is the hardest of all depressions to fight against. I was silly enough to have a delightful dream last night. As a rule my sleeping dreams are jumbled, inconsequential things in which I am generally trying madly and vainly to get dressed to go somewhere or find the music for a hymn the minister has given out in church. But this dream—why, I was *happy* in it! And when I wakened from it to the cold gray dawn of another lifeless, pointless day, I felt as if I *could not* get up and live it—or rather *exist* through it. It turned me sick at heart to think of having to do it—a day with not a spark of pleasure or even interest in it—nothing but a monotonous routine of dull duties seemingly fulfilled to no purpose but to prepare for a similar dreary morrow. Oh, I fear this life will spoil me completely—it will make me secretly bitter and resentful. I hate to feel this—I struggle against it, trying to keep my mental attitude sane and wholesome in spite of all—but it is hard—hard. I am so utterly alone. I have not *one* real, helpful friend near me—not one to say a cheery word in my moods of discouragement, or double my few pleasures by sharing them. When I can get out for a walk these dark moods don't control me so; but, cooped up like this, they get the better of me in spite of myself. I am not naturally morbid or discontented. I have kept myself cheery and hopeful in some very hard and discouraging periods of my life. But then I had the assistance of freedom and wholesome society. It was *life*, even if it was hard, not stagnated existence, and so I came out victorious. But now my endurance seems *frayed out*. There doesn't seem to be any *reserve strength* to fall back upon when the dark days come. The happy hours, the little fugitive gleams of pleasure, I have had since last fall could be compressed into a day.

There, I'm going to stop growling. I've had my growl out—and I feel a little less bitter. I believe I've enough grit to go and do a little sewing now—I hadn't before. It just seemed that I must pitch *everything* away with a scream and fling myself into bed. But I never *do* scream for all—I shut all this up in my heart and journal. I couldn't live if it wasn't for this poor old doleful journal!

I'm always glad when the end of the day comes—these days at least—and I can get to bed. I like to curl up by myself and dream gorgeous waking dreams—brilliant affairs where I have everything. I haven't got in the real world. They help me a lot, those blessed dreams.

Monday, May 20, 1905
Cavendish, P.E.I.

Such a long period of non-grumbling means no particular cause for grumbling. Spring has come and "newness of life." I have always been glad to see spring come but I never sounded such deeps of gladness as this year. I know exactly what I shall feel like on the resurrection morning!

My dear garden! Early in April I took the boughs off my tulip and daffodil bed. I didn't expect to see anything growing so soon; but there were tiny darling baby spikes up two inches! Oh, the joy of it! The way I felt was a prayer!

Since then every day has its own dear miracle of growth. I feel as if I were assisting at creation. I have a big yellow daffodil on the table beside me now—a very star of the year. All the lost sunshine of old summers has gone to colour it. Of course flowers have souls! I've known roses I expect to meet in heaven.

The long-delayed library books arrived about a fortnight ago, also a few I had sent for for myself. I broke all decent bounds and read day and night.

I bought Kipling's "Jungle Books"[1] this spring. They are glorious. I'm sorry I couldn't have had them when I was a child. But the next best thing is to have them when grown up. I also bought and re-read "Pickwick Papers" and "David Copperfield."[2] I first read the immortal "Papers" when a child—there was an old racked, coverless copy lying around the house and I revelled in it. I remember that it was a book that always made me *hungry*—there was so much "good eating" in it, and the folks were always celebrating with ham and eggs and "milk punch." I generally went on a cupboard rummage after I had been reading "Pickwick" for a little while.

I brought home a library book the other night—"Elizabeth and her German Garden"[3]—taking it as Hobson's choice because I couldn't get anything else. I didn't know anything about it, didn't think it was worth much, and made no haste to read it. Finally last Thursday I began it. Before I had read a chapter I was ready to kick myself for not having found out what it was before.

Lover's Lane

It was delightful—the whole book. My "twin soul" must live in *Elizabeth*—at least, as far as gardening is concerned. She has said a hundred things that I always meant to say when I had thought them out sufficiently. I shan't have to say them now—*Elizabeth* has done it so well.

I escaped to Lover's Lane as soon as I could. I hadn't been able to get to it since December until May 5th. It was like a new birth to find

---

1. *The Jungle Book* (1894) and *The Second Jungle Book* (1895) by Rudyard Kipling contain stories about a child brought up by animals.

2. *The Pickwick Papers* (1836–37) was Charles Dickens's first work; *David Copperfield* (1849–50), his best-known novel, includes a strong picture of unhappy childhood.

2. Elizabeth von Arnim blends humour and sentimentally in this story (1898) about the life of a woman withdrawn into a country estate, with three children, a beautiful garden, and a domineering husband.

myself in it once more—I don't know what I'm ever going to do without that lane in heaven!

I have moved upstairs again—which means that I have begun to *live* again. It seems odd that such a thing can be brought about by simply changing rooms! But it is so. To me it means the difference between happiness and unhappiness. I almost live up here—what time I don't live in my garden. It is such a pleasant life I thus shape for myself that I am almost contented in it.

Tuesday evening
May 21, 1905
Cavendish, P.E. Island

I've been doing so nicely of late that it is a pity that the demon whose special office it is to torment me should have contrived to lure me this afternoon into a Foolish Deed—namely, that I should read over the part of my journal written in Prince Albert. It wrung my very soul because it was about Laura and Will. I realized how lonely my life is, comparing it with those old riches of friendship. I long for Laura and Will as they were in those old days. The entries in my journal brought back the flavour they gave my life so vividly that it emphasized the present bareness for vital savor—a bareness which I do not generally realize, so accustomed to it have I become, except on such occasions as these.

I sometimes say that I would like to revisit P.A. But I doubt if I really would. It is the P.A. of the old days I wish to see, not the P.A. of today. With father and Will gone it could never be the same. Laura, too, is now an "old married woman" with *three* boys. Could we again meet on common grounds? I fear not. The years, and our different experiences must have pushed in between us.

Still, I think I would probably go if it were possible, if Mrs. Montgomery were not there. I do not wish ever to see her again. My resentment of her treatment of me is as deep and bitter as it ever was—my memory of it as vivid! Oh, my dear father. How far away your grave is! You should be lying by my young mother's side over yonder in the churchyard.

There, I'm crying. I suppose the moral of all this is that I should never read old records. I suppose it would be wiser not to; but I know I shall continue to do so at intervals, for the reading brings a keen, strange pleasure while it lasts and the price of the pain that is paid for it never seems too much in prospect although it always seems too much in reality.

July 30, 1905, Sunday Evening
Cavendish, P.E.I.

Over two months' silence! Not a grumble! Not a "blue"! What does this mean? Well, this has been a pretty good summer—I've been less worried than usual and I feel quite happy and cheerful. But it does seem a pity to fill this journal up all winter with moans and groans and not put in a single bit of summer pleasantness.

For one thing we are alone this summer. Uncle Leander's family did not come over—and that means a great deal to me! I write and read and ramble and dream and revel in my garden—and life is so pleasant and peaceful that it actually frightens me.

I feel that it *can't* last—that it is the calm before a storm.

My garden—oh, the delight it has been to me this summer! I am positively revelling in flowers. Roses—such roses! My big bush of blush doubles, which never did anything before, flung all its hoarded sweetness of three years into bloom—dozens of the most lovely blossoms. There is a big vaseful on my table before me now. And behind me are other vases full of the sweetest of sweet peas and yellow poppies, and nasturtiums like breaths of flame. It is the greatest pleasure my days bring me to go out to my garden every morning and see what new blossoms have opened overnight. At such moments my heart fairly bursts with its gladness. Oh, what a wise old myth it was that placed the creation of life in a garden. Oh, you dear pink rose, here is a kiss for you! I think that long ago in heaven you and I were sister spirits. You were born a rose and I a woman. You are the happier, perhaps. But yet I'm glad to be a woman with a garden and a work and a sorrow. Three blessings,—ay, three blessings all!

I must try to write oftener in this journal this summer because I'm sure to be grumbling next winter again and I don't want this dear old journal, which I love as if it were a living friend, to be *all* grumbles.

This afternoon I was looking over an old scrapbook[1] made years ago when I was going to school and college. I had many a laugh over it—and many a sigh! It seemed to hold the jests and merriment for those old days. Selena Robinson, who was teaching here when I began it, made one at the same time and we collected "screwveneers" for those scrapbooks with zeal and diligence. On the first page of mine is a tiny shoe-buckle which once

---

1. The two earliest scrapbooks, formerly on display at LMM's birthplace, are now in the archives at the Confederation Centre Art Gallery, Charlottetown.

adorned one of Selena's slippers and which she gave me for a mascot for my scrapbook because it was in the shape of a horseshoe. Underneath it is a little fancy calendar which Will P. sent me the year I was at P.W.C.

Here's another calendar which "Aileck" of "Hotel de MacMillan" fame gave me one day. Poor "Aileck," I wonder what has become of him. What fun Mary C. and I used to have over him. But then, was there *anything* in those times that Mary C. and I did *not* have fun over!

A page or so is given to time-tables and pass lists of my entrance exam. What a lot of heart-throbs they stand for! I don't believe I could pass that exam now—but—well—I could pass some others.

There are any number of fancy "cards" in the book. These cards, where the name of the owner was concealed under a gorgeous cluster of flowers held in a slender hand cut off at the wrist, were a beloved fad of our school-days. Anybody who at all aspired to be fashionable sent for a packet of these cards and exchanged them with her mates. Nowadays "picture postals" have usurped their place. "Other times, other fads."

Here is a programme of my first opera. Hedley Buntain's sharp, prim little face rises up before me, also that frantic *fiancée* of his who came to town in such hot haste because she heard I was "cutting her out" with Hedley. I was entirely innocent of the deed or wish. But I daresay Hedley needed looking after for he slipped through her fingers after all and married some other girl.

A piece of wood chipped from my desk in Dr. A.'s room—what a Vandal I was!—is cheek by jowl with a card of Mr. Mustard's—a *bona fide* visiting card, for Mr. M. was never guilty of anything so frivolous as a "fancy card" of course—and a piece of one of Laura P's ball-dresses. A burned out match— relic of some frolic of Mary C.'s and mine—is next to the account of Florrie Murchison's wedding.

Here's a splinter from the famous old lamp-post on Prince St. and next to it a bit of the fringe of a cream-coloured shawl I wore the very first night I ever had an escort home. No girl ever forgets *that* momentous occasion—at least no country girl. I stepped over the threshold of young ladyhood that night. Cream coloured shawls—or "squares" as they were called, were "all the rage" that fall. Every girl had one or wished she had. When new and soft and fluffy they were very pretty and becoming.

"Prince of Wales College Commencement Programme," with a scrap of red and blue college ribbon fastened thereto! I read an essay that night— which a kindly reporter, glory be to his memory, puffed fulsomely in the next mornings daily. Here is my name, and here are the faded flowers I wore that night. And then a "License" time-table! Up come all the faces of those "examinees"—Mary C. here—Ida over there—Nellie McGrath in front of me—Fannie Wise at the right—Nell Rodgerson yonder. Pshaw! Nell had her *fourth* baby christened the other day—named after me! That puts the license exam very far back!

Here are a squirrel's tail, a four leaved clover and a piece of McGill ribbon. Surely there's no lack of variety. And "Firefly's" fur—*Firefly* of old Prince Albert—days. Any more cats? Bless you, yes—"Coco's," "Carissima's," "Max's," "Mephistopheles," "Tom's," "Lady Katherines," "Topsy's"—a whole host of dead and gone pussies of whom only these scraps of fur remain.

What is this? A piece of ornamentation—a woollen rose, to be exact— taken from a sofa cushion. Yes, I was sitting on that cushion the night Lem McLeod proposed to me at Park Corner! Lem is out west now—a spruce business man with the beginning of a bald spot. He was married last winter to Maggie Sellars of Ch'town. Of course she knows nothing of that momento in my scrapbook—nor of another further on, a piece of poetry Lem once sent me in a letter. He didn't write it himself of course—Lem was never guilty of writing poetry or of reading it either, for that matter—but he clipped it out of a paper and sent it with a "them'smy-sentiments-too" letter. It's very sentimental.

> What need of light? By far too bright
> The fire your dark eyes show
> Mine must reveal the love I feel
> So let the lamp burn low.
> Leave me the dark! Too fair a mark
> For Cupid's cruel bow,
> And archer art is my fond heart
> So let the light burn low.
> For, if my love should hopeless prove
> Then must I learn to know
> Darkness alone till life be flown
> So let the light burn low.
> And if you say the word I pray
> That one sweet word would show
> My fate to me so bright to see
> 'Twere best the lamp be low.

But Lem didn't devote himself to "darkness alone till life be flown" after all—and very sensible of him, too!

A time-table of Bideford School—did *I* ever make out such a fiercely tabulated document with every minute accounted for—and the address my Bideford pupils gave me when I left.

Ladies' College ribbon—Halifax looms up now. And oh, yes, more poetry! Lou Dystant eclipsed Lem in sending poetry in his letters. Lou's taste in verse was fearfully sentimental and he underlined like a school-miss. Here is one gem:—

> She was so small—
>> A wee, pure bud from God's own garden lent
>> To fill my life with one bright dream of joy.

Did Lou really consider me "a wee, pure bud?" How Bertha Clark and I used to scream over those frantic clippings!

An old-time fashion plate with big sleeves! The big puffed sleeves are in again now. When I put on a new dress the other day with big sleeves it gave me the oddest sense of being a Dalhousie girl again—for that was the year they came to their fullest balloon-like inflation, stiffened out with "fibre-chamois" etc. "Stuff me in" was an inelegant phrase constantly heard when one girl wanted another to poke the huge sleeves of her dress into the sleeves of her coat.

Friday, Aug. 4, 1905
Cavendish, P.E.I.

This August day was a great golden dulcet dream of peace through which the heart of summer throbbed with lazy rhythm. I went far afield in it to gather ferns. I put my lips to the cup of the day and drank deep—deep—deep. What a world to be glad of—and in!

Tonight was lovely. An August night, calm, golden, dewless, can be very beautiful. I went for a walk over the hill. On its crest I *saw* a poem. Two spruces were clasping dark hands over an arc of silvery twilight sky; and right under the arch formed by their boughs was the new moon, like a sickle of red gold. I looked at it—and thanked God for life in a world where such a sight could be seen. Will there be no new moons in heaven? No twilights? Oh, yes, there must be!

Nasturtiums, who coloured you, you glowing, luxurious things? I could steep my soul in the richness of your hues. You must have been fashioned out of summer sunsets.

Today was sung the requiem of the roses. I picked the last bud. They have been so lovely this summer—I have steeped my soul in roses until I am even willing to let them go, knowing that too much delight is not for this world.

The yellow poppies are out now. It has taken the sunshine of the summer to colour them. Every morning they hold their golden chalices up to me. And the dear sweet peas! They must be the souls of good butterflies. My own soul seems filled with flowers.

Sunday, Aug. 6, 1905
Cavendish, P.E.I.

This morning early I went back to Lover's Lane for ferns to decorate the church. It is so beautiful back there in the fresh morning. I walked all through it and it brought me nearer to God than the service in the church did.

This evening I found an old packet of Nate's schoolboy letters in my trunk. I took it out, untied the ribbon around it, and read them all.

What a correspondence we carried on to be sure! Every evening I wrote him a letter, secure of receiving a similar epistle next morning in school, passed over in a "Bryce" or "Fasquelle"[1] and read down under the maples.

Lover's Lane

I had to laugh a little over those letters. They were so intensely in earnest. Besides, they did not seem to be written to *me*; it was as if I were reading old letters written to another girl.

I wonder what Nate is doing tonight. It is a safe guess that he is *not* reading my letters. I wonder if he has kept them. That is not likely either. I sincerely hope he hasn't; not that there was much combustible material in them—they were rather cool, intellectual epistles as I recall them now; but still, I'd rather they were all in ashes. *I* wonder if *he* wonders what *I* have done with *his* old letters, and what he would say or think if he could read some of them over now. Well, they were nothing to be ashamed of. They were frank, pleasant, clever epistles and they were very delightful reading *then*. Even tonight his boyish compliments gave me one of the old pleasant little thrills, the secret joy with which a woman recognizes her power to please—a joy measured by the gauge of the man. And Nate, even as a schoolboy, was worth pleasing. His was the homage of intellect and spirit as well as of mere sense. I feel no interest in the Nate of *today*. I don't even want to see him. But the Nate of long ago—I'd like to see *him*. I wonder if he is as dead as the Maud of long ago. And how strange to be speaking of it all as "the long ago." Reading those letters made it all seem as of yesterday or, at the most, last year or so. No memories of my life are more clear-cut than those. They were written upon virgin pages.

---

1. David Bryce of Scotland published standard text books on history and education early in the twentieth century; Éditions Fasquelles (now merged with Grasset publishers) provided French texts for schools.

Those letters were full of allusions to old jokes, old incidents, old mates, old doings in C. society that are ancient and forgotten history now. The boys and girls mentioned in them are scattered far and wide—some married, some dead. The old hates have ceased to burn, the old likings to glow, the old friendships are half forgotten. Yet they were none the less intense and real while they lasted.

The Lane

There was a wonderful sunset tonight—so beautiful that it hurt. I walked down the lane to look at it after I had read Nate's letters; and so strong was their resurrective power that I half expected to hear a whistle coming up the old church hill and later see Nate swinging around the curve with his cap on the back of his head and his thin clever face alive with the old quizzical smile. Anything seemed possible in the magic of that sunset.

Good-night, journal. I'm going to bed. I'm lonely and I've got a heartache. Not for anything in particular but just on general principles. Stirring up old memories always gives me one. Like sleeping dogs they should be let lie. I believe it would be far better not to have old letters and such fry but just to forget comfortably, as we go along. Nature probably meant us to do that. And when we defeat her purpose by keeping such records she punishes us with a heartache.

Friday, Aug. 11, 1905
Cavendish, P.E.I.

I have been re-reading *Eugene Aram*.[1] I read it for the first time when I was fifteen and never since. Nate read it at the same time and we were both enraptured with it—we were Lytton-crazy at that romantic period. I remember us both sitting down under the firs on the school hill discussing that book, and it is inseparably connected with those firs and Nate's memory ever since. One of Nate's letters the other night, in which he wrote about the book, aroused in me a wish to read it again.

I found that I still liked it—though not with the frantic adoration of fifteen. Much of what I admired then seems strained and florid now. But I think the book is written in a purer style than most of Lytton's and with all its faults there is something in it that holds the interest. It is very sad—perhaps

---

1. Bulwer-Lytton's novel (1832) about a murderer redeemed by love.

that was why I liked it so well long ago; youth revels in sadness—and leaves a certain haunting impression like a cadence of dying minor music. Nate was fascinated with the character of Aram. I wonder if it is still his ideal. It is not in the least likely. Our ideals change as we grow older—change and, alas, *lower*! We are driven to compromise with the insistent *Real*.

October 1, 1905
Cavendish, P.E.I.

The summer is over! How I shrink from facing that fact! I look forward to the winter with inexpressible dread!

I am half sick now with anxiety and worry and have been so for the past two months. Uncle John and Prescott have been using grandmother shamefully all summer. In short, they have been trying to turn her out. Prescott, forsooth, wants to get married and get this house to live in! Grandmother is nearly broken hearted and I have had a terrible time with her. Grandfather's absurd will put her completely in their power—the power of selfish, domineering men eaten up with greed. Grandmother told them she would *not* leave the home where she had lived and worked for sixty years and since then Uncle John has never spoken to her, or visited her, and all the mean, petty spite they have shown in a score of ways would be unbelievable.

What the outcome will be I do not know. For my own part I care little. It is on grandmother's account I worry. It will, of course, hurt me deeply to leave this old home which I have always loved so passionately even in years when I have been far from happy in it. But I have known, ever since grandfather's death, that the time would come when I would have to leave it, and the reality can scarcely be much worse than the long anticipation has been. Indeed, I believe that, were the final wrench over, it would be a relief not to have such a sword of Damocles[1] hanging over my head any longer.

Uncle John and his brood detest me because I have been the stumbling block all along in their scheme of ousting grandmother from her home. If I had not been here she could not have stayed here alone and they know it and hate me because of it. I shall never forget and I feel I can never forgive the way they have used me ever since grandfather died. They have shown their petty spite and jealousy in a thousand ways. Uncle John is a man whom, from my earliest recollection, I have disliked. When I was a child I feared him unspeakably. He never spoke a kind word to me. He was a domineering, insulting, unjust, bad-tempered man, without one spark of

---

1. In classical mythology a naked sword is suspended above the head of Damocles by a single hair.

consideration for the rights and feelings of other people. When I grew up he had to treat me civilly for, like all bullies, he only bullied those who were too weak to defend themselves. I ceased to fear him but I have never ceased to dislike him. My success in literature has further embittered him against me. His family are brainless—and he knows it and hates me because of it. However, I care nothing how they regard me. It is only on grandmother's account I am worried.

Oct. 15, 1905, Sunday Evening
Cavendish, P.E.I.

Today was a beautiful autumn day—a day on which a heart ought to be glad and grateful and joyous. That mine cannot be so is not its fault—for it could appreciate it to the full if it were care-free.

This evening I went alone to the shore, under the sunset. I have not been much to the shore this summer. Yet it is so wild and lovely there that when I do go I always wonder why I don't go oftener and resolve that I will. It was so beautiful there tonight that I lingered until the sunken sun

"The crash o' white turmoil"

had sucked all the rosy light out of the great blue bowl of the sky and twilight came down over the crash and white turmoil of the breakers—for the tide was high and the winds were out and the sea was thundering its mighty march of victory.

I spent a whole afternoon back in the woods a week ago. If I could have left care behind me it would have been perfect. Even with such a dour companion I found a joy and a happiness in those crimson and yellow soli-

A sunny nook

tudes where the red leaves were falling and the winds purred softly in the tree-tops and went to sleep in sunny nooks. I wished that I might lie down there among the bleached ferns and fall into a pleasant dream that might have no ending and no return to unrest and anxiety. Oh, those dear old woods and fields! I love them with all my heart and have found in them fullness of joy in all my years.

Frede Campbell spent last Saturday and Sunday here and was an unspeakable comfort to me. I had been so lonely and sad-hearted but felt so much better for her visit. I am not naturally a blue or melancholy person but

I do not think even *Mark Tapley*[1] himself could keep his spirits up under my present circumstances.

My garden's glory is departed. The last sweet peas and asters bloomed this week. I bade them farewell very sadly for I do not expect ever to have a garden here again. I do not feel welcome even to so much soil as would suffice for—a flower plot. It is very bitter to think of giving up my garden—my one sole pleasure apart from books and pen. Ever since I can remember I have had my little plot of annuals. It seems to me that every pleasure is being stripped from my life. It is terribly hard to keep from growing bitter and sullen. But I *do* strive against *that* at least. These things shall not—*must not*—creep into and poison my soul.

Wednesday, Nov. 8, 1905
Cavendish, P.E.I.

It has been a raw, damp, dreary day, with showers of mist and snow. I think the rawness and the dreariness have crept into my being. I write here because I feel lonely and comfortless and want a friend. Yet I have nothing to write.

I've been reading "The Bonnie Brier Bush" all the evening—and crying over it. I am not to be pitied for those tears, however, for there was no bitterness in them. They were born of a certain pleasure in the sweetness and pathos of the tales—simple, wholesome tales, like a sweep of upland wind or the tang of a fir wood on a frosty night.

I have two chrysanthemums and a rose out. I look at my rose and I think "God's in His Heaven, all's right with the world." It is a song and a hope and a prayer all in one. The mums are very pretty, too, but it does not do to have them and the rose too near together. Seen by themselves they are handsome, bright, big blossoms, pink and yellow, looking very well satisfied with themselves. But set the rose beside them and the change is actually amusing. They then seem like vulgar, blowsy kitchen maids beside a stately white queen. It's not the fault of the poor mums that they weren't born roses, so to be fair to them I keep them by themselves and enjoy them that way.

I speak of *enjoying*—but this fall I really enjoy nothing. I hate to waken every morning. At night I am thankful another day is done. What a pitiful state of affairs in a beautiful world we were meant to delight in! But perhaps things will be better some day. That hope and my writing are all that keep me alive.

---

1. Character from Dickens's *Martin Chuzzlewit* (1943–44), determined to be jolly under trying circumstances.

Sunday, Nov. 12, 1905
Cavendish, P.E.I.

We have had a week of typical November weather—dull, wet, sodden. The world seems tired and outworn—too tired even to think about a possible spring. It wants a rest—a long rest first. But perhaps we read into the world only the alphabet of our own mood.

Yet it is certainly looks weary and dreary. The sky is gray and so are the trees and fields. The ground is littered over with dead leaves. The year is an old housewife who has ceased to take an interest in her domicile and has grown slovenly.

This Sunday has been very dull. I had nothing new to read so fell back on an old book and tried to convince myself that it and my rose and my mums made the day worth while.

There was service in our church this afternoon. Rather a dull affair owing to the poor day but I was thankful to get away for an hour and see a few cheerful faces. I am thankful for very small mercies and pleasures these days. Pleasures? Nay, rather say momentary reliefs from the hundred petty and maddening annoyances of my life. But thank God for books and flowers. They can drug, if they cannot satisfy, the hunger for life.

Thursday, Nov. 16, 1905
Cavendish, P.E.I.

The mums are purged on the rose now, for it is faded and brown and unsightly, while they are so brilliant and buoyant as ever. Still, wouldn't you rather be a rose than a mum?

My dear dead rose! Tomorrow I must cut it off. But I shall shred its withered petals lovingly into my rose jar—a sweet death for a sweet flower friend.

It's a wild weird night of wind and rain. I don't want to go to bed, but since I have to I mean to shut my door, say good-night to my books and pictures, blow out the light, creep into my nest, and there have wonderful adventures—waking dreams all gay and brilliant and beautiful. My body shall be pent in here but my soul shall fly far beyond the rain and the dark to "cloudless realms and starry skies."[1] Thank God for the Ideal. "With it is immortal hilarity—the Rose of Joy."

---

1. Misquoted from Lord Byron's 1814 poem, "She walks in beauty, like the night / Of cloudless climes and starry skies."

Friday, Nov. 24, 1905

I'm sleepy. Last night there was a party at Wedlocks'[1] in Stanley and I was invited. Jim Simpson took me up. It's no difference who Jim is or how he came to take me. He's *nil*. And I was bored to death.

I had a chat with Frede which made the evening worth while to me. I didn't know many of the guests and wished I knew fewer for I had to talk to those I did know and they were sinfully uninteresting. How *can* people live in such an interesting world and be such bores?

The Wedlocks evidently thought the supper they served would delight people. It was very lavish. If the table didn't "groan" it should have. There was so much piled on it that one couldn't decide what to eat before the time was up. My right hand neighbour was a man who made "funny" speeches all through the meal and kept me wondering for what good purpose God had ever fashioned him. I would like to have a house of my own just to see if I couldn't set a table as it should be done and bring together some people who could talk and be interesting.

But then there isn't the least likelihood I ever shall have a house of my own. I suppose, when grandmother has gone, I shall migrate to Ch'town or some similar burg, get a cheap boarding place, and write pot-boilers for a living. A pleasant outlook, truly! But I suppose it's better than charity or the poorhouse and so, thanks be!

Sunday, Dec. 10, 1905

A big snowstorm! Dear me, I suppose this is the beginning of sorrows. How I hate the winter! And yet how I might love it, the wonderful white thing under other conditions! I used to love the winter as I loved the seasons. Will I ever love it again I wonder?

I've been quite busy these past three weeks. Bertha Mackenzie[2] is to be married on Christmas day and I am to be her bridesmaid. So I'm having a little pleasure for a change. But today I can only look at the dismal side of things. I'm not feeling well and all the world is one thick, blind whirl of snow.

My mums are still blooming but are beginning to fade. I shall miss them like human friends when they are done. But I have some hyacinth and

---

1. John Wedlock and his wife Mary Lamont, Presbyterian family at Stanley Bridge.

2. Bertha McKenzie was a cousin on the Woolner side, her grandfather having married Margaret Woolner, sister of LMM's grandmother. A newspaper clipping in LMM's scrapbook notes that the Rev. Ewan Macdonald performed the ceremony.

narcissi poking their dear heads up in window boxes and I have great hopes of them by and by.

Later On

I feel better. Fancy why? Because it is raining out now and it will stop the drift and I shall not have to turn out and shovel snow in the morning.

The bookcase in my room

When I've nothing new to read I generally go prowling in an old trunkful of books upstairs. My best books I keep in a little bookcase in my room; but the aforesaid old trunk is full of school and college books, paper covered novels etc. I came across a book tonight—*The Safe Compass*[1]—and brought it down for old associations.

That book was a classic of my childhood. It had belonged to my mother and her name was written on the fly-leaf. It was very religious; but it was also interesting and consequently a great stand by for Sundays. The frontespiece had a gruesome fascination for me. It was the picture of a boy lying under a tree, with the legend, "His neck was broken and there lay the young Sabbath breaker, *dead*." The heinous crime which the defunct had committed was climbing a tree to eat some cherries on Sunday!

The book had the faults of its class but its virtues were its own. Probably it helped to form what good then is in my character—although I'm afraid I'd eat cherries on a Sunday even yet! I must keep that little red book forever. The child I was haunts every page and story of it. I remember what a fascination the chapter on "garden" had for me. The "garden" was the "heart" and I used to struggle desperately—by fits and starts, after I had been reading the book—to root up the "weeds" of temper, selfishness etc. and plant the "flowers" of all the virtues instead. I wonder if it really did me any good—any lasting good, at least.

Dec. 24, 1905, Sunday night
Cavendish, P.E. Island

Tomorrow is Christmas and Bertha's wedding day. I am sitting here with my hair tortured up into a dozen or so braids and "bids" so that it may be properly fluffy and fashionable tomorrow. May my hair be naturally curly in my next incarnation!

---

1.   Evangelical sermons (1863) by the Rev. Richard Newton, an American Episcopalian.

My bridesmaid dress is lying in chilly state on the spare room bed; it is a sweet thing of flowered silk organdy, all frills and puffs and laces, looking somewhat unseasonable in a world of snow and frost; and my bouquet of white carnations and white hyacinth and asparagus fern—which latter in spite of its kitchen gardeny name looks like the soul of a fern—is in a vase on the sitting room table. It came yesterday and reconciles me to much I dislike in the fuss and details of this marrying and giving in marriage.

Weddings seem, for the most part, to be rather vulgar things, stifled in a dust of sweeping and scrubbing and baking and borrowing, with all the various harrassments thereof. The beauty they should stand for seems wholly lost sight of.

I know how I would like to be married—and never will be for even supposing I should ever marry I should have to conform to the conventionalities. But that doesn't prevent me from having an ideal of what a wedding should be, and—if I lived in an ideal world—this would be mine.

In the morning—a June morning when a glorious sunrise should be blossoming over the silvery east and the roses in gardens and wilding lanes should be as sweet as roses could be—I would rise early and dress—dress for the one man in all the world and for the eyes of no other and make me as fair as might be for his delight; and then in the expectant hush of dawn I would go down to meet him, unknown of any others and together we would go to the heart of some great wood where the arches were as some vast cathedral aisle and the wind of the morning itself sang our bridal hymn; and there we should pledge to each other a love that should last for all time and all eternity. Then we would turn, hand in hand, back to the busy world that would forevermore be glorified because of our life together!

Well, there's my *ideal*. But the *Real* is quite another thing.

Only—I *swear* that *if* I ever do marry I will *not* be married under an "arch" of tortured spruce boughs, decorated with pink and white tissue paper "roses" and looking like nothing that god ever thought about! If I were to outrage my ideal as flagrantly as *that* I should be looking ahead to the divorce court while the minister was reading the marriage service!!!

Yesterday, Friday, and Wednesday I spent with Bertha, mixing and icing cakes, making candy, sweeping, dusting, decorating. These things made me physically tired; but what wearied me mentally and robbed life of all its "bouquet" was having to talk to Bertha's two brothers, Bob and Milton. Milton is a cub and a bore, and does more than anything I've every read or seen to make me disbelieve in the existence of a soul. Bob is a decent enough fellow but he, too, is a hopeless bore. I can tolerate him along the lines of acquaintanceship but when he inflicts his unwelcome attentions on me—the nauseating attentions of a country *clod*—I feel as if I were being spiritually smothered.

Yet I have to be civil to him on Bertha's account—and even on my own; since he is one of the few folks I can depend on to take me anywhere I have to go. I loathe these necessary makeshifts and the galling dependence they imply. But in this world of material facts such things have to be reckoned with.

Tuesday Evening
Dec. 26, 1905
Cavendish, P.E. Island

It is all over and I have just arrived home feeling that the greatest blessing life can offer is a warm bed and a good sleep!

Yesterday was quite the merriest Christmas I have ever spent. I went down to Bertha's in the morning and must say I enjoyed everything to the full. The ceremony was at twelve and then we had dinner and a very jolly afternoon. At three we—Bertha and Will, and Bob and I—left for *Ebenezer*. Ebenezer is the name of the place where Will lives, but that is his misfortune not his fault! As the day was fine and the roads good we enjoyed our drive very much. When we got there, however, the fun was over. There was a reception that night and as I didn't know the people—or want to know them—I was bored to death. The only fun of the evening was a drunken fiddler. It sounds rather awful; but he *was* drunk and he *was* funny. At two o'clock

Bob. Mr Green. Bertha. Me.

I went to bed, so tired that I couldn't sleep. Everybody seemed dragged out the next day. Bob and I came home this afternoon.

Well, it's been pleasant, getting all this up. I daresay I'll be lonely for awhile—and, what is worse, have time to worry again! Oh, how sick I am of worry. It is the hardest thing in the world to endure. I've had so much of it here since grandfather died that my strength to bear it seems getting frayed out.

1906

Monday, Jan. 1, 1906
Cavendish, P.E. Island

A lovely New Year's day. But I do feel so sad tonight. I was over to New Glasgow today with Russell Macneill to see Pensie. Poor Pensie is dying of consumption and I do not know when I have made a more sorrowful visit.

It is wonderful how old ties formed in childhood hold. They may grow so slack and be so overlaid with newer interests and affections that you forget their existence. But suddenly some wrench reveals it. Pensie and I have seen very little of each other since her marriage because she lived too far away for frequent meetings. But now when she is ill our old friendship revives. How we talked today of our childish games and schooldays. We were so often together then and had such jolly times.

We are on the threshold of the New Year. Oh, I wonder what it will bring me! I only ask release from worry—I would be content with that.

I feel tired and lonely and discouraged. Patience, sad heart. There is eternity. This life is only a cloudy day in what may be a succession of varied lives.

Pensie and husband and child

Sunday, Jan. 14, 1906

So far we have had a lovely winter; really, it does not seem like winter at all—just enough snow for good roads and such mild lovely days. It is such a blessing. I could not endure what I endured last winter under my present circumstances. But there is plenty of time left yet for rough weather and I have dismal forebodings.

Just now my flowers are a great joy and comfort to me. I have a window garden of bulbs and they have begun to bloom. Some white narcissi and yellow crocuses are out and they are very beautiful. I fear I love them idolatrously but I can't help it. And I have had more unworthy idols!

Oh, my beautiful, wonderful, star-like, fragrant flowers! You are teachers and companions and beloved friends.

Thursday, Jan. 26, 1906

This past week has been a gayer one socially that often falls to my lot. Annie Stewart is home for a visit and last Saturday evening George R. and I were invited up for a game of whist. We had it and it was very enjoyable. Then we had a "seance" and made a table rap. Of course this was lots of fun. But it is a curious thing and a little uncanny, give it what scientific "explanation" you please.

Monday evening Mrs. J.R. Stewart gave a "goose supper" to the members of the Literary Programme Committee. Both the ministers, Messrs. Belyea and Macdonald,[1] were there and we had another table rapping. We made the thing do various stunts, such as standing up on one leg, walking round the room etc.

Last night there was a dance at J.R. Stewart's and I took it in also. Had a very nice time. That is, as nice as I can ever have nowadays with my subconsciousness of worry grumbling away under everything else, like a partially disregarded aching tooth.

Thursday, Feb. 1, 1906

January has gone out—a most perfect and lovable January, like a very fine April. There is no snow and no frost. How abjectly thankful I feel for it.

Today I had the pleasure of receiving an autographed novel from the writer thereof. For several months I have been corresponding with a Mr. Gerald Carlton of New York, introduced to me by a mutual friend in Halifax. Last letter he said he was going to send me one of his books and today it came. I've read it—"Her Mad Love"[2]—this afternoon. It is absolute trash—not even interesting. I thought him rather a clever man from his letters but he can't write at all, at all.

Saturday, Feb. 3, 1906
Cavendish, P.E.I.

Yesterday I spent the afternoon with the Belyeas in the Parsonage. Mr. and Mrs. Belyea are both very nice and particular friends of mine. I borrowed

---

1. John G. A. Belyea (b. 1854) came to Cavendish with his wife Violet in 1903, becoming pastor of the Baptist Church, following the Rev. "Craw" Wilson. Ewan Macdonald (b. 1870) became the minister in the Presbyterian Church in Cavendish in 1903, but did not take up residence in Cavendish until 1905. This is the first mention in the journals of the man who at about this time began courting LMM.

2. *Her Mad Love: A Psychological Novel of To-Day* (1890), a story of love and murder as well as madness by Gerald Carlton. Years earlier LMM had pasted an article about Carlton in her red scrapbook (see *Imagining Anne*, 160).

Baptist Parsonage

a much talked-of book from Mr. Belyea—"The Law of Psychic Phenomena"[1]—I began it at ten o'clock last night upstairs in bed and found it so fascinating that I read until one and then only stopped because I was too cold to go on. Today I finished it. It is a wonderful book and I am intensely interested in some of its theories and conclusions.

My flowers are so lovely now. Every day brings a fresh miracle of opening loveliness. Every morning I make new discoveries of bud and bloom. If it be true that flowers do better with those who love them mine ought to flourish superlatively for I stand adoring them ten minutes at a time and go to the length of praying for them most devoutly and earnestly.

February 25, 1906
Cavendish, P.E.I.

This is different from last winter with a vengeance. I was glancing today over the part of my journal written last winter and it seemed nothing but a record of storms and blues. Well, it was not exaggerated.

February has been another perfect month—no cold, no snow, excellent walking—this last item being an important one for me. And I have summer in my window garden where my glory of daffodils are the talk of the community. One box in particular—it's a wonder something hasn't happened to it, for I'm sure I think too much of it. There are nine big double "Van Zions" out in it, each looking like a veritable sunburst. I cannot express what those flowers have meant to me this winter. When I look at them I *almost* forget my constant, carking worry.

This is Sunday night and I feel lonely. I expected Frede and Jim Campbell down last night but the roads broke up in Friday's thaw so they could not come. I was much disappointed for I was longing to have a good talk with Frede. Still, in another way, it was a relief that they did not. If Jim had come he would have had to go over to Uncle John's to put his horse in, for Uncle John has left no place in our barn for a horse. Ever since grandfather died, if any friends came here with a horse they had to be sent over there.

---

1. Dr. Thomson Jay Hudson, Ph.D., LL.D., lawyer, journalist, and government official, discussed mental therapeutics in his book (1892) to help readers avoid letting "the subjective mind overthrow the throne of reason."

I have always hated this, and now it has become unendurable. Moreover, poor grandmother seems to hate to see my guests come here. Frede she will tolerate as a relation but anyone else is under a ban. So I was glad Jim did not come because I could have done nothing to make his visit pleasant and would have been hampered and harassed in tendering even the smallest civilities.

I long intensely for summer when I can live more or less in my own room and call my soul my own in some small measure.

Tuesday, Mar. 2, 1906
Cavendish, P.E. Island

Today I went to New Glasgow to poor Pensie's funeral. I never saw anybody so pitifully wasted as she was. I looked at that emaciated face in the casket and tried to believe it was the face of my old rosy merry schoolgirl chum but I could not link the two together at all.

Saturday, March 6, 1906

This evening was lovely and Wilbur Clark and I went up to Stanley to visit Wedlocks. I sometimes wonder what I would have done if Darnley Clark had not had a family of boys!!! They have all been so kind to me and they are nice brotherly chums, always ready to do a good turn, with no nonsense of sentiment in the matter.

I saw Frede and had a little confidential talk which did me more good than I can express. These little occasional out pourings to a trusty and understanding friend are veritable safety valves for my intense nature and keep my worries from moth-eating my soul. There is no one in Cavendish to whom I can turn for advice or assistance. I cannot bear to expose the seamy side of my life to the gaze of any outsider. To all here I preserve the same unbroken front of smile and jest and composure. But *some* outlet I must have and between Frede and my journal I continue to muddle along quite respectably. But oh, life is such a starved, ugly, thing when, if I possessed even the average measure of freedom, I could make it a rich beautiful thing. I *know* I could; it is in me.

Thursday, April 5, 1906

I feel rather too seedy to amount to anything today after the party at Joe Stewart's last night. Wellington MacCoubrey[1] was there. He has been living in Sydney[2] for three years and he told me some news about Nate who was practising law down there during the same time.

Nate, as I saw by the papers some time ago, is *married*. Actually! He married a Miss Mabel Saunders[3] of Wolfville and immediately thereafter left for Sydney to practice his profession there. His many friends etc. etc.

Wellington M. told me two things about Nate that amazed me. One is that he is *very gray*. Nate *gray*!!! What an idea! Why, wasn't it only the other day that he was a curly-headed schoolboy? What business has he to be getting gray? Nate! *Gray?* The other thing was still more surprising. Wellington said Nate had not done much in Sydney, that he seemed "such a dull fellow without a spark of life or ambition." This amazed me. Nate, who used to be simply full of life and ambition and energy! Is it possible he can have changed so? It does *not* seem possible. I know he had a long and hard struggle to get through college. Perhaps it was *too* long and hard and ate up all his supply of energy and pluck. I should certainly have thought Nate just the man to succeed in law.

Poor Nate, I hope he is happy and that he has a nice little wife. Wonder what he said when she asked him if he had ever loved anyone before her—for of course she *would* ask him. But I daresay he had loved a dozen—*I* was only the first; and I daresay he would assure her he had never *loved* anyone; and I daresay again that he would honestly think he was telling the truth—which is all as it should be! World without end! Amen!

But—Nate—is—gray! Verily, the next thing that I will hear about him will be that he is a grandfather!

Tuesday, April 18, 1906
Cavendish, P.E.I.

Frede went back to Stanley this morning after being down since Saturday. We had two golden days together and they put new grit into me, which was fortunate, as my stock was running rather low.

---

1. The McCoubrey family had come originally from Newfoundland. Wellington (1874–1950) was born in PEI but died in Sidney, NS.
2. Nova Scotia mining town.
3. A cousin of Margaret Marshall Saunders, author of *Beautiful Joe* (1893) and a string of other best-selling children's stories.

Spring is here. It's nice—but not half the joy it was last year because the winter was really just like one long spring. I'm glad it's over, though. How dismally I looked forward to it last fall! Well, fortunately my forebodings were not all fulfilled.

I don't think Prescott will try to meddle with grandmother for awhile at any rate. He is very ill—has been ill all winter—and looks ghastly. I believe his doctor is afraid of some variety of tuberculosis. It is hard to feel sorry for him after the way he has acted. It is almost enough to make one believe that there *are* such things as "judgments."

Sunday Evening
May 13, 1906

Why am I writing in this diary tonight? This is not a conundrum. I really know of no reason why I should be, except that I am blue and lonely and worried. And *that* is too common a state now with me to be worth writing about.

I found myself wondering today what it would be like to be free from care. It is so long since I was that I have forgotten the sensation. I know there was a time when I was comparatively free from care just as I know there was a time when I was not born. But both states seem equally mythical to me.

I think I could bear some great trouble or sorrow tolerably well. But for me life consists of one unending series of pin-pricks,—petty annoyances and vexations from dawn to dusk. I hate to wake up and come downstairs in the morning. I breathe a sigh of thankfulness when I creep into bed at night.

This is Sunday and Sundays are apt to be drearier than any other day. Poor grandmother can't work then and so has nothing to take up her attention and prevent her from crying and lamenting the most of the time. Much of this is due to the behaviour of Uncle John and his breed—and I love them for it proportionately.

I have a Bermuda lily out—and it is something to dream about. It makes me almost happy to look at it. I have set up a lot of house plants this spring to console me in a measure for the lack of my garden. But oh, how great the lack is. No dear green things to poke up their sweet-heads this spring, no visions of poppies and asters in the months beyond! Well, there is no use in feeling badly over that. There are so much worse things to be faced every day.

At least I have some mayflowers—vases of them everywhere about my room that there is a place for them. Amanda and I went up to the barrens mayflowering yesterday afternoon. It is no pleasure to me to go anywhere with Amanda now. But she asked me to go with her so I went. But there are times when I wish simply that I need never see Amanda again. Our friendship died long ago. I realize this if she does not. Yet I would wish to retain respect and tenderness for its memory; but every time I am in Amanda's company she robs this memory of its meed until I often fear that she will eventually fill me with disgust for everything connected with her. How sad it is that our old girlish friendship, which was once so beautiful and pleasant a thing, should have come to this! Yet I can honestly say that I have nothing with which to reproach myself in regard to her. I never said an unkind thing to or of her. I struggled for years to keep our friendship alive and vital. I suppose Amanda cannot help the unlovable traits and qualities that have developed in her—certainly she does not try to help them. She sets the teeth of my soul on edge with her odd ways and remarks. I say "odd" but it would really be more correct to say "malicious." She seems to be literally eaten up with *jealousy* of everybody. Yesterday she spoiled for me the golden day and the south wind among the little firs and the mayflower stars in the sere grasses. I would have enjoyed them alone—enjoyed them doubly with a real friend—but with *her* I felt *raw* all the time. Oh, I am so sorry! How pleasant it would be if our friendship were what it once was! What a bright spot in my busy, lonely, harassed life! And I could bring something into her life too, if she would let me. But when things are dead there is no use wishing them alive again.

Sunday Evening
October 7, 1906
Cavendish, P.E.I.

Never a word since last May! Well, I've been too busy most of the time. Now, in the moon of falling leaves there are long evenings when I have some spare time. This evening it is too windy to go up to the Baptist church as I had planned so I'll pick up my dropped threads. Yet there really isn't a great deal to write.

x Bertie

The summer is over. It has been for the most part a pleasant one with fewer worries than last year. I look forward to the winter with no pleasurable anticipations. It promises to be a lonely one.

I have not roamed much abroad this summer. In June I had a brief but very enjoyable trip to town. I went in one day and out the next. As Bertie and I had only one night to talk we made the most of it. We never went to bed at all—just sat up and talked. How I wish it were possible to see her oftener.

A month ago I drove over to Park Corner one Sunday morning and back again in the evening. I had not been over for a year and a half and I was overjoyed to see the dear old spot again.

Uncle Leander, Aunt May and Kennedy spent five weeks here in July and August. Their sojourn was not as disagreeable as it was the last time. Uncle L. has found a drug which alleviates his trouble and consequently his temper. Aunt Mary and I had lots of fun bathing and visiting together. I was rather sorry to see them go. Uncle John and his family never dare to show their meannesses quite so blatantly when they are here.

One afternoon in August we had a picnic on the manse grounds. While I was crossing them on an errand I met Edwin Simpson!

Well, there is not much to say about it. All at once, I found it did not matter. I simply felt utter indifference. There was no pleasure in meeting him and as a mere matter of preference I would rather not. But all the old shame and humiliation and restraint were gone. The past was—at last—dead.

I stood and talked for an hour to him before all the crowd and didn't mind it in the least—that is, as far as onlookers were concerned. In one way I *did* mind it for, to confess the whole truth, I was *bored*. But I couldn't escape so I stood first on one foot and then on the other and listened perforce. I should not have said that *I* talked to *him*. It was entirely the other way round—*he* talked to *me*. He evidently was bent on showing me while he had a chance how vastly much he had crammed into his head during the past eight years. His whole personality seemed to exhale as a breath, "See what you've lost, young lady!" Meanwhile, in the back of my head I was saying "Thank God, I've escaped this man. Why, in a week he would have me talked to death."

He is as good-looking, as clever, as conceited, as superficial as ever. He is pastor of a city church in Illinois and from one standpoint he is a successful man. But nobody seems to like him and he talks entirely too much about himself—what *he* has said, thought, done, etc. He spent Monday afternoon here and took tea with us. He left Cavendish next day and that was the end of it. Poor Ed, what a pity he is so conceited! But I daresay it makes him very comfortable!

Friday, Oct. 12, 1906
Cavendish, P.E. Island

This afternoon Ewan Macdonald[1] called to say good-bye before leaving for Scotland, where he intends studying for the winter at Glasgow University. And I am sitting here with his little diamond solitaire on my left hand!

FICTION
L. M. Montgomery—a face of balance and refinement. The smooth high forehead shows love of stories and sympathetic perception, the height and squareness above the temples and the arched eyebrows suggest poetic feeling and artistic taste, while the full eyes show facility of expression.

Yes, it is a surprising thing. And I think nobody could be more surprised at it than I am myself. I wonder if I can analyze clearly the events and motives that have led up to it.

"Me, mineself"

Three years ago, our congregation called Ewan Macdonald as its minister and he was inducted in September 1903. He had preached here in the preceding spring, just after his graduation from Pine Hill, and made a very favourable impression. He was an Island man and belonged down east near Valleyfield.[2] His people were Highland Scotch and although he was Canadian born he had a pronounced but not unpleasing Scotch, or rather Gaelic, accent. He was considered a handsome man by many but I should rather call him fine-looking. He is of medium height, with a good but somewhat stiff figure which is erect and dignified now, but may become "paunchy" in later life. He has thick black hair, black, roguish eyes, a clean rosy wholesome face, a fine profile and a very pleasant smile which brings out engaging dimples in his cheeks—altogether a very personable young man of about 34.

His induction service was held in Cavendish church on Tuesday, Sept. 1, 1903. It was a social function quite as much as a religious one and the church was crowded. Rev. Edwin Smith of Cardigan[3] preached the sermon *and* Rev. Edwin Simpson sat in the audience and thought, as he told me a few days later, that, Mr. Macdonald struck him as "a good-looking boy whose mother had told him to put on his best suit for his ordination." I had no earthly interest then in Ewan Macdonald as a man; but I did not think the remark in very good taste, coming from an outsider to a member of the

1. Ewan Macdonald (1870–1943), the newly inducted Presbyterian minister, born in Bellevue in the central-eastern section of the Island, and educated at Prince of Wales College and Dalhousie University's Pine Hill Theological College, was hailed in Cavendish as "an indefatigable worker and a genial companion." LMM misspells his name in this entry and errs regarding his age—he was 36, not 34.

2. A settlement near Bellevue, PEI, about 50 miles (80 km) east from Cavendish near a river that flows into Cardigan Bay.

3. On the east coast of PEI.

congregation which had just called him, and who therefore would not care to hear criticism or ridicule of her minister.

I "sensed" somehow that Edwin Simpson did not altogether relish the idea of a young unmarried minister being let loose in the community where *I* lived and thought that a timely bit of a sneer might prejudice me against him.

Mr. Macdonald could not get a boarding house in Cavendish so he boarded in Stanley until the spring of 1905. During those years I saw little of him socially but considerably of course in the church services and work. Gossip, always ready to buzz about an unmarried minister, used to link up his name with those of the only girls in the congregation, who, by reason of age, some modicum of cleverness, and aptitude for church affairs, seemed "suitable" for ministers' wives—Margaret Ross of Stanley, Mabel Woolner of Rustico, and "me, mineself" of Cavendish.

Rev. Ewan Macdonald

I do not know Margaret Ross, save by sight, but I doubt if she were in any sense a candidate for his favour. She was then, I believe, in the throes of an unhappy love affair of her own and had little thought to spare for other men. Mabel Woolner, however, looked upon him with favour and, as I have since discovered made no scruple of letting him see it. But, according at least to the gentleman himself, when he first saw me he made up his mind that if I were not already "bespoke" he would try his luck. The poor fellow could not, however, find out very easily whether I was or whether I wasn't. Gossip was always engaging me to somebody and the Edwin Simpson tradition lingered, reinforced occasionally by Ed's appearance in C. and his calls on me.

Interior of Church

As for me, I was most certainly not in the field to get me a husband. Neither had I the least hankering to be a minister's wife. The life of a country minister's wife has always appeared to me as a synonym for respectable slavery—a life in which a woman of any independence in belief or character, must either be a failure, from an "official" point of view, or must cloak her real self under an assumed orthodoxy and conventionalism that must prove very stifling at times.

Why, she wouldn't even be able to play whist!!

I did not want Mr. Macdonald for a lover; but I rather hoped at first that I might find a friend in him. But after meeting him a few times I decided I could not. He was likeable and pleasant but I did not discover any especial congeniality in him and was not in the least attracted to him. He was not an intellectual man and had no culture in spite of his college education. He preached good, solid sermons but out of the pulpit he possessed no fluency of speech; he was somewhat shy and awkward in society with a very narrow conversational range. He was very well liked by all—I liked him very well— but he was, and remained a practical outsider as far as my life was concerned until the spring of 1905, when he came to live in C., boarding at John Laird's. He came up for the mail very frequently and before long fell into the habit, of lingering for an hour or so and talking to me. As I came to know him better I found more in him than I had expected—a certain depth of thought and feeling that was generally hidden and repressed, partly by his natural reserve, and partly I think by the poverty and stiffness of his vocabulary. I began to enjoy our chats on theology and philosophy—the only subjects he had a real grasp of—and moreover, I began to be attracted by the man himself—just why or how I could not say. I liked him—I was glad to see him—I felt the loneliness of my life more keenly when he went away. But, although gossip was by the ears over his calls, I did not think seriously about him until last spring. After all, he had never done anything but call in the afternoons to talk on impersonal subjects, and once or twice drive me home from Literary. I had no reason to suppose that he meant anything but simple friendliness. He had never made the slightest attempt at love-making—had never looked, or implied, or hinted at any such thing. In most men this would have indicated an utter absence of any wish to be more than friend. I was not quite sure that it indicated this in the case of Ewan Macdonald, however. There were times when I *felt*, without any valid reason at all, for so feeling, that he cared for me and would, sooner or later, ask me to marry him. And, by this time, I was interested in him to the extent of asking myself very seriously what answer I would make if, and when, he did.

I found it an extremely difficult thing to decide and for months I could not make up my mind. Last spring was a troubled and rather unhappy time for me.

As aforesaid, I did not care for the idea of marrying a minister. On the other hand, viewing marriage in the abstract, *I* would be glad to marry *if* the right man asked me to marry him. I wanted a home and companionship; and more than all, to be perfectly candid, I wanted children. It has always seemed to me a terrible thing to go out of life leaving no life behind you to which you gave birth; and a childless old age is a bitter thing to contemplate.

But much as I wanted all these things I did *not* want them badly enough to marry anyone if I could not be reasonably happy in such a marriage—*reasonably* happy, I repeat. Perfect and rapturous happiness, such as marriage with a man I loved intensely would give me, I have ceased to hope for. I would be content with a workaday, bread-and-butter happiness—so humble has the unhappiness of these past eight narrow, starved years made me in my demands on life.

But suppose a marriage with Mr. Macdonald would not give me even this. I would make him unhappy, too, in that case. Or, worse still, suppose that, having married him, I met a man whom I could love as it is in me to love, with an overmastering passion and devotion. For a few years after I put Herman Leard out of my life I was so numb from the anguish of it all that I believed I could never love again. But now I know I could if I met a man of the type which attracts me strongly. The type is uncommon and the chances are a hundred to one against his ever coming into my life. Yet, if the thing should happen the results, I am absolutely certain would be tragedy of one kind or another to me and it might be to others. There were times when I said, "I will not risk it."

On the other hand, I dreaded unspeakably the *loneliness* of the future when I should be alone, absolutely alone in the world, and compelled to make a new home alone in some strange place among strangers. There were moments when I could not face *that* alternative either. Viewed in the abstract, without reference to any particular man it honestly seemed to me a choice of evils—and which was the least? I balanced them one against the other—but could come to no decision. In some moods—my morning moods—I inclined to think that I would be wiser to keep my freedom and trust life. In other moods—my evening and three o'clock at night moods—I inclined to marriage. In one mood loneliness seemed the greater evil, in another a companionship from which I could never escape even if it should prove to be uncongenial.

Again, I was considerably worried over this problem:—I cannot in any case marry as long as grandmother lives. Would I then be acting fairly to bind a man down to wait for me for an indefinite time—perhaps till my youth and bloom were entirely gone. But, after all, this was for him to settle not me. If he cared enough to do it well and good. If he did not he was quite free to seek a wife elsewhere.

Again and again I asked myself did I care enough for Ewan Macdonald to justify my marrying him. There were moments when I was intrigued by his smile, and by a certain undeniable, though not overmastering or especially subtle, physical attraction which he had for me, into thinking I did. But generally it seemed to me that I did not. I liked him—I respected him—I saw all his good qualities of heart and character; to put it plainly, I was *very* fond of him. But I knew that was all.

Suddenly, during the summer, in the midst of my perplexed self-grilling, came news that he had resigned and was going to Scotland. Somehow then,

I felt that I could not let him go out of my life. He seemed to *belong in it*. I couldn't face the thought of the emptiness and blankness he would leave.

One evening he called for me and we drove down to Will Houston's. On the way home, through a dark, rainy night, he said suddenly,

"There is one thing that would make me perfectly happy but perhaps it is too much to hope for. It is that you should share my life—be my wife."

I told him that I would marry him if he could wait until I was free. He said he would willingly do that rather than give me up. So it was settled at last.

I think I have done the wisest thing in assenting. But the future alone can prove that. One takes a risk in any marriage—the very "for better or worse" of the ceremony shows that. I feel content.

Sunday, Nov. 4, 1906
Cavendish, P.E.I.

Such a horrible day! It has blown a most fearful hurricane from the north and is bitterly cold. It has also rained hard from Wednesday afternoon until last night. I can't help feeling blue for the weather has got on my nerves and it is so lonely here in this dreary time of year. I miss Ewan's cheery calls so much. I suppose he is in Scotland tonight. It will be a fortnight yet before I can hear from him, I suppose.

We have had no service in our church for over a month and there is absolutely nothing going on in C. at all. Stella was down for a fortnight in October. We had a jolly time. How I wished they lived nearer to us. And how I wish the winter were over. I do so dread it under existing circumstances. How the wind wails and howls and shrieks tonight! When I am not lonely I love the wind; when I am I hate it because it seems to be the soul of all the unrest and wretchedness and dreariness the world has ever known.

November 6, 1906
Cavendish, P.E.I.
One o'clock Tuesday Night

One o'clock is a somewhat unearthly hour to be writing in a journal! The truth is I'm undergoing a "white night." I can't sleep and I'm tired of lying in the dark fancying things—unpleasant things—so I've lighted the lamp and got out this diary to "write it out."

The causes of my white night are two. Firstly, the weather! It is still raining and blowing fiercely. This poor old house is leaking like a sieve. There are half a dozen different "drips" in my room alone. I've been getting up to put basins under them ever since I came to bed. Then, just as soon as I had crawled in again and begun to get warm I'd hear a "s-plud" in a new place and up I'd have to get again.

The second cause is far worse. I had a letter yesterday from Edwin Simpson!

Did I say the past was dead? Well, he has evidently a ghoulish propensity for digging it up. His letter has upset me completely.

When grandmother handed it over to me yesterday there came across me the same horrible old sensation I knew so well and experienced so often eight years ago. It was an hour before I could summon courage enough to open it.

Of course, I knew before I opened it that his motive in writing was simply to find out if there was anything between Mr. Macdonald and me. He naturally heard the gossip when he was home last summer and it seems to have affected him more than I could have supposed was likely or even possible.

He did not avow this motive, of course. I would have more respect for him if he had done so instead of employing the roundabout way he did. He began by saying,

"You will be surprised to receive this letter but often since my call last summer, which I very much enjoyed, I have felt tempted to write you. You will pardon my presumption for the sake of Auld Lang Syne."

That reference to *Auld Lang Syne* is in Ed's usual felicitous taste! Surely the "auld lang syne" which was between him and me was not of such a nature as would be likely to appeal to me.

He then goes on for several pages describing his work, aims etc. It is not until the sixth page that he gets down to the real object of his letter.

"Has the Pres. church settled another dominie since Rev. Macdonald departed for Scotland? I wonder how he is getting along among the heretics of the old world. I must not ask you, yet *Dame Gossip* once mentioned that you would know. I gave her story little credence—why I do not know. I remembered all too well a promise or a threat—which shall I call it?"

Ed has a certain astuteness in seeking what he wants to know. He dared not ask me any open question on the subject so he very skilfully frames some sentences which he thinks will *provoke* me into denying or affirming the truth of "dame gossip's reports." But he is mistaken. When I answer his letter—for I mean to answer it, having some things I want to say to him—I shall completely ignore his reference to "gossip." He can draw what conclusion he likes from that.

Then he goes on:—

"I wanted to ask you some questions this summer but remembered your prohibition and did not dare. It was imposed eight years ago—why, I am still wondering and I presume, among almost endless presuppositions, I shall go on wondering until the end of this world's time for me."

Now, in every letter Edwin Simpson has written me since our engagement was broken he has voiced this same reproach, more or less pointedly—the reproach that my reasons for my behaviour have been left a "mystery" to him—that I have kept him in the dark as to the real reason for my change towards him. Well, perhaps he has only too much right on his side there. But I am going to write to him and offer to answer those "questions" fully and candidly, if he really wishes to ask them. Eight years ago I could not have done so—it was a psychological impossibility then for a girl of my training and temperament to have told him certain things. But now I can and will. It will not be a pleasant thing to tell him the whole truth about that miserable old story—to tell him that I never loved him but only fancied I did and that the fancy was dispelled in three or four *days* by the physical repugnance I felt for him. It will be as unpleasant writing for me as it will be reading for him. But it will be for the best, though it will be a hard thing to do. I wonder if every woman who makes such a mistake has to pay such a long drawn out penalty as I have had to pay.

Ed concludes his letter thus:—

"I hope these past eight years have been happy ones for you. To me they have brought many unexpected prizes; yet not all that I wished for has come, as I once believed it should. I sometimes wonder if it lives only in the past. If thus, better there than not at all. I must close what I fear you will call a cowardly letter written today from a motive not clear even to the writer."

There is a note of insincerity there. Ed is merely *posing*—trying to protect his vanity; he knew perfectly well why he wrote.

"May I hear from you in answer to this if you feel like it. Rest assured that my promise of friendship which I once requested you to accept when you felt you must reject anything further shall ever be kept and I shall always consider it a privilege to serve you. Our meetings for me have been pleasant since then but exceedingly difficult—such a fearful self-consciousness will ever arise. I have wondered if it was so with you. Pardon this unlocking of the skeleton closet which to me is very real still though not as unsightly as it once was. Time is 'the beautifier of the dead' but it will not grant oblivion. I can scarcely pray that it should or should not."

Much of Ed's letter annoyed and irritated me; but some of it also saddened me and barbed the sorrow with remorse. I feel that I have done him a great injury. I had surely thought that the oblivion he speaks of had come long ago. I regret that it has not. And I cannot understand how Ed *can* have any such feeling left for me. I would expect him to feel only resentment and contempt for me, if he retained any feeling whatever concerning me. Yet it is only too evident that he does not and I fear that he still hopes that the future will re-unite us—a hope utterly vain even if there were no question of Ewan Macdonald.

Well, Ed shall have his belated explanation. We shall hold a coroner's inquest over our dead past. It will be a gruesome proceeding but if it will lay the old ghosts forever it will be justified.

Well, it is two o'clock. I'm going to put out the light and try to get to sleep.

Sunday, Nov. 11, 1906
Cavendish, P.E.I.

Things are better! I've had a good sleep since Tuesday night and feel more like looking my perplexities in the face. Besides, I had a letter from Ewan yesterday and that has made the world seem brighter. He is in Glasgow and likes his college and surroundings very much.

As for Ed's letter, I haven't answered it yet—haven't been able to get up enough courage to do so. Of course it will not grow any easier by procrastination. But there are some things I want to say as wisely and carefully and decisively as they can be said and they will bear a good deal of thinking over. I don't want to make any more mistakes.

We had service today—the first for a long while. It was a real treat to get out and see a few familiar faces. The world is a cheerless sodden place just now—constant rain for ten days and not a glimpse of sun, moon, or star. What wonder I get a bit downhearted—I, who, years ago seldom knew what a blue mood meant. Perhaps my old cheerfulness will return some day. Even yet when I have half a chance I'm not really a dismal creature.

Monday, Nov. 12, 1906
Cavendish, P.E.I.

Still pouring rain from dawn till now! I feel like screaming aloud—I feel smothered—stifled. Oh, to live in a world where there were no Novembers!

I am tired wandering around the house setting basins under leaks—which is about all I've done today. I didn't feel well physically either—hadn't even enough "sauce" to "dress up." Consequently, I feel dowdy, lustreless, uninteresting! I even bore myself! I had partly planned to write Ed tonight but I did not. I want to feel *well* and in decent spirits when I do it for it will be a depressing performance at best. I wish it were over. Oh, and there are moments when I wish life was over, too. It seems so full of perplexing problems and harassing penalties. When I get as tired and nervous as I am now I haven't the strength to face them. I just feel as if I wanted to lie down somewhere and fold my hands and go to sleep and never *think* again. This is mostly the morbid result of bad weather, *leaks*, and loneliness. If the sun ever comes out and dries things up I'll be much better. But just now I'm *blue*. I keep thinking of all the mistakes I've ever made. I dread the thought of the night. I feel sure I'm not going to sleep and besides I think one of my periodical headaches is coming on—indeed, all this morbid unrest is one of the symptoms. Between an oncoming headache, Ed's letter, Ewan's absence— I *do* miss him exceedingly—twelve day's rain, leaks uncounted—but I *did* count them today and there were *fifteen*—I am a miserable creature and life doesn't seem worth living.

This all comes of living alone. I say "alone" advisedly. For all practical purposes of companionship I am alone—far more alone than if I really had nobody living with me—for then at least I could do as I liked and amuse myself in some fashion. I would light a fire in the room, make candy, read, talk, think, dream aloud. As it is, I must sit here in silence, too tired to sew or re-read old books. And at nine I must meekly trot off to bed, whether I'm sleepy or not. Poor grandmother, what a pity she cannot be convinced that people grow up.

Bed Time

I have just discovered five more leaks. That makes twenty in all. We shall be drowned I think. Uncle John's will not fix the leaks and I cannot persuade grandmother to get any outsider to do it for fear they will make a scene. I hope the way Uncle John has used his mother will be visited on him some day!

Tuesday, Nov. 20, 1906
Cavendish, P.E.I.

This has been a *good* day. Good every way! It was fine and sunny and mellow. I felt well physically and mentally; got a good day's work done; had a charming walk tonight.

But Sunday and yesterday were bad bad days. I did not get my expected letter from Ewan Saturday and that made me feel disappointed. Then Sunday night I wrote to Edwin Simpson. It was so unpleasant a task that it made me feel actually ill. I had to lie down for awhile after I had written it. It is certainly unfortunate that these things should have such power over me. But thank "whatever Gods there be"[1] it is written. I would feel more thankful still if I did not fear that it will bring another letter from him which will be still harder to answer.

Still, it is quite possible that it may not do so. I have told Ed that what I have to say will not be pleasant reading for him. His colossal vanity will quite likely take alarm at this and he may not choose to run the risk of having it wounded. It will be a conflict between his vanity and his desire to know the truth and it is quite possible that the former will win. But even so I shall have robbed him of his weapon of offence. He will never again be able to reproach me with not having told him my real reasons if he refuses now to take advantage of my offer to do so.

Of course the writing of this letter upset me to such an extent that I had another white night—couldn't sleep at all, tossed miserably, and imagined vain things. As a result I had a headache all day yesterday. Wasn't fit to do anything. But Ewan's belated letter arrived and cheered me up somewhat. I went to bed, got a good sleep and so felt like something worth while today.

It was lovely out this evening. I went up over the hill in the clear pure November air and walked about until twilight had deepened into a moonlit autumn night. I was alone but not lonely. Thought was quick and vivid, imagination active and bright. I held a series of imaginary conversations with imaginary comrades, and thought out so many epigrams that I was agreeably surprised at myself. Then I came in, still tingling with the strange, wild, sweet life of the spirit, and wrote a chapter of my new serial—wrote it easily and pleasurably, with no flagging or halting. Oh, it is *good* to feel well and vivid and interesting and all alive!

Sunday Evening
Dec. 2, 1906
Cavendish, P.E.I.

We are having the first real snowstorm of the season. It has snowed and drifted all day and consequently has been very lonely and dull.

I've been jogging on of late in a rather uninteresting rut. But a nice thing happened last Tuesday. *Everybody's*[2] accepted a short story of mine—"The Quarantine At Alexander Abraham's"—and sent me a hundred dollars for it.

---

1. From "Invictus" (1875) by W.E. Henley, the "unconquerable soul."

2. New York magazine founded by Wanamaker's, a leading ten-cent general illustrated magazine, noted for popular serials.

Everybody's is one of the big magazines and to appear in it is a sign that you are getting somewhere.

Today I was reading a new book, "The Future Life."[1] It was very interesting but after all did nothing to solve the problem. There has never been any authoritative answer to that old, old question. "If a man die shall he live again?" Yet man will keep on asking it from age to age.

Today, too, I read in the earlier pages of this old journal wherein I had written concerning my love for Herman Leard. What a mad infatuation it was! And yet it taught me some lessons it was well to know. I am not sorry I felt it—nay, I'm glad. Every experience enriches our life and the deeper such an experience the greater the richness it brings. I am a deeper-natured, broader-minded woman than I would or could have been if it had not been for that old love, that old temptation, that old anguish. It stirred my soul to depths that I would never otherwise have sounded or been conscious of. I am glad I knew it. It would have been a sorry thing to go through life and never have known love, even though it was an unhappy and unsatisfied love. I shall never know the *fullness* of life—to love absolutely and give myself to the man I so loved, knowing he loved me as well. But I have not been cheated out of everything.

Tuesday, Dec. 4, 1906
Cavendish, P.E.I.

All day a storm has been raging as bad as any we had during that dreadful winter two years ago. We are drifted completely up. It is bitterly cold, too. Of course there was no mail and I am lonely. Oh, are we going to have another awful winter? My soul cringes at the thought. Altogether I'm disgruntled. The only thing I had to pass the time away today—for I couldn't write amid so many discomforts and worries—was fancy work. What a solace that is to a woman!!!! It's well I have something to help me for I'm harassed by a score of worries—all more or less petty, of course. But the "cumulative effect" is not petty. I don't experience one placid care-free moment from waking to sleeping. I am "cabined, cribbed, confined," mentally and emotionally as well as physically.

---

1. The 1906 translation of a French dissertation (1905) by Louis Lucien Baclé (pseud., Louis Elbe) based on "ancient wisdom and modern science."

 1907

Sunday Evening
Jan. 20, 1907

I wonder if, sometime in the future, I shall ever again find Sunday evenings pleasant. For the past six years they have for the most part—in winter at least—epitomized for me all that was dreary and lustreless in my existence. This is a typical one. There was no service today and it is raining heavily and blowing. Grandmother is reading hymns and crying over them. Her continual "sniffing," which has none of the dignity or pathos of real grief, keeps me rather nervous and "raw."

I have not written in this journal for a long time. Somehow I haven't had the heart. I have felt depressed and worried. For the past six weeks Ewan's letters have only made matters worse. He seems dreadfully blue and downhearted. He says he is troubled with headaches and insomnia but he tells me nothing else and I cannot find out what is the cause of this. I cannot help fearing that something serious is the matter with him, for otherwise why should he be so depressed and discouraged. His letters give me the dismal feeling that he is *compelling* himself to write them and has no real interest in writing them—as if his mind and thoughts were exclusively taken up with something else. I didn't know how much I had been counting on his letters to help me through the winter until they failed me. As it is, I really dread getting them, they worry and depress me so. I have asked him repeatedly if he has been to a doctor but he will only say doctors cannot help him—nothing more, to all my questions. It would not be so hard if I only *knew* but as it is I disquiet myself with all sorts of harrowing suppositions and fears. One thing is certain, he is not able to study and his time is being wholly wasted. I have really only one thing to cheer me just now—a big box of golden daffodils out in luxuriant blow. It calms and heartens me just to look at them.

We are trying to get up a concert and "supper" for the church debt. It is a sickening piece of business, with this one getting "mad" and that one feeling slighted and half the choir at loggerheads with the other half. I am sick of trying to keep the peace and smooth down ruffled plumage. I detest these petty affairs for raising money anyhow. Religion ought to be above such sordid things. If it doesn't mean enough to people to make them put their hands in their pockets and pay properly for their churches it doesn't mean much. But I suppose we must take people as we find them in this world and do the best we can under their and our limitations. *These* worries, at least, are only external and don't go very deep—unlike the others in my life. I wouldn't mind them—I'd merely laugh at them in a normal existence. But when one is miserable and harassed all the time even an added pin-prick seems unbearable. This journal of mine is certainly my "blue" book.

There are times when I hate life! Other times again when I love it fiercely with an agonized realization of how beautiful I *could* make it if I had only half a chance. It seems to me that every instinct of my nature is thwarted except that which urges me to literature and which is fortunately beyond the power of anybody or anything here to thwart. Everything else is denied me. I cannot garden, I cannot have any social life, I cannot have any friends visit me. I cannot travel.

But, thank God, the soul, the mind, is *free*—nothing can trammel it. At a bound it overleaps the prison of the material and soars among the stars.

Our Literary Society this winter has been a failure, as all but two of the nights were stormy. I don't care muchly. I only go to it now because it is easier to go than to explain a hundred times why I don't go—especially as I couldn't after all give a truthful explanation but would have to concoct some decent fib.

There is no pleasure in the Literary for me now—or so little that it is lost amid the annoyances. I have to walk up alone over a mile of bad roads through the dark. Yet I don't mind this half as much as the coming home with a crowd of giggling girls and gawkish boys among whom I feel wretchedly out of place. None of my old set are left to go to the Literary now.

I haven't been very well physically of late. So I'm blue and lonely and discouraged, except for a few rare hours when a young moon shining through darkling firs or the white hush of a winter twilight wrapping me around lifts me out of myself for a space. Or when I look at my daffodils! I have looked at them just now and they make me ashamed of my blues and my despondency. After all I've lots to be thankful for—I'm not hideous—I'm not stupid—I'm going to do something with my pen yet—I've got a lovely gray cat—and I wouldn't be anybody but myself for all the world—not even a better or nobler anybody. *I* want to grow better and nobler—to root out faults and prune off unsightly growths—but I want to be *I* and nobody else through all the ages of eternity, through all the lives that are to follow this. Sometimes I take a queer, whimsical comfort out of the thought, "Never mind! Next time I'm born I'll have what I've missed in this life."

I'm reading Gibbon's "Rome"[1] just now. It is a massive work. What millions of men and women have lived and toiled and suffered and succeeded and failed!! What is *one* among such a multitude? Isn't it presumptuous even to hope for an individual immortality?

---

1. For *The History of the Decline and Fall of the Roman Empire* (1776–89) Edward Gibbon used modern research methods in his use of notes and primary sources. LMM read through this large text more than once.

Sunday, Jan. 27, 1907
Cavendish, P.E.I.

Another week has gone. I am thankful for that! What a melancholy statement! When life is so short to be glad that another week of it is gone!

It has been a hard week of bitter cold. Our concert came off Thursday
night. It was a worry to get it up but at the last it was a success and a
pleasure. However, I've had a cold ever since and feel miserable physically,
for the cold weather still continues. It snowed last night so I could not get
out for a walk this evening. I would not have felt so blue if I could have.
But here I sit, suffering from all the mean little discomforts of a cold—
"snuffles," headache, sore throat, chapped lips etc. etc. Cheer up! Better
times will come. You'll get well of this cold and nothing can prevent spring
glory be! When I can once more get out to my dear fields and woods and
hills nothing will seem unbearable. Just now everything seems so—except
my darling daffodils that look as if they were compounded of the sunshine
of a hundred summers.

Tuesday night
Feb. 5, 1907
Cavendish, P.E.I.

It's very cold and there's a northeast storm on. But I don't feel as blue and
lonely as usual tonight for I had a nice letter from Ewan today—the first
cheerful letter he has written since November. It cheered me up at once.
How different it used to be when I received Ed's letters! How I hated to
read *them* and answer them! I never read one of them twice. How strange
some things are in life. Nothing seems really in accordance with the theory
of it.

> There's a lot of things that never go by rule—
> There's an awful lot of knowledge
> That you never get at college,
> There are heaps of things you never learn at school.[1]

That isn't poetry but it's truth! One doesn't learn *anything* at school. *Life*
is the only real teacher. One doesn't forget *her* lessons. They are branded in
too deeply.

---

1. LMM quotes this jingle in a letter to George Macmillan, April , 1907 (see *My Dear Mr. M.* [1992])
   and again in *Anne of the Island* (1915), ch. 37. Compare the college song, "It's not for knowledge /
   that we go to college…"

Monday, Feb. 25, 1907
Cavendish, P.E.I.

I *must* have a good fierce grumble! I've been keeping it off as long as possible but it has got to come tonight or I shall *burst*. We have had " a dreadful cold spell"—five days away below zero. The house has got so cold that it is really not fit to live in, as grandmother will not have a fire anywhere but in the kitchen. I've been shivering for twenty four hours. When physical discomfort is added to mental and emotional discomfort the last stage is reached in my endurance. I *have* to succumb and growl it out in this journal.

This is the most utterly lonely winter I have ever put in. And Ewan's letters, after that one cheery one early in the month have been so gloomy. *What* can be the matter? And why won't he tell me? There *must* be something worse than headache and insomnia to account for his despondency. Day after day drags by, cold, lifeless, monotonous. Oh, if it were *only* spring!

One really nice thing happened a week ago, though. I had never seen Frede since the middle of October but last week I got a chance up one evening. It did me good, mentally and emotionally, yea, and spiritually and physically. Frede and I got in her room, wrapped shawls about us, squatted on the floor with a box of chocolate caramels between us, and talked ourselves out. Oh, it was jolly! I've been living on the memory and taste of it ever since.

Today it has stormed all day in addition to being very cold. I haven't felt well, so couldn't work with much satisfaction to myself. Winter is a four month's nightmare under my present circumstances. But "it's bound to clear up sometime." I suppose it is. But just now the clouds are very black and the gloom and chill of the storm are creeping into my very heart. There, I *will* stop grumbling for I'm ashamed of it. But when I've smiled outwardly all day and tried to be bright and cheerful I've just got to work off the internal bitterness by an explosion in this journal.

Wednesday, Feb. 27, 1907

In an old book—a very old and very wise and very wonderful book—is a saying that often comes to my mind of late—"Pray ye that your flight be not in the winter."[1]

But *I* should rather pray that my flight—from this old home—when it comes might be in the winter because then it would not have half the pain

---

1. Matthew 24:20.

it would have in summer. In winter I almost turn against the place; but in summer I love it still, as I shall always love it, despite the bitterness that I have gone through here. I shall never love any place as well, not even

The old home in winter

though I may be far happier elsewhere than I have ever been here. I am *rooted* here, and though the soil may be ungenial and the blasts piercing still it is *home* and can any other spot in the world ever be that to me?

We have had a great storm and no mail since Monday. I have been quite ill and have felt miserable in mind and body. This evening I was reading over my old Prince Albert journal, full of Laura and Will. How vividly those old days came back—their jokes and laughter—oh, how we *did* laugh then!—and our little outings and—what shall I say? I hate the word "flirtation"—it sounds cheap and vulgar and those little moonshinings were sweet and innocent and harmless. Reading over those old days always stirs my heart and nature to their very deeps and touches the "source of tears."

Sunday, March 10, 1907
Cavendish, P.E.I.

Up to Friday I was blue all the week, for it was so extremely cold that one could not exist even in physical comfort and Thursday "capped the climax" with a furious storm. It was not *very* pleasant having to wade out and shovel snow in the teeth of such a blizzard to get in coal and water. Really, if Friday had been stormy, too, I don't believe I'd have had the courage to get out of bed at all. But it was a lovely day, sunny and calm, and so were yesterday and today—the first really pleasant days we have had for eight weeks. Instantly new courage poured through every vein of me and I felt like something worth while again. I had the loveliest

Lover's Lane in winter

walk last night—the first I have had for over six weeks. I went over the fields to dear Lover's Lane I seemed to be walking through a spellbound world of diamond and crystal and earl, so white and radiant were fields and hills and sky. The air was so clear and pure that it was half intoxicating. I felt a wonderful lightness of spirit and a soul stirring joy in existence—a joy that seemed to spring fountain-like from the very deeps of my being and to be independent of all earthly things. I was alone and I was glad of it. Any human companionship, even the dearest and most perfect would have been alien to me there—would have been a flaw in those peerless moments. I was sufficient unto myself, needing not love nor comradeship nor any human emotion to round out my felicity. Such moments come rarely—but when they do come they are very wonderful and beautiful—as if finity were for a second infinity—as if humanity were for a space uplifted into divinity. When I came out to the main road and a sleigh flashed by, bells tinkling, voices laughing, the spell was broken and it seemed to me that I was leaving behind me a world that had nothing in common with the one to which I was returning—a world where time was not, which was young with immortal youth, where there was neither past, present, nor future but only the great "I-Am." I shall go there again tonight, for it promises to be fine, and there I shall keep tryst with all that is best in me and all that is best in life.

Friday, Aug. 16, 1907
Cavendish, P.E.I.

Here is a gap with a vengeance! But there has not been much to write about and I've been very busy and contented. Since spring came I haven't been dismal and life has been endurable and—by spells—pleasant.

One really important thing *has* come my way since my last entry. On April 15th I received a letter from the L.C. Page Co. of Boston[1] accepting the MS of a book I had sent them and offering to publish it on a royalty basis!

All my life it has been my aim to write a book—a "real live" book. Of late years I have been thinking of it seriously but somehow it seemed such a big task I hadn't the courage to begin it. I have always hated *beginning* a story. When I get the first paragraph written I feel as though it were half done. To begin a *book* therefore seemed a quite enormous undertaking. Besides, I did not see just how I could get time for it. I could not afford to take time from my regular work to write it.

I have always kept a notebook in which I jotted down, as they occurred to me, ideas for plots, incidents, characters and descriptions. Two years ago in the spring of 1905 I was looking over this notebook in search of some

---

1. This company had published Marshall Saunders, Bliss Carman, Charles G.D. Roberts, and many other Canadian authors.

suitable idea for a short serial I wanted to write for a certain Sunday School paper and I found a faded entry, written ten years before:—"Elderly couple apply to orphan asylum for a boy. By mistake a girl is sent them." I thought this would do. I began to block out chapters, devise incidents and "brood up" my heroine. Somehow or other she seemed very real to me and took possession of me to an unusual extent. Her personality appealed to me and I thought it rather a shame to waste her on an ephemeral little serial. Then the thought came, "Write a book about her. You have the central idea and character. All you have to do is to spread it out over enough chapters to amount to a book."

The result of this was "Anne of Green Gables."

I began the actual writing of it one evening in May and wrote most of it in the evenings after my regular work was done, through that summer and autumn, finishing it, I think, sometime in January 1906. It was a labour of love. Nothing I have ever written gave me so much pleasure to write. I cast "moral" and "Sunday School" ideals to the winds and made my "Anne" a real human girl. Many of my own childhood experiences and dreams were worked up into its chapters. Cavendish scenery supplied the background and *Lover's Lane* figures very prominently. There is plenty of incident in it but after all it must stand or fall by "Anne." *She* is the book.

I typewrote it out on my old second-hand typewriter that never makes the capitals plain and won't print "w" at all. The next thing was to find a publisher. I sent it to the Bobbs-Merrill[1] firm of Indianapolis. This was a new firm that had recently come to the front with several "best sellers." I thought I might stand a better chance with a new firm than with an old established one which had already a preferred list of writers. Bobbs-Merrill very promptly sent it back with a formal printed slip of rejection. I had a cry of disappointment. Then I went to the other extreme and sent it to the MacMillan Co. of New York,[2] arguing that perhaps an "old established firm" might be more inclined to take a chance with a new writer. The MacMillan Co. likewise sent it back. I did not cry this time but sent it to Lothrop, Lee and Shepard of Boston,[3] a sort of "betwixt and between" firm. They sent it back. Then I sent it to the Henry Holt Co. of New York.[4] *They* rejected it, but not with the formal printed slip of the others. They sent a typewritten

---

1. A famous house of bestsellers. In 1903 they had taken over the copyright of L. Frank Baum's *The Wonderful Wizard of Oz* (first published 1900 by George M. Hill).

2. Published the 1902 bestseller Owen Wister's *The Virginian*, and in 1903 Jack London's *The Call of the Wild*.

3. Lothrop published the bestseller of 1900, Irving Bacheller's *Eben Holden*.

4. Publisher of LMM's old favourite, *The Prisoner of Zenda* (1894).

screed stating that their readers had found "some merit" in the story but "not enough to warrant its acceptance." This "damning with faint praise" flattened me out as not even the printed slips could do. I put "Anne" away in an old hat box in the clothes room, resolving that some day when I had time I would cut her down to the seven chapters of my original idea and send her to the aforesaid Sunday School paper.

The MS lay in the hat box until one day last winter when I came across it during a rummage. I began turning over the sheets, reading a page here and there. Somehow, I found it rather interesting. Why shouldn't other people find it so? "I'll try once more," I said and I sent it to the L.C. Page Co.

They took it and asked me to write a sequel to it. The book may or may not sell well. I wrote it for love, not money—but very often such books are the most successful—just as everything in life that is born of true love is better than something constructed for mercenary ends.

I don't know what kind of a publisher I've got. I know absolutely nothing of the Page Co. They have given me a royalty of ten percent on the *wholesale* price, which is not generous even for a new writer, and they have bound me to give them all my books on the same terms for five years. I didn't altogether like this but I was afraid to protest, lest they might not take the book, and I am so anxious to get it before the public. It will be a start, even if it is no great success.

Well, I've written my book. The dream dreamed years ago in that old brown desk in school has come true at last after years of toil and struggle. And the realization is sweet—almost as sweet as the dream!

Ewan came home in April. He seemed very well and quite recovered from his headaches and insomnia.

Wednesday, October 9, 1907
Cavendish, P.E.I.

This evening I went to the shore. Yesterday we had a wild storm of wind and rain but today was clear, cold, sunny, with an air of marvellous purity. This evening the sunset was beautiful beyond words. I drank in its loveliness as I walked down the lane. My soul was filled with a nameless exhilaration. I seemed borne on the wings of a raptured ecstasy into the seventh heaven. I had left the world and the cares of the world so far behind me that they seemed like a forgotten dream.

On the old North Shore

The shore was clean-washed after the storm and not a wind stirred, but there was a silver surf on, dashing on the sand in a splendid white turmoil. Oh, the glory of that far gaze across the tossing waters—the only restless thing in all that vast stillness and peace! It was a moment worth living through weeks of storm and stress for.

There is a great solitude about such a shore. The woods, now, are never solitary—they are full of whispering, friendly beckoning life. But the sea is a mighty soul forever moaning of some great unshareable sorrow that shuts it up into itself for all eternity. You can never pierce into its great mystery—you can only wander, awed and spell-bound, on the outer fringe of it. The woods call to you with a hundred voices—but the sea has only one—a mighty voice that drowns your soul in its majestic music. The woods are human but the sea is of the company of the archangels.

I thought of Emerson's lines as I stood there tonight in that wonderful place.

> The gods talk in the breath of the wold,
> They talk in the shaken pine,
> And they fill the long reach of the old seashore
> With a dialogue divine.
> And the poet who overhears
> Some random word they say
> Is the fated man of men
> Whom the ages must obey.[1]

I shall never hear that random word—my ear is not attuned to its lofty thunder. But I can always listen for it and haply by times I shall catch the faint, far-off echo of it and even that will flood my soul with music and my heart with supernal joy.

Oh, you dear earth! Tonight I loved you so much that I could have flung myself face downward on you, my arms outstretched as if to clasp you, and kissed your clods for very gladness in you.

Yesterday I wrote the first six pages of my new book—the sequel to "Anne." I have been busy all summer collecting material for it, blocking out chapters, devising incidents and fitting them into each other, and "brooding up" the characters. This is the disagreeable part of the work but it is done now and the rest is pure joy. To breathe the breath of life into those dry bones and make them *live* imparts the joy of creation. *Anne* is as real to me as if I had given her birth—as real and as dear.

---

1. From Emerson's "The Poet" (1841).

Sunday, Nov. 3, 1907
Cavendish, P.E.I.

In the old school woods

I like to walk through the old school woods in the twilight. The twilight is so much kinder to them than the mid-day. In broad sunlight they are old and unlovely—at least on a near view. All the lower boughs have died and are jagged and unsightly. The ground is strewn with broken branches and the open glades show bare, rotted stumps. But in the gloaming none of this is seen and I can so easily imagine that the woods, full of lurking shadows, are as they once were—green and blithe, full of dear little winding paths fringed with ferns and starflowers, and sunny glades carpeted with moss. They are peopled, too—my old schoolmates are lingering there, calling to me from behind the trees and among the shadows to join them at their old games. I love to walk down the school hill at dusk in the company of such fancies.

There was a Hallowe'en party at Darnley Clark's Thursday night. I went because they were my friends and I did not want to insult them—as they might consider it—by not going; but the whole thing was distasteful to me. I disliked walking up alone in the dark. Few of my old set were there and those few were not congenial. The rest were all mere youngsters, of a very shallow type at that. The evening passed playing games which might amuse children but were rather infantile stuff for men and women. Finally I had to take "a chance" home with a young imbecile of not even the average farmer boy intelligence. When I got home I went thankfully up to my dear white room and thought that the whole evening had seemed like a nightmare. I would not exchange one of my solitary twilight rambles with its airy fancies for a thousand such parties. It is one of the things I love Cavendish for that it offers so many places where one can have such rambles unnoticed and unhindered. Yet I am no recluse by nature and no one enjoys intercourse with congenial friends more than I do. But books and flowers and trees are better friends than *most* of the people I meet with here. When I speak of *loving* Cavendish it is the place I love not the people. Of course, I *like* the greater part of them well enough and a few of them a good deal but none of them are of vital importance to me. But oh, I do love Cavendish the *place*!

My dear room

Wednesday, Nov. 13, 1907
Cavendish, P.E.I.

Something so good and sweet and lovely came my way tonight that I must write about it! And what was this good and sweet and lovely thing? The world would laugh to hear—but the world shan't hear it, I shall tell nobody about this lovely thing—for it *was* lovely to me beyond words, and gave me more real pleasure than all the parties I ever attended all put together, as well as furnishing a vivid picture of my mental gallery that shall be mine as long as memory endures.

Tonight at twilight I went for my usual walk. The evening was very mild and calm. As I loitered along the road between the school and the graveyard I saw, away beyond the little brook valley below me and half way up the opposite slope, a brush fire burning brightly and clearly in the old orchard beside the maple grove in Geo. Macneill's field. There was something undescribably alluring in that fire, glowing redly against the dark background of wooded hill and twilight fields. A wood fire at night has always a great fascination for me and I must go to this. I hurried down one hill, up the other and along a lane until I reached a gap that let me into the field. I was as breathless with delight as a pleased child and when I reached the old orchard I was so perfectly happy that I could have sat down and cried for pure, unearthly joy. I wanted some new language, full of unused, unstained words, to express my rapture.

Oh, it was beautiful! The fire, composed of red apple boughs, burned with a clear steady glow and the long arcade beneath the trees was illuminated with rosy radiance, beyond which lurked companies of enticing gray and purple shadows. And everything was so still and remote and dreamy. It was an hour when *anything* might come true—when pixy folk might have crept out to join hands and dance around the fire or wood nymphs stolen from their trees to warm their white limbs by that blaze. I don't think I would have felt any surprise if I had seen something of the kind—some queer little elfin face peering at me around the tree trunks or the flash of an ivory shoulder through the gloom.

And there I sat and enjoyed it all, with a sort of wondering pity for the people out beyond in all the various farmhouses who weren't there to see it and didn't know anything about it—and wouldn't have cared if they had. Oh, I shall never forget that hour! I shall be homesick whenever I think of it. It would make a year worth living, even if it were all dull and gray but that hour! It makes me feel afraid to think that I might have missed it—might not have gone out tonight—might have taken another road—a dozen "mights" that *might* have holden my eyes from it. When I pray tonight I shall only talk to God about that hour and thank Him for it. There was *everything* in it—things the most widely sundered and diverse—the beauty of classic myths—the primal charm of the silent and the open and the gloom—the lure of mystery and the beguilement of fancy—the love of all life, past, present and to come—ideal friendship—ideal love! Oh, when I reluctantly turned away—when I left the shadows and the glow and went down the lane into the twilight—I felt as if I were leaving Fairyland behind me and all my heart and soul yearned back to it.

Monday, Nov. 18, 1907
Cavendish, P.E.I.

Lover's Lane

I had a walk through Lover's Lane at dark tonight—or just as the dark was coming down. I was never there so late before and while I enjoyed it I was really a little bit afraid, with a not unpleasant fear. The whole character of the lane seemed changed. It was mysterious, sibilant, remote, eerie. The trees, my old well known friends, were strange and aloof. The sounds I heard were not the cheery, companionable chorus of daytime—they were creeping and whispering and weird, as if the life of the woods had suddenly developed something almost hostile—at least alien and unacquainted and furtive. I could have fancied that I heard stealthy footsteps all around me and I felt the old, primitive unreasoning fear that was known to the childhood of the race—the awe of the dark and the shadowy, the shrinking from some unseen danger lurking in the gloom. My twentieth-century reason quelled it into a rather piquant watchfulness—but it would not have taken much to deliver me over to a blind panic in which I would have turned and fled shamelessly. As it was, when I left the lane I walked more quickly than my wont and felt as if I had escaped from some fascinating but not altogether hallowed locality—a place still given over to paganism and the revels of fauns and satyrs. None of the wild places are ever wholly Christianized in the darkness, however much so they may seem by daylight. There is always a lurking life in them that dare not show itself to the sun but regains its own with the night.

Sunday, Dec. 14, 1907
Cavendish, P.E.I.

Tonight I did something which twenty years ago I could never have imagined myself doing. What was this startling thing? Why, I walked *alone* through the "Cavendish Road woods" *after dark*.

When I was a child I had the greatest horror of those woods. A mile in along the road lived a family of "Jacks," who kept a small—a very small—shop where they sold tea, sugar etc. I was frequently sent in to buy some household supplies and I shall *never* forget the agony of terror I used to endure going along that wooded road. The distance through the woods was not more than a quarter of a mile but it seemed endless to me. I never dared tell anyone of my terror for I would have been laughed at and ridicule was even more dreadful to me than the nameless horrors that lay in wait for me in those woods. I cannot define just what I was afraid of—I could not have put my dread into words. It was just the old primitive fear

Entrance to the woods

handed down to us from ancestors in the dawn of time who were afraid of the woods with good reason. It was on my part just a blind, unreasoning terror. But this was all in the daylight. To go through those woods *after dark* was simply not to be contemplated. I could not understand how anyone *could* do it. I remember a young schoolteacher who boarded here and who used to go in there at night to transact school business with a trustee who lived on the other side. In my eyes he was the greatest hero the world has ever seen.

But tonight I came through them. I don't remember ever coming through them after dark *alone* before. They are out of the way of my twilight peregrinations and I've always had company on that road. But I was alone tonight and I liked it. I never even remembered that I used to be frightened of those woods long ago until I came home. I don't feel at all heroic.

I wonder if all the things we look forward to with dread in the future will not be like this. When we come to them we shall not mind them—we shall not be afraid.

Tuesday, December 17, 1907
Cavendish, P.E.I.

Once—and even yet in summer—I did not think that the Bible verse telling us that there would be no night in heaven contained an attractive promise. No night—no soft twilight enkindled with stars, no white sacrament of moonlight, no mystery of velvet shadow and darkness, no ever amazing miracle of dawn! The night was as beautiful as day and heaven would not be perfect without it.

But now, in this dreariest time of the year I almost at times wholly—share in the hope of the old Patmian seer.[1] The nights are *so* dreary now and so long, and there is such a brief space of gray, sunless day. I work and think all day; and when night comes early dour gloom settles down on my soul. I cannot describe the feeling. It is dreadful—worse than any actual pain. In so far as I can express it in words I feel a great and awful *weariness*—not of body or brain, but of *feeling*, coupled with a heavy dread of the future—*any* future, even a happy one—nay, a happy one most of all, for in this strange mood it seems to me that to be happy would require more effort, more buoyancy, than I shall possess. The fantastic shape my fear assumes is that it would be *too much trouble* to be happy—require too much energy. At such times the only future to which I could look forward with resignation would be a colourless existence making absolutely no demands on my emotional nature. At such hours I am bankrupt in hope or belief. I become convinced that I am a creature whom no one could love. Every hateful thought that ever came across my mind creeps out of its lurking place like some slimy hateful thing to which I had given birth. Every error and mistake of my life—and my accursedly good memory retains every one from the earliest dawn of consciousness—comes back to shame me.

I try to reason myself out of this. I say, "Now this is morbid nonsense, induced by certain abnormal conditions in my present environment. I have plenty of faults and shortcomings; but I am on the whole an average person with the average share of lovableness and the average number of friends." It is all no use. I might as well be reciting the alphabet. Another curious thing about these moods is that while I am in them I am thoroughly convinced that I will always feel like that. It is no use to tell myself that I have often felt so before and got over it. "Yes, *those* moods passed away but *this* will be permanent," is the unreasonable answer suffering consciousness makes. This condition lasts until some pleasant happening or outing, or even a sound sleep, restores me to my normal state. Then I am quite likely to re-act to the opposite extreme—to feel rapturously that the world is beautiful and mere existence something to thank God for.

I think I must be more sensitive to my environment than most people. I suppose it is the fatal shadow of the imaginative temperament. "The gods don't allow us to be in their debt."[2] For all their so-called gifts they make us pay roundly.

---

1. St. John the Divine wrote the book of Revelations on the Greek Isle of Patmos.
2. From John Godfrey Saxe, "The Gifts of the Gods." Quoted also in *My Dear Mr. M.* and elsewhere.

1908

Sunday, Jan. 12, 1908
Cavendish, P.E.I.

This afternoon I did something I haven't done for years. I went up and through the old barn. I have never cared to go near the barns since Uncle John got them into his possession.

x. Old barn. xx. New barn.

The poor "old barn" is a mere shell now and in a most desolate, wind-winnowed condition. Long ago it was a cosy delightful old place full of attractive dusky corners and dim, high heaped, swallow-haunted lofts where I delighted to climb and prowl with my cats. The old barn was a favourite haunt of mine there and I wonder I did not break my neck climbing the rafters and scrambling along beams and through holes. I can see yet the long golden dusky shafts of light falling through the crannies of the roof athwart the shadowy recesses of loft and gable. The memories of those old childish play hours came back in their old surroundings so vividly that they hurt me.

I had a letter recently that amused me. Not long ago an article of mine entitled "The Old South Orchard"[1] was published in an American magazine. It purported to be the history of an old homestead orchard, with all its associations of sorrow and romance, and was wholly imaginary from beginning to end. But this letter was from a gentleman who had "greatly enjoyed" the article and wished to know where the orchard was because he had "a great desire to visit it if such a thing were possible." I had to write back and tell him that I was very sorry the orchard existed only on the estates of my castle in Spain.

One of my Christmas gifts was a delightful volume entitled "The Heart of a Garden."[2] It consists of a series of essays by a woman who loved her garden and is illustrated by several photographs of beautiful old gardens. I revelled in it. One of my dearest wishes is to have a garden—a *real* garden. I shall never have my *ideal* garden—it would require more land and money than I shall likely ever have at my disposal, not to speak of a hundred years history behind it. But I do hope I shall be able some day to have some sort of a garden where I can at least grow all the flowers I want.

---

1. Published in *Outing Magazine*, January 1908; adaptation of the material appears in *The Story Girl*.

2. A collection of essays (1906) by "Graham R. Tomson" (Rosamund Marriott Watson, 1860–1911), an author recovering from a nervous breakdown, who turned from a scandalous private life to write books on gardening.

But oh, my garden of dreams—what an enchanting place it is! What dear old trees and shady pleasances, what velvet turf and trim walks, what vine-hung walls and pergolas, what nooks and shadows and sweetnesses! All the heaven I would ask is such a garden with its spring and summer and autumn—yea, and its winter, too.

I am pegging away at my new book,[1] but it is rather discouraging work in winter. I have to write in the kitchen, as none of the other rooms are warm enough, and there is so much coming and going in connection with the post office. I am constantly interrupted. There are six unused rooms in this house and there is no good reason why I should not have one fitted up and warmed as a library—no reason except the all-potent one that grandmother would not hear of such a plan for a moment.

The old kitchen

I have my ideal library, too, and have more hope of attaining it than my ideal garden. If I ever have a house of my own I shall see what I can do towards making it real. But likely something will spoil it, too. I'm afraid I've grown pessimistic in these hard later years. At least, the unafraid hope of youth can never again be mine.

I seem to be *tired* all the time—not physically or mentally, but *emotionally*. I feel a strange, woeful shrinking from life. For years, if I wanted the simplest thing, such as other people have as a matter of course, I have had to plan and worry and often humiliate myself to attain to it—in short, expend as much energy to bring it about as would have sufficed for some great enterprise. As a result, I seem to be bankrupt of energy and to shrink from the thought of being called upon to need or show any. I have of late let many things go that I thought desirable simply because I did not seem to have enough "grit" to hold them. And the worst of it is I feel too "tired" to care that I am losing them.

Sunday, May 3, 1908
Cavendish, P.E.I.

Spring has come once more. I am glad—or rather, I am thankful. *Gladness* is something I never seem able to feel now.

The winter was a very mild and open one, which, under my present conditions, is a great blessing indeed. Yet it has been very dreary. And the worst

---

1. *Anne of Avonlea* (1909). The story of Anne as a teacher draws on journal entries about Bideford and Belmont.

of it is this life is shaping me to itself and unfitting me for any other—at least, without great pain in the transition. I am like the "prisoner of Chillon"[1]—my chains and I have grown friends and when I regain my freedom it will not be merely "with a sigh" but with positive anguish.

I have not felt well for weeks and am haunted by the fear that I am on the verge of nervous breakdown. This may be merely a morbid fear, induced by certain unwholesome conditions present in my life but I cannot shake it off. There really is something wrong, whether it is merely nervous strain or the forerunner of some physical trouble. For the past three months I have been *tired*—that is all there is to say: A deadly weariness, utter apathy, listlessness, indifference. I care for nothing—find interest in nothing—not even my dear writing. I shrink from seeing people, even my friends. Sometimes I feel just as tired when I waken in the morning as when I went to bed, although I sleep like a log. Other mornings I feel a little better when I waken and have enough "grit" to carry me through the tasks of the forenoon. Then the strange languor returns and grows worse, until at bed time I can hardly spur myself to the exertion of undressing. I feel as if I wanted to *drop right down* wherever I was and lie there for a hundred years, feeling, thinking, hearing, seeing nothing.

But now spring has come and I may be better, when I can get out to the companionship of my dear nooks and woods, so well loved—*too* well-loved, since the thought of parting with them seems more than I can bear.

All winter I have been shut up, going out very little and working hard. I have been compelled to watch poor grandmother constantly grieving over various things and feel myself powerless to mend matters any. I have had to conceal my own depression and assume a cheerfulness I did not feel, so that I might not add to her troubles. I suppose it is no wonder I am played out. But if I break down what will I do? There is no one to take care of me and I could not afford to go away for treatment or to stop work and rest.

Some passages I came across lately in Nansen's "Farthest North" have cheered me a little. He seems to have felt, at times, in the gloom and solitude of an Arctic winter much as I have felt this winter. If Nansen, the strong and skilful and successful, felt so is it any wonder that I, who am only a weak, harassed woman, feel so? It has really given me a better opinion of myself. He says:—

"My mind is confused; the whole thing has got into a tangle. I am a riddle to myself. I am worn out and yet I do not feel any special tiredness. I have no inclination to read, draw, or do anything whatever. The only thing that helps

---

1. A poem (1816) by Lord Byron about the trials of a sixteenth-century monk imprisoned in Switzerland: a fixture in school readers.

me is writing, trying to express myself on these pages and then looking at myself as it were from the outside. Yes, man's life is nothing but a succession of moods. I have not the courage to think of the future. I know this is all a morbid mood; but still this inactive, lifeless monotony wrings my very soul."

How true that touch about writing it out is! It *does* help. But I have "written out" so many moods in this journal that it is merely repetition now, and I get ashamed of it. I would not feel so badly if I were sure that when the strain is lifted I shall return to my normal state. But I cannot help fearing that I shall not—that something has been crushed out of me forever and that I shall be unfitted to assume new duties and to adapt myself to a new life.

But enough of grumbling. I'm going to get a tonic and take long walks in the fresh air. We'll see if that won't help.

One day in February I started out in the morning and walked to Stanley. I was longing to see Frede and I was sick of looking for "chances up" and humiliating myself to get them. So I resolved I'd never ask for one again as long as I possessed two feet. I started out one fine morning when the roads had frozen after a thaw and walked the five miles, easily and pleasantly feeling happier and more like myself than I had done for many a day. I reached Mrs. Ross's[1] in an hour and fifty minutes and spent a delightful day. In the evening I walked back, Frede coming half the way. I expected to feel very tired and stiff the next day but I was neither.

Mr. Macdonald was down in March for a brief visit. He is settled up west at Bloomfield[2] so I see him very seldom. I wonder if I am fit to be his or any-body's wife—so hopeless, so "played-out" do I feel. Perhaps this is only temporary. But if it should not be? There are moments when I feel that I can never undertake the responsibilities of marriage.

There! Didn't I say that I wasn't going to grumble any more?

I went back to Lover's Lane Thursday evening for the first time in many weeks, as the mud has been too bad. It was as lovely and peace-giving as ever in those wood-brown depths,

Lover's Lane

where the spring brooks were foaming along every little channel. Every voice of the woods called "spring" in tones of old primal gladness. But I was too tired to respond. I only felt a little more peaceful and soothed.

---

1. Perhaps the mother of Margaret Ross Stirling. Hedley Ross wrote a history of Stanley bridge in 1904.

2. Inland village, on the railway line in the most westerly area of PEI, about 80 miles (129 km) from Cavendish.

My birthplace at Clifton

The old home of childhood

Of late I have been reading over this foolish old journal from the first and seeing the effect all my various experiences have had on me much more clearly than when I lived them.

I was fourteen when I began it. Before that time I had kept a little childish diary in various "notebooks" since I was nine. When I grew older I burned them. I shall always regret having done so for they would have been interesting to me now. But I remember my childhood with great vividness.

I was born in Clifton but my mother came home to die when her fatal disease took hold on her. I was only about 21 months old when she died but I remember seeing her in her coffin and I have earlier memory still of seeing her lying on the bed. After her death father went to Boston and I was left here with grandfather and grandmother and Aunt Emily. I went to school at six. I don't think I liked going to school very well for the first

Myself at six

few years. I was an extremely sensitive child and such, I think, have always a hard time in a public school.

Aunt Emily married and went away when I was seven. I don't recall having missed her at all. Soon after the two Nelson boys came here to board and stayed till I was eleven. They were the nicest playmates I ever had. I never liked Uncle John's or Uncle Leander's boys but Well and Dave were as brothers to me. We used to have glorious fun together.

I was a dreamy, delicate child, very impulsive, heedless, shrinking from an unkind or sarcastic word as from a blow—and I received many such for Uncle John never lost an opportunity of saying something unkind to me and grandfather was also very hard on me. The latter did not mean to be, I think—but he was extremely irritable and had no consideration for the feelings of anyone.

I was fond of books and lonely rambles and these were a great comfort to me. On the average my childhood was not an unhappy one—but it was not wholesome. Looking back now, I see clearly how unwholesome it was and how easily it might have ruined forever the disposition of so sensitive, "highly-strung" a child. I was constantly "nagged." Other children, who in sober truth were not a bit better than I was, were cast up to me as paragons. I received an impression of which to this day I have never been able quite to rid myself—that everybody disliked me and that I was a very hateful person. A more unfortunate impression could hardly be made on a child's mind.

Father came occasionally to see me and his visits were bright spots for me. I loved him so deeply and felt myself beloved in return. I think now that grandfather and grandmother resented this very love of mine for him. They saw that I did not turn to them with the out gush of affection I gave him. And it was true—I did not. But it was their own fault. I know now that they loved me after a fashion. But they never expressed or showed that love in word or action. I never thought they loved me. I felt that the only person in the world who loved me was father. Nobody else ever kissed me and caressed me and called me pet names. So I gave all my love to him in those years. And my grandparents did not like it. They thought that, as they were giving me a home and food and clothes and care that I ought to have loved them best. Perhaps I should. But alas, love doesn't go by "ought" in this world. And after all, "ought" I to have? "Life is more than meat"—they gave me "meat" but they did not give me "life." They did certain things because they thought it was their duty; they did them well and kindly. "But if I give all my goods to feed the poor and have not love it profiteth me nothing."[1] I did not *know* these things then; I only felt them and felt them unconsciously.

Father was not successful in business and was never able to do much for me in a financial way. Grandmother cast this up to me very frequently and I resented it—and resent it—bitterly. Nothing *could* be said except in this regard for not a word could be said against him as a man. He was beloved by all who knew him.

When I was eleven the boys went away and I lost my little playmates. One year I was laid up all winter with a succession of colds.—I had night sweats and a constant cough and everybody thought I was in consumption. I remember grandfather telling me "You will be in your grave before spring"— a cheerful and kind thing to say to a sick child! I cried bitterly about it night after night. But I got well when spring came. Sometimes I think it would have been better for me if I had not!

---

1. From I Corinthians 13:3.

From ten to thirteen I went to school to James MacLeod.[1] He used to whip us unmercifully and had a vile habit of making a feint or two with the ruler before he finally brought it down on our tingling, outstretched palms. But I rather liked him in spite of this. He was never sarcastic and the pain of his "hand cuts" never lasted beyond their infliction. When I was thirteen Izzie Robinson came here to teach and boarded with us.

She was very sarcastic and her sneers cut like lashes. She disliked me from the first—why, I was honestly at a loss to know, since I was not a bad pupil though inclined to be a rather talkative one; and at home I kept out of her way all I could. I understand now that she vented on me her dislike of grandfather and grandmother.

I cannot blame her for disliking them or at least grandfather; for he acted in a most absurd fashion towards her. He took a dislike to her and showed it very childishly in the most unreasonable sneers and jibes. Grandmother, too, was very unwise in some respects.

That winter I went up for a long visit to Aunt Emily. While I was away Miss R. flew into a rage at something grandfather said, made a scene, declared he had "insulted" her, and left. When I came home in the spring grandfather and grandmother were so petty and unwise as to refuse to let me go to school. I cried bitterly at this and pleaded wildly to be allowed to go but all in vain. I shall never forget the humiliation of that

Aunt Emily's

summer. Poor grandfather and grandmother had set the whole community against them by their behaviour and it was visited on me. It was very wrong of them to fill a child's life with their own spite and bitterness. I resent it now more keenly than I did then—for I was then still young enough to think that they were right in everything and that all others were wrong.

When I was fourteen Miss Robinson left and Miss Gordon came. A new era began for me. I loved going to school to her as I had never done before. She was a good friend to me and I owe her

Miss Gordon

---

1. Teacher noted for discipline, perhaps the original of Mr. Phillips, the teacher in *AGG*.

2. Harsh teacher from first year in school, not to be confused with friendly Serena Robinson.

much. For the first time it dawned on me that I was not so unlovable as I had been made to believe. I found myself one of Miss Gordon's favourite pupils and this fact alone did more for me than all my previous years of "schooling" put together. As far as school went those two years I went to Miss Gordon were very happy ones. In other ways, however, they were not so happy. I was growing up and I felt all the natural—and innocent—wishes of a girl of my age. These were persistently denied and thwarted. I had no company and was seldom allowed to go anywhere, even to a concert or lecture. As

Grandfather

for my boy friends, poor grandfather nearly tore the house down if I went for a drive with one of them. Of course I never asked them to the house. If they came they were generally insulted.

Besides, I began to feel worried about my future. What was I to do? My grandparents were old and I could not count on always having a home here. I felt it was necessary to fit myself to earn my own living but what could I do? I had no one to advise me or help me. Miss Gordon wanted me to study for a teacher and I liked the idea. But grandfather and grandmother opposed the notion bitterly. Grandfather hated teach-

ers because of Miss Robinson. Uncle Leander, with his accustomed selfishness, advised against it also. I think I can guess at his motive pretty well!

I almost lost heart. But I managed to get a Latin, an algebra and a geometry,—borrowing two of them—and began to learn "the branches" with very little hope, however, of ever getting any further on.

I do not mean to say that I was actually miserable for that would be very far from being the truth. I had "lots of fun" in school and away from home. That winter of 1890 was a pleasant and jolly one. School was full of big boys and girls and we had very merry times together in our games and classes.

About this time father began, in his letters, to express a wish that I should go out west and spend a year with him. I was girlishly eager to go. I wanted to see father—I wanted the trip; and besides, I cherished a secret hope of getting to school or finding something I could do. Grandfather Montgomery offered to pay my way

Grandmother Macneill

out, so Grandfather and Grandmother Macneill could not refuse to let me go although they did not like the idea very well.

Well, I spent a year in the west—and I was with father which atoned for everything. But my dreams of getting an education were soon dispelled. I had to stay home and be Mrs. Montgomery's household drudge—that is the plain English of it. Father could not help it—I never blamed him.

There were many pleasant things in that western year and I shall never be sorry that I spent it. But I was very glad to come back home. The little peculiarities of Grandfather and Grandmother were nothing compared to Mrs. Montgomery's jealousy and bad temper. But I felt depressed, too. All avenues seemed closed to me.

That winter I spent at Park Corner giving Clara and Stella music lessons. It was a happy jolly winter indeed. It would not appeal to me *now*; but to a girl of seventeen with all a girl's law-ful longing for fun and pleasure it was delightful in truth.

Park Corner

The next year I finally obtained grandmother's consent to study for a teacher's license. Grandfather simply ignored the whole matter and never, from first to last, gave me any assistance financial or otherwise. Grandmother and father between them paid my expenses at college.

That last winter I went to school here was a happy one. I studied hard but I had pretty good times, too, and I had *hope* to carry me over all trials. In the summer I passed my entrance exam and the next fall I went to P.W.C.

I studied very hard for I was taking two years' work in one. But that year was the happiest of my life, I think. The next, when I taught in Bideford, was also happy and successful. For the first time I found myself unhampered by clan jealousy and inherited traditions of dislike and aversion and prejudice. I was a stranger and stood on my own merits or demerits. As a result I made friends everywhere and found myself popular and successful. It warmed the cockles of my heart with a glorious glow! Here in Cavendish I had always had to struggle against influences and traditions I was not to blame for. These big family connections are by no means a wholly good thing. They produce too much heart burning and jealousy. Each member of the clan seems to resent bitterly another member's surpassing him in any way, whereas in the case of a stranger, nothing of the sort would be felt.

My salary in Bideford was the usual one of a second class teacher in those days—one hundred and eighty dollars a year plus ten dollars supplement given by the district. As I did not get the school until a month of the school year had passed I lost fifteen dollars of this, so that my year's work there brought me in one hundred and seventy five dollars. Fifty paid my board, twenty five stood me my other expenses, and I saved one hundred dollars. Grandmother gave me eighty dollars more and that gave me my Dalhousie term. How I longed to take a course in Arts and get my B.A. degree! But there was no hope of that. Then the next year I went to Belmont and the comedy of life turned to tragedy.

Well, I was not the first foolish girl to mistake flattered vanity, intellectual attraction and the "strong necessity of loving"[1]—oh, surely Byron was inspired when he penned that phrase!—for love itself. But surely no girl every suffered more over it.

As for the next year in Bedeque—well, that was folly and madness if you like. But I would rather let every other year in my life be blotted out than lose that. It is dead and done with now: but it was the nearest I have ever come—or ever will come now, I suppose—to life's supreme glory.

Then grandfather died and I had to come home. There is no need to say more. Since then life here has grown harder, grayer, barer, drearier every year. Yet I have had many happy and beautiful moments in them all. And I would have been happy and contented here if it had not been for the way Uncle John and his family have used us. Even grandmother's unfortunate bias of thought and habit would not alone have embittered life.

May 19, 1908
Cavendish, P.E.I.

This morning I felt more like myself than I have for many a day. I got out for a walk over the hill. It was a very mild, still, misty morning, with the *smell* of spring in the air. I seemed to have left all care and worry behind me, like a cast-off garment, and I felt peace and gladness—no, not *gladness* exactly but the *possibility* of being sometimes glad once more. The ground felt good under my feet. The young spruces along the hill were so green and friendly, with pearl-like beads of moisture fringing their needles. Oh, "nature never did betray the heart that loved her"[2]—she has always a gift of healing for us when we go humbly to her.

---

1. From Byron's *Childe Harold's Pilgrimage* (1812–18), canto 4, cxxv. The stanza begins "Few—none— find what they love or could have loved."
2. From William Wordsworth, "Lines Composed a Few Miles above Tintern Abbey" (1798).

Sunday, May 24, 1908
Cavendish, P.E.I.

I am so much better now. Perhaps it is the tonic I've been taking—with many grimaces—that has helped me. But I believe it is rather my escape from the bondage of cold and wet and gloom to the beautiful—oh, so beautiful!—outdoor world—my darling lanes and woods and fields. Oh, *how* I love them—love them more every day of their dear companionship. It breaks my heart to think of ever leaving them.

SCENE ON THE NORTH SHORE

Tonight—this lovely May night—I walked to the shore. It was as beautiful as ever. I think the Cavendish shore is the most beautiful in the world. This is not merely my fond and foolish fancy. I once heard a man who had been all over the world say he had never seen a more beautiful beach than that of Cavendish sandshore, as far as natural advantages were concerned. As I sat there alone tonight—alone but not lonely—I felt keenly and clearly that I can never *love* any place as I have loved Cavendish. And I have never been really discontented here. At times, when ill or worried, I have had moods of discontent and written them out in this journal to get rid of them. But such moods were passing and comparatively few. And even then, they were with existing conditions, not with the place. If I could have a wish granted to me it would be to live here all my life but freed from the painful environment of the past few years. If Uncle John's family did not exist and if I had an independent home and existence here I should never in sincerity wish for any lasting change.

The day has gone by when I could make changes—even desirable ones—easily. I am thirty three; my tastes and habits are formed—or rather have been formed for me by the irresistible pressure of circumstances; I am bound to this spot by all the thousand ties of old associations and natural affections—bonds, not of the intellect, which sees and admits the flaw and drawback, but of the heart which cries, "Yes, I see them but I love in spite of them."

Saturday, June 20, 1908
Cavendish, P.E.I.

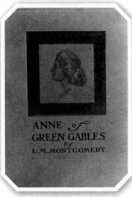

Cover design of "Anne"

Today has been, as *Anne* herself would say "an epoch in my life." My book came today,[1] fresh from the publishers. I candidly confess that it was for me a proud, wonderful, thrilling moment! There in my hand lay the material realization of all the dreams and hopes and ambitions and struggles of my whole conscious existence—my first book! Not a great book at all—but *mine, mine, mine,*—something to which *I* had given birth—something which, but for me, would never have existed.

As far as appearance goes the book is all I could desire—lovely cover design, well bound, well printed. *Anne* will not fail for lack of suitable garbing at all events.

On the dedication page was the inscription "To the Memory of my Father and Mother." Oh, if they were but living to be glad and proud. When I think of how father's eyes would have shone!

June 30, 1908
Cavendish, P.E.I.

I cannot recall such a beautiful June as this. It has been the sweetest month of sun and shower imaginable and the greenness of everything is something to steep your soul in. It is a benediction to walk past a clover field.

Caraway in the orchard

I am feeling much better. The depression and nervousness of last winter have passed and I feel hopeful and cheerful, once more. It would cure anybody to walk over the hill every morning as I do before sitting down to write, with the spruces on either hand and the green meadows beyond. I tramp along "thanking the Lord for a life so sweet."

Our old house is billowed about with caraway just now—great, lacy waves, swaying in the June winds and sprinkled with buttercups.

---

1. LMM copied this passage, with some stylistic changes, into "The Alpine Path."

And I have been picking early strawberries. I went this evening down the shore lane and picked a cupful during those windy, sweet smelling grasses. I love picking strawberries. The occupation has something of perpetual youth in it. The gods might have picked strawberries in high Olympus without injuring their dignity.

These days are perennially interesting because of the reviews of my book. So far they have been very favourable. *Anne* is already in her second edition. My publishers are hurrying me now for the sequel. I'm working at it but it will not be as good as *Green Gables*. It doesn't *come* as easily. I have to force it.

July 16, 1908
Cavendish, P.E.I.

A busy fortnight has slipped away. Uncle Leander and Aunt Mary have been here since the first of the month. Aunt M. and I have had several delightful "dips" on the old, dear shore. Alma Macneill has been home for a month and we have had some jolly chats and walks and one glorious bathe. I am feeling quite well again and the change is unspeakably delightful. We are having such a beautiful summer that one could hardly help feeling better.

I had an encounter tonight which was at first disagreeable, then amusing, and finally rather upsetting.

Amanda called for the mail and I went to her gate with her for a walk. On my return I met—Edwin Simpson and *his bride*!

I heard last winter that Ed was to be married. I did not hear the name of the lady nor have I heard it since. Ed, I may say, never took advantage of my offer to tell him the real reason why I broke my engagement. I was not surprised at this. He was not sincere in asking for it—or rather *hinting* for it. He merely thought I never would tell and that he could always make use of it as a matter of reproach to me. I daresay he was very much taken aback at my offer to do so. Moreover, my utter disregard of his hints regarding Mr. Macdonald would lead him to believe that there was something after all in those "rumors" to which he "gave little credence."

The news of his prospective marriage in so far as it affected me at all, gave me a feeling of relief. I was glad for his sake. I do not flatter myself that Ed has remained unmarried all these years on my account. From my knowledge of his character I should be very much surprised if such were the case. But I certainly did do him a wrong and the sense of it has always been an uneasy one to me. I was also glad for my own sake. I would henceforth be free from any dread of meeting him or getting letters from him.

I thought no more of the matter until one day in June when I saw a newspaper notice of his arrival on the Island with his bride. This rather disturbed me. I knew he would visit his Cavendish friends and I should probably meet them somewhere. I would not at all mind meeting them in a strange place— nay, I should have liked to do so, for I was naturally curious regarding *her*. But I did *not* like the thought of meeting them before *their* friends and *my* friends, who knew or suspected our old relationship and would be watching to see "how I took it." Altogether, the meeting could not but be embarrassing to at least two out of the three of us, and so I wished to avoid it, while at the same time I *did* want to have a peep at Ed's bride.

They came to C. and Ed preached last Sunday evening in the Baptist church. We had service in our church that evening also, which neatly prevented my going to the B. church or his coming to ours. I had not heard anything of them since and supposed they had left Cavendish by this time.

After parting with Amanda at her gate I walked back briskly. As I came down David Macneill's hill I was aware of a buggy with two people in it coming down Pierce's hill. But I did not suppose it was "anyone in particular," and I was so interested in trying to make out who was on the pond in a boat that I never looked around at the buggy until it was right by me, when I turned my head indifferently to see if it were anyone I ought to speak to I found myself looking at Ed and his bride.

I shall never forgive myself for not having turned my head sooner. Had I done so I could have had a good look at her and seen what she was like. As it was, I had just barely time to bow and smile to Ed, before they were past. I had not a moment to look at his wife. I simply got a fleeting impression of a woman in a gray suit, "merry widow" hat,[1] and thick chiffon veil. For all I saw of her face she might just as well not have been there at all.

In spite of my surprise I had presence of mind enough to make my bow and smile very cordial. But there was no cordiality about Ed—not the shadow of it. I rather suspect the very fact that I *was* cordial would seem an insult to him as indicating an unflattering indifference to the fact that I had finally lost him through my own unreasonable stubbornness in refusing him. At any rate he did not even smile. He merely raised his fingers very stiffly to his hat and gave an almost imperceptible bow. As for his expression—well, it really looked "plain mad," as the children say; but of course it was merely the result of his embarrassment at the sudden and unexpected encounter. I knew my own feelings and could guess with tolerable accuracy at his. What his wife's were is problematical. Likely she had none at all, never supposing

---

1. One with a wide curved brim, as worn in Franz Lehar's operetta, *The Merry Widow* (1905).

that the woman who had just passed had any connection with her husband's "past." If I know Ed, he has never told her of his affair with me.

By the time I had reached the bridge my breathlessness of surprise had passed and amusement had set in. I laughed softly to myself. What an encounter! A little over a year ago Ed had written to me that "time had not brought oblivion and could not"—that "the skeleton in his closet was still very real to him" etc. "Oblivion" must have been nearer than he fancied. Well, well, he is not the first man to have been led by his love of fine phrases into saying much more than he meant. It is not fair to laugh at him for it.

After the amusement came the "unsettling" part. Edwin Simpson is not anything to me now, not even a disagreeable anything. But still, the sight of him always brings back the past so vividly, with all its hatefulness and anguish, that I seem to live it over again and I cannot endure doing so.

My curiosity regarding Mrs. Ed was not doomed to be wholly unslaked. When I was down at Alma's day before yesterday she, having seen her in the B. church, told me some things about her, not knowing at all how keen my interest was. She is "not pretty but is said to be very clever and to have money." I had to choke back a smile over this. It reminded me of one of Ed's felicitous speeches to me long ago. In speaking of his early "dreams" he said he always thought he would be "quite satisfied if he could marry a lady who was nice looking and *had money*." I might have claimed to be passable as far as "looks" were concerned but I certainly had no "money" or the prospect of any! Ed was really trying to pay me a Simpsonian compliment—to convey the idea that I was sufficiently charming to make him forego this requirement; but he only succeeded in making me feel that *he* thought *I* should be very grateful for his condescension in waiving this important qualification in my case. The vanity and sordidness revealed in his speech disgusted me.

Well, his shadow has at last gone out of my life. I wish him prosperity and happiness and that is all there is about it.

Friday, July 31, 1908
Cavendish, P.E.I.

We had a most exciting and unpleasant sensation here this morning. I feel so shaken over it that the mere recollection makes me tremble.

It was a very hot morning with a high wind. After I had finished the morning's work I went for my customary walk over the hill before sitting down to write. When I came back I mounted to my den and had just begun work on the last chapter of my new book when I heard Aunt Mary run through the sitting room screaming, "Maud, the house is on fire!"

I don't know how I got down and out—I don't remember that part at all. A space about two feet square was ablaze on the kitchen roof, evidently having caught from a spark. There was no decent ladder about the place, everything of that sort having been long since carried off by Uncle John's. But I recalled an old rotten ladder with half its rungs missing which had been lying in the woods behind the pighouse for three years. Somehow or other, Aunt Mary and I dragged it to the house and lifted it against the roof. There I seized a bucket of water and scrambled up it. Fortunately the rungs did not give way under me as I had feared they would. I could not get very near the fire but I stood on the top rung and flung the water at it. Luckily, my aim was good. The water struck the very centre of the flames and put them half out; another bucket passed up by Uncle Leander completely extinguished them, as the fire was only on the surface and had not had time to eat in. I feel sure that ten minutes later would have been too late.

When I realized that the danger was over my sustaining excitement left me and I went to pieces—burst into tears, trembled from head to foot and had to go to bed. In my present condition of nervous weakness such a shock is rather a serious thing. I don't seem to have the reserve strength to meet it.

I have such a horror of fire. And all my life I have been haunted by an ever recurring dream that the house in which I am living is on fire and that I have to stand and watch it burning, unable to make any effort to quench it. I wonder if this means that I am some day to be "burnt out."

Monday, Aug. 3, 1908
Cavendish, P.E.I.

Today I finished my second book. I've been mulling over it so long that I'm not capable of judging it correctly but I know it is not nearly so good as *Green Gables*. I began to write it last October but was blocking it out and collecting and arranging materials for it all last summer. All this time I've been the prey of worry and nervous ills—not very favourable circumstances for the production of a good book. Anyhow, I am thankful it is done—though after all I enjoyed writing it. There still remains much of revision to do—and then the worst job of all, typewriting it. That is so tedious and slow.

Saturday, Aug. 29, 1908
Cavendish, P.E.I.

Uncle L.'s went away Tuesday. Thursday morning I went to town to meet two American ladies, friends of a literary friend of mine in Boston, who were touring the Island and wished to meet me because they had read my book. It was difficult for me to go to town just now. But I could not ask them to come to this tumble-down place. They would not understand why I, a successful writer, should be living in a house in such wretched repair, surrounded by outbuildings almost falling to pieces. And I could not explain to strangers why it was. So I vexed my tired soul making arrangements to go to town and meet them. I had a pleasant trip and enjoyed meeting them. They were boarding on a farm out at Brighton—the prettiest spot I ever saw in my life.

I came home Friday night to find Frede Campbell and Clara and Clara's husband, Fred Wilson, here. Fred is a fine looking fellow and seems nice and kind. Clara is fat and jolly. I was

Mr. and Mrs. Fred Wilson

glad to see her; but the gulf between us now is too wide to be bridged. We have *nothing* in common now that girlhood is past—neither ideals nor opinions nor tastes nor hopes—I was going to write "ambitions" but it would be absurd to talk of Clara having ambitions. She seems very happy and satisfied with her life and her husband and I am sincerely glad that it is so; but I would soon weary of her society now. It is hard to believe she and Frede can be sisters—they are so utterly unlike in all vital respects.

September 1, 1908
Cavendish, P.E.I.

The past four weeks have been dreadful ones for me. Ever since the fire my nerves seem to have been growing worse every day. I feel even worse than I did last spring—wretchedly tired, body and soul, despondent, worried, morbid. Oh, *morbid*! I seem utterly incapable of taking any just view of life—I seem to view everything through a perverted or distorted medium. I know perfectly well that it *is* perverted and distorted, but so disjointed is my internal economy that the knowledge of my intellect seems to have no effect on my feelings. I could lie down and do nothing for a whole day, content if I am only let alone. This is unnatural in me who am such an active creature normally that I could never lie still for ten minutes in daytime. But something seems to have gone out of me—some mainspring of purpose or energy snapped. My physical system seems well enough—except that I am much troubled by a dull headache. But I have no energy—none at all—and *don't want to have.* I don't want to do anything—go anywhere—see anybody—I want only to lie down and sleep for a hundred years! Of course, there are days and hours when I feel better; but for the most part I'm miserable. The shock of the fire was too much for me, I suppose, and this is the result.

Thursday, Sept. 24, 1908
Cavendish, P.E.I.

The days have been dragging on. They should have been beautiful for the weather has been so lovely. I do not remember such a perfect September. But I do not seem much better—I am tired, tired, tired.

I had a pleasant little outing this week, though, which did me good while it lasted. George R. went to town Tuesday to hear Fielding at the great Liberal rally[1] and I went too. We stayed in till Wednesday and I enjoyed every minute of my trip. The political meeting was interesting but I enjoyed most my visit with dear Aunt Mary and Bertie. They are so lovely and sweet and jolly, and that little home at Brighton is one of the Meccas of my heart.

Thursday, Oct. 15, 1908
Cavendish, P.E.I.

I had a delightful trip over to Park Corner on Tuesday, getting an unexpected chance over with Will Houston. It was two years since I had been over. It did me so much good to see the dear old place again and have a jolly afternoon with Stella. I have been feeling a good deal better this past fortnight—have a better appetite and more energy, and have lost much of my morbid aversion to seeing people. But I dread the winter. I feel that I have not strength to face it and the worries it is sure to bring. Grandmother is already suffering much from rheumatism and I fear she will have it badly this winter. I do hope it will not be a severe one.

I had a letter from Page today asking me for my photo and a personal sketch of how "Anne" came to be written to give "inquisitive editors." It seems that *Anne* is a big success. It is a "best seller"[2] and is in its fifth edition—I cannot realize this. My strongest feeling seems to be incredulity. I

---

1. Wilfrid Laurier led the Liberal Party to his fourth victory in 1908, on a pro-imperialist platform. William Fielding was the defending candidate in Nova Scotia. Francis Haszard supported him in PEI. *Grit* is a Canadian term for a political Liberal.

2. LMM's account book records sales in the first year, 1908, as follows: Canadian, 77; Australian, 500; English, 500; U.S., 18,286; total: 20,061. Sales would double in the second year.

can't believe that such a simple little tale, written in and of a simple P.E.I. farming settlement, with a juvenile audience in view, can really have scored out in the busy world. I have had so many nice letters about it—and no *end* of reviews. Most of them were very flattering. Three or four had a rather contemptuous tone and three were really nasty.

One of the reviews says "the book radiates happiness and optimism." When I think of the conditions of worry and gloom and care under which it was written I wonder at this. Thank God, I can keep the shadows of my life out of my work. I would not wish to darken any other life—I want instead to be a messenger of optimism and sunshine.

Pleasant? Yes, of course it is pleasant. It is a joy to feel that my long years of struggle and unaided effort have been crowned with success. But that success has also evoked much petty malice, spite and jealousy. It does not hurt me, because none of my *real* friends have been guilty of it. But at times it has given me a sort of nausea with human nature.

Friday, Oct. 23, 1908
Cavendish, P.E.I.

Today I finished typewriting "Anne of Avonlea"; and heartily glad I am, for it has been a tedious and back-breaking job in very truth. These past few days have been hard ones. I've been feeling badly again—depressed, tired, broken, a prey to indescribable and unconquerable unrest. These attacks must have a physical cause. They seem to be growing worse and of longer duration. I ought to have medical advice; but I cannot consult any doctor here, for that would mean running the gauntlet of gossip and surmise; and it is difficult to consult one far away. But if I get much worse I shall have to try. Oh, the misery of these past few days and nights. Generally I can sleep but one night I could not and it seemed as long as a year. I could not even *think* to pass the time. My personality seemed turned wrong side out and I disliked everything I normally like and shrank from the thought of all I normally desire.

Wednesday, October 28, 1908

Feeling a little better today I went for a walk back to the woods, through the beautiful day. A friend I met on the road called out, "Just like spring, isn't it?" I nodded—but I did not think it in the least really like spring. It was as warm and sunny and blue-skied as spring—but the whole *spirit* of spring was lacking—that indefinite, keenly-felt spirit of growth and awakening. Instead, there was abroad in the world a spirit of rest and peace, of work accomplished and over, of a folding of the hands to slumber. It fitted in with my mood— I, too, would like to lie down and sleep. When the worst of these fits of gloom and unrest pass they leave me feeling "played out," as if I had just passed through some severe struggle—a wrestling with "principalities and powers" of evil and darkness.

View from my window

I saw a pretty thing tonight as I looked from my room window in the twilight—a new moon just over the slender top of the big larch tree on the dyke. I am glad I happened to glance out of my window just then—and I'm glad I live in a world where there are new moons.

Saturday, Oct. 31, 1908
Cavendish, P.E.I.

Our beautiful October has not gone out beautifully. Yesterday and today have been days of storm—heavy rain, showers of snow, and high winds. The trees are lashed and ragged and the world looks unsightly. I haven't felt at all well either of these days. I seem to be haunted by a vague, teasing dread of impending evil—as if I were expecting a blow and shrinking from it. This feeling visits me very often now. It has no foundation in fact but reason has no effect on it. As a result, I cannot do anything—not even read—with pleasure or satisfaction. I compel myself to work, read, sew, talk—and under it all I am nervous and tense with this absurd and reasonless dread which I cannot control or banish. It is harder to bear than anything else.

I suppose I am too much alone. My temperament has a natural bent toward introspection and self-analysis and it has become morbidly intense of late. Some of my present mental, or rather psychic, processes are as curious as they are disagreeable. For instance, as I have said before, when I was a child I received many harsh words and cruel "cuts" and not less cruel teasings from many of the members of my mother's family. At the time they hurt me; but the pain soon passed and I cannot recall ever feeling any resentment or sullenness towards those who had caused it after it had passed. I forgot it promptly. Well, of late all these incidents seem to have returned vividly to my memory, as if they had been churned up from some lower depths by some disturbance in my inner consciousness. And the curious part is, the intense, unforgiving, *bitter* resentment I *now* feel against those who inflicted those injustices and "harshnesses" upon me. I feel as if I could *never* forgive them or look upon them with any feeling but anger and hatred—emotions which I never felt at the time of the infliction with anything like the intensity I feel now. This is unnatural, whatever the cause.

Writing this out, or talking it out to an understanding friend, always helps me. It is like lancing a fester and letting out the pus which is causing the pain. I always feel a good deal of relief for the time.

But nothing seems to help this vague dread of evil much. I can't write *it* out because I cannot find words to express it with any nearness to truth. I shall be glad when it is bedtime so that I can go to sleep and be oblivious to this misery for a time. It is such a blessing that I can generally sleep well. Time was when I chafed somewhat over having always to go to bed promptly at nine o'clock simply because grandmother so decreed. But now I'm only too glad to go—ay, and earlier if I can. It is such a relief to get upstairs alone and *let myself go*—not to feel that I must be bright and smiling and cheery. It is a real relief to lie down on the bed and feel that I can be just as miserable as I want to be.

Poor grandmother, she has to endure a great deal in many ways. I try to do my best for her, but I am very helpless in many respects, partly owing to Uncle John's shameful behaviour, partly to poor grandmother's own stubborn childishness in adhering to all her old ways and customs in defiance of changed circumstances. There are times when I feel a sort of savage despair over my helplessness. Grandmother has five living children and not one of them makes, or ever has made, any attempt to share the responsibility of her care. It never seems to occur to them that grandmother is not the capable woman she was twenty years ago, with a husband to protect her. Aunt Emily has had a houseful of grown-up girls for ten years and she has never once offered to send one of them to take my place for a week or two while I get away for a change. Her children are almost strangers to grandmother; she herself has visited her mother *once* in the past three years and written *twice*. Yet she lives only 26 miles away.

Tuesday, Nov. 3, 1908

I have felt better today but very tired. The high cold wind went down and the sun shone out. I got out for a walk tonight which did me good. It was a wierd purple shadowy world I roamed in, with great cold clouds piling up above a yellow sky, hills brooding

Ocean tumbling on a rocky shore

in the silence of forsaken woods, ocean tumbling on a rocky shore. The whole landscape seemed

> as those who wait
> Till judgment speak the doom of fate.

It was beautiful and sad and dignified. I looked on it and loved it. Its tragic peace entered into my soul and possessed it, and I came in soothed and calmed.

Thursday, Nov. 5, 1908

This afternoon I went for a long ramble "back in the woods." What would I do without those woods to ramble in? What shall I do when I have to bid them farewell? But I did not ask myself, any disagreeable questions while I was there. I rambled along at will, idly, lingeringly, drinking in the tang of the golden frosty air, exploring a couple of woodland lanes, picking a "chew" of gum from a lichened old spruce, sauntering through sere

Birches back in the woods

fields, sitting for dreamy half hour on a sunny old fence. I came home feeling as if I had exchanged my shop-worn soul for a fresh one, fire-new from the workshops of the gods. But alas, such feelings don't last very long now.

Tuesday, Nov. 10, 1908
Cavendish, P.E.I.

These two days have been hard ones for me. They have been cold, wet and dull; and though this is not the cause of my suffering it aggravates it. That

horrible feeling of dread has returned. I have a morbid horror of seeing anyone and feel like *hiding* when anyone comes to the house. Besides, I have felt
physically miserable. There was a strange feeling in my head as if something
were grinding back and forth continually. I
had neuralgia in my face and a nasty, irritating
"cold sore" on my mouth. I wanted to walk
fiercely all the time. I couldn't even read. Last
night I couldn't sleep until nearly morning.

This lasted all this forenoon. But this afternoon I felt better again. I could think, read,
and enjoy a twilight walk over the hill.

Ewan is much concerned over my condition and has insisted that I do no writing for
a month. I have yielded to please him but I

A sunny old fence

do not think it is a wise thing after all. When I am writing I am happy for
I forget all worries and cares. If I do not write I have all the more time for
morbid brooding.

I had a letter today from a Toronto journalist who had been detailed to
write a special article about me for his paper—wants to know all about my
birth, education, early life, when and how I began to write etc.

Well, I'll give him the bare facts he wants. He will not know any more
about the real *me* or my real life for it all, nor will his readers. The only key
to *that* is found in this old journal.

I've been reading *Waverley*[1] this evening. Splendid old Scott! His magic
never fails. After a surfeit of glittering, empty modern fiction I always come
back to him as to some tried old journal who never fails to charm. What a
delight the few novels of Scott which I could get to read in early life were to
me! There was one around the house—an old paper-bound *Rob Roy*—over
which I pored until I read it to pieces. Then I got hold of *The Talisman* and
Ivanhoe, thanks to Nate, who got them out of the hall library and lent them
to me—a very unlawful proceeding of course! I was not allowed to attend
the Literary or become a member of the society, much as I yearned to do
so. This was another mistake of grandfather and grandmother. It would not
only have been a great and innocent pleasure to me but a real and lasting
benefit if I had had access to that little library. But now and then I got a book
of it to read and what a delight if was! To me, Scott's novels are blent with
the brightest memories of those old days and so have the added charm of
old associations.

---

1. Beginning of a list of the series of bestselling novels published between 1814 and 1825 by Sir
    Walter Scott.

Wednesday, Nov. 11, 1908
Cavendish, P.E.I.

I am the helpless victim of "moods" these days, moods following one another so periodically that I can almost count ahead for a fortnight and predict just how I shall be feeling on any given day. In one mood I am possessed by a horrible unrest and a dread of something I don't know what. I cannot eat, read, sleep, work or do *anything* unless I drive myself to it and then I feel as if I were trying to do it with somebody else's hands or brain and couldn't work very well with them. This mood is generally followed by a "hopelessly tired" one when I feel as if I just wanted to creep away into some unseen corner and lie there undisturbed for *years*. Then I'll probably react into the worst mood of all—a mood when I seem possessed with a sullen, fierce, unreasonable resentment against fate. I feel an acrid hate against those who have used me ill. I feel as if I hated the world and it hated me. Then the fourth mood comes—I grow tender and mild and sad. A mood of kindness, a thought of old happier days and associations will bring tears to my eyes. I feel no wish to look forward to the future but only back to beloved things passed away, yearning after them bitterly. This is the least unbearable mood of all but it is so intense that it makes me suffer keenly, too. These dreadful alternations of feeling seem to be racking my life out.

Saturday, Nov. 21, 1908
Cavendish, P.E.I.

The worst week I ever lived through without exception—a week of intolerable nervous distress combined with unusual worry about certain things—came to a climax yesterday in a sick headache of the most severe type. I had a dreadful day. In summer when I have these headaches I can endure them because I can lie on my bed upstairs. But now the house is too cold for that, because I can't go to bed altogether owing to the *unrest* which attends these headaches and which compels me every few minutes to get up and walk fiercely to and fro. So I have to lie on the kitchen sofa and be stared at every few minutes by some "kid" who comes in to get the mail or by some "grown-ups" who have to ask what the matter is and discuss it and suggest useless remedies when I feel that every word or look jars my very soul. However, I dragged through the day and slept well at night. To-day, I woke up, feeling refreshed and hopeful. The relief is unutterable after the suffering of the previous ten days. Thank God for it—and for the exceptionally wonderful sunset I saw tonight. It was a page from His own Scripture, lettered in splendor indescribable. I looked at it over the leafless trees in the old front orchard and felt as if my soul were hovering in it, free from the damps and mists of earth.

Now, I'm going to read Kipling's glorious "Jungle Tales." I *can* read tonight. Two nights ago I couldn't. It seemed as if I were trying to read a foreign language, seeing and pronouncing the words but getting no real meaning out of them. Oh, if I could only keep as well as I feel now!

Tuesday, Dec. 1, 1908
Cavendish, P.E.I.

I heartily wish I could see a competent doctor whom I could trust and discuss my condition with him. I cannot go to the nearest doctor here—Stuart Simpson of Stanley. He takes "sprees" now and again and at such times tells the first person he meets all about his patient's ailments, with smutty comments. And in any case he would not be competent to treat a nervous disorder. Yet some medical advice I believe I ought to have and that soon. Thursday, Friday, and Saturday of last week, were, in all calm decision, the most utterly wretched days I have ever passed in my life. Nothing I have ever before experienced at the worst of times could compare with them. During the earlier part of the week I felt quite well and cheerful—almost my normal self. Wednesday evening the change came again, suddenly and without warning. It was as if a black cloud settled down over my soul. I felt the most intolerable nervous unrest, coupled with an equally intolerable dread of coming disaster. I could not sleep at all that night. Thursday was worse. I could not do anything—read, work, or eat. Thursday night again no sleep. Friday, still worse—Friday night, no sleep. As for Saturday, it was indescribable. Every moment was an agony. I shut myself in a cold room and walked the floor for hours. By this time I was also physically ill from lack of sleep and utter inability to eat anything; but it was the hideous nervous distress that nearly killed me. Oh, I cannot describe how I felt and it is puerile to try. But in all candor I'd rather die than go through such a time again.

Then all at once, about dusk, the cloud lifted. The horrible feeling passed away and in a few minutes I was lying on my bed utterly exhausted but so blessedly at *peace, at rest*. No words can describe the relief of it. As soon as I had enough strength to move I undressed and went to bed. Oh, it was so blessed to sleep soundly,—nay, more, it was so blessed before going to sleep just to lie there at ease and think happy thoughts! Since then I've been improving steadily, although I still feel the weakening effects of that dreadful time and am not good for much yet.

Thursday, Dec. 3, 1908
Cavendish, P.E.I.

This has been another bad day, but this time the suffering was physical, the consequences of a very bad cold. I began to feel it coming on last evening and passed a very bad night. My head ached so severely that I could not sleep. Then it was very cold—several degrees below zero and a strong wind blowing. The air in my room was so cold that I could not endure my face over the clothes and consequently passed the seemingly endless hours alternately freezing and stifling. Today I spent on the kitchen sofa, racked with cough and headache, with people coming in for the mail all the time. However, ill as I feel, it is as nothing to those dreadful days last week.

The mail, as usual, brought me a grist of letters about my book and a bunch of favourable reviews—hard, cold, glittering stones to a soul that is asking vainly for the homely bread of a little human companionship and tenderness in its hard hours.

Sunday, Dec. 13, 1908
Cavendish, P.E.I.

That terrible mood of a fortnight ago seemed to be the "crisis" of my moods. At anyrate, I have had no return of them since and the relief is indescrib-

A little gate

able. To be sure, I'm not really well for I'm tired all the time and have no energy: but that seems nothing compared to those horrible attacks of nervous unrest. Perhaps, if those moods do not return, I'll gradually get rested. I seem to expend all my strength wrestling with them and they leave me exhausted.

This has been a beautiful day, mild and sunny with splendid walking. At dusk I betook myself to Lover's Lane, going across the fields. One can go to that dear place by so many different dear ways. You can go around by the road and up David Macneill's lane till it ceases to be "David's lane" and becomes Lover's Lane. You can go across Pierce's field, through the spruce grove, over a brook, through David Macneill's orchard, and out into Lover's Lane by a little gate. You can go over Pierce's field and over David's field, striking the lane just above the first bridge—my favourite way of going. You can go up "Laird's Hill" to the top, then strike across the fields to the lane just below the second bridge, or you can go "in along the road" to the site of the old Baptist church, plunge "down" through the woods, over the brook and "up" through the woods to the field where the lane ends. And every way has beauties of its own.

Just above the first bridge   Where the lane ends

It was exquisite back there tonight and exquisite thoughts came flying to meet me like birds as I tramped along under the bare boughs of the lane. When I reached the field beyond I walked around it half a dozen times. There is not a house or sign of human habitation in sight from that field and is almost wholly

"The field beyond"

surrounded by dark spruce woods, faintly flecked with snow, whose pointed tops came out against the saffron of the western sky. I had an hour of happiness in which I felt as I used to feel always long ago. Ah, "Nature never did betray the heart that loved her." Then it grew dark and I came away regretfully.

Sunday, Dec. 20, 1908
Cavendish, P.E.I.

Today has seemed long—no service and too much light snow for outdooring. I *did* take a walk over the hill tonight in defiance of the snow. The world was very lovely, in creamy, lustrous atmosphere, a fair sunset and ranks of spruces faintly powdered with snow. But I was too tired to enjoy it. I *saw* the beauty but could not *feel* it.

I passed part of today reading Burrough's "Locusts and wild Honey"[1]—a delightful book of simple essays on outdoor themes, written by a close and sympathetic observer of Nature in her sky and hidden ways which must be

---

1. John Burroughs wrote in the Thoreau tradition of essays, detailing in this work (1879) the attraction of bees and strawberries and the joys of camping and fishing.

trodden with reverent feet and scanned with loving eyes if you would read their intimate scrolls. I am thankful above all else for my love of nature and my capacity for finding fullness of joy in her companionship. I would rather lose everything else I possess than that. I could not have lived these past ten years without it.

 **1909**

Jan. 10, 1909
Cavendish, P.E.I.

The New Year is ten days old. It brought me a new sorrow for its guerdon. On the second of January I received a letter from Bertie McIntyre telling me that her mother had died New Year's morning.

To me it was a bolt from the blue. I had known Aunt Mary was not quite well, as she was suffering from a return of her chronic throat trouble; but I had no idea that she was seriously ill; and indeed, she did not die from that, although it would probably have been fatal in the end, but from heart failure induced by an attack of pleurisy.

It was a bitter grief to me. Of all her generation there was no one so dear to me. I never really knew Aunt Mary until the year I went to P.W.C. I had met her only once or twice in my whole life before; and I am sorry to say that I felt against her a prejudice and distrust which had been early instilled into my childish mind by the things I had heard grandmother and Aunt Annie say about her. I know now that most of those things were either untrue or so warped and distorted by the prejudice and narrow mindedness of those who uttered them as to be worse than falsehoods. But I did not know this then; I was still under the delusion that grandmother and Aunt Annie were quite infallible in all their judgments and that their opinion on every point was the last word.

But I had only to know Aunt Mary to realize what injustice they had done her. Never was there a braver, sweeter, pluckier, kinder, more loving and loyal soul ever pent in flesh—and the circumstances of her married life called for all the bravery and loyalty she possessed. Uncle Duncan was a very dissipated man and the care and upbringing of her large family fell wholly on her.

I loved her from the moment the scales of prejudiced ignorance fell from my eyes and in all the years that have followed every meeting has drawn us closer together.

I went into town on Thursday to the funeral, which was to have been Saturday but as James and Laura were delayed by washouts and did not arrive home until Saturday afternoon it has to be put off till Sunday and I could not stay having to come home Saturday evening. At such times I feel keenly being tied down as I am. I do not mind so much giving up pleasures but it is hard not to be able to stay by my friends in their time of trial.

Still, I saw dear Aunty in farewell. She was always a beautiful woman and she looked more beautiful than every lying among her flowers with a face of perfect peace and sweetness. Then there was a sorrowful pleasure in meeting my cousins and Aunt Maggie again. It was so long since I had seen them.

Harry and Cuthbert are such dear boys.

When I came away I felt as if my heart would break. I had never before left there that Aunty did not come to the gate and wave her hand to me with her little characteristic gesture of farewell. I could almost hear her saying, as always, "Come back soon." But there was nobody there, only poor Harry, standing in the wintry sunshine and I felt as if I should never care to visit Ch'town again.

Sunday, Jan. 31, 1909
Cavendish, P.E.I.

This has been an unwholesome day. It has stormed all day and stirring out was impossible. We saw no one. There was nothing to do but write letters and read, both of which I did until I could do no more of either. My brain grew very tired. Vexing thoughts began to swarm through it like teasing gnats. I could not prevent them or escape them and I had no companionship to exorcise them. It is at such moments I long bitterly for a friend with whom I might talk were it but nonsense. Nay—could I only get out for a walk it could help me.

A stormy day

Still, I am very glad to say, that I have really been a great deal better this month than I have ever been since the day of the fire. I have had no return of those terrible moods of unrest. True, I feel very tired and spiritless most of the time but that is not so hard to bear and I think I am slowly improving in every way.

Last week I was laid up three days with a bad sore throat. It certainly was unpleasant; but I can endure physical suffering tolerably well when it is not combined with mental. Besides, I can own up to *it*. I can say simply "I have a sore throat" and lie down, not expected to eat, work, or be cheerful. Poor grandmother can understand physical trouble, having endured a good deal of it herself. She had no understanding of or sympathy with nervous disorders or mental suffering. So I always try to conceal it—to eat and talk and laugh as usual. It is not very difficult to hide it from her for she is not very sensitive to the moods of other people and never suspects anything if complaint is not made in words. It is better for herself that it is so and I would not have it otherwise. Yet often, when my dark moods come, I have felt that I could have mastered them had I but a sympathetic friend to express them to—one who would not meet my effort at confidence with the scornful remark that she "didn't see what *I* had to be blue about," as grandmother years ago met my first, last and only attempt to discuss any of my troubles and perplexities with her. Poor grandmother has never realized that "man does not live by bread alone." She has always thought that if you had "bread"—food, clothes and a roof over you—there was nothing else that any proper person could desire.

Today I read the book of Job, along with Froude's essay on the same. What a magnificent thing it is—that old Oriental poem of which we do not even know the author. I wonder who and what he was—how he lived and suffered—for the writer of that book suffered terribly—and dream of mighty things and saw unspeakable visions in the watches of the night. His brain has been dust for thousands of years; yet the thoughts of that brain have come down to us and are as grand and fresh and beautiful as when they first burned their way through his soul to his pen. The question he asked in his anguish are as unanswerable then as now—what is the meaning of undeserved suffering and pain—"If a man die shall he live again?"[1] "Canst thou loose the bands of Orion?"[2] Nay, we cannot. We are as powerless as job to pierce the mystery of the most. High or translate the hieroglyphics of human agony.

February 1, 1909
Cavendish, P.E.I.

'Nother unwholesome day. No mail—no stirring out. However, one could work today so the hours did not seem quite so unfriendly. It is bitter cold and my only amusement has been to get a flower catalogue and pick out all the dear things I'd grow if I had a garden. By the aid of a little imagination this can be made quite a fascinating occupation.

Tuesday, Feb. 16, 1909
Cavendish, P.E.I.

I have had another hard week—a return of my nervous malady—unrest, insomnia and depression, aggravated by several worries and by confinement to the house on account of the bitter cold and the impossible walking. I have been trying desperately today to struggle with my evil genius but it has got

---

1. Job 14:14.

2. Job 38:31.

the better of me. It has been so cold, so dull, so lonely. I couldn't work or write or read—I could only walk the floor and wrestle with black, cankerous thoughts that infested my mind. I would have been glad for *anybody* to have come in and talked to me for a little while—glad of any diversion. I used to think that I could never feel very lonely, as long as I had a book to read or a pen to write with. That used to be true—is true enough even yet generally—but in these nervous attacks I *can't* read—I cannot gather any meaning from the printed page or assimilate the thoughts contained in it.

Last night was *dreadful*. I couldn't sleep—I seemed burning up with strange nervous pulsations, and I thought around and around in a circle of misery. The night was so cold that I couldn't bear my face above the clothes and the physical discomfort aggravated the nervous disorder. When the days on which I feel better come I look back with wonder to these miserable sensations and marvel that I could not overcome them. But the fact remains that I cannot, try as I will and do. I have been dosing myself with emulsion all winter but though I am gaining a little in flesh I cannot see that it is helping my nerves any. A talk with Frede Campbell if I could get it would do them more good than all the drugs in the world.

Daffy

My gray cat "Daffy" has just come in and climbed up on my knee. I don't know what I'd do without him, the big gray furry fellow. He is three years old and the mere touch of his soft sides and sleek head is a comfort to me. But Daffy can't talk and I just want somebody—sealed of the tribe—to talk with and to. *You* can't talk, old journal, who have gone through so much with me, but you are a help for all that. It is wonderful what a relief it is to write this stuff out.

I've been turning over the pages of your first volume and reading those written during the winter I taught in Belmont. Certainly, that winter was the most uncomfortable one, from a physical point of view, that I ever passed. I had a wretchedly cold room and an equally cold school, one crowded with rough, unlovable pupils, so different from my Bideford pupils that it was hard to believe they belonged to the same species. The people with whom I boarded were uncouth and eccentric. They kept a very poor table. Two thirds of the time I was cold, hungry and solitary—much of the time physically unwell. Yet I was very seldom blue or despondent—I was full of hope and energy even in the hardest hours. I never complained to anyone outside of my journal. I knew I should meet with no sympathy at home, where grandfather was so bitterly opposed to my teaching; and I was too thankful to get any sort of a school for those were the days of a surplus of teachers before the west opened its gates. Yet there is no doubt that what I went through that winter took much away from my strength. If I had a daughter I should be wild if I thought she had to undergo any such experience.

I remember one evening in particular. I was coming home from school. It was nearly dark for I had stayed in late as usual with Edmond Campbell. There had been a thaw and the gutters along the road were full of water but it had turned very cold and was freezing fast. I stepped on what I thought was solid ice and it broke. I went through so suddenly that I lost my balance and fell. The ice gave way wholly and I went "souse" into the bitter water beneath. I was wet to the skin and I had to walk half a mile in that condition with my wet clothes freezing on me. When I reached Frasers I was so utterly tired out that I had hardly strength enough left to change my clothes.

On another occasion I wakened up in the night, feeling rather cold and moist, and discovered that my pillow was covered with snow which had drifted in through the cracks of the window at the head of my bed.

Oh, it was all hard enough; but I had plenty of spirit and courage then and could laugh at my tribulations even while I groaned under them—laugh at them as I cannot laugh at them now when they are past and gone—for when my dark moods come on I seem to live all the suffering of my whole life over again in a strange, horrible fashion—as if I were haunted and possessed by the ghost of dead wretchedness.

But never mind! Just wait till a thaw comes when I can get out to the balm of the fir trees and the peace of the white places and "the strength of the hills"—what a beautiful old Biblical phrase that is!—and I shall be made whole once more.

And yet—and yet—and yet—I'm very tired. My whole life seems to have been one long struggle against unequal odds and I'm wearied out.

Feb. 20, 1909
Cavendish, P.E.I.

This afternoon I read a very beautiful book—Bliss Carman's "Making of Personality,"[1] which Ewan sent me recently. It is one of the most helpful books I have ever read and has done me a vast amount of good—I feel better, braver, more hopeful, more encouraged, more determined to make the best of myself and life since I have read it. It is a series of lessons on "the oldest of all arts—the art of living"—a subject on which most of us require a good deal of instruction and which is never taught in the schools. The book is a

---

1. Bliss Carman (1869–1929), Maritime poet turned transcendental philosopher, author with M. Perry King of *The Making of Personality* (1908).

mingling of glorified commonsense and starry aspiration. The first essay is on the "meaning" of personality. He tries to define it—I hardly think he succeeds. It is a very elusive thing—and the greatest force in the world. It is not to be commanded by wealth or education.

Carman insists on the tri-une cultivation of soul, mind, and body—and he is right. The great lack of Christianity—its cardinal mistake—lies in the fact that it has *over*-emphasized the spiritual—taught that the body must be mortified—or at best, disregarded as of no importance—a false and ugly—yea, and a blasphemous doctrine—blasphemous because it lowers the "image of the Creator" below the brutes. Mind and soul can express themselves only through the body and therefore we should try to make it and keep it as perfect an instrument for their expression as possible.

The essay on the value of Instinct is exquisitely true—as I too well know, having disregarded instinct many times to my cost and in my bitter punishment having learned what a safe guide it is. One sentence was peculiarly vital. "We often over-persuade ourselves, against the subtle intimations for instinctive preference, to enter into relationships that turn out disastrously for all concerned and *to attempt friendships that could never be worth while.*"

How often I have done this and how I regret the wasted effort now. I have done it in childhood when I was *not* to blame for it. I had a child's natural craving for companionship. The right sort was not to be had so I took what I could find and formed schoolgirl intimacies which did me no good—nay, did me positive harm—and which cling around me now, hampering and valueless. I have done it in mature years when I *was* to blame for it, because I disregarded my instinct, trying to find friendship in someone who was pronounced by other people to be good, or clever, or nice, and I thought it must be of value to have companionship with such.

I am wiser now. I never try to cultivate *intimacy* with anyone in whose society I do not feel *thoroughly at ease.* I shall always try to be cordial to all but I shall never try to open the gates of my soul to anyone who, as my instinct warns me, is not in sympathy with me—who is not, in Frede's favourite phrase, "of the race that knows Joseph."[1]

Wednesday, March 3, 1909
Cavendish, P.E.I.

Oh, I *do* wish spring would come! It seems to me that winter under my present circumstances is just one grim, ceaseless *endurance* of physical and mental discomfort, worry and loneliness. I can get out so seldom even for a

---

1. An inversion of the phrase from Exodus, also quoted February 10, 1901.

walk and this last fortnight has been a hard one. I do really feel better than I did some time ago. I don't suffer so many dark moods. But I feel so very tired most of the time—too tired to take an interest in anything. Some days I feel tolerably bright and like myself—the next my soul will be a bleak, gray desert, without colour or music, and I'll want to lie down in it and die. That is just how I feel tonight—and yet if I could have got out for a tramp over the hill the desert would blossom like the rose of joy—a thousand flowerets of fancy and hope and illusion would fling their garlands over it. But it is too cold and the snow too deep for that.

This evening I have been reading Mrs. Browning's poems. Some of them are very beautiful, though she is really too long-winded. She is essentially a poet of feeling, though not of passion, and some of her poems are among the very few which bring tears to my eyes—their truth is so poignant and their pain so real—I suppose because she herself was so long schooled of pain. My favourite among her poems is "The Lay Of The Brown Rosary"[1]—and I am much more in sympathy with *Onora* than Mrs. Browning was!

I am sorry I did not know and grow into her poems when I was a child. Poetry pored over in childhood becomes part of one's soul and nature more thoroughly than what is first read in mature years can ever do. Yet I was rather fortunate in this respect in childhood for I had access to many poets—Longfellow, Tennyson, Whittier, Scott, Byron, Milton, Burns—and as poetry was not frowned upon as fiction was I could revel in them as fully as I wished. Their music was woven into my growing soul and has echoed through it, consciously or unconsciously, ever since—"the music of the immortals"—of those great beautiful souls whose passing tread has made of earth holy ground.

Tuesday, Mar. 16, 1909
Cavendish, P.E.I.

I'm good for nothing tonight, I am so tired. So, as usual, I'll seek a refuge from brooding and carking thoughts by writing in this journal. A fortnight ago the Page Co. wrote me asking for a later photo than the one I had sent them last summer as a prominent book magazine wishes to publish it as a frontispiece. I wrote back that I couldn't conveniently get to town before spring; but last week I had another letter urging me to have one taken at once if possible, as the matter was urgent and important. I hardly think it so very "urgent and

---

1. Elizabeth Barrett Browning's hectic poem (1838) of love, temptation, sin, and death. LMM explores its impact on a young reader in *Emily Climbs*, chapter 19.

important" that the great American public should see my face; but I wearily surrendered and set about putting the necessary machinery in motion.

When I was a child a trip to town and a trip to Park Corner were the only outings that ever entered my life and both were looked upon as great pleasures. A trip to Park Corner was of comparatively common occurrence—usually twice a year. A trip to town was a very rare treat—once in two or three years—and loomed up in about the same proportion of novelty, excitement and delight as a trip to Europe would now. It meant a brief sojourn in a delightful and fascinating place, where everybody seemed always dressed up and able to get all the nuts, candies and oranges they wanted, to say nothing of the exquisite delight of looking at all the wonderful things in the shop windows.

I remember the first trip to town of which I have any recollection. I could not have been more than six at most and I think I was only five. Grandfather, grandmother, father and I all went to town in a big double seated wagon. To go anywhere with father was sheer happiness for me. I had a glorious day of it but the most delightful part was a tiny adventure I had just before leaving for home. The others had met some friends at a street corner and stopped to talk. Finding that I wasn't being "looked after" I promptly shot down a nearby street in search of adventures. It was *so* jolly and independent to be walking down a street alone! It was a wonderful street. I've never seen it since—not with the same eyes anyhow. No other street has ever had the charm that had. The most amazing sight I saw in it was a woman shaking rugs *on the top of a house*. I felt dizzy with astonishment over such a topsy turvey sight. We shook our rugs in the back yard. Who *ever* heard of shaking them on the top of a house?

Arriving at the bottom of the street I coolly ran down the steps of an open door I found there and discovered myself to be in a most charming dim spot full of barrels, with a floor ankle deep in beautiful, curly shavings. But just as I reached the foot of the steps I saw a man over in a corner and, overcome, not by fear but by bashfulness, I beat a prompt retreat. On my way back I met a little girl with a jug in her hand. We both stopped and, with the instinctive, unconventional *camaraderie* of childhood, plunged into an intimate confidential conversation. She was a jolly little soul with black eyes and two long braids of black hair. We told each other everything about ourselves, except our names which neither of us thought about. When we parted I felt as if I were leaving a lifelong friend. We "never met again."

When I rejoined my grown-ups they had not missed me at all and knew nothing of my rapturous voyage into wonderland.

But there is no such romance about a trip to town nowadays. I got up at five yesterday morning and by the time I was ready the team which I had engaged to come down for me from the station had arrived. This way of getting to the train is a vast improvement on going up with the mailman as I used to have to do when I was poorer. But it isn't pleasant. The driver is always some stupid French boy and the drive is long and tiresome. It was particularly so yesterday morning for the roads were so rough and full of slews.[1] I was tired out when I reached Hunter River—tireder still when I got to town. There I was overcome by a sudden sense of desolation. Always before the first thing was to go to Aunt Mary's where a warm welcome waited for me. But there was no doing that now. Bertie would be at her school and the dear little aunt with her sweet face and voice, was out in the cemetery. Feeling curiously heartsick I went uptown and sat for a picture, hoping that I wouldn't look in it as tired and hopeless and out-at-elbows as I felt. Then I rushed feverishly about town getting some necessary shopping done. I seemed to be wandering in a species of nightmare with much the same feeling I occasionally have in dreams when I am roaming in some strange place unable to find my way out. I hated to meet people—to force animation of voice and manner, receive congratulations gracefully and talk small talk. At two I met Bertie in the library and we had a chat, the only pleasant spot in my visit. At three my train left. Reached Hunter River at four and drove again over the eleven miles of rough road.

When I got home I was more utterly tired out than I ever remember being in *all* my life before, and *so* wretchedly nervous. I was too tired even to lie down. I felt as if I must scream at the slightest noise—the ticking of the clock seemed unbearable. I went to bed and had a wild, passionate fit of nervous crying, the result of my intolerable weariness. But it calmed me so that I fell asleep as soon as it was over, but suffered from distressing dreams all night. Today I've been miserable enough. It is dreadful to feel so tired. Pain is really easier to bear. I shall not recover from the effects of yesterday for some time.

Wednesday, March 31, 1909
Cavendish, P.E.I.

It is fortunate that I've been feeling a good deal better of late or I think the past ten days would have been hard on me. Things have been all wrong in the weather line—snow, rain, sleet continually. Stirring out is next to impossible and is no pleasure when it is possible. We had no foreign mail for a whole week until Monday when a huge pile came and gave some tang to life once more.

---

1. Variant of *sloughs*: patches of mud or mire.

I *am* much better and feel so unutterably thankful for it. I haven't had any of those distressing moods for a long time, and although I still get tired easily and have not a great deal of energy I seem to have regained a certain peace and poise of mind to which I have long been a stranger; and even in regards to the feeling of weariness I am improving. Oh, it is so blessed to feel better. I do hope it will continue.

Saturday, April 3, 1909
Cavendish, P.E.I.

Last night was a beautiful one and as I was coming home in the afterlight I saw a sight that filled me with rapture. I was in the field behind the church. To my right was a grove of tall, gently-waving spruces. Seen in daylight those spruces are old and uncomely—dead almost to the top, with withered branches. But seen in that enchanted light, against a sky that began by being rosy saffron and continued to be silver green, and ended finally in crystal blue, they were like tall, dark, slender witch maidens, weaving spells of magic in a rune of elder days. How I longed to share in their gramarye—to have fellowship in their twilight sorceries.

Lover's Lane

Today I went back to Lover's Lane and the woods beyond. I knew the walking would be dreadful but I was so homesick I couldn't keep away any longer. The walking *was* bad—a vile compound of slush and mud and ice. But it was only my feet that were concerned with it. The rest of me revelled in the soft April charm of the world. Old Mother Nature is a rare artist. Back there today the woods were a symphony of greens and grays, so subtle that you could not tell where one began to be the other. Gray trunk, green bough, gray-green moss. Yet the old gypsy doesn't like unrelieved monotones—she must have a dash of colour and here it is—a broken dead fir branch of a beautiful ruddy brown swinging among the beards of moss.

The white birches out on the edges were so dear, with a transparent mist of purple twigs over their bare limbs. The white birches are beautiful pagan maidens who have never forgotten the Eden secret of being naked and unashamed.

Sunday, April 11, 1909
Cavendish, P.E.I.

Haven't been very well again this past week. Had a dull dizzy headache most of the time and felt miserably nervous and morbid. *All* my thoughts and emotions seem to be morbid nowadays, even those that are normally good. Everything I hate I hate with trebled bitterness; everything I love, whether place, person or thing, I love with a passionate intensity that has more pain than pleasure in it, everything I dread I shrink from with an agony out of all proportion to its real importance. All this is unnatural. Oh, I long so for spring and good walking. I have not been able to get out for a walk this week and that is half what is the matter with me. I had a bad night of sleeplessness last night. But I feel better today and think the attack is passing for this time.

If anyone wants to find out what has become of her submerged friends let her write a book. They will then "bob up serenely" from the deeps of the lost years in all quarters of the world. Yesterday I had a letter from Lottie Shatford—now Mrs. Handy of Vancouver. I had not heard from or of her for seven years. Now she has read *Anne* and writes to me. Her letter was, like all her epistles, a frank, kind, and generous one. I always enjoyed Lottie's letters—much more than her personal society indeed. Our *intellects* seemed to be perfectly in accord; it was something in our *personalities* that was out of tune. Lottie had a nature free from all envy or pettiness—a candid, sincere, and honourable one. I always recognized and admired her good qualities, even while I felt that there was not in her that subtle "fitness" which is the very essence of real friendship. I was pleased to receive her letter and shall write in return. But I do not think any real good or pleasure could accrue to either of us from a re-opening of our correspondence and I shall make no attempt to do so.

Yesterday also a copy of the London *Spectator*[1] came with a two column review of *Anne*—the most favourable review of any yet. I *do* feel hugely flattered—I admit it frankly. The *Spectator* is the biggest of all the "big" literary reviews and praise or blame from it carries tremendous weight.

Friday, April 16, 1909
Cavendish

Two days of this week the weather was really heavenly. The rest—well, they were the place-opposite-to-heavenly!

---

1. Founded in 1828, this English weekly newspaper was highly respected for its political and literary criticism.

Tuesday and Wednesday were the lovely days—sunny and warm as June. Whether it was the effect of the weather or if it just happened so I don't know but for those two days I felt perfectly well and like my "old self"—hopeful, peaceful, all the bitterness gone out of my memories of the past and my feelings of the present. I had some lovely evening walks—one of them to the graveyard! Not exactly a cheerful place for a walk one would sup-

Part of the graveyard

pose? But I always like to wander over that westward sloping hill of graves in the gentle melancholy of a spring evening. I like to read the names on the stones and note the ages, and think of all the loves and hates and hopes and fears that lie buried there. I would like to be buried there myself, when my time comes—by mother's side.

After my walk that evening I came in and studied a new book on astronomy—just plain, every night astronomy that anybody can understand. It was so fascinating that I carried the book to bed with me and sat up on my pillows half the night, poring over the charts of the constellations. Astronomy has always been a subject possessing a great charm for me. I would give much for a peep through a telescope.

On Thursday evening I received a telegram from my half sister Kate announcing her mother's death on the previous day—a very sudden and unexpected death.

I had no reason to love Mrs. Montgomery but I never wished her ill and I was very sorry to hear of her death for the sake of her children. They are now doubly orphaned at an age when they most require a parents' care and counsel. But at least they will have plenty to provide for them, as I understand Mrs. Montgomery has made a great deal of money these past few years in real estate business; and they have many near relatives near them to look after them.

Today I received a letter from a Toronto journalist asking me to read a paper before the International Council of Women,[1] meeting in Toronto in June. The honour is to my book, of course. I cannot go—and what is worse, I do not wish to go. All my old desire for travel seems to have died out completely. I shrink from any change, even a desirable one.

---

1. Founded in 1888 in the United States as part of the suffrage movement.

Sunday, April 18, 1909

The very name of "Sunday" at the head of an entry in this journal presupposes a dismal "growl." It is as usual. This has been a dreary day. All yesterday I was wretchedly ill and although I feel better today I am very weak. It snowed last night which made sloppy walking today so I could not venture out. This evening I have read over the entries made in my journal in my old schooldays and when I had finished I was heartsick. Oh, if I could only go back to those dear days! They were not without their trials—trials inseparable from the condition of a sensitive child in my circumstances. But after all they were only the thorns on the roses of the days—they pricked me all too often but it meant only a smart, not a deep seated, enduring pain and between the smarts I was free to drink the perfume of the blossoms. I had a scores of sweet little joys and delights and a merry circle of young friends. Now I have no pleasure but my rambles and my books and few congenial friends within "get-at-able" distance.

When I put the volume of the journal away I could hardly restrain myself from bursting into tears. I did not let myself, however, because I did not wish to annoy grandma, so I've written it out here instead and it has helped me, as it always does. I feel calmer again—more patient to endure, as it did not seem I *could* do half an hour ago.

Saturday, May 1, 1909
Cavendish, P.E.I.

Last week I felt wretched, being ill most of the time and suffering from headache. This week, however, I have fortunately felt much better—fortunately, because one of the worries that have been harassing me all winter has suddenly assumed an acute form. Aunt Annie has been very miserable since last August. At intervals of a few weeks she has suffered attacks of intense pain. This has now developed into appendicitis and she has to go at once to the hospital for an operation. This latter fact is, in one way, a relief, since it is what I have felt would be wisest all along. But her condition is critical after her exhausting winter of suffering. I shall be racked with anxiety until the operation is over. If anything should happen to Aunt Annie—but I dare not think of it, much less put it into words.

Saturday Morning
May 8, 1909
Cavendish, P.E.I.

If I wanted to make this journal a cheerful record I should always and only write it in the mornings. As a rule, I feel "like myself" in the mornings, and even at the worst of times much better than I usually feel in the evenings. But then I do not want to "make" this journal any particular sort or kind. I look upon it as a faithful old confidant to whom I can go in my dark moods for relief—and seldom fail to find it.

But this morning is lovely and I have just come in from a walk over the hill. It is the first day this spring that it has been warm and dry enough to resume my old habit. And oh, it was delightful! All cares and worries seemed left behind and I walked with the loveliest and sweetest of winged thoughts.

Friday, May 14, 1909
Cavendish, P.E.I.

The first gleam of sunshine in a very dark week came today. A letter from Frede announced that the operation was safely over and her mother was doing well. It was such a relief. Grandmother has been very ill this week—so ill that I insisted on sending for the doctor. She is a little better now but she has failed in a good many ways of late and every recognition of it saddens my heart.

Aunt Annie

I feel very much alone. It is a great responsibility to be all alone with an old person who is not well. Aunt Annie's illness, coming at such a time, makes it harder, since I cannot look to her or her family for any help just now.

Friday, May 21, 1909
Cavendish, P.E.I.

The first few days of this week were bitterly cold and wet. They seemed endless. It was very delightful to see the sun again this morning. And this evening we had one of the most beautiful spring twilights imaginable, with a young moon in the midst of it. I prowled about the fields till long after dark, studying the stars with my field-glass. When I came in I felt as if I had been millions of miles away in the blue ether and all my old familiar surroundings seemed momentarily forgotten and strange.

One of the roads

I love roaming about by myself in these spring twilights. My continual state of worry and unrest unfits me for ordinary human companionship. But when I am alone in the dusk I find a strange peace, as if I had gone backward into old years. It is a sad peace—I feel sorrowful in it—but it *is* peace and that seems the most desirable thing in life to me now—peace of mind, freedom from worry and dread. I walk up and down the long roads, between the silent ranks of the spruces, or over the still fields. I am companioned by thoughts of old laughter and joys, shadowy footsteps of dead or absent friends, voices of the vanished years. I cannot think much about the future; the present is only to be borne by escaping from it in thought. So I seek for happiness and comfort, in "the light and warmth of the long ago."[1]

Physically, however, I am much better than I was. I have not had my bad nervous attacks for a long time and am not so often tortured by headaches. I've been taking tonics and emulsions all winter and I believe the result is being seen at last.

Tuesday, June 1, 1909
Cavendish, P.E.I.

This evening I had a good hour. I went in over the hill to call on a friend. *This* was not the hour referred to. My friend, so called, is merely an old acquaintance whom I like well enough. The good hour came as I was walking home alone. Before me arched the afterlight of a glorious sea-sunset. The tall slender firs along the moist red road came out against it in a grace and beauty that made me ache for joy; and behind me a full moon deepened until the white radiance mingled with the gold and flame of the west. I came down the hill and up the lane. The birches hung out young-leaved boughs over me. The apple trees crowded lovingly about the old house. The moonlight softened all until it looked as it used to look long ago—a bowery "haunt of

---

1.   From James Russell Lowell's "The Vision of Sir Launfall" (1848).

The Lane

ancient peace."[1] It is at such moments that I realize how deeply rooted and strong is my love for this old place—a love of instinct and passion, blent with every fibre of my soul.

It is terrible to love things—and people—as I do!

Today I began work at my new book "The Story Girl."[2] The germinal idea has been budding in my brain all winter and this evening I sat me down in my dear white room and began it. I think it is a good idea and I think I shall be able to make a good piece of work out of it. But I feel sad, too, for I cannot be sure that I shall be long enough in this old house to finish it and it seems to me that I could never write it as it should be written anywhere else—that some indefinable, elusive "bouquet" will be missing if it is written elsewhere. I suppose this is a foolish fancy. And perhaps I shall be able to finish it here. But I cannot banish these thoughts and they are very saddening.

Yet it is a joyous young world now and its beauty is as new wine to me. The improvement in my health continues and I feel again my old joy in mere existence—in the blue sky, the greenness of the southern slopes and the airy charm of pussywillows.

"As it used to look long ago"

I am re-reading Andersen's Fairy Tales[3] and find them as delightful as ever. I am glad I had the privilege of reading them in my childhood. The child who has not known them has missed much. Mr. Fraser, one of my early teachers, offered prizes in school for various things. The offer made great excitement. In the fourth class—mine—the prize was for the pupil who was "head" oftenest. I won that. Wellington Nelson won the prize in the arithmetic class and his was a volume of Andersen's Tales. I shall never forget the happiness the perusal of them gave me. After Wellington went away I never read them again until now, for I never could get a complete edition.

1. Alfred Lord Tennyson's description of the painting of "an English home" in "The Palace of Art" (1833).

2. LMM weaves a collection of stories into this novel (1911), which would remain her favourite among her works. In it a young girl enchants a happy circle of cousins with tales of Prince Edward Island.

3. Hans Christian Andersen's *Tales* (1835), first translated into English in 1846.

At last I have succeeded in doing this by sending to England for it. It is the same edition Wellington had and the stories have lost none of their charm. I am glad I can find pleasure in fairy tales still.

My own prize was also a volume of fairy tales of which "The Honey Stew of the Countess Bertha"[1] and "Gaffer Wind and Dame Rain" gave me no end of delightful "thrills." I have it yet. The "Honey Stew" abounded in ghosts and ghosts had a special fascination for me then. Indeed, to this very day I like nothing better than a well-told ghost story, warranted to send a cold chill down your spine.

Thursday, June 3, 1909
Cavendish, P.E.I.

A scene on the shore

This evening I went to the shore. As usual now, it was very quiet and lonely. When I was a child it was not so. Those were the days when the mackerel fishing was good and the shore was dotted with fishing houses. Grandfather and Uncle John fished together at the latter's shore. "Tony" Wyand, a peculiar local personage, also had a fishing house there, and Geo. R. had his close by. A few yards along the shore, at the end of the "Big Lane," where the rocks left off and the sand hills began was quite a little colony of fishing houses. This was called "Cawnpore"—owing to the fact, I believe, that on the day the last nail was driven into the last house news arrived of the massacre of Cawnpore in the Indian Mutiny. There is not a house left there now and the name is forgotten, too.

"Where the rocks leave off"

When I was a child I spent much time at the shore. The men would get up at three or four and go out fishing. Then we children had to take their breakfast down at eight or nine—later on, their dinner and, if it were a good day for fish, then teas also. If they

---

1.   A tale by Alexandre Dumas père, translated into English in 1846 by Mrs. Cooke Taylor. Mentioned in *Pat of Silver Bush* (1933).

were not "in" when we went down we had to wait—sometimes for hours if the mackerel were biting. I soon, therefore, came to know every cove, headland and rock on that shore. We would take the spyglass and watch the boats, paddle in the water, gather shells and pebbles, or sit on the rocks and dream dreams. The pebbles were many and beautiful and some were curious.

The rocks at low tide were covered by millions of "snails" as we called them. I think periwinkles is the correct name. They had shells of all sizes, from those as big as a hazel nut down to shells as tiny as a pin head. I used to think—perhaps I was right—that these tiny ones were baby snails which would afterwards grow big. And I could not understand how the *shells* could grow, whatever their occupants might do. And I don't understand it yet, for that matter, if it be really the case. We often found great empty "snail shells," as big as our fists, which had washed ashore from some distant strand or deep sea haunt.

Then there were mussels, which were thought quite a delicacy by most people when brought home and baked. I never really liked them but used to eat them because it seemed rather the fashion. For the same reason I ate dulse, not caring a bit for it. I liked better to gather the long shirred ribbons of "kelp" or a queer little seaweed with clusters of grape-like things that exploded with quite a noise when pinched.

The sea, constantly dashing against the soft, sandstone cliffs wore them away into many beautiful arches and caves. Somewhat to the east of our fishing houses was a rather bold headland. Through the "neck" of this headland a hole became worn—a hole so small that we could hardly thrust a hand through it. Every season it grew larger. One summer Pensie Macneill and I adventurously crawled through it. It was a tight squeeze and we used to exult with a fearful joy over having done it and speculate as to what would have happened if we had got stuck half way through!

In a few years we could walk upright through the opening. Still a few more years and a horse and cart could have been driven through it. Then the thin bridge of rock at the top gave way and the headland became a sort of island, as if a gateway had been cleft through its wall. It is a spot I have always loved.

The "gateway"

There were many stories and legends connected with the shore which I heard older people tell and talk of. Grandfather liked a dramatic story, had a good memory for its fine points and could tell it well. There was the history of the terrible American Gale or "Yankee Storm" in the early '50's—so called because hundreds of American fishing vessels out in the gulf were wrecked along the north shore. One of the most striking and pathetic tales of this great storm was that of the *Franklin Dexter*. I never tired hearing it. The *Franklin Dexter* was a vessel which went ashore down at Cape Turner. All on board were lost, including four brothers, one of whom was captain and owner of the ship. They were the only sons of their father, a man in Portland, Me. After the storm their bodies came ashore and were buried, along with many others, in Cavendish churchyard. Their father, a broken-hearted old man, came up and insisted on having the bodies exhumed, saying that he had promised their mother that he would take her boys home to her. The coffins were put on board a trading vessel at New London, while the father returned home in a passenger vessel. The trading vessel was called the *Seth Hall*. She left New London harbour with the four bodies on board—*and was never heard of again*. It always seemed to me as if it were a thing fore-ordained—that the bodies of those boys were doomed to the sea. There was also a story that the captain of the *Seth Hall*, a profane man, had sailed out of the harbour at a time when the tide rendered it difficult to get out. He was told that he wouldn't be able to get out that night and he retorted that he would sail out of New London Harbour that night if he sailed straight to hell, and God Almighty shouldn't prevent him!

Then there was the Cape Leforce story—a bit of tragic, unwritten history, harking back to the days when the "Island of St. John" belonged to France. It was some time in 1760s (I can never remember dates. The only two dates that remain in my memory out of all those so painstakingly learned in schooldays, are—Julius Caesar landed in England 53 B.C. and the Battle of Waterloo was fought in 1815).

France and England were at war. French privateers infested the St. Lawrence gulf and plundered the commerce of the New England colonies. One of these was commanded by a Captain named Leforce. One night it anchored off what is now Cavendish shore—at that time, of course, a wooded solitude. For some reason the crew came ashore and spent the night, camped on a headland. The captain and his mate shared a tent and endeavoured to come to a division of their booty. They quarrelled and it was arranged that they should fight a duel at sunrise. But in the morning, as the Captain was pacing off the distance, the mate treacherously raised his pistol and shot him in the back. I do not know whether the mate was ever punished for this in any way. Probably not. It was a mere sentence in a long page of bloodshed and piracy. But the captain was buried by his crew on the spot where he fell. I have often heard grandfather say that his father, old "Speaker" Macneill, had seen the grave in his boyhood; but it had eventually crumbled off into the waves.

Nowadays the headland I have referred to as having the hole in it is called Cape Leforce, probably because it is the only striking looking headland on the shore. The real Cape Leforce is an insignificant little point further down.

The headland called "Cape Leforce"

Away to the westward six or seven miles the view was bounded by New London Point, a long, sharp tongue of land running far out to sea. In my childhood I never wearied of speculating what was on the other side of that point—a very realm of enchantment surely, I thought. Even when I gradually grew into the understanding that beyond it was merely another reach of shore like our own it still held a mystery and fascination for me. I longed to stand out on that remote, lonely, purple point, beyond which was the land of lost sunsets.

I have seen few more beautiful sights than a sea-sunset off that point. Of late years a new charm has been added to it—a revolving light which, as seen from here, flashes on the point in the dusk of summer nights like a beacon

O'er the foam
Of perilous seas in fairylands forlorn.[1]

The wreck of the *Marcopolo* occurred within my own remembrance. I was only seven years old[2] but I have a very vivid recollection of the dramatic event, and of the exciting summer that followed it—a summer so different from the usual quiet, sleepy summer of Cavendish.

The *Marcopolo* was a very famous old ship—the fastest sailing vessel of her class ever built, her record never having been beaten. She had a strange, romantic history and was the nucleus of many traditions, some reliable, others mere flights of fancy, or pertaining to other ships. She had finally been condemned in England, under the Plimsoll Bill.[3] Her owners evaded the bill by selling her to a Norwegian firm and then chartering her to carry a cargo of deal planks[4] from Canada. On her return she was caught in a furious storm out in the gulf; she sprang a leak and soon became so waterlogged

---

1. From Keats's "Ode to a Nightingale" (1819), lines 69–70.

2. LMM's son Stuart Macdonald corrected this in the typescript to "eight years old."

3. The Merchant Shipping Act of 1876 decreed that a mark on the hull indicated the maximum loading-level of a ship: Samuel Plimsoll had agitated for this kind of measure and designed the "Plimsoll line."

4. Fir or pine cut into 6-foot (1.8-metre) lengths.

that the captain—Mr. *Bull* of Christiania[1]—determined to run her on shore to save crew and cargo.

That day, the 25th of July, 1883, was a terrible windstorm here. We were in school; suddenly through the noise of the wind came the sound of a crash. The boys said it was a tree blown down in the woods. But to me the sound seemed to have a certain quality of *distance*—as if it had happened so far away that no crash of a fallen tree could reach our ears.

Meanwhile, although we did not know it, a crowd of people were already gathered on the sandshore, watching a magnificent sight—a sight I shall always regret not having seen—the sight of a large vessel coming straight on before the north gale with every stitch of canvas set. She grounded about 300 yards from the shore and as she struck the crew cut the rigging and the huge masts, one of them of iron, went over with the crash that we heard in the schoolroom a mile away.

The next morning the crew of 20 men got ashore. They found boarding places about the settlement and being typical tars, painted our quiet village a glowing scarlet for the remainder of the summer. It was their especial delight to crowd into a truck wagon and go galloping up and down the roads yelling at the tops of their voices. They were of many nationalities—Norwegians, Swedes, Dutchmen, Germans, Irishmen, Englishmen, Scotchmen, Spaniards and—most curious of all—two Tahitians, whose woolly heads, thick lips, and gold earrings were a never failing joy to myself and the little Nelson boys who were here then.

Captain Bull boarded here. He was a Norwegian, a delightful, gentlemanly old fellow who was idolized by his crew. He spoke English well but was apt to get mixed up in his prepositions and was as likely to thank you for your "kindness against" him as "to" him. The three mates boarded down at "Uncle Jimmie's."[2] Owing to the captain being here, the crew haunted the place also. I remember on the night they were paid off, seeing them all sitting out on the grass under the parlour window, feeding our old dog "Gyp" with biscuits and trying to pronounce his name—"Yip," "Ship" and "Schipp." Well and Dave and I saw, with eyes as big as owl's; the round mahogany table in the parlour literally covered with gold sovereigns, which the captain paid out to them. Never had we imagined there was so much wealth in the world. The whole summer was a series of "pictures" to me.

Finally, after an immense amount of "red tape" the business was concluded. The ship and cargo were sold to a St. John firm and Captain Bull and his motley crew took their departure.

---

1. The former name of Oslo, the capital of Norway.
2. James Macneill (1822–99), younger brother of LMM's grandfather; village poet and eccentric, perhaps the original of Emily's cousin in the *Emily* trilogy.

A company of men were hired to take out the cargo, most of them being people belonging around here. Eighteen schooner loads of plank were taken out of her. The planks had so swelled from the wet that it was found necessary to cut through her beams to get them out. Consequently she was soon a mere shell, with half her cargo still in her.

Meanwhile, I was having a delightful time of it. The huge cables, as thick as a man's body, were coiled in our barnyard and made the most delightful playhouses imaginable. Then came a big auction which was held at our barns. That was quite a tremendous day for us small fry. The thing I most clearly remember was that a big sail was spread on the ground in the barnyard and piled with "hard tack," to which all and sundry might help themselves. It was about as easy to chew as a board but it was all gone by night. If you could succeed in gnawing some of it off it had a very sweet taste and Well, Dave and I chewed away at hard tack all day.

One fine evening the wreckers decided to stay on board all night—a very risky proceeding. By dawn another furious storm was raging and soon the shore was lined with a horrified crowd. You may be sure that "Well, Dave and I" were on hand. It was a never-to-be-forgotten scene.

Almost everyone there had a friend or relative on the vessel but nothing could be done. It was realized that the ship must soon break up. Three of the men on her, mad with fear, got into their boat, despite the fact that it had been "stove in" by the waves, and tried to reach shore. Of course the boat was instantly swamped. Two of the men managed to regain the wreck. The third was drowned before our eyes.

Suddenly the ship parted in two at the forecastle head and went down. But the windlass and a small piece of bow still remained, held by the anchors and the men clung to this.

Meanwhile the beach was a sight to behold, heaped with deal plank for miles.

By evening the storm abated somewhat and a rescue party contrived, at much risk, to reach the wreck and bring ashore the exhausted sufferers.

Soon after, in another gale, the last vestige of the old ship disappeared. Divers were brought over to try to raise her copper bottom, valued at $10,000.

Geo. R.'s place

They could not do it; it is there yet, covered from sight by the drifting sand, and there it will probably remain until "the sea gives up its dead."[1]

---

1. From the prayer for the burial of the dead at sea.

There are many Marcopolo relics around Cavendish to this day. George R. has the name board on one of his barns and is therefore frequently referred to as "Marcopolo George." There are also many gate posts of the enduring pitch-pine of her masts—two of them in our barnyard to this day.

Our barnyard

Tonight I watched the flashing light on my mysterious headland and thought over all those "old, forgotten, far-off things,"[1] gleaming in the light that never was on sea or land.[2]

Friday, June 4, 1909
Cavendish, P.E.I.

Last night there was an eclipse of the moon. I had an hour of pure enjoyment watching it. I have always found a wonderful fascination in eclipses. No matter how many I have seen I am always just as interested in a new one as if I had never seen one before. To watch that strange dark shadow creeping over the brightness, slowly, steadily, relentlessly, until the whole disc is covered and glows redly through it, like the smouldering ember of a burned-out world! Then to see it retreating, vanquished, and the "orbed maiden" coming out radiantly, and calmly from her ordeal by darkness! Oh, one feels, as Emerson says, that one has been present at the creation of light and of the world.

I have always loved the moon. I suppose everybody does. We owe far more to the sun; in fact for all practical and essential purposes, we could get along quite as well without the moon altogether, while the loss of the sun would mean the extinction of our very lives. Yet nobody feels any particular affection for the sun. It is the moon we love. Her cold, silvery light irradiates the pages of old romance. Her never ceasing changes have all the charm of variety in a beautiful woman. There is no more exquisite sight in the universe than a young moon in a sunset sky. I have seen some new moons setting over dark hills that I shall remember in the halls of eternity.

And the magic of moonlight—the evasive, white-woven enchantment of moonlight—ah, we have all been intoxicated with it now and again—we

---

1. Misquoted from "old, unhappy, far-off things" in William Wordsworth's "The Solitary Reaper" (1805).

2. From Wordsworth's "Elegiac Stanzas" (1805), line 15.

have all walked in a world of faery "with the moon's beauty and the moon's soft pace."

Saturday, June 5, 1909
Cavendish, P.E.I.

This afternoon I spent at Russell Macneill's. It is necessary that I do these things occasionally—and how I dislike them!

I dislike—as I have always disliked—the country custom of going somewhere to "spend the afternoon." It is very seldom that it is anything but dull; and at Russell's it is worse than dull. Russell is a typical "clodhopper." His wife is a stupid, petty-minded woman. They are people with whom I have nothing in common. Yet I have to visit them now and again, else they would be offended. And that would not do, grandmother has to get Russell to haul her coal for her and do various other things which Uncle John refused to do for her. Hence, for her sake, I have to keep on friendly terms with people in whose company I find not one spark of interest or congeniality—people who can talk nothing but gossip and not

Russell and Mrs. Russell

even entertainingly of that. For gossip is *sometimes* interesting, if it is skilfully and delicately handled; but when it is infused with misunderstanding and jealousy and spite—Good Lord, deliver us! It is dreadful to visit at a place where you have to say every word over to yourself before you utter it aloud to make sure it is harmless and won't involve you in mischief if reported elsewhere.

Saturday, June 25, 1909
Cavendish, P.E.I.

Tonight I had to go to a choir practice. I have been going to choir practices for six years and I do not think I have grumbled to you—or anyone about it. But tonight I *must* grumble—and so get those six years out of my system.

Choir practice is one of the most unpleasant duties I have to fulfil. Six years ago, when the former organist went away, I had to step into her place. I say *had* to. There was absolutely no one else in the church who could play the organ at that time and although I was bitterly averse to becoming organist I was urged by minister and choir until I was driven to consent.

I have always disliked the position. I have no real musical gift and so feel like "a square peg in a round hole." Still, the playing of simple hymns and Psalm tunes on Sunday does not demand any great talent and I do not so much dislike *that*. It is the choir practice I dislike. Some of the members of the choir are no friends of mine and I always feel the atmosphere disagreeable. Some of them are no friends of each other and are always getting slighted or offended. In the winter I have to walk long distances alone to the practices. Yes, I hate it all. I look forward to every practice night with aversion. It is so apt to be disagreeable in one way or another. Tonight it was especially so. Uncle John's daughter "Tot," an impudent, ill-bred girl, justly disliked by all the members of the choir was, as usual, a disturbing element and annoyed everybody.

Wednesday, June 30, 1909
Cavendish, P.E.I.

I was away picking strawberries this evening down the shore lane—a delightful occupation truly, in a world of green grass and blue sea, and cloud curdled sky and breezy fields. I picked and was at peace with my soul.

June has been a very lovely month. Yet I am thankful it is over. For reasons connected with Uncle John's family I looked forward to June with dread and every day of it I have lived under the shadow of an expected annoyance. But it is over now and what I dreaded has not happened. Yet it might very easily have happened and the dread of it spoiled June for me. It is a shame to have a June spoiled. There is only one June in the year and to lose the delight of it through fear and worry is too bad. Shall I every again know a life free from *constant* worry and dread? I never wake up in the morning without wondering "What disagreeable thing will happen today?" And it is rarely that some disagreeable thing does *not* happen, either in connection with Uncle John's or with poor grandmother's unwise ways.

We are expecting Uncle Leander and Aunt Mary over soon and I am glad, simply because their mere presence takes a little of the responsibility from my shoulders. There are times when I feel utterly crushed under it. The care of a woman of eighty five, who is too old to act with judgment and too "set in her ways" to listen to any suggestion or advice is a serious matter. I never go out of sight of grandmother without feeling worried and anxious about her—I have seldom in the past eleven years known a moment untinged with care and worry. I am stating this not as a complaint but merely as a fact—as an explanation of my position and condition. I never complain elsewhere—to the world I keep my usual front of silence and smiles. But there are times when I must have a little outburst in this journal to save me from breaking out somewhere else.

July 11, 1909
Cavendish, P.E.I.

Today I finished reading Keats' poems. I got the book in March and have been reading so many pages per day ever since. On the whole, I do not like Keats. Perhaps if I had known him in childhood I might have so grown up with him as to love him, tinging his lines with the hues of my own life as I lived it. But I did not and he comes to me too late.

It is not because I find his poems lacking in beauty that they leave me indifferent. They are, in reality, *too full of beauty*. One feels stifled in roses and longs for a breath of frosty air or the austerity of a mountain peak towering to the stars. There is little in Keat's poems except luscious beauty—so much of it that the reader is surfeited. At least, that is how they affected me.

This is not to say that Keats has *no* lines that appeal to me. I found them rarely but some I did find, and for those few rare lines I admit him a great poet—and he would have been as great a poet if he had never written anything except those lines. There is the oft-quoted stanza about,

> Magic casements opening on the foam
> Of perilous seas in fairylands forlorn[1]

which has in it some indefinable witchery that never fails to charm, even when quoted for the thousandth time. And I found three other lines, never quoted—at least; I have never heard or seen them quoted—which are as a gleaming star of exquisite truth shining down from a far crystal sky on the languid loveliness of the rose garden:

> He ne'er is crowned
> With immortality who fears to follow
> Where airy voices lead.[2]

True, most true! We must follow our "airy voices"—follow them through bitter suffering and discouragement and darkness, through doubt and disbelief, through valleys of humiliation and over mountains delectable where sweet things would lure us from our quest—ever and always must we follow them if we would reach the "far-off dime event" and look out thence

---

1. From Keats's "Ode to a Nightingale" (1819).

2. From Keats's "Endymion" (1818).

over to some fair, fadeless land of promise—to the aerial spires of some City Beautiful—*our* City of Fulfilment, whatever it may be.

Aug. 1, 1909
Cavendish, P.E.I.

This evening I spent in Lover's Lane. How beautiful it was—green and alluring and beckoning! I had been tired and discouraged and sick at heart before I went to it—and it rested me and cheered me and stole away the heartsickness, giving peace and newness of life.

I owe much to that dear lane. And in return I have given it love—and fame. I painted it in my book: and as a result the name of this little remote woodland lane is known all over the world. Visitors to Cavendish ask for it and seek it out. Photographs of its scenery have appeared in the magazines. The old lane is famous.

Lover's Lane

September 1, 1909
Cavendish, P.E.I.

My new book "Anne of Avonlea" came today. We very soon become used to things. When my first book came to me I was much excited and half intoxicated with joy. But the new book only interested me mildly. I liked its "get up" and glanced over it with calm approval—and then went for a walk in the woods and thought no more about it.

I have dedicated it to my old teacher, Miss Gordon, in gratitude for her sympathy and encouragement in the old days. Whether she will ever see it or not I do not know for I have lost track of her. I have not heard from her for over three years and all my efforts to locate her present abode have been in vain.

September 4, 1909
Cavendish, P.E.I.

I have been reading Tennyson today. I like Tennyson, although I cannot think he is a supremely great poet. There is something lacking in him. He is very beautiful—not *too* beautiful, as Keats is—very graceful, in short, the Perfect Artist. But he seldom lets us *forget* the artist—we are always *conscious* of the art—we are never swept away by some splendid mountain torrent of feeling. Not he—he flows on serenely, between well-ordered banks and carefully laid out pleasaunces. And that is good. But an occasional bit of wild nature would make it better still. No matter how much one loves a garden one does not want to be cooped up in it *all* the time—one likes an excursion now and then to the waste places.

I detest Tennyson's *Arthur*! If I'd been *Guinevere* I'd have been unfaithful to him too. But not for *Lancelot*—*he* is just as unbearable in another way. As for *Geraint*, if I'd been *Enid* I'd have *bitten* him. These "patient Griseldas" of women deserve all they get!

Speaking to a friend once of Tennyson I said, "I *like* Tennyson because he gives me nothing but pleasure. I cannot *love* him because he gives me nothing but pleasure."

My friend did not understand the epigram. But it held truth. I love best the poets who *hurt* me—who offer me the roses of their thoughts with the sharp thorn among them, piercing to the bone and marrow. When in reading a poem I come across some line or couplet that thrusts itself into my heart with a stab of deadly pain—then is my soul knit unto the soul of that poet forevermore. Browning hurts me worse than any poet I have ever read—and so I love him most.[1] Even Wordsworth, "as soft as evening in his favourite May," occasionally says something so vital and poignant that I am ready to cry out with the agony of it—and so I love him too, in spite of his much balderdash.

But I think I shall have some love for Tennyson after this—for today I read a verse in *In Memoriam* which I do not think I can ever have read carefully before—which scorched me with a sudden flame of self-revelation and brought to me one of those awful moments when we look into the abysses of our own natures and recoil in horror from the shapes of evil we see there,— as if, while treading over garlands, we had inadvertently peeped into a foul nest of knotted snakes.

The verse was—

> Do we indeed desire the dead
> Should still be near us at our side?
> Is there no baseness we would hide,
> No *inner vileness* that we dread?[2]

---

1. LMM had not included Browning in her list of favourite poets in college days.

2. From Tennyson's *In Memoriam A.H.H.* (1850), LI.

I stopped to repeat the question to myself and forced myself to answer it. Did I really wish *my* dead to be near me—at my side—*always*—to know all my thoughts and hear all my words and see all my deeds? No—no—no! A thousand shuddering times no! And in that admission was the shame and shrinking of the realization that I do or think things every day of my life which I would not be willing to have them know or share in.

Tuesday, Sept. 21, 1909
Cavendish, P.E.I.

Lover's Lane

This evening Oliver Macneill and I were walking in Lover's Lane under its whispering maple boughs and balsam breathing firs. The air was warm and wood-fragrant; the moonlight fell down through the boughs in splashes of silver. It was all very beautiful. But tonight I realized that I must walk no more in Lover's Lane with Oliver Macneill.

He is a second cousin of mine, home from Dakota on a visit. He came the first of the month and I have seen a good deal of him. There were a great many things in him I did not like, and several more that I laughed at but he was pleasant, companionable and, in some ways, interesting. It didn't occur to me that there was any danger in our friendship. I knew that he had recently divorced his wife on the ground of her unfaithfulness and that gossip reported him to be "looking for" another one—probably thinking that he might find a more satisfactory one among our simple unspoiled P.E.I. girls. And I knew that in the first week of our acquaintance he had shown some unmistakeable signs that he hoped to find her in me. But as I had snubbed all his advances and as he has since been paying marked attention to Campsie Clark I did not suppose there was any reason why I should not accept and enjoy the pleasant companionship which thus offered itself for a time in my lonely life.

Oliver Macneill

But tonight I found that I was again playing with fire. Oliver Macneill told me he loved me and asked me to be his wife. Now, I would not marry Oliver Macneill for any inducement that could be offered to me—I do not feel the slightest wish or temptation to marry him. So our intercourse must cease. He is one of those impulsive, passionate men who rush to extremes in everything and a further indulgence in our companionship might bring real suffering into his life. I don't want to do this. His love, springing up thus suddenly in a few weeks, cannot as yet have taken much hold on his nature and he will soon forget me.

There is another reason—and a humiliating one—why I must put an end to our companionship. Tonight I realized clearly that Oliver Macneill is one of those men of whom I have met a few in my life—men who, without being able to inspire in me one spark of real love or even admiration, yet have the power to kindle in me a devastating flame of the senses. I have a horror of feeling thus towards any man I cannot marry. It seems to me a shameful, degrading, dangerous thing—and it is. Tonight I thrilled from head to foot under the caressing tones of Oliver's voice and his physical nearness to me as we walked in that shadowy lane. *He* did not know or suspect this—I succeeded in hiding it. But the very repression of such intense feeling made it burn more fiercely. I was ashamed of it—and yet, too, I knew there was in it

> The poison and the sting
> Of things too sweet.[1]

It *was* sweet, with all the deadly sweetness of the pleasures of sense, blent with the spiritual charm of the moonlight and the whispering shadows.

Oliver took my answer hardly and pleaded passionately, but I do not think there is much lasting harm done as far as he is concerned. I think he is a man who falls in love easily and quickly, loves wildly for the time being, and gets over it just as easily and quickly.

He is a curious compound psychologically—an odd mixture of the most contradictory characteristics.

And must not the same thing be said of myself? Do not extremes meet in my nature also? Can it be that the woman who stood on the shore last night and felt her very soul caught up to the seventh heaven in an unspeakable rapture of pure aspiration and unearthly joy be the same woman who walked in Lover's Lane tonight and burned with the wild flame of sense that scorched me? How can such things be? Is it because the higher the tree reaches towards the stars the deeper must its roots strike into the soil of earth? Perhaps that is the explanation.

---

1. From Adelaide Procter's poem *"Per Pacem ad Lucem"* (1892).

October 13, 1909
Cavendish, P.E.I.

Today Oliver Macneill left on his return to Dakota.

These last three weeks have been a species of nightmare to me. There was no use in trying to avoid Oliver—he sought me out everywhere and came here almost every evening. I had to go out walking with him or he would have made a scene before anyone who happened to be about. He would not take no for an answer. I have never seen such a reckless, desperate man. I think he tried every possible means to induce me to marry him, even to trying to bribe me with his wealth—of which it seems he has a goodly share. He made all sorts of absurd propositions—if I would marry him and live with him three months out of the year I could go where I liked and live where I pleased the rest of the time! If I would be his wife for *one year* he would take himself out of my life at the end of the time etc.

At last, however, I convinced him that he was wasting his breath. He is gone—and the whirlwind of passion that has so suddenly swept over my life will speedily die away. I know that and am glad of it. Yet just at this moment there is something in me that is crying out for him with a hideous desire and longing. My higher self is thankful he is gone; but my lower self is writhing in agony and would leap up with a fierce joy if Oliver were at this instant to appear before me.

October 20, 1909
Cavendish, P.E.I.

Thank God, I am my own woman again—and wondering at myself! I feel as if some evil demon had been exorcised out of me. For the past week I have lived in an anguish of smothered emotion. And then, all at once, it was as if a fever left me—as if some unclean spirit had been cast out. On my bended knees this morning I prayed that nothing like this might ever enter my life again. It costs too much to conquer it. The crushing down of such powerful impulses does a violence to Nature which is not slow to avenge. "Another such victory and I am undone."[1]

---

1. From Plutarch's *Lives*, Pyrrhus 21.

November 7, 1909
Cavendish, P.E.I.

This evening I walked in Lover's Lane—
and enjoyed it for the first time since Oliver
Macneill went away. For some time after he
left I could not go there. One evening I tried.
I got as far as the fence by Mr. Webb's field
and I had to turn back. A week later I made
another attempt. This time I forced myself to
go to the lane, for I knew that was the only
way to exorcise the memories that were spoil-
ing it for me. I went through it from end to
end in the twilight. Every step was an anguish.
Longing and loneliness possessed me.

Lover's Lane

But the next time was easier; and tonight
the lane was my own again and there was nothing in my thoughts or feelings
to come between me and the soul of the woods.

Sunday, Dec. 5, 1909
Cavendish, P.E.I.

We have had a week of dreadful weather—storms of wind, snow, and rain in
the earlier part, days of fog and mud in the latter. Today was very foggy and
dull. This evening I went to the shore but the air was so damp and the walking so bad that there was no pleasure. It was very different last Sunday night.
That was a beautiful evening, mild, gray, still. I went far up the sandshore
to the sea-run, walking in a weird, uncanny, twilight kingdom. The sea was
like gray satin afar out, but washed on the sands with little swishing ripples.
The sky was clouded, with rifts from which a strange, pale light shone. I was
shut in between the misty sea and the high, dark sand-dunes. And I was
happy—oh, so happy!—lifted far above all material or cankering things by
the intoxication of that wild scene—a scene thoroughly in harmony with my
mood. Yes, for two hours that night I was perfectly happy.

I am much better physically this fall than I have been for some time. I
have been, as usual, much worried, overworked mentally by reason of having nothing to do but work, and at times very lonely. But so far this season I
have had none of those terrible attacks of gloom and restlessness. In October

I was in town and consulted Dr. Jenkins.[1] I have been taking his medicine ever since and probably that is why I feel better. When I think of November last year I cringe. What a hideous month it was for me! I am very thankful indeed that this year has not repeated that experience.

Yet I dread the winter more than I can express. Grandmother is suffering so from rheumatism now. I feel so alone and helpless when I realize our position. Well, I suppose I have to live only one day at a time and one always seems able to do *that*. It is the "tomorrow" we can't live through! If I can only keep physically well and nervously unbroken I shall not mind anything else so much.

Thursday, Dec. 23, 1909
Cavendish, P.E.I.

So far this week has been a hard one. I must write a bit of a growl tonight to relieve my feelings. I fear I am going to be very nervous again this winter just as I was last.

I have been over-working of late. The Page Co. wish to bring out in book form a serial of mine which ran in a magazine last winter. It was called "Una Of The Garden." But it was not long enough to please them, so I have had to re-write and lengthen it—a business I dislike very much. I began it in mid-November and as it had to be in the publisher's hands by New Years I had to hurry. A fortnight ago I saw that I would not be able to finish it at my regular rate of progress, so I have been writing at it every spare minute since, until I would fairly feel faint with fatigue. But I shall have it done on time. Its name is to be changed to "Kilmeny Of The Orchard."[2] It is a love story with a psychological interest—very different from my other books and so a rather doubtful experiment with a public who expects a certain style from an author and rather resents having anything else offered it.

Monday it snowed all day. I wrote from morning until bed-time. Tuesday it snowed all day, I wrote from

May

---

1. Stephen R. Jenkins, M.D. (1858–1929), educated in Philadelphia, returned to Charlottetown and became a leading physician there. In 1928 he became President of the Canadian Medical Association.

2. Kilmeny was a heroine of Scottish folklore; her story is told in James Hogg's *The Queen's Wake* (1813).

morning until dark. Then I dressed and went with Alec and May Macneill to spend the evening with friends in Rustico. I was so tired I could not enjoy myself and as usual was worried about grandmother at home alone. We had an unpleasant drive home and I got snow-damp and chilly. I could not sleep when I went to bed and got up yesterday morning with a sore throat. It snowed all day and I wrote all day. My throat grew worse and at dark I had to drop my pen and lie down on the sofa. My head ached and I was feverish, and that feeling of dread and weariness I know so well again took possession of my mind. I hated the thought of going to bed. I knew I would not sleep and the thought of lying there in the darkness, feeling as I did, seemed unbearable. At last I resolved not to endure the darkness anyhow but to leave my lamp burning all night. I was afraid to do so, for grandmother often prowls about the house after night, to seek out the cause of mysterious noises she hears or fancies she hears, and if she were to discover my

light burning would think it a dreadful extravagance or would think I was up to some unlawful doings—and would never be able to sleep in peace again. But last night I determined to risk it. It was well I did for I had a bad night, sleeping fitfully with oppressive dreams, and then waking up in mental and physical distress. At such times it was a great comfort to *see* my own dear room, with my pictures on the walls and my books on their shelves.

My own dear room

I think I was a little light headed with the fever of my cold, for it seemed to me that the *sight* of those familiar objects was all that kept me from falling into some horrible abyss of strangeness.

Today it snowed all day. There is a great deal of snow down. No mail came. I wrote from nine o'clock in the morning until eight in the evening. My throat is still sore, but my headache is better and I hope I shall sleep tonight. But I am very tired and weary and sick at heart. Every morning I set my teeth to endure the day. Every evening I wonder how I am to face tomorrow. I am very morbid and nervous. I know it is mainly from lack of exercise and too-constant work. But what can I do? It is impossible to go walking in soft snow four feet deep. And if I don't work there is nothing to pass the time. I am so thankful I *can* work. I hope and pray *that* capacity may never be taken from me, for if it should be I would not be able to go on with life.

I have some lovely bulbs in flower. They are a great comfort and sweetness to me.

Christmas Eve 1909
Cavendish, P.E.I.

Christmas Eve! The very name seems like a mockery to me. A time of good-will and peace and rejoicing—and I feeling as I do! I must "write it out" before I go to bed, or I shall not sleep tonight—and I do want to sleep, for I haven't slept well this week and if I do not tonight what shall I do tomorrow—Christmas day?

As it was impossible to stir out I wrote all day. My throat is better but I am tired and spiritless. I forced myself to work because working is one degree *less hard* than not working. Of course I could not have done any original work but fortunately I had my *Kilmeny* manuscript ready to copy out and I wrote at it until my hand grew too stiff and tired to write more.

The mail came at dark—a heavy Christmas mail. It was full of Christmas boxes and greetings for me and the pleasure and excitement of these might have roused me out of my depression if a letter from Frede Campbell had not been among them, telling me of the serious illness of her father. Aunt Annie is as yet none too well, though better than last year; and I feel as if she and Uncle John Campbell were the only ones in the world to whom I can turn for any help in regard to grandmother.

My condition this evening alarms me—I feel so bitter and *vindictive*. I can't even cry—it would be a relief if I could. I know this is a morbid mood and not the real *me*—but it has me at grips for all that. I feel like a trapped creature, tortured by every movement, ready to bite savagely even at the hand of a deliverer.

In years past I asked of fate happiness and joy. Now all I ask is peace of mind and release from my load of care and worry. It is crushing the life out of me—and, worse still, it is making a bitter woman of me. I find myself tonight wishing that I had been born a hard, entirely selfish person, with no regard whatever for the feelings of others and no sense of duty or hesitancy in inflicting pain. That wish is dreadful. I *know* it—and I shall *feel* its dreadfulness when this black mood is past. But just now it is surging up in my soul and drowning out everything else.

I feel utterly *rebellious*. I feel tonight as if God were indeed the cruel tyrant of Calvin's theology, who tortures his creatures for no fault of their own at His whim and pleasure. I feel like shrieking at Him defiantly, "Why did you create me to suffer like this? Why did you thwart every wish and instinct and sensibility you implanted in me? I will not give you reverence or love any more than a creature strapped to the rack will love or reverence his tormentor."

Like Byron's *Cain*, I feel like saying that I could

> dare to look
> The Omnipotent tyrant in the face and tell Him
> His evil is *not* good.[1]

In days to come I shall read over this record with horror. But it shall stand—I shall always let it stand to make me more gentle in my judgment of rash deeds in others, when I recall the fearful thoughts that surged into my own soul, like some foul brood engendered in darkness.

My common sense tells me that all this is mainly the result of a week's confinement to the house and distressing conditions in that house. Very true. If this had brought about physical illness my common sense would indicate the cause just as truly. But that would not remove the illness—or dull the pain—or assist recovery.

Saturday Night. Dec. 25, 1909

Christmas is over. I am glad!

Last night I could not get the sleep for which I hoped. I had a wild fit of crying after I went to bed. Then I spent the rest of the night in fitful doses made wretched by bad dreams and a terrible sense of physical oppression. This morning when I wakened I felt as if I *could not* get up. Up I did get, however. I felt badly until the middle of the forenoon, when the feeling of dread and "blackness" suddenly left me. I was better for the rest of the day. In the afternoon I went to William Laird's where I had been invited for tea. I did not feel like going but I forced myself to go because I thought it might be better for me.

I walked down over a very bad road, through a dead, stirless white world, under a chill gray sky. I cannot say I enjoyed myself. There was in my mind and soul something cold and hard and bitter that prevented that. And to compel oneself to talk and laugh and jest when feeling wretched is not pleasant. But still I felt better for going. The brood of black thoughts that had infested my heart scurried out of sight when laughter and companionship shed light on them, as rats will hide from the light. I felt as if I had been released from the grasp of an evil thing.

---

1.   From Lord Byron's *Cain: A Mystery* (1821), line 138.

Sunday, Dec. 26, 1909
Cavendish, P.E.I.

We are in the grip of a terrible winter storm and will I fear, be all drifted up by morning. I am suffering from a very severe cold. I can hardly breathe, my head aches and a hard tight cough racks me continually. It would not be much wonder if I were nervous and depressed but I am not. I certainly do not feel very cheerful but the "black mood " is not on me tonight.

I passed the day reading and writing letters.

> I sought for shelter from cold and snow
> In the light and warmth of long ago.[1]

by reading over the journal of my schooldays. Some days this has a bad effect on me but it did not have today. I found myself dwelling on what was bright and happy in those old years and the better and more lovable qualities in those with whom I lived and mingled. I have temporarily lost the power of lightening present ills by looking hopefully forward to the future. Somehow I cannot do that now. If life yet holds any good thing for me it can only be reached by a passage through pain and worry and anguish of parting such as in my present condition of nervous weakness I shrink from intolerably. "Forward tho' I canna see, I guess and fear."[2] So it is easier to look backward to the sunny spots in the past.

Nevertheless, owing to my physical distress it has been a long day. This evening, as I paced the floor in the twilight, listening to poor grandmother groaning with rheumatism, I smiled rather grimly as I contrasted my lot with what the world doubtless supposes it to be. I am a famous woman; I have written two very successful books. I have made a good bit of money. Yet, partly owing to Uncle John's behaviour, partly to grandmother's immoveable prejudices I can do *nothing* with my money to make life easier and more cheerful for grandmother and myself. And there is so much I *might* do if I could—fix up this old home comfortably, furnish it conveniently, keep a servant, travel a little, entertain my friends. But as it is I am as helpless as a chained prisoner.

I think I have coughed once for every sentence written here.

---

1.   Quoting again from Lowell's *The Vision of Sir Launfall* (1848), 2.III.

2.   Robert Burns, "To a Mouse" (1787), line 46.

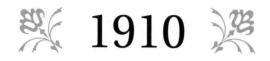

1910

Saturday, Jan. 1, 1910
Cavendish.

I always used to wish my journal "Happy New Year" long ago. Well, I will do so still. I cannot think the New Year will bring me much happiness. But if it brings peace of mind and capacity of good work I shall not ask more.

This has been a hard, dull week—such a week as we have not experienced since the stormy winter five years ago. All last Monday it stormed heavily and although Tuesday was fine the drifts were so deep that no one could move out. I was very ill both days with the cold. But all these things were bearable because I did not feel nervous or despondent—quite the reverse in fact. Had I felt as I did all the preceding week it would have been dreadful.

Wednesday we had four days' mail in one. We did not have any more mail until today, as we had another storm Thursday. Today I was much relieved to get a letter from Frede saying that her father was much better and that the worst is over. So that anxiety is lifted and I am very thankful.

But how I wish I could get out for a walk!

Thursday, Jan. 6, 1910
Cavendish, P.E.I.

I re-echo the wish with which I closed. But it is a vain one. At present walking is as much out of the question as flying. It snows a little almost every day and as a result I have been a prisoner all the week. It has not had a good effect on me. Tonight I cannot work or read and I feel indescribably wretched. I am again overcome with feelings of gloom, dread and unrest which I cannot conquer. Dr. Jenkin's medicine does not seem to be helping me as much as I hoped. A brisk walk in the open air, or an hour of cheerful conversation with some congenial friend, would help me more than all the drugs in the world. But both of these are out of the question.

We are having such a dreary succession of "dirty" days. It rains or snows almost constantly and we rarely see the sun.

I finished and sent off the MS of *Kilmeny* last week. I miss it for I cannot settle down to any work which requires concentrated thought. *Kilmeny* did not. I had merely to copy and amplify existing thoughts. I am making very poor progress with *The Story Girl*. The hours are rare when I am in a mood for creative work and I do not wish to spoil it by working at it when I cannot do my conception of it justice.

Tonight I feel that life is *too hard*—that I cannot endure it any longer.

Friday, Jan. 7, 1910
Cavendish, P.E.I.

Today I have spent on the sofa all the time I was not doing necessary work. I was too weary to lift my head. I lay there—and *thought*—and—*thought*. I seem to have been living over my whole past life today, from my earliest recollection. I have been haunted and tortured by old memories. I do not know which hurt the most—the pleasant ones or the unhappy ones. I think the former. My mood is very morbid. I wonder if it would do any good to write out all the recollections that have crowded into my thoughts today, like a series of pictures and sensations, at which I could not choose but look and which I could not choose but feel. Besides, I am always being bothered by publishers and editors for "information" regarding my childhood and "career," and it will be handy to have it all ready for them at the cost of copying out.

I have always had a somewhat remarkable memory—an advantage which, like everything else, has its shadow. I can remember when I was no more than twenty months old. As I have written before in this journal I remember seeing my mother in her coffin. She died on September 14, 1876, when I was 22 months old. But in July of that summer Uncle Leander and his family were here. One of them was my cousin Cassie, a child slightly older than myself. I remember sitting on the sofa in the room and seeing Cassie, in a white, embroidered dress, going through the hall door. I have

The mantel in the old sitting room

three other memories, which I think must have antedated this, but I have no means of determining just how old I was at the several times. In the very nature of them, however, they must have belonged to the first dawning of consciousness. I think they occurred before I could talk. On one occasion I remember myself in father's arms, being carried about the sitting room to look at the pictures and other ornaments. On the mantel was a glass vase with a border of deep scallops. On these scallops were markings somewhat resembling a human face. As father held me up to see this it seemed to me that the face on one of the scallops made a hideous grimace at me. I was terrified beyond endurance. I broke out into screaming and would not be pacified. I remember that terror—and *feel* it—vividly at this very moment.

The parlor where I was shut up

The second memory is similar in its nature. We had company to tea. I behaved badly in some fashion at the table and Aunt Emily took me away and shut me up alone in the parlor. It was very dusky for the slat blinds were down. I stood inside the door, a cold, terrified mortal, sobbing in fear and shame. Then it suddenly seemed to me that all the chairs in the room, headed by the big haircloth rocking chair, were dancing around the table in the centre, making faces at me as they passed me. Oh, the horror of it! I broke into frenzied screaming and I think someone came and took me out.

The third memory is of father taking me to town to be photographed. The photographer brought out a big fur robe to fling over the chair. Again I was terrified. I cried and screamed; nothing, not even the taking away of the fur, could pacify me. So no picture was taken of me that day. I am sure I could not *talk* at the time of these memories. I have no recollection of *saying* a word—only of things *seen* and sensations *felt*.

The first six years of my life are very hazy. I do not seem to have any *connected* memories of them. Here and there a picture like scene stands out in vivid colours. Many of these are connected with visits to Grandfather Montgomery's place at Park Corner. They lived in the "old house" then—a most quaint and delightful old place as I remember it. I recall in particular a certain long "back hall," with cupboards on one side and a window on the other. At the end of this was a short flight of steps going up to a little private sitting room of Grandmother Montgomery's. Out of this another flight of steps led down to Grandmother's bedroom. "Grandmother" Montgomery was my father's step mother. His own mother had died several years before.

Grandfather Montgomery   Grandmother Montgomery

It was there, when I was about five or six that I had typhoid fever. I remember it very distinctly. The night before I took ill I was out in the kitchen with the servants. I was sitting before the stove—an old "Waterloo"—and the cook was "riddling" the fire with a long straight bar of iron used for that purpose. She laid it down on the hearth and I promptly picked it up, intending to do some "riddling" myself—an occupation I much liked, loving to see the glowing red embers fall down on the black ashes.

[L.M. Montgomery as a child]

Alas, I picked the poker up by the wrong end! As a result my hand was terribly burned. It was my first initiation into physical pain—at least the first of which I have any recollection. I suffered horribly and cried bitterly, yet I took considerable satisfaction out of the commotion I had caused. For the time being I was splendidly, satisfyingly important. Grandfather scolded the poor, distracted cook. Father entreated that something be done for me; frenzied folks ran about suggesting and applying a score of different remedies. One of these—to hold the burned hand in a saucer of kerosene oil—made the burn far worse. Finally I cried myself to sleep, holding my hand and wrist in a pail of cold water—the only thing that gave me any relief.

In the morning I wakened with a headache. Father dressed me and carried me out to the breakfast table. I could not eat and began to cry. They took me into the little bedroom off the sitting room and put me to bed. I remember nothing more of my hand. It was well long before I was. I had typhoid fever.

I do not know how long I was ill but I was very low and several times they thought I could not possibly recover. Grandmother Macneill was sent for and came up. I was so delighted to see her that the excitement increased my fever and after she had gone out father, thinking to calm me, told me that she had gone home. He meant well but it was an unfortunate statement. I believed it implicitly—too implicitly. When Grandmother came in again I could not be convinced that it was she. No, *she* had gone home. Consequently, this tall thin woman by the bed must be Mrs. Murphy, a woman who worked frequently at grandfather's and whom I did not like. Nothing could convince me as to the contrary. From that out, all through my illness, I would not suffer grandmother to approach me or do anything for me—no, she was Mrs. Murphy and I would not have her near me. This was put down to delirium but it does not seem to me that it was. I was quite conscious of everything else. It was rather the fixed impression made on my mind in its weak state by what father had told me. Grandmother had gone home, I reasoned. *Therefore*, the woman who looked like her *must* be someone else.

It was not until I was able to sit up that I got over this delusion. One evening it simply dawned on me that it really was grandmother. I was so happy and could not bear to be out of her arms. I remember stroking her face continually and saying in amazement and delight, "Why, you are *not* Mrs. Murphy after all—you are grandma."

Everybody seemed very glad when I recovered. I think it would have been much better for me if I had died then. How much suffering I would have been spared!

Typhoid fever patients were not dieted so strictly during convalescence in those days as they are now. I remember one day, long before I was able to sit up, that my dinner consisted of fried sausages—rich, pungent, savory, home-made sausages. I felt hungry and I ate ravenously. Of course, by all the rules of the game those sausages should have killed me. But they did not. These things are fated. I feel sure that nothing short of predestination saved me from those sausages.

I remember a terrible fright I got the next summer. It was announced in a Charlottetown paper that a certain man who set up to be a prophet had predicted that the coming Sunday would be the judgment day. I believed this—or almost believed it—and my agony of mind was dreadful. I dared not ask the opinion of the "grown-ups" because I was almost as much afraid of being laughed at as I was of the Judgment Day. But all the Saturday before the fateful Sunday I vexed Aunt Emily to distraction by repeatedly asking her if we would go to Sunday School the next afternoon. Her impatient assurances that of course we would were a great comfort to me. If she really expected that there would be Sunday School she could not believe that the next day would see the end of the world. Nevertheless the next night and all Sunday was a period of intense wretchedness for me. Sleep was entirely out of the question. Might I not hear "the last trump" at any moment? I can laugh at it now—anyone would laugh. But it was real torture to a credulous child—just as real as mental agony in after life.

Sunday was even more interminable than Sundays usually were. But it came to an end at last and as its "low-descending sun" dimpled the purple sky line of the Gulf I drew a long breath of relief. The beautiful green world of blossom and sunshine had not been burned up. It was going to last for awhile longer. But I have never forgotten the suffering of that Sunday.

The next summer I began to go to school. I had learned to read and write before going and was in the "second book" of the old *Royal Reader* series in vogue then. I had learned the "primer" at home, and then gone into the second reader thus skipping the "first" reader. When I went to school and found out that there was a "first" reader I felt greatly aggrieved to think I had never "gone through" it. I seemed to have missed something—to suffer, in my own estimation at least, a certain loss of standing because I had never had it. To this day there is a queer, absurd regret in my soul that I missed that first reader when all the other children had it.

However, there I was in the Second Reader; and I remember—with a little thrill to this day—the compliment the teacher paid me on my reading—the

Cavendish School, but rebuilt after my time. Originally it had only two large low windows on each side and the roof was lower.

first compliment I have any recollection of receiving. We were standing up in the side aisle and our lesson was the immortal rhyme, "How Doth the Little Busy Bee."[1] We all read in turn and then "the master" said of me, "This little girl reads better than any of you, although she is younger and has never been to school before." How my heart swelled! Truly, the trite old words of the trite old song are as true as most trite things are—"Kind words can never die."

I have no especial remembrance of my first day in school. Aunt Emily took me down to the schoolhouse—which was just outside our gate—and gave me into the charge of some of the "big girls" with whom I sat that day. The next morning I was late. Very shyly I slipped into the schoolroom and sat down beside one of the "big" girls—Pensie Macneill, I think. At once a wave of laughter rippled over the school.

I had come in with my hat on!

As I write, the fearful shame and humiliation I endured at that moment rushes over me again. I felt that I was a target for the ridicule of the universe. Never, I felt certain, could I live down such a terrible mistake. I crept out to take off my hat, a crushed morsel of humanity.

The big girls—they were ten years

The school woods

old and seemed all but grown-up to me—soon tired of my novelty and I gravitated down to my own age. That first summer I sat in the front seat with

---

1. First line of Isaac Watts's "Against Idleness and Mischief" (1715).

Maud Woodside. Mimie[1]—short for Jemima—Kesley also sat with us for a short time. We "did" sums and learned the multiplication table and wrote copies and read lessons and repeated spellings. At recess we played for the most part in the "bush." I shall always be thankful that my school was near a grove—a spruce grove with winding paths and treasure trove of ferns and mosses and violets. It was a better educative influence in my life than the lessons learned at the desk in school. And there was a brook in it, too—a delightful brook with a big, deep clear spring where we went for buckets of water. It was a great treat to be allowed to "go for a bucket" of water.

We had playhouses in the bush—two or three girls sharing one between them. And great was the rivalry between the various establishments in broken dishes, mossed cupboards and stone seats. We picked gum, too, which the teacher remorselessly confiscated when he saw us chewing it.

My first teacher was Kaye Ross. I went to him only a few days as I had begun going near the close of the school year. He was followed by George Simpson who taught only till New Year's. I remember nothing at all of him and very little of his successor—a man named Lamont, who had red hair, *whiskers*—also red—and a *wife*. That a schoolmaster should have whiskers and a wife seemed two uncanny and unnatural things to those of us who were used to the beardless youths in their teens who had been the Cavendish pedagogues.

I remember very little of Mr. Lamont beyond his red side-whiskers and the fact that he tried to make me, a child of seven, learn off by heart the long complex formulae in the arithmetic. They were totally incomprehensible to me and he might as well have tried to make me memorize Greek. But at the time I supposed, with a seven year old's pathetic faith in the wisdom of grown-ups, that he was quite right in trying to make me learn them. But now I feel indignation and contempt for a man who would set a child a task so impossible—and useless if possible! I can't imagine what his motive was. No other teacher ever thought of such a thing. Even Lamont himself never asked any of the other children to do it.

In the winter following my seventh birthday Aunt Emily married and went away. I remember her wedding as quite an event, as well as the weeks of mysterious preparations beforehand and all the baking and "frosting" of cakes that went on. Aunt Emily was only a girl then but in my eyes she was as old as all the grown-ups. I had no conception of age then. Either you were grown-up or you were not—that was all there was about it.

The wedding was one of the good, old-fashioned sort—all the big "connection" on both sides being present, the ceremony at seven o'clock,

---

1. This appears to be "Minie" in LMM's journals. Unclear if it's an error.

supper immediately afterwards, dancing and games until the wee sma's,[1] and another big supper at one o'clock. Aunt Emily was dressed in brown silk. A silk dress was a great rarity in those days and nobody expected to have more than one in a lifetime. My mother's was a bright green silk. To my mind it was very ugly; but I believe it was thought very handsome at the time. It was trimmed with bands of green satin and green fringe. And the skirt was very voluminous. Aunt Emily's, eight years later, was furnished out with pleatings and flounces and overskirt. And it had a train, with a white ruching sewed all around it! Of course she had a bonnet. Whenever a young girl was married in those days she immediately donned a bonnet, no matter if she were still in her teens. It was not until five years later that this fashion died out. I was about twelve when the last bride wearing a bonnet "appeared out" in Cavendish church. It was a bonnet of brown silk with "drab" bows and long satin ties. Aunt Emily's bonnet was of black jet[2] with a white feather. It seems absurd enough now; yet those dressy little bonnets were very becoming to fresh young faces; and nothing is ridiculous when it is the custom!

Her bridesmaid was Grace Macneill, also arrayed in brown silk. Uncle John Montgomery was a great favourite of mine. He was a kind, generous, open hearted man. Aunt Emily's wedding was the last festivity in this old house. With her went all the social life that had ever centred here. Grandfather and grandmother were left to settle into the indifferent routine of age and I to grow up in that routine.

The next summer Mr. Lamont went away and William McKay came. I have very little recollection of the year he taught here, as far as school goes and, in spite of the fact that he boarded here for the first six months I remember little of his personality. I could not have disliked him however, or I should remember it. Neither could I have been much attracted to him. We "small fry" did not come in for much notice from the teachers then, so they made no great impression on us. He was a very dark, black-haired, thick-browed man, commonly known as "Bill Buffer," from the fact that his father

Will McKay in later life

who lived at Clifton was known as "Buffer" McKay—to distinguish him from the many other McKays there.

To digress for a moment—the subject of those McKays was a humorous one. I remember having heard that when father kept store at Clifton

---

1. Scottish dialect: very early morning.

2. Polished black lignite used as beading.

there was *twenty six* William McKay's on his books. To differentiate so many of the same, name nicknames were resorted to, some of which were ludicrous enough. "Geordie Bain," "Geordie Squires," "Geordie Bush," "Geordie Creek" were all legally George McKay. Sandy Long Jim and Sandy Big Tom were others. They were never spoken of in any other way. It is a matter of record that a minister in Clifton once gravely called upon "Alexander Big Jim" to lead in prayer! And Alexander Big Jim as gravely complied. Nobody even smiled.

To return to our mutton[1]—that is, the year Mr. McKay taught here. Time was then reckoned in Cavendish by the year of the reigning pedagogue, much after the fashion of ancient Rome with her consuls.

That was the summer the *Marcopolo* came ashore and the Nelson boys came here to board. It was a very happy summer for me. There was so much going on—so much excitement—that I was left pretty much alone and not teased or nagged. I had constant playmates, too, for the first time, and this was rare good fortune. I have described my life with the Nelson boys elsewhere in this journal, so there is no need to repeat it here. But those three years of their stay in Cavendish comprise the brightest and happiest memories of my childhood—unclouded memories, for we never had a quarrel in all those three years and we *did* have fun in abundance—simple, wholesome fun, with our playhouses and swings, our games in the beautiful summer twilights when we ranged happily through fields and orchards, or in the long winter evenings by the fire.

After Mr. McKay went away Mr. Fraser came. He was a boyish young fellow and boarded here. He was not a successful teacher for he could not control the big turbulent boys, as old as himself, who attended then. But we little folk loved him because he was so good and kind to us. Soon after he came he created an enormous sensation by offering prizes. How excited we all were! I made up my mind to win the prize in my class—offered to the one who was "head oftenest." I *did* win it and I have it yet. It was a volume of delightful fairy tales and even yet I can read them with pleasure.

Early in the winter following my ninth birthday I took a severe cold which settled on my lungs. I was miserable all winter and did not go to school. I was not allowed to go outside the door—somewhat different from the present day method of treating lung troubles!

Father was home that winter and spent much of his time here. His visits were periods of unclouded delight for me. He had come home from the West after a three years' absence and remained home till March, when he went west again leaving his native Island forever although he knew it not.

---

1. Gallicism: to get back to the subject.

Apart from father my principal pleasures were dolls and books. Of dolls I had quite a family and I was very fond of playing with them. I had two "china" ones and three wax ones. One of the china ones had half her head broken off and the other had lost an arm. But how I loved them for their very misfortunes! One of the wax dolls was a small one I had found in my stocking on my sixth Christmas. The second was quite a large one which Mrs. Cunningham, the aunt of the Nelson boys, had sent me. I was very proud of her because she was so beautifully dressed in red cashmere trimmed with lace, but I never gave her as much love as I gave my broken china ones. The third was a huge doll as large as a baby, also the gift of Mrs. Cunningham. I was proud of this doll because of her size but I don't think I loved her at all. All my dolls had very fancy names but I have forgotten them all except that of the largest one which was called Roselle Heraldine. I had a little doll bedstead which father had given me, with a complete outfit of sheets, pillows and blankets. I learned to sew, making patchwork quilts for my dolls, and I had a goodly supply. Then I had a little china tea set and a tiny frying pan and a little iron, all of which were a great source of pleasure to me.

But I was always fonder of reading than of anything else. There were not a great many books in the house but, as we kept the post office, there were generally plenty of papers and a magazine or two. And what books we had were well and often read. There were two, red-covered "Histories of the World," with crudely coloured pictures, which were a perennial delight to me. I fear that as histories they were not especially reliable but as story books they were very interesting. They began with Eden, went through "the glory that was Greece and the grandeur that was Rome" down to Victoria's reign. Then there was a book called "Little Katey and Jolly Jim"[1] which was much to my taste and a missionary book dealing with the Pacific Islands. The pictures in this book of cannibal chiefs with their extraordinary hair arrangements had a great fascination for me. *Pilgrim's Progress*[2] was read and re-read with never failing delight. Many a time did I walk the strait and narrow path with *Christian* and *Christiana*—although I never liked *Christiana's* adventures half so well as *Christian's*. For one thing there was such a crowd with *Christiana*; she had not half the fascination of that solitary intrepid figure who faced all alone the shadows of the dark valley and the encounter with *Apollyon*.

I am proud of liking *Pilgrim's Progress*; I am not quite so proud of the fact that I found just as much delight in reading Talmage's sermons.[3] That was

---

1. Children's book by an anonymous author (London: Nisbet, 1865).

2. John Bunyan's allegory (1678) about religious striving toward heaven; in Part IV Christiana, her children, and her neighbour Mercy go on the same pilgrimage.

3. Thomas DeWitt Talmage's evangelical *Sermons, Delivered in the Brooklyn Tabernacle* (1872).

Talmage's palmy day. All the travelling colporteurs[1] carried his books and a new volume of Talmage's sermons meant then pretty much what a "best seller" means now. It was not the religion in them which attracted me—though I liked that then, too—but his vivid word-paintings and dramatic climaxes. His sermons were as interesting as fiction. I couldn't read them with any patience now and Talmage is dead and discredited. But I owe him a very real debt of thanks for pleasure given to a child craving for the vividness of life.

There were not many novels to be had. Those were the days when novels were frowned upon. *Pickwick Papers*, *Zanoni*, and *Rob Roy* were almost the

The old sitting room

only novels in the house and I pored over them until I almost knew them by heart— I *did* know whole chapters of *Zanoni* by heart. Grandmother took a magazine called "Godey's Lady's Book"[2] and its monthly advent was a great event. I remember the preposterous fashion plates of bustles and overskirts which I thought very wonderful and beautiful. I used to pore over them, imagining myself arrayed in them, and firmly determined to have something just like them when I grew up. Mrs. Cunningham sent Wellington a monthly magazine called "Wide Awake"[3] which contained splendid stories. It possessed a distinct literary quality and was one of the best formative

influences in my childhood. The serials in it, by the best writers of the day, were a never-failing delight and the illustrations were almost as good.

Wellington had won Hans Andersen's tales as a prize and they were rare food for my fancy. I had a few "Children's Books" which contained much good reading for a child. Fortunately I could read anything I liked over and over repeatedly, extracting fresh interest and sweetness from it every time. In the long winter evenings, when the

The bedroom off the sitting room

---

1. Book-hawkers, especially Bible salesmen.

2. Best-known women's magazine (1830–98), offering sentimental stories, with coloured illustrations of fashions.

3. Founded in 1875 by Daniel Lothrop, who also published *Pansy* and *Babyland*.

fire was lighted in the sitting room, I sat and pored over my dear stories, while grandfather read his paper and grandmother knitted or sewed, and the boys studied their lessons by candle light out in the kitchen. They were very pleasant evenings and shine with a soft glow of beauty in my memory. But the thought of them hurts me unbearably in these sad moods of evenings so different. At 8 o'clock I was sent to bed in the bedroom off the sitting room. There I lay, pleasantly watching the light from the sitting room on the ceiling and dreaming waking dreams. For I had already begun to live that strange inner life of fancy which has always existed side by side with my outer life—a life into which I have so often escaped from the dull or painful real. It is one of the hardest things now, in these moods of nervous pain and sadness that overwhelm me that I cannot so escape, even for a time. The pain prevents the play of the imagination and holds me prisoner from that life of dream where I have roved in fairyland and had wonderful adventures and tasted strange sweet happiness unmarred by any cloud or shadow. Ah, yes, many a happy hour I spent, lying there on my pillows in the dim room. The memory brings bitter, stinging tears to my eyes as I write. It is not good to recall such things in my present mood of loneliness and soul-ache. "A sorrow's crown of sorrow is remembering happier things."[1]

That winter I first began to keep a diary and write "pieces" on "letter bills" and in the little yellow notebooks sent out by a patent medicine firm—Dr. Pierce's of Buffalo fame, to be precise. I owe old Dr. Pierce a real debt of gratitude! As I had no place in which to lock them up then and as I was very much averse to their being seen I used to hide them on two little "shelves" formed by two boards which had been nailed across the underside of the ends of the room sofa. I fondly believed nobody knew of the existence of these shelves but myself. They were soon packed full of MSS. I wish heartily that I had those same MSS now. They would be invaluable to me. But every year, as I used to read them over, some seemed to my maturing intelligence too silly to be kept. I was ashamed of them and burned them— as when I was about fourteen I burned all the "note book" diaries I had kept—something I shall always regret having done. They were quaint little documents, as I remember them—quaint and naive and painfully truthful and sincere, whether I wrote of my own doings or of others. Poor little diaries, long ago ashes, what pages of a child's life you were—a little simple life of dreams and childish pleasures. Not quite as happy as childhood should be—and as it might so easily have been—but seeming very bright now to my backward—glancing eyes, so used to the dullness and dreariness of my present existence.

---

1. From Lord Tennyson's "Locksley Hall" (1842), line 76.

I suffered a good deal that winter from my "conscience spells." I had described them before. When they came on I discarded all books except the Bible, Talmage's sermons, and a certain slim little volume entitled "The Memoir of Anzonetta Peters." I shall never forget that book. It belonged to a type now vanished from the earth fortunately—but much in vogue at that time. It is the biography of a child who at five became "converted," grew very ill soon afterwards, lived a marvellous patient and saintly life for several years, and died after great suffering at the age of twelve.

I must have read that book a score of times if I'd once. I don't think it had a good effect on me. For one thing it discouraged me horribly—for Anzonetta was so hopelessly perfect that I felt it was no use to try to imitate her. Yet I *did* try. She never seemed by any chance to use the ordinary language of childhood at all. She invariably responded to any remark, if it were only "How are you today, Anzonetta?" by quoting a hymn or Scripture verse. Anzonetta was a perfect library of hymns. She died to one, her last faintly whispered utterance being,

> Hark, they whisper! Angels say,
> Sister spirit, come away.

I dared not make the attempt of using verses and hymns in current conversation. I had a wholesome conviction that I would be laughed at and moreover I doubted being understood. But I did my best—I filled my little "diary" of the time with them—I even went Anzonetta one better and wrote out whole hymns, whereas she seldom if ever went beyond two verses. My favourite hymn of that time was one descriptive of heaven with the refrain,

> But what must it be to be there?[1]

I remember writing under this hymn in my journal, "I wish I were in heaven now, with mother and George Whitefield and Anzonetta B. Peters."

But I did not really wish it. I hated the very thought of it. But I believed I *ought* to wish it and so I tried to!

In the spring my health improved and after the spring vacation I returned to school. Vacation came then in spring and fall—three weeks to each. Mid summer holidays were unknown, except perhaps a week at the first of July. Before Mr. Fraser came we had only every alternative Saturday as a holiday. During his term the trustees decided upon what many people considered a daring and dangerous innovation—they decreed that every Saturday should be a holiday.

---

1. From the Hymn Book (1753) of George Whitefield (1714–70), one of John Wesley's Methodist evangelical preachers.

School life begins to grow distinct and interesting in my memory that summer. The great events of the year were the two semi-annual "examinations," one at Christmas, one at the end of June. Then the trustees and the ministers came to examine the school. Mr. Fraser was the first teacher under whom I took written examinations. We looked upon these as serious and dreadful things. I am afraid we sometimes cheated a little in them to the extent of asking questions of each other. We were always put in separate seats and all the text books were given to the master. But there were such things as notes. I don't think it ever occurred to us—or ever was told us, that this was dishonourable. It seemed a quite justified evasion of what we then considered the useless tyranny of written examinations.

I was never allowed to "go barefoot" to school, and as all the other children went so I felt keenly that this was a humiliating difference between them and me. I wanted to be "like the rest." I think it would have been wiser if I had been allowed to "go barefoot." My pleadings availed not. At home it was permitted under protest; but in school I must always wear "buttoned boots." Not long ago a girl who went to school with me confessed that she had always envied me those "lovely buttoned boots." Human nature, I suppose—always desirous of what it has not got. There was I, aching to be barefoot like my mates; there were they, resentfully coveting my buttoned boots!

Another thing that worried me with a sense of unlikeness was the fact that I had to go home to dinner every day while the rest took their dinners. *This* was rank foolishness on my part. It was much better and nicer in every way that I was near enough the school to go home to a good warm dinner. But it did not seem half so interesting as taking lunch to school and eating it, sitting in groups on the playground or under the tree with a bottle of milk that had been kept cool and sweet in the brook water. Great was my delight on stormy winter days when I had to "take my dinner, too." I was "one of the crowd" then, not set apart in any lonely distinction of superior advantages.

I do not think that the majority of grown people have any real idea of the tortures sensitive children suffer over any marked difference between themselves and the other denizens of their small world. I remember one winter when I was sent to school wearing a new style of apron. I think still it was very ugly. Then I thought it hideous. It was a long, sack-like garment *with sleeves.* Those sleeves were the crowning indignity. Nobody in school had ever worn aprons with sleeves before. When I went to school one of the girls sneeringly remarked that they were "*baby* aprons." This capped all! I could not bear to wear them—but wear them I had to, until they were worn out. But the humiliation never grew less. To the end of their existence—and they *did* wear horribly well, never getting any fortunate rents or tears—those "baby" aprons marked for me the extreme limit of human endurance.

I had nothing else to complain of in regard to my clothes. I was always kept nicely dressed and my clothes were generally pretty and becoming, though occasionally a little old fashioned owing to grandmother's inability to adapt herself to changing modes. *Materially*, I was well cared for. *Mentally* I had the power of foraging for myself to a certain extent. It was *emotionally* and *socially* that my nature was starved and restricted.

Child life, in a country settlement, is necessarily simple and quiet—and this, with some modifications, is as it should be. Life in Cavendish was markedly so. Day school and Sunday School made up a child's life. At the time of which I write Sunday School was as much of a social function—to us—as a religious one. We thought, I regret to say, quite as much of displaying our own good clothes and seeing those of our friends as we did of our lessons. Yet the latter were not neglected. We were strictly made to learn our "golden texts," our catechism questions,[1] and our "paraphrases" at home. I remember one thing that always puzzled me. The "Shorter Catechism" which was used in the "big" classes was five times as long as the one we used in our "little" classes!

Church where I went to Sunday School

The use of the Catechism has almost gone out in the Sunday Schools of the present day. This is deplored in some quarters but I think it is a good thing. I doubt if the memorizing of those dry formulas ever did anyone any real good. Certainly it never did me any. I did not understand the meaning of half I learned and it was never explained to me. Moreover, the Shorter Catechism teaches things that are no longer believed—and never should have been believed. When one comes to think of it it was a hideous thing to teach children the doctrines of "election" and "predestination." What a conception of God to implant in a child's mind! Fortunately I think I did not take any real hold on our minds. We did not comprehend the real meaning of the terrible answers we so glibly recited. The "catechism" was something that had to be learned, but its doctrines slipped over our minds like pebbles over ice, making little impressions.

I was not fortunate in my Sunday School teachers. They were three old maids in succession and their personality was neither lovable nor helpful to a child. One of them, I remember, became insane a few years later and drowned herself. Yet she was a kind, gentle woman and I liked her the best

---

1. The Presbyterian Shorter Catechism contained 107 questions and answers concerning doctrines and duties (the Anglican Church had 24), beginning with "Q: What is the chief end of man? A: To glorify God and to enjoy Him forever."

of the three. One of them was the homeliest woman I ever saw with a face spotted with moles and a pendulous lower lip. None of them did anything to make Christianity beautiful or appealing or even clear to me. Indeed, they rather prejudiced me against it, since they were "Christians" and I somehow had the idea that to be a Christian meant to be as ugly and stupid and—and—well, as *unromantic* as those "good" women were. They made me feel—and I believe that this feeling is still firmly embedded in my subconscious mind—that *religion* and *beauty* were antagonists and as far as the poles asunder. They gave me the same feeling towards it as they did towards matters of sex—that it was something necessary but ugly—something you were really ashamed of, although you had to have it—or go to hell! As for "heaven," I don't remember that they ever discussed it but I thought it was a rather dull though gorgeous place where we did nothing but stand around and sing. Not even my dearly beloved "what must it be to be there" could counteract this impression. As for the personality and teachings of Christ, I had as little idea of their real meaning as the young heathen for whom I occasionally gave my "five cent pieces" or went around collecting with a "Mission Card."

A pensive Sunday School scholar

But I liked going to Sunday School and would have been sorry to miss a day; and some of my sweetest memories are of those hours spent in the old church with my little mates, with our "testaments" and "lesson sheets" held primly in our cotton-gloved hands.

That was the summer of "Pussywillow and Catkin."

I have always been very fond of cats. I do not know how I came by the taste. Father hated cats, mother did not like them, and grandfather and grandmother detested them. They never liked to see me petting cats but did not actually forbid my having one. I had had several before this but I do not remember them very clearly. My cats had a precarious tenure of their lives. We had a dog "Gyp"—a nice old dog, with one very bad fault. He, too, hated cats and pursued them to the death! He killed several kittens for me. This summer when I got two kittens, a sweet little gray one and white one spotted with black I determined to keep them shut up in the granary until they grew big enough to defend themselves. I called them by the names I had found in "The Letter Box" of "Wide Awake" and thought very beautiful and appropriate.

I fear my poor little pets had rather dull lives in the granary. They were well fed but did not grow rapidly. But they were a great pleasure to me and I loved them both especially the gray Pussywillow—with all the devotion of my passionate little heart. For it is my doom to love whatever I care for with such intensity that there is as much pain as pleasure in my love. Catkin was a little too meek and pink-nosed to suit me but Pussywillow was the cutest little scrap of striped fur ever seen. By the fall they were allowed the run of the barns. But one bitter morning I found Pussywillow dying of poison, caused by eating a poisoned rat. My little pet died in my hands. Never shall I forget my agony!

It was the first time I *realized* death—the first time anything I really loved left me forever. At that moment the curse of the race came upon me—"death entered into my world"—and I turned my back on the Eden of childhood where everything had seemed everlasting. I was barred out of it forever by the fiery sword of that unforgettable and unforgotten pain. Yes, I feel that pain still as I write—the sickening soul convulsion and anguish with which I beheld my little pet's bright eyes glazing and its tiny paws growing stiff and cold. It is twenty five years since that day and the scar of that hurt is still on my soul.

I mourned my little gray playfellow longer and more bitterly than most human beings are mourned. I remember that I used to dream that it came

"Bobs"

back to life—and how bitter the awakening always was.

Catkin lived until the winter and then disappeared. I felt sorry over her loss but I had never loved her as I loved Pussywillow, and her loss was softened by the lingering hope that she was still living and would come back.

I decided that it was no use trying to "keep a cat" as long as Gyp was alive. Gyp lived until I was about twelve. Then he died and I grieved over that, too, for I was very fond of old Gyp. But the next spring I got a gray-and-white kitten whom I named Topsy—also after a cat in "Wide Awake." She grew up into a beautiful and intelligent cat and lived for seven or eight years. She finally "disappeared" the winter I was teaching in Bideford. One of her first "batch" of kittens was a handsome gray with white paws and breast. I kept him and named him Max. He was a dear cat but when he was about two years old he went away and never returned—the fate of so many roving Thomases. Since then I have had four pet cats—all grays, for I have come to think that

Daffy the Third

the only real cat is a gray cat! The first was "Coco," a pretty light gray, whose name I changed to "Bobs"[1] in a fit of hero worship during the Boer War. The second was Daffy, the First—a dark gray. Then came Daffy the Second—a silver gray, the dearest and handsomest cat I ever had. All these died of poison. When Daffy the Second died I felt almost as badly as I had felt over Pussywillow's death long ago. Now I have Daffy the Third whom I got as a kitten from Alec Macneill's. He is four years old, a very large, handsome fellow and stays home so closely that his days have been long in the land. I do not know what I would do without him. I would be ashamed to say just how much I love that cat. And he doesn't love me at all! There isn't a particle of affection in him. But he is so handsome that he is his own excuse for being and he knows more than would be wholesome in a human being but is quite lawful in a cat. He is fond of rocking chairs and cushions and has had a perfectly happy life, viewed from a cat's standpoint. Grandmother pets him almost as much as I do. Formerly she did not like my pets and seemed to resent the affection I gave them. But in these lonely, later years, neglected by her children, she seems to have changed in this respect and grown fond of the Daffies and almost indulgent to them. Well, there are many worse friends than the soft, silent, furry, cat-folk.

I like dogs also and would like to keep one but it is impossible under my present circumstances. There are so few things that are *not* impossible!

The summer after my ninth birthday Mr. Fraser went away and James McLeod reigned in his stead. He taught here for three years. We did not like him—at least, while he was here. He used to whip us very unmercifully. Everything was punished by a "cut" or so, across the palm, with a hardwood pointer. But he never wounded our souls with sarcasm and the physical pain was soon forgotten and forgiven. I cannot discover any bitterness in my soul towards him for it. He was a fairly good teacher in some respects. But I had not yet awakened to a love of study for its own sake. I learned my lessons because I had to and as I was quick of perception and retentive of memory this never meant much work to me; but I took no especial pleasure in it. My ambition was always awake however; it was a desirable thing to "keep head" and a terrible disgrace to "get down" in class.

As the school was large, "Jim" as we called him that behind his back— could not always overtake his classes. Consequently he often sent some of the older scholars to "hear" the second and third classes. This was thought a great pleasure. But we soon discovered that if "Jim" thought we *wanted* to hear a class we would not be asked to. At first he used to glance over the

---

1. Named for Lord Roberts, British hero against the Indian Mutiny, and commander-in-chief in the South African Boer War.

room and if he saw a pupil idling send him or her to take the class. But when he found that this was far from being considered a punishment he changed his tactics. For my own part, I invented a scheme which worked "like magic." When "Jim" called out the class I stopped work and gazed into vacancy. Then, when I caught his eye, I would snatch up my pencil and fall to "ciphering" furiously. "Jim" rarely failed to fall into the trap. Here was a pupil who was evidently *afraid* that she would be sent to hear a class for her sins. Consequently, that pupil must be sent and was. Trying to look cross and reluctant but inwardly jubilant I would go out to the aisle and proceed to "hear" the class.

Notwithstanding "Jim's" strictness, he could not be everywhere, or see everywhere, at once and we had much unlawful fun behind his back. A very fashionable game of the time was "knifey," played with a jack knife on the sod of the playground. Amanda and I used to play it in school hours, with a huge pin on our laps or on the soft wood of our seat!

We had many games for recesses. "Ball" was the standard in spring and fall but the summer days were too hot for it. Then we played "Knifey," "Jackstone," "King, King, come along," "Bar on," "Stepstone," "Little Sally Water," "Oh, Love it is a dangerous game" and "Drop the handkerchief." There was a large school and there was always enough children for real fun. In winter we played "Blind Man's Buff" in the school porch, or went coasting. We used to have some glorious coasts on the "school hill," Pierce Macneill's field and our "big hill field." Upsets added to the fun. How short the dinner hours seemed those days!

The Nelson boys went away that winter and I missed them much. The following summer Uncle Leander's boys, Fred and Murray, came over for the first time. I looked forward to their coming with delight for I expected

Fred

they would be Well and Dave over again. But I was disappointed. Not totally so in Fred. I rather liked him and in that and many following summers we were tolerably good friends, though we had plenty of quarrels. There were some very petty things about Fred, but on the whole we agreed. I never liked Murray. He was a selfish boy with a very exaggerated idea of the importance of Murray Macneill. Unless a girl bowed down to him and worshipped him he had no use for her. Unless you looked upon Murray as a wonder and flattered him unstintedly he did not care for you. I was much too independent—for this; the frank comradeship which I had felt for Well and Dave and which was all I could offer him did not please him. So we were never friends; and in the course of a few years, during which I had found Murray out in various mean and petty deeds and speeches, I grew to dislike him heartily and had as little to do with him as I possibly could. We would have had very little company if it had not been for the frequent visits of my uncles and aunts. Grandfather and grandmother seldom went anywhere and rarely had anyone come here. I was never allowed to visit anywhere save at Pensie's and Amanda's. If we had not had the post office very few of our neighbours would ever have been in the house.

But the family visits were quite frequent in those days. Uncle John and Aunt Annie Campbell, Aunt Emily and Uncle John Montgomery often came. The former were my favourites. I was always glad to see them, all the more if Clara and Stella came, too. Aunt Emily was less welcome for she generally thought it her duty to reform all my faults during her visit. And she was one of those unlucky people who would rather make others worse than improve them, by arousing a sort of impatient contrariness in them. But I liked Uncle John Montgomery very much.

Lover's Lane

Uncle Chester, then a lawyer in Ch'town, and Aunt Hattie came out two or three times a year. I liked Uncle Chester fairly well but I disliked his wife. Aunt Hattie was a cold, selfish woman who lived only to be amused. Uncle Leander, and his family always came over from St. John N.B. in summer. His second wife, Aunt Annie, was a very sweet woman. Uncle Leander generally brought a supply of novels with him and I used to have a glorious reading debauch after his coming. I was never quite "at home" with any of them, except Aunt Annie's family, but still their coming was always welcome, as meaning brightness and excitement of a sort.

A woodsy corner

Bridge where I caught my "big" trout

The summer of my twelfth year was I think, the first summer we had mid summer vacation. I lived much outdoors in summer. We—the Nelson boys and I, and, later on, Fred and I—were very fond of going trouting up the brook in the woods. It was on one such expedition with Well and Dave, one exquisite summer evening that I had my first walk through Lover's Lane. I enjoyed its beauty to the full, little dreaming how much it was to mean to me in after years. The two bridges that crossed it were capital trouting places. And there was another spot equally good—the Birch Pool under the roots of an overhanging clump of white birches in a woodsy corner. We fished with hook and line, using worms for bait. Sometimes I managed to "put my worm on" for myself, but I expended a fearful amount of nervous energy in doing so. How I hated it! The Nelson boys always put the worms on for me but Uncle L.'s boys were not so nice about it. I preferred to go through the agony myself than have it done for me with some jibe about my sex. But I loved trouting and often made good catches. I remember the thrill of pride I felt one day when I caught quite a large trout—as large as some caught in the pond. Fred Macneill was with me and I felt that I went up ten percent in his estimation. He respected me much more thereafter. A girl who could catch a trout like that was not to be altogether despised.

Next to trouting berry-picking was my delight—and to pick berries in "Sam Wyand's" field was the crown of delight. This field was "away back" behind "Jimmy Laird's woods." It was a veritable "beauty spot," almost encir-cled with thick, rustling maple woods which were thickly carpeted with ferns. We went to it through wood lanes fragrant with June-bells, threaded with sunshine and shadow, banked by green mosses. We saw foxes and rab-bits in their native haunts. And I have never heard anything sweeter than the whistling of the robins at sunset in the maple woods around that field. Oh, how the sweetness of those old days, when I was so near to nature, comes back to me as I write of them, and makes me homesick for them.

"Sam Wyand's field!" It was not a beautiful or romantic name in itself but it stands for exquisite beauty in my memory. The mere name calls up all the old loveliness connected with it—and I ache in every fibre of my lonely soul for the sweet, simple delights that were never marred or darkened by any past pain or fear of future shadow. To childhood, as to God, *all* is the present. There is neither past nor future.

That summer of my twelfth year was the summer Grandfather went to England to a great Exhibition held there. Uncle Chester went with him and Aunt Hattie and her baby stayed with us while they were away. I remember the delight and excitement when grandfather and uncle returned—the gifts and pictures and souvenirs they brought and the wonderful tales they had to tell. It was nice to have grandfather home again. In those days he was not so irritable and unreasonable as he became a few years later in the childishness of advancing age. There were many fine things about grandfather Macneill. He had a rich, poetic mind, a keen intelligence and a refined perception. He was a good conversationalist and a lover of nature. His faults were an irritable temper, a vanity that sometimes made him a little ridiculous and at other times smarted under imaginary slights, and, worst of all, an utter disregard of the feelings of other people—or, rather, a failure to realize that they had any feelings. He had no patience with anything that fell short of his ideals, and never seemed to have any conception how harsh and brutal were some of the things he said, especially to children. In some things he was very unreasonable and prejudiced. He was really very fond of and proud of all his grandchildren but he showed that fondness and pride in a very unwise manner. For example—he never said a kind or encouraging word to me; he said many sneering and unkind ones; and he constantly held up to me as paragons my other cousins. Consequently I believed for years that I was the only one of his grandchildren that he disliked. Later in life I discovered that he was just the same to them—saying harsh or sarcastic things to them and praising me—a proceeding which naturally aroused their jealousy and tended to make them dislike me. If he had only reversed the process—at least to the extent of saying his kind things to our faces and holding his tongue to others about our faults—he would have been a much more lovable man and would have exercised a much stronger influence for good over us.

The winter I was twelve father wrote me that he was soon to be married again—to a Miss Mary McRae of Ontario. I was delighted over the news. I fondly believed that I would have a real mother to love and be loved by. The many stories I had read of "cruel stepmothers" had not infected my mind at all. I knew only one stepmother in real life—Uncle Leander's second wife. No mother could have been kinder and more affectionate than she was to the sons of her husband's first marriage. She furnished my conception of a stepmother, and I thought mine would be like her. After father's marriage I wrote her affectionate letters wherein I poured out my childish soul to her and sent her pressed flowers from my favourite haunts. When I afterwards came to know the sort of woman she was I smiled at myself for the sentiment I had lavished on a creation of my own fancy. Such a woman could care nothing for my poor tributes of ferns and June-bells. But I was blissfully ignorant of this as yet. It gave me exquisite joy to search the woodlands until I found something I deemed perfect enough to offer her and I fondly supposed that she would feel on receiving it the same joy I had felt in sending it.

That next summer James MacLeod went away. All we girls cried ourselves half blind at his departure. All at once we discovered—or thought we did—that we were deeply attached to him. And truly, a tie of three years—three years is a long time in childhood—could not be broken without pain. But I think his affecting farewell speech, beginning "The time has come for us to part" had much to do with our lavish luxury of tears. Annie Stewart began to cry first and it spread from one to another like a swift infection, until we were all crying stormily. But our tears were quickly dried after all was over—as the tears of children ever are.

The trustees then engaged a "lady teacher." No "lady teacher" had ever reigned in Cavendish school before and wise heads were shaken in doubt over the experiment. "Izzie" Robinson was the one selected. There was some doubt for a time between her and another candidate; I remember that I was much delighted when Miss Robinson was chosen. I knew nothing of her; but her brother had once taught in Rustico and had been here once or twice to get his papers "signed" before grandfather, who was a J.P.[1] On one occasion he had helped me with my geography lesson so nicely that I thought him "lovely." I argued that his sister would probably be just as nice. I was doomed to disappointment.

Miss Robinson came here to board—literally forced herself on us, indeed. Grandmother did not wish to take her and only yielded to much entreaty on Miss R.'s part. It was a pity she did so. Grandfather behaved very unwisely in regard to her—very childishly. Yet there was something to be said on his side, too. Miss Robinson was a very inferior person, with a very exaggerated notion of her own importance. She could not "take a joke" at all, resenting it as an insult to her dignity. Grandfather was fond—far too fond—of teasing people—"giving them bars," as he called it. If Miss Robinson had been a different type—for example, had she been like her successor, Miss Gordon—she might have taken this in good part and won grandfather over. But she did not. She betrayed her petulance and resentment, and Grandfather took a dislike to her. He was not to be blamed for that. But he was certainly blameworthy for the way he showed it. His "bars" became mordant and insulting. He and she were constantly bickering. Miss R. vented her dislike of Grandfather in all her dealings with me, especially in school. She never lost an opportunity of lashing me with sarcasm—often totally undeserved—before my mates. She was the only teacher I ever disliked—and I did dislike her intensely. She would stoop to the pettiest deeds and speeches. One example must suffice. It was characteristic of her whole demeanor towards me.

We were in the class, "analyzing" a poem, verse about.[2] Clemmie Macneill was analyzing her verse. My turn was next and I was intent on the analysis of my verse, to have it in readiness; and, as was my custom in thinking over

---

1. Justice of the Peace: lay magistrate, appointed to notarize deeds.
2. Taking turns at reading.

anything, I was gazing before me into space, seeing nothing of the objects before my eyes. Meanwhile—as I was told afterwards for I was quite unconscious of it at the time—Clemmie came to grief over the parsing of a word in her verse. Miss R. accordingly parsed it for her. Then, I suppose, she happened to encounter my probably puzzled gaze; and I, amid my wonder as to whether a certain clause were adverbial or adjectival, was suddenly recalled to a sense of my surroundings by this biting remark, delivered in such a tone as only "Izzie" Robinson could use. "Well, I suppose *you* think that isn't right, Maud. That is what your face says. You have *a very expressive face.*" The venomous sneer of her last sentence is quite untransferable to paper.

I stared at the vulgar woman like one stunned, utterly ignorant what offence I had committed, unable even to say a word in my own defense. A giggle ran around the class at my expense. My soul burned within me over the cruel and wanton injustice of her attack—and it burns yet as I write. I should like to meet that woman today and tell her exactly what I think of her for uttering such a speech to a child who had not been doing or saying anything to provoke it. But this was only one of many such insults.

In March I went for a long visit to Aunt Emily in Malpeque. I had a very nice time and do

Aunt Emily's home

not recall ever having been lonely or homesick. The Malpeque people were noted for their sociability; there was always plenty of company; Uncle John Montgomery was very kind and jolly; and Maggie Abbott, an orphan girl who had been brought up there, was my companion. Despite the difference in our ages—Maggie was 18—we were "chums." Maggie's parents belonged to a low and immoral class. But Maggie herself was a sweet-natured, pureminded, sensitive girl. We had "great fun" together that winter and spring.

In May I came home to find, as before related, that Miss Robinson was gone, and I was not allowed to go to school. This was an unwise and undignified course of conduct on the part of my grandparents. It inflicted much needless suffering on me. Though I did not like Miss R. and though she would probably have treated me worse than ever, I still wished to go to school. I was interested in my studies. I was lonely and wanted the companionship of my mates. I was subjected to much mortification from the significant questions which were always being asked me. Altogether, that summer was a very unhappy one for me, made more so by a quarrel between Uncle John and Grandfather which lasted till the fall, when they were reconciled.

Uncle John was wholly to blame in the affair and ran true to form in his behavior from start to finish. But grandfather's lack of tact precipitated the quarrel. It made us all terribly unhappy.

That summer I began to take music lessons. As we had no organ I used to go down to "Uncle Jimmies," just across the road, and practice. My music teacher was a Miss Snowey, a very young girl who was not at all a good teacher although she had considerable natural talent. Later on, when father and grandmother between them gave me my organ, I took lessons from Mrs. Spurr. I liked the lessons and did not dislike practising. But now I think it was all rather a waste of time and money, because I had no real musical gift. And certainly, if I had never learned to play I would have been spared a good deal of annoyance and bother in later life when, by reason of being able to play a little, I have been forced or drawn into uncongenial and vexatious positions.

At the end of the school year in June Miss R. engaged to stay for another year—much to my despair. A year seems an eternity when one is twelve. It seemed to me that I could *not* bear another year of loneliness and exclusion from the world of my mates.

But in the autumn came good news. Miss R. was to leave at the New Year. Life grew roseate and hopeful again for me. The first day of the new teacher's advent found me in my old seat with Amanda, and oh, how happy I was! It makes my heart ache now in these hard days of monotonous pain and loneliness to remember how happy I could be and often was in those old days. I cannot conceive it possible that I could feel so now under any circumstances.

Hattie Gordon was a very different type of woman and teacher from Izzie Robinson. She was not faultless; but she was a lady, which Miss R. was not, and she had a certain stimulating personality which I have never found in any other teacher. She had the power of inspiring a love of study for its own sake and of making the dry bones of the school routine alive with interest.

What a worker she was! I realize that now, although at the time I took it as a matter of course. I owe her a great debt for the sympathy and encouragement she always showed me.

Miss Gordon was the first of our teachers to require the writing of compositions. Every week we of the advanced classes had to write one at home on a given subject, sometimes selected by ourselves, sometimes by the teacher. I revelled in this; but, naturally, most of the scholars detested it. The honour of writing the best compositions generally fluctuated between Nate Lockhart and myself. We had always had recitations on Friday afternoons and this—also dreaded by most of the pupils—was a great delight to me. With my flexible memory it was no trouble to learn a piece of poetry "off by heart" and it was a dramatic joy to recite it. Miss Gordon added to the ordinary recitations the variation of dialogues and songs, and we often had quite a little concert on Friday evenings, as well as much fun in preparing the dialogues. It was all very good training, too.

Miss Gordon it also was who organized a "Mayflower picnic" each spring. Delightful festivals they were. The school was large ranging from 40 to 50 pupils. This meant jollity and intellectual stimulus as well.

The Cavendish school of today seems to me a very forlorn institution. I feel sorry for the few children who attend it. There are only about a dozen in the district and half of those are French. They never seem to have any of the real, good, wholesome "fun" school children should have. They never play games—there isn't enough of them. They never coast or play ball or build playhouses. And they don't learn as well or as much as we did, for there is no competition to inspire them.

The year I was fifteen—and when I found myself fifteen at last I thought I was grown up!—was in the main a happy one, at least in its earlier months. True, I had little social life. I was never allowed to visit anywhere except at Amanda's and Pensie's. That was one of the Literary Society's palmy winters but I was seldom permitted to attend a meeting. Now and then I was let go to one, under protest, and always enjoyed it hugely. Miss Gordon took an active interest in the Literary and encouraged her pupils to recite or read at its meet-

The hall where I recited

ings. Finally I was asked to recite. I felt as I should now feel if I were asked to read before the crowned heads of Europe. I wished to recite because of the kudos of it—but I was very nervous and frightened. How anxiously I practised my selection—"The Child Martyr"—before my mirror! How excited I was when the night of the concert arrived! I remember every incident of that evening. How I trembled as I mounted the platform when my name was called out! How faint and faraway my voice sounded in my own ears! But, thanks to my faithful rehearsals it seemed to sound all right in other people's ears. Several of Miss Gordon's other pupils recited that night, too. I do not think we did her training any discredit. She was proud of us all and never hesitated to give her meed of commendation. I can see her yet, smiling on us, dressed in the brown velvet coat and smart little toque she wore that winter. She was considered to be very "dressy." We were always much interested then in what our teachers wore and how they dressed their hair. Miss Gordon had pretty hair, fair and wavy. Her face was not at all pretty but it was striking, and she had a peculiar and interesting smile. She had a very quick temper, easily roused by trifles, but she seldom voiced it. It was betrayed only in her suddenly crimsoning face and ominous silence. But it passed as quickly as it came. She was never sarcastic or vindictive. She made some mistakes as we all do, but they were not of the kind that last or rankle.

All that winter I was looking forward to going out to Prince Albert with Grandfather Montgomery. I was naturally much excited and delighted. I had never even been on a train. My heart thrilled at the idea of seeing father again; and at that time, filled with the impression made on my mind by my few trips to Ch'town, I thought it would be quite heavenly to live in a *town*.

We went in August. The journey out was an unqualified delight. I enjoyed every moment of it. But when I reached Prince Albert the glamor vanished. For the first few weeks I suffered from homesickness to a degree that makes me shudder even now. The discovery of what my stepmother was like naturally increased this. But in any case I should probably have suffered keenly, because it is my nature to love a spot where I have long lived very deeply and passionately and feel keen anguish when removed from it. Yet I did not dislike Prince Albert as a place to live in and after the first keen edge of my nostalgia wore away I liked it well enough.

I did not like the High School very well. Mr. Mustard was a very poor teacher. The pupils—three girls and six boys—were an odd chance medley. There was no system about our studies. I was far ahead of the other pupils in most of the branches, but far behind them in two or three. I had never studied—bookkeeping for instance. I do not think I learned one thing of any value at that school. But I might have got a teacher's certificate by spring if I could have gone regularly. But after Bruce was born I could not go at all.

I disliked Mr. Mustard professionally and personally—or it might be more correct to say that I felt a contempt for him. It has always given me a disagreeable feeling to recall that he fell in love with me and suggested marriage. I did not, and do not, consider that it was at all a compliment. He was, as we girls bluntly said, "A ninny and a bore," and I resented his clumsy attentions far more bitterly than I would have resented his dislike.

I did not care for, or find much pleasure in, the society of my stepmother's people except her mother, Mrs. McTaggart who was a dear old soul. Edith Skelton was a jolly companion and after she left the Pritchards were my friends and the only ones I cared much for. Laura's friendship meant a great deal to me that year. So did Will's. We had many happy and pleasant hours together, filled with the unthinking joy of youth. The few days I spent with Laura out on their farm were the brightest of my western sojourn.

In September I came home, travelling alone from Prince Albert to Ottawa—a girl of sixteen! I don't know how I dared do it. Yet I did not feel in the least dismayed or alarmed at the prospect when I set out. And I got along all right. I had plenty of spirit and dauntlessness then and I enjoyed my journey home.

Miss Gordon was still teaching in C. She got up another concert that fall and I, as well as some others, of her former pupils helped. It was a very pleasant affair all through and the concert was a success.

That winter grandmother went over to Park Corner for a week—the last time she ever went from home for more than a day. I kept house while she was away and it was not a pleasant experience in some respects for grandfather behaved in a fashion which I can only call absurd. He was always more irritable and unreasonable than usual when grandmother was away. He was lonely without her—which was natural but was no excuse for his outbursts of temper and his impatience with those who were trying to do their best. Nothing I did pleased him. If, by reason of inexperience, I made some little mistake he railed and sneered at me, as if I had done something really dreadful and inexcusable. I can never forget his tone, look and words on some occasions. When I try to recall him in his more amiable moods these more deeply branded impressions seem to obliterate all else. It was his *injustice* which rankled most deeply. When I really did wrong and was scolded for it, no matter how severely, I might feel badly at the time but it never left any bitterness. But to be stormed at or sneered at because of some trifling mistake or accident—for example, such as letting a bit of ham slip into the fire through the bars of a much delapidated old gridiron while turning it—*did* leave a bitterness that has never been effaced. I was glad indeed when grandmother came home.

Then I went over to Park Corner to give Clara, Stella and George music lessons. I did not dislike giving the girls lessons, but I could make nothing of George. He was a spoiled, headstrong, bad tempered boy and these qualities had been intensified by his parents' unwise indulgence. However, this meant only two disagreeable hours a week and for the rest we all enjoyed ourselves heartily. Our amusements certainly seem to me now rather crude and frivolous but they satisfied at seventeen.

Clara, Stella and I were just at the age when the opposite sex are more interesting than they ever are before or after. We each had two or three "beaux" who "saw us home" from meetings, took us driving and kept up a not unfriendly rivalry with each other over

Park Corner

George   Clara   Stella

our favours. I am very much afraid that we delighted in all this, and I blush to think how much we talked about those boys and how large a share "he said" and "he did" played in our conversation. We liked to be teased about them, too—oh, yes, we did! It was all very silly and harmless—if anything silly can really be harmless which I doubt. A wiser training and a different environment might have saved us from this silly age—but possibly not. I have since seen it manifested just as strongly in girls who had both advantages. It seems a sort of phase in natural development which few girls escape. At all events, we were in the thick of it that winter.

I came home early in June, was lonely for a week, then slipped back into my old groove once more. I had a pleasant summer though not without some troubled hours. In September I at last obtained grandmother's somewhat reluctant consent to study for P.W.C. and a teacher's certificate.

Selena Robinson taught here that year. She was a rather nice girl personally and we were chums. But she was a very poor teacher. Had I stayed home that year and studied by myself I would have got on just as well. I did not much enjoy going to school. It did not seem like Cavendish school to me. Very few of my old set were left. But outside of school I had a pleasant winter. The disagreeable things were obscured by the glitter of starry hopes; and I had a little circle of friends and duties which satisfied me then. The Literary Society and the Prayer Meeting were the only "social functions" and it was considered a great disappointment if a stormy night prevented one or the other. So I lived my double life, as it seems to me, I have always done—as many people do, no doubt—the outward life of study and work and social intercourse and the inner one of dreams and aspirations.

In July I went to town to take the P.W.C. entrance exam. It was an anxious time. I was so sure that my whole future depended on it. And when it was over there was a more anxious time still—three weeks of waiting for the result. I was very dubious and the longer I waited the more dubious I became, until I felt sure that it was impossible that I could have passed. I was afraid I had failed in arithmetic—and arithmetic was one of the "vital" subjects. If you failed in it you did not "pass" no matter what your other marks were.

Then one day the long agony of suspense came to an end. The papers came out with the list of successful candidates and I had passed well up. What a relief it was! And what a happy girl went dancing to the shore that night! I do not think it would be possible to feel *now*, no matter under what circumstances, as I felt then. Only youth can feel so.

In September I went to P.W.C. It was, I believe, the happiest year of my life. Yet it was not all sunshine either. I had a very poor boarding house. That room was bitterly cold and the table the poorest that could be imagined, the food of wretched quality, idly cooked and served, were the smallest of the evils. The MacMillan family were most vulgar and ill-bred people; the majority of their boarders belonged to their own class; the whole atmosphere of the place was the worst possible for a young girl in the formative period of her life.

These drawbacks, however, did not cloud my P.W.C. year very darkly. I was too young and inexperienced to realize what living in such an environment might mean, and the material hardships were borne patiently because I knew they were only temporary. It is wonderful how much difference it makes in the endurance of anything if we can believe that it is only temporary. Mary Campbell and I extracted endless fun out of our very tribulations. I remember Mary staggering across the room one day and pretending to faint because when we came home from college we discovered clean slips on our pillows—a *very* rare occurrence!

But there was nothing to mar the college side of my life. It was all a delight to me. I was happy every minute I spent in the old college, *except* when in the geometry class. I enjoyed my studies—and I studied hard. When the year drew to a close I was conscious only of regret.

They had a very barbarous custom in regard to exams at that time. Nowadays it is changed; but then the college exams and the "license" exams were entirely different things. At the end of the year we had a hard fortnight of college exams. Then, tired and fagged as we were, we had to go over the whole ground again in a breathless week of "license" exams.

The License exams that year were very hard—so hard that out of many candidates an absurdly small percentage passed. I shall never forget that anxious, driven week. But at last it was over; and how delightful and impossible it seemed to be free.

I came home but had a somewhat unhappy and anxious summer. It was so difficult to secure a school. The country was swarming with teachers especially the host of "third class"[1] ones let loose by the failure of so many candidates, who would take any school gladly for no "supplement" at all. Unless you applied in person you had very little chance of getting a school. This I could never do, as grandfather would not assist me in any way to secure a school, even by so much as letting me have a horse to drive to a district. I had to depend on written applications. I sent out dozens of them and tasted each mail day the bitterness of repeated disappointment when no answer came from any.

It was the last of July before I finally got the Bideford school. What a relief it was to me! With what interest I looked forward to my work. It seemed a great thing to me then—much greater, I suppose, than it really was. With a heart full of courage and ambition I packed my trunks and went to Bideford.

My first week there was a miserable one. I was bitterly homesick; I was unsettled and worried about finding a boarding house; and I found it hard to get my school organized and in running order. I was assailed by a horrible suspicion that I was not going to like teaching, after all my struggles to become a teacher. I used to be so tired and discouraged every evening when I got home from school that I could not help crying for sheer sickness of heart.

But that passed; and with the exception of that week my year in Bideford was a happy and hopeful and enjoyable one. I worked very hard in my school. I was enthusiastic and had many "ideals"—which suffered a good deal from contact with the real; but I was never wholly false to them nor they to me.

I had a large—a too large school—especially in summer. I had 21 in the primer class alone. But the majority of my pupils were nice and lovable. They liked me and I had the satisfaction of knowing that I was a successful "schoolma'rm."[2] I was also fortunate in my boarding house. I had a comfortable room, good table, and refined companionship. Mrs. Estey was a dear. In spite of her sixteen years seniority we were "chums." I did not like Mr. Estey. And to tell the plain truth I don't think his wife liked him either. But he was absent so often and so long on circuit visitations that he seemed to count for very little. He was inferior in every respect to Mrs. E. There seemed to be no affection or comradeship between them. They called each other "Mr." and "Mrs." Estey, even when alone and Mrs. Estey never seemed like herself in his presence. I had neither liking nor respect for him. He was a selfish, uncultured, high-tempered man who had had, and has since had, trouble on almost every circuit he ever was on. But he was, as I have said, away a great deal and Mrs. E. and I were very happy in his absence.

---

1. Refers to PWC graduates who had not successfully passed the teachers' license exam with first or second class standing. Elsewhere in this entry, "class" refers sometimes to a grade in school, sometimes to social standing.

2. An American derivative from "schoolmadam." ·

The worst drawback of the winter was the bad road I always had to school. A great deal of snow fell that winter. The road was never broken as all the travelling was by the river ice. I shall never forget some of those walks, especially when the spring thaws set in. I sometimes arrived at the school wet to the waist and had to spend the day in that condition.

Socially I had a nice time. Lou D. gave me plenty of pleasant drives and outings. But I have always been sorry that I went with him. I fear it did spoil his life. He was never married. I met him on the street in town last fall and hardly knew him, he looked so old and careworn. He walked out to Bertie's with me and when we parted at the gate he turned up his coat lapel and showed me under it a little "button pin" on which was a picture of myself copied from a photo I gave him when I left Bideford. I had not the heart to tell him that I objected to his wearing it even unseen. Yet I certainly did not like the idea. However, even if it were seen, nobody would recognize me by it now, so I suppose it does not matter. But it does matter that his life has been made unhappy through me.

But I could not foresee this in the Bideford days. I was only a careless young girl with a girl's liking for fun and frolic. It was country custom for the girls and boys to drive about with each other in friendly fashion and half the time it meant nothing. I do not now think it a good custom; but at the time I simply accepted it as a matter of course.

Yes, that Bideford year was a pleasant one, both as regards my school and my social life. It was, although I knew it not, the last happy year of my life.

From Bideford I went to Halifax for a year at Dalhousie College. I should have dearly loved to have taken the full Arts course. But that was out of the question. I could not afford it. So I had to content myself with a year in special courses.

Looking back on my life with the insight which comes from riper experience I think my going to Dalhousie was a mistake—a waste of time and money. I do not think I received any good whatever from that year as far as educational value went. But I did not see this at the time. I wished to go to Dalhousie for two reasons, of which perhaps the second was the more potent though kept very secret. In the first place, I thought a special course

In my Halifax year

in English, languages etc. would help me in my ambitions to be a writer and also help me to obtain better schools; and in the second place I hoped that it might be possible to find some entrance into journalism while in Halifax— "get on a newspaper" or something of the sort. This hope was disappointed.

No such opportunity came my way. And in regard to my classes at college I cannot see that I gained any good from them that I would not have gained just as effectually and much more cheaply in the solitude of some country school district with my books and my pen. If I had taken that money and taken a cheap little run over England and Scotland it would have been of far more value to me. But everybody of my home circle would have thought me crazy and extravagant to do that—I would have thought I was myself!

I did not quite like boarding at the Ladies' College. Accustomed as I had been for two years to much greater personal freedom I found the restrictions irksome and the unmitigatedly feminine atmosphere rather stifling. The girls who formed my immediate circle I liked passably well but I did not find in any of them a really congenial associate. Miss Clark was the only *real* friend I had there—the only one in whose society I felt really at home, or found any real satisfaction. Yet I enjoyed many things in that year. It is not because I did not enjoy it that I consider it a wasted year. It is simply because I do not think it advanced me in any way. But I have many pleasant memories of it—and that, after all, is no mean legacy for a year to leave.

When I came home I had another mortifying summer, vainly trying to get a school. I had hoped that my Dalhousie year would be of some assistance to me in this respect. But it was of no weight against the plethora of teachers who could make personal applications. It was not until the fall that I obtained the Belmont school.

That year, even apart from my unhappy engagement to Edwin Simpson, was the hardest I ever lived. It was hard in almost every way a year could be hard. I did not like my school. The majority of the pupils were rough, ill-bred, ignorant little creatures whom it was neither a pleasure nor a satisfaction to teach. Of course there were a few exceptions but they were in truth very few. The school was large and the work very heavy. I had one pupil whom I had to take through the first year course of P.W.C., extra work which meant much extra toil and worry for me but, of course not a cent of extra pay—nor as the sequel showed, extra gratitude either.

I had very little social life. The Simpson, Campbell and Allan Fraser families were the only ones with whom it gave me any pleasure to associate. The rest of the Belmont people were of a very inferior caste. I had a poor boarding house, a cold room, poor table, rough, illiterate people. My health was not good. The days were a routine of drudgery. Yet my spirit did not fail me. I believed there must be something better further on and I struggled towards it.

In the spring came the agony of my mistaken engagement, swallowing up all other ills, as a dreadful physical pang blots out the consciousness of gnat stings. For a whole year I lived in such anguish of mind as I pray may never fall to my lot again. The memory of it has lost none of its keenness in all these years.

That year in Bedeque! What a strange year it was. A year of mad passion! And how I suffered! "To love where we esteem not," it is indeed torture. And yet—I am not sorry I had that love, in spite of all the suffering it brought me. I *cannot* be sorry. For all its pain there was in it, too, a wild potent sweetness that somehow means more to me in recollection than all the rest of the ordinary happiness of my life put together. It is a bitter thing to love vainly. But a drab life with no love in it—that would be the worst thing of all!

Monday, Feb. 7, 1910
Cavendish, P.E.I.

I wonder if anything could be offered me which would—supposing it were possible induce me to live this past month over again. There are, perhaps, one or two things which might be potent enough. But even if I were offered the most intense and perfect happiness of my most daring dreams as a reward for enduring such another month I should hesitate to take the risk—because in all truth, I do not think I *could* live through it without going insane.

"That which I feared" has come upon me—I have had a month of nervous prostration—an utter breakdown of body, soul, and spirit. The hideous suffering of it, especially of the first fortnight, is something of which the mere remembrance curdles my blood. I thank God I do not come of a stock in which there is any tendency to insanity. If I had I believe that my mind would have given way hopelessly.

It came on very suddenly after my last entry. A new and dreadful worry[1] which preyed on me for a week or two, precipitated the crisis I suppose. At all events I broke down completely.

I could not sleep. For a week I hardly slept a moment. I can never forget the agony of those sleepless nights and the resulting days. For the ensuing fortnight I dozed fitfully. But this past week I have begun to sleep fairly well again.

The days were only one degree less hideous than the nights. I could not eat; every mouthful had to be forced down. I could not work or think or read or talk. I was possessed by a very fury of restlessness, only to be endured by walking the floor until my limbs failed from very exhaustion. Hitherto, when I have had similar though slighter nervous attacks I have been able to conceal my condition from grandmother. But this time it proved impossible

---

1.   Later disclosed as a fear of cancer.

and the resultant worry and alarm of the poor old soul was an added wretchedness to me.

I dreaded to see anyone coming to the house. When people came I had to hold myself still and talk to them—and I think death would have been easier. It was only by sheer will power that I could concentrate my mind sufficiently to understand what they were saying or make a coherent reply. Then when they had gone I was worse than ever.

Some days I would feel slightly better—so that I *could* compel myself to do such things as *had* to be done. Other days I could only walk the floor like one possessed of devils. Everybody noticed my wretched appearance but attributed it to the facial neuralgia from which I was indeed suffering severely enough but which seemed a very trifling ill compared to my nervous suffering.

I wanted to die and escape life! The thought of *having to go on living* was more than I could bear. I seemed to be possessed by a morbid dread of the future. No matter under what conditions I pictured myself I could only see myself suffering unbearably. I have heard *hell* defined as "a world from which hope was excluded." Then I was in hell for those three weeks. I had *no* hope. I could not realize any possible escape from suffering. It seemed to me that I must exist in that anguish forever. This is, I believe, a very common symptom of neurasthenia—and it is the hardest of all to bear. We can

[L.M. Montgomery]

endure almost any pain if we can *hope* that it will pass. But when we are convinced that it will never pass it is unbearable.

I could not in a hundred pages detail all my sufferings during that awful time. I understand now what drives some people to suicide.

I went to Dr. Simpson and told him I was suffering from insomnia and nervousness. He gave me some medicine which has already helped me a good deal. The worry which precipitated the attack has also been partially removed and I feel that I am recovering. I can *work* again—oh, the blessedness of it. But I am far from well yet and some of my days are very miserable. Oh, if I could only see Frede for a few hours and "talk things out" with her. But she is away down at Cape Traverse[1] this winter and I cannot see her.

I have come to the last page of this book, and I feel a curious regret as if I were parting from some real old friend and confidant. This book *has* been

---

1.   On the South Shore, the nearest point to the mainland.

a friend to me. Without it I verily believe I should have gone under. It is a rather tragic volume. From cover to cover it gives a record of unhappiness. It began with my mistaken engagement to Edwin Simpson—who, by the by, oddly enough, is at present suffering from nervous prostration, also, as I heard recently.

Nearly thirteen years ago I began this volume of my journal. Now it is ended. They have been in most respects a hard thirteen years. Yet I have won literary success and fame in them; and hard as they have been they have been salutary in many respects. Perhaps in no other way could their lessons have been taught; perhaps, had I been happier I had not climbed so high, lacking the spur of pain. But I *would* like a *little* happiness, just for a change. Whether it will ever be mine I do not know. Just now I am too discouraged to have any hope of it.

Good-bye old journal. You have been in all these long hard, lonely thirteen years almost my only comfort and refuge.

JOURNAL
Volume III

L.M. Montgomery

February 11, 1910–March 12, 1916

L.M. Montgomery

Friday, Feb. 11, 1910
Cavendish, P.E.I.[1]

Somehow, it is with a curious feeling of reluctance that I begin this new volume of my journal. Why I feel so I do not know. Perhaps it is because the last volume—or rather, the life it reflected—was so bitter and tragic; and hence there is a subconscious impression that the next volume must be so, too, and therefore I shrink from entering on it. Yet this is foolishness; and even if it were so I must go on with it. I could not live without my journal now. Temperaments such as mine *must* have some outlet, else they become morbid and poisoned by "consuming their own smoke."[2] And the only *safe* outlet is in some such record as this.

I have just been reading over my first two volumes;[3] and the thought uppermost in my mind is that, after all, in spite of my free confessions and self-analysis, a stranger perusing these journals would receive from them a quite misleading impression of my real character and life.

The first volume seems—I think—to have been written by a rather shallow girl, whose sole aim was to "have a good time" and who thought of little else than the surface play of life. Yet nothing could be falser to the reality. As a child and young girl I had a strange, deep, hidden inner life of dreams and aspirations, of which hardly a hint appears in the written record. This was partly because I had not then learned the art of self-analysis—of putting my real thoughts and feelings into words; and partly because I did not then feel the need of a confidant in my journal. I looked upon it merely as a record of my doings which might be interesting to me in after years. Hence, I kept to the surface of existence and thought, in the writing of it, and never attempted to sound the deeps below.

Again, the second volume gives the impression of a morbid temperament, generally in the throes of nervousness and gloom. Yet this, too, is false. It arises from the fact that of late years I have made my journal the refuge of my sick spirit in its unbearable agonies. The record of pain seems thus almost unbroken; yet in reality these spasms came at long intervals, when loneliness and solitude had broken down my powers of endurance. Between these times I was quite tolerably happy, hopeful and interested in life.

Well, I begin the third volume. I am going to try to strike a better balance in it—to write out my happiness as well as my pain. And I mean to try, as far as in me lies, to paint my life and deeds—ay, and my thoughts—truthfully, no

---

1.   Here begins the third handwritten journal.

2.   Thomas Carlyle, *Sartor Resartus*, II chapter 6.

3.   LMM copied her handwritten journals into legal ledgers.

matter how unflattering such truth may be to me. No life document has any real value otherwise; the worst as well as the best must be written out—*and the best as well as the worst*, since we are, every one of us, whether we own to it sincerely or not, angel and devil mixed up together, now the one predominating, now the other—in the endless struggle of Ormuzd and Ahrimanes.[1] In one mood we are strongly tempted to acknowledge only the angel and disown the devil; in another mood we grovel and lash ourselves in the miserable conviction that we are *all* devil. But one mood is as false to truth as the other. The only thing to do is to look the matter squarely in the face—and then to try to keep the devil in subjection—starve him out eventually by giving all the nourishment of our nature to the angel. Yet he can live on so little—this demon of sense and hate and anger—and often when we think him dead, or at least so weakened as to be shorn of his power, he will rise up in seemingly renewed might and rend our souls with his bestial impulses.

So, for good or evil, I begin this volume. I turn over its blank pages with a shrinking wonder. *What will be written in them?*

I have been fairly well since my last entry until yesterday, when I had a very dreadful day of nervous unrest. Today I felt much better; and, according to an unwilling promise I went in to Mayfield to spend the afternoon with Amanda Macneill—now the wife of George Robertson. She married him last July. How she *could* do it I do not know. He is a most ignorant, uncouth man, lacking little of being absolutely hideous and in intellect so sub-normal as to narrowly escape being in the class of pronounced mental defectives. I know that she neither loved nor respected him.

He used to try to go with her off and on since they were grown up. In her early girlhood she would have none of him and snubbed him most unsparingly and openly. He was then a gaunt awkward creature, short-sighted and uncanny looking, the butt of the community. As long as Amanda had any hope of getting anybody else—she had a couple of unhappy love affairs which came to nothing, both the men jilting her after leading her to think them in earnest—she would have nothing whatever to do with him. She told me once that she could never spend her life with him. Why her two affairs petered out I don't exactly understand but I have reason to believe that Amanda disgusted her lovers with over-eagerness. She did too much of the courting! However it was, she lost them and then she fell back on George, who meekly accepted her, knowing he could not get a wife anywhere else.

I was at the wedding and it was a weird performance. Amanda was deucedly cranky and mysterious. She was a ghastly-looking bride for when

---

1. Zoroastrian twin-deities: the lords of good and of evil.

Amanada's old home, x window of parlor

Her new home

she stood up in the parlor to be married she turned—not pale but the most gruesome *livid green*. I never saw such a color in a face in my life before. As for George, he looked as much like a monkey, short of the tail, as any supposedly human creature could. But they were married and Amanda went to live in at Mayfield, about three miles from here.

Her departure from Cavendish was a decided relief to me, since I would no longer be compelled to meet her frequently. She has of late years developed such a dreadful disposition that any intercourse with her was a real misery to me. It is impossible to realize that she is the same Amanda Macneill I loved in childhood and young girlhood. But she is *not* the same. She is not the same in *any* respect. *That* Amanda does not now exist. I think of *her* as of a dead and buried friend of youth.

But some slight intercourse has still to be kept up. Amanda was here one afternoon lately and I promised to return the visit. I went today to get it over. There was no pleasure in the afternoon. I cannot even talk gossip with Amanda. I am oppressed by the spirit of malice with which she seems to utter and hear every word. And there is nothing else she can talk of. The only pleasure of the outing came when I was walking home alone with my good friends the stars. I also had the delight of seeing for the first time the mysterious, phantom-like Zodiacal Light.[1]

But recently I have had to drop my studies in astronomy for a time. In my present nervous condition they had a bad effect on me. The effort to realize those dreadful, enormous distances between the stars crushed me. In the midst of such an unthinkable assemblage of suns, *what was I* that God should be mindful of me? I felt lost—I felt like *nothingness*. And, as such feelings were intolerable in my present condition, I have stopped trying to plumb the universe until I return to my normal state.

---

1.   Faint illumination of the sky, elongated as a band of light on each side of the sun, in the northern hemisphere best seen at twilight in February and March.

Yet my study of the stars has a great and indescribable fascination for me. I never took up anything that gained such a hold on me or that gave me such strange, eerie, unearthly pleasure—the most purely spiritual pleasure I have ever known since there is indeed nothing of earth about it!

Tuesday, Feb. 15, 1910

I have had four very hard days, yesterday being the worst. Yesterday afternoon Tillie Macneill[1] sent her brother over for me, saying that she was ill and lonely and wanted company. Under the circumstances I could not refuse to go but the afternoon was a misery to me. I was burning up with nervous restlessness, yet I had to force myself to sit still, to sew, to talk brightly to Tillie, to laugh and jest. I did it but such a day ages one more than the passing of years. When I came home I felt completely exhausted. After I went to bed I cried passionately for an hour, then spent a night of tossing wakefulness. Today I have been dreadfully weak and filled with a horrible dread of life. *Everything* seems to hurt me. I have no strength for anything.

Saturday, Feb. 19, 1910
Cavendish, P.E.I.

After a very miserable week I feel slightly better today though very dull and tired. I received my publisher's report today and the year's royalty check[2]— over seven thousand dollars! It seems like mockery that this money should come to me now when I am perhaps too broken ever to enjoy it. If I could only have had one tenth of that sum when I was a young girl, struggling for an education and enduring many humiliations and disappointments because of my lack of money. A little of it then would have saved me much. Nevertheless, I suppose it is not to be despised even now, if I ever regain health and spirit to enjoy it.

There are as yet very few days when I can work. My new book is at a standstill and my correspondence is very far behind. But all this matters little if I can regain a measure of health and energy. The trouble is, that when I

---

1. Matilda McKenzie Houston (1853–1911), a cousin on the Woolner side; her mother was Grandmother Macneill's sister.

2. LMM recorded all payments in an account book, now at the University of Guelph. The total royalties for 1909 for *Anne Green Gables* were $5,396.53.

cannot work there is nothing else here to take up my thoughts or pass the time, and then I am apt to fall into morbid brooding. I cannot even get out for a walk.

Feb. 28, 1910
Cavendish, P.E.I.

All this week I have been very ill with grippe. I am feeling slightly better now, both physically and mentally. What a wretched month February has been! God grant I may never have to undergo such another. But *will* God grant it? I have so often prayed for suffering to be averted or relieved but He has not answered my prayer. Does He ever answer such prayers? Somehow I cannot believe it. He may do what is best for us—I cling to my old faith that He does—but His way seems to be different from our way and I cannot really believe that it is any use asking Him to change it.

Saturday, March 19, 1910
Cavendish, P.E.I.

I have, as a rule, continued very miserable this past fortnight. Some days I was able to work and therefore able to endure. Other days I could not work and then it seemed that I could *not* endure. I have had a very bad cold and sore throat and I cannot get rid of it.

Have been busy reading the proof of *Kilmeny*.[1] It is to be out in May. Recently I received a copy of the Swedish edition of *Anne*[2]—interesting as a curiosity. Anne is portrayed on the cover as a black-and-white damsel, lugging a huge carpet-bag, and having hair of a literally *scarlet* hue—a startling contrast to the black and white. Of course I cannot judge as to the merits of the translation since I know no Swedish.

Oh, I am so very tired! If I could only feel *rested* once more. It does not seem to me just now that I would ever ask anything else. But of course I would! If I felt like my old self there are many, many things I would ask—and keenly desire.

---

1. Reworked from an earlier serial published in the Minneapolis *Housewife* in 1908 titled "Una of the Garden," *Kilmeny of the Orchard* (1910) presents an artistic but voiceless girl, released by the love of a young man from a different world.

2. *Anne på Grönkulla*, translated by Karin Jensen (Lund: Gleerup, 1909).

Monday, March 21, 1910
Cavendish, P.E.I.

Today I received a MS copy of a song "The Wild White Cherry Tree,"[1] which was composed by an English lady, once a noted concert singer, and which is to be published dedicated to me. She wrote me that the music seemed to her to express her feelings on reading *Anne*. The song, so far as I can judge, is very beautiful and the compliment is a rare and delicate one.

Wed. March 23, 1910

It is dreadful to feel so tired all the time as I do. This afternoon I went to the Sewing Circle at Alec Macneills[2] and sat and sewed little dresses and trousers for small heathen in Trinidad[3] when it seemed to me I would fall from my chair with sheer weariness if I relaxed a muscle. Then we had choir practice in the evening and after it I walked home alone hardly able to drag one foot after another.

Tuesday, Mar. 29, 1910

Frede Campbell came up from Cape Traverse—where she is teaching—on Tuesday to spend Easter with me. I believe that all I need is companionship. I felt like a different being when she was here. We talked out all our difficulties and worries and they did not loom so blackly and menacingly when put into words. I feel strengthened and able to go on. I think if Frede had not come to see me I must have given up completely. What a great blessing faithful friendship is—the friendship of a true woman on whom one can depend and in whom one can trust. I fear it is a rare thing. Yet I have found some such friends—not many but enough. I do not, since

Frede

---

1. Song based on Anne's chatter to Matthew in chapter 2 of *AGG*, about "a wild cherry tree, all white with bloom in the moonshine."

2. Alec MacNeill (1870–1951), a second cousin, brother of Penzie, became LMM's dear friend in later years, as did his wife May (1876–1947).

3. The Presbyterian church in nearby New London maintained a mission in Trinidad, British West Indies.

girlhood passed, make friends easily or lightly. But I no longer desire many friends or a superficial popularity. Rather do I wish a few, kin to me of soul, whom I can grapple to my life with bonds not to be broken, on whose honor I can rely, and in whose companionship I can find satisfaction. For such friends I say "Thank God," with all my heart.

Thurs. Mar. 31, 1910
Cavendish

This was a dull damp day and the inspiration of Frede's visit having worn away I felt broken and dispirited all day. This evening I ventured out in desperation and betook me to the woods. The walking was as bad as it could be but the influence of the woodlands and the silent places was consoling and uplifting and strengthening. I felt much better mentally when I came in. It had not helped me physically, however, for the damp air aggravated my cold and I coughed rackingly all the evening. I cannot throw off this cold and it alarms me. I never before had a cough which kept me awake at nights, but this does.

The silent places

Sunday, April 3, 1910

I am no better. The hardest task in the day is getting up in the morning. It always seems as if I could *not*. And I feel so tired and sick at heart. Absurd as it sounds, I feel *homesick*—that is, I feel just as I have felt when I have been really homesick. A morbid fancy persists in picturing myself as away somewhere among strangers and strange scenes, miserable, incapable of adapting myself to new conditions, and yearning ceaselessly back to my old life and associations. I cannot shake off, or escape from, the tyranny of this mood—I cannot picture myself as contented anywhere than here, or under any conditions differing from those by which I have so long been shaped. My reason tells me that this is probably an utterly false belief but reason has little effect on feeling when it is tortured into morbid activity. The mere thought of making radical changes in my life or accepting new responsibilities fills me with a very terror—the terror of weakness which cannot answer to such demands. I have, for the last twelve years, borne a heavy responsibility here; but it is one to which I am accustomed—one which I have gradually learned to bear. It seems to me, in my weakness and heart-sickness, easier to bear old sorrows than new joys!

Monday, Apr. 4, 1910
Cavendish, P.E.I.

Today, in going through an old trunk I came upon a "crazy quilt."[1] And I took it out and unfolded it and sat me down to study it and the memories of the past it recalled. When I was about twelve years old "crazy patchwork" had just come into vogue. It was "all the rage." Everybody made at least a "crazy" cushion. Some few attempted quilts. I was among the latter.

The name was certainly an inspired one. "Crazy" such work certainly was—nay, more, rankly insane. To my present taste it is inexpressibly hideous. I find it hard to believe it possible that I could ever have thought it beautiful. But I did so think it; and I expended more "gray matter" devising ingenious and complicated "stitches" than I ever put into anything else.

I was from twelve to sixteen completing the quilt—five years; and verily it was "Love's Labour's Lost"[2] for by the time I had finished it crazy patchwork was out of the fashion. My crazy quilt has been lying folded in that trunk ever since—and will continue to lie folded. Perhaps future generations may regard it as a curiosity as we look upon old samplers now.

Nevertheless, I felt many a tug at my heart as I looked over it today. It was compact of old memories; almost every gay piece or bit of embroidery called up some long-ago incident or place or face. As for the dreams sewn into that quilt, they were as thick as Autumn leaves in Vallambroso.[3]

A great part of the delight of "crazy" work was the excitement of collecting pieces for it—silks, satins, velvets—for of no meaner materials might genuine crazy patchwork be made. Old boxes and drawers were ransacked and long hidden bits of finery joyfully found and used. Contributions were levied on all my friends. Did one get a new dress or hat a bit of the trimming must be begged. Sometimes the work was at a standstill for weeks because of lack of scraps. But eventually enough were collected and the quilt completed—a quaint cipher of many and many an old gayety and vanity and heartbeat. Sometimes I sent away a dollar to an American silk firm and received a package of pieces about four inches square cut from remnants.

---

1. An example of LMM's handwork, a quilt with samples of embroidery marking the seams between patches of richly coloured material, is preserved in the University of Guelph Archives.

2. LMM misquotes the title of Shakespeare's play (*Love's Labor Lost*).

3. From John Milton's *Paradise Lost* I, line 302.

They were always very rich and beautiful, with the glamor of the outer world about them—the world of wealth and fashion where "grande dames" disported themselves in whole robes of these materials. It was a never failing diversion of my chums and me to "choose out" the various dresses we would have if given our pick of those gay samples.

There are many pieces from dresses of my mother and aunts in that quilt. Many wedding dresses figure there. And all are covered with intricate stitching. The result is a very nightmare of jumbled hues and patterns. And once I thought it beautiful!

Well, after all, it gave me pleasure in the making and so what matters if the result was not worth while? I had "the joy of the working" and that was the essence of heaven.

Sunday, Apr. 24, 1910
Cavendish, P.E.I.

April has been a very hard month. I have been for the most part very miserable. But this past week I have felt much better. We have had an early spring and the walking is good. I have got out for long rambles and the result has been wholesome. How thankful I am that the winter is over! I never endured such misery as I have suffered since New Year's. Nervous prostration is a hideous thing. And to bear it all alone with no one to aid or comfort is hard!

Monday, Apr. 25, 1910

Today was beautiful. We have had a very early and very lovely spring. I began housecleaning today. I have always enjoyed housecleaning. There is something very pleasant in getting rid of the winter's dust and grime and making the rooms sweet and fresh.

I did the north room today. It is an unfinished room, rough plastered, and has always been used as a store-room for clothes, blankets, and cast-offs. It looks out on a wilderness of young poplars and spruces. I remember when I first began to take charge of the housecleaning what a task it was to clean that room, so full of useless odds and ends it was, not one of which would grandmother suffer to be disposed of. They might "come in handy sometime." It was vain to argue with her so I took matters into my own hands and quietly burned some of the trash at each successive housecleaning, with the happy result that in a few years it was all gone and cleaning the north room simplified by half.

Tonight I walked over the hill and washed my soul free from dust in the aerial bath of a spring twilight.

Tuesday, April 26, 1910
Cavendish, P.E.I.

Today was the turn of the "look-out." This little room was where I used to sleep in summer until I was about twelve or thirteen. I remember that I was always very careful—in my thoughts and diary, *not* in my conver-

View from hill

sation—to call it "my boudoir"—as a "boudoir" figured largely in all the fashionable fiction of that day. One never hears of "boudoirs" now. But I had mine and in it I kept my few books and magazines, my dolls and work-box and all my little knick-knacks. There was a beautiful view from the low

x. The "look-out"

window over the trees of the "front" garden to the far green hills and woods of western Cavendish. Nowadays the little "look-out" serves as a trunk-room and Daffy looks upon it as his "boudoir," for he spends most of his time there, sleeping on the bed. Poor little room! I dreamed many a bright dream there—and none but the dream of fame has ever been fulfilled!

Wednesday, Apr. 27, 1910
Cavendish, P.E.I.

Today I cleaned my own dear room. It is a white peaceful nest tonight. Alas, that I should ever have to leave it! No spot on earth can ever be to me what it is. Here, by its window I have sat in grief and joy and looked afar to those green hills in rapture and in heartbreak. Many a night I have wept myself to sleep here and

Daffy asleep in "look-out"

many nights I have been happy here. But there have been many more sorrowful nights than happy ones; and perhaps that is why I love it so—as we love what comforts us in sorrow more than what merely shares in joy. Oh, little room, when I leave you I fear my heart will break.

This evening I walked up to the barrens and picked an armful of Mayflowers. They are even more beautiful than usual this year. I never saw such large pink-and-white clusters. As somebody said of strawberries so say I of Mayflowers, "God might have made a sweeter blossom but God never did." I enjoyed my walk and gathering so much. There was a sweetness in it not to be put into words. Like the Mayflowers, it had the sweetness of the past and the dream of the future commingled.

Monday, May 3, 1910

Parlor and door of "spare room"

Today I cleaned the parlor and "spare room"—those solemn rooms of state which seemed such princely apartments to my childish eyes. Never in my recollection was the parlor much used. After Aunt Emily went away it was never used at all. Her wedding was the last festivity ever held in it. The spare room was quite frequently used however. I remember when I was a child I had an avid desire to sleep in it—just because it *was* the spare room and such a wonderful-seeming place. My desire was never given me. And when I grew old enough to compass it if I had wished—lo, the desire was not.

The parlor was a large, pleasant room, with south and west windows, with green slat-blinds of a kind I have never seen elsewhere. It had also long lace curtains which were considered very elegant in those days and which very few people in Cavendish then had. The carpet was very gorgeous—all roses and ferns. It is not "my idea" of a carpet now but once on a

The parlor and old mantel

time I thought it left nothing to be desired. There is an old black "colonial" mantel piece which I admire now; but in those long ago days it did not appeal to me. I thought much more highly of the "lambrequined" mantels in other people's parlors. The furniture was simple and old-fashioned. A horsehair sofa and rocker were thought quite elegant. The rest of the chairs were plain, cane-bottomed ones. There were many gay tidies and cushions. The old room has never changed. Every chair stands precisely where it always did and every tidy is placed on the same cushion at the same angle. There always seems to me a certain pleasing dignity about the room, born of its very simplicity and old-fashionedness. I like occasionally to step in there and sit on the old rocker and just dream.

May 4, 1910
Cavendish, P.E.I.

My third book "Kilmeny of the Orchard" came today. Like the others it is nicely gotten up. Who would have thought that a book of my own would so soon become a commonplace to me? The advent of "Anne" in cold type seemed a wondrous event. But *Kilmeny* is "all in the day's work"—nothing more.

Monday, May 23, 1910
Cavendish, P.E.I.

Tonight I succeeded in seeing Halley's comet.[1] It was a sorry spectacle—little more than a dull white star. There has been so much concerning it in the newspapers and periodicals of the past 6 months that everyone expected a wonderful sight and we have been proportionately disappointed. Tonight I gazed at it and tried to feel enthusiastic, remembering that this self-same star I gazed at hung over doomed Jerusalem during its memorable siege and lighted Norman William to his English conquest ere the fatal day of Senlac Hill.[2] It will be seventy-five years before this comet "calls" again. By that time I shall not be searching for it in the tremulous spring-time skies. I shall be lying somewhere under the grasses and eyes now unborn will be gazing at the famous vagabond of space.

> Get leave to work;
> In this world 'tis the best you get at all,
> For God in cursing gives us better gifts
> Than men in benediction.[3]

---

1. A comet named for the English astronomer, Edmund Halley, who observed it in 1682. With its tail of gas and dust, it orbits between Mercury and Venus every seventy-six years.

2. William the Conqueror, whose troops from Normandy defeated the English army in 1066 at the Battle of Hastings.

3. From Elizabeth Barrett Browning's *Aurora Leigh* (1857); LMM quoted the same lines in 1900 at the time of her father's death.

So wrote Elizabeth Barrett Browning—and truly. It is hard to understand why work should be called a curse—until we remember what bitterness forced or uncongenial labor is. But the work for which we are fitted—which we are sent into the world to do—what a blessing it is and what fullness of joy it holds! I felt this today as I wrote a chapter of my new book and experienced the creator's subtle, all-embracing joy in creating. "Leave to work"—one would think everyone could obtain so much. But sometimes suffering and trouble forbid us the leave. And then we realize what we have lost and know that it is better to be cursed by God than forgotten by Him. If God had punished Adam and Eve in the old myth by sending them away to idleness—by *forbidding* them to work, then indeed would they have been outcast and accursed. But He sent them out from Eden to *labor*—and not all their dreams of Paradise, "whence the four great rivers flow" could have been as truly sweet as those which crowned their days of toil.

Oh God, as long as I live give me "leave to work"—thus pray I—leave and courage!

Monday, July 11, 1910
Cavendish, P.E.I.

In April our minister, John Stirling,[1] married Margaret Ross[2] of Stanley and they are now living in the manse. This means a great deal to me. Margaret has been an intimate friend of mine for the past two years and it is very pleasant to have her so near me. I like her very much and we have "awfully good times" together. She is what may be called "a sweet woman." She is rather lacking in strength and a certain reticence which I would like to see in her; and I am far from thinking it

x. Margaret

is wholly safe to tell her *everything*. But she is a very congenial companion. She does not love John Stirling. She likes him very well—and she is "getting on." For the matter of that I somehow can't fancy any woman *loving* John Stirling. He is one of the nicest men I've ever met—clever—absolutely good and *sincere*—which is a rarer thing among ministers than I once fondly believed; so that in spite of his marked homeliness of feature everyone likes

---

1. Born in Scotsburn in Pictou County, NS, this Cavendish minister was briefly gossiped about as a suitor to LMM.

2. One of the three women whose names had been linked with Ewan Macdonald's by local gossip before his engagement to LMM.

him. I like him tremendously—and I could never have the slightest fancy for him as a man. Not because of his marked homeliness, either. He *is* very homely; but the refinement and goodness of his features prevent his plainness from being in any way repulsive. When you come to know him well you never think of it. But he simply isn't one of the men whom women love though they may marry them from some other motive.

The Manse

In spite of his fine mentality he is a poor preacher and is rather lazy, too—which things will always militate against him. But his extreme *likeableness* is a huge asset. I think he and Margaret will get on very nicely in the parish and I am exceedingly glad to have them near me.

This evening I was invited to tea at the manse to meet Dr. Pringle[1] of Yukon fame. He is a voluble talker and as his conversation is wholly about life in the Yukon it is very entertaining. But I do not think he can talk of much except Yukon life and I am sure he is very egotistical. He is not a man with whom other people can be conversationally at their best. He is one of those men who listen absently to anything you may say, as if they were just waiting for you to finish to break in with what they are thinking of saying. You feel that your remarks have slipped over their consciousness without making the slightest impression on it, as a pebble might slide over ice. Dr. Pringle complained several times that I "wouldn't talk"—he kept calling me "Anne" and seemed to think I must or should be as big a chatter box as she was. But the truth was he didn't give me or anyone else the slightest chance to talk.

Uncle Leander, Aunt May and Kennedy are here for the summer.

Wednesday, Aug. 10, 1910
Cavendish, P.E.I.

This morning Tillie Houston and I drove down to Shaw's Hotel[2] at Brackley Beach and spent the day. Marjory MacMurchy[3] of the Toronto "News," with

---

1. The Rev. G.C.F. Pringle (1873–1949) later published his Yukon stories as *Tillicums of the Trail* (1922).

2. A long-enduring family-run hotel at Brackley Beach, east of Rustico Bay.

3. Literary editor of the Toronto *News* between 1903 and 1917, and founder of the Canadian Women's Press Club and its president, 1905–13, Marjory MacMurchy (1870–1938) was a promoter of women writers and took an early interest in LMM.

whom I have had some correspondence since my books came out, was there and I wished to meet her. She and her sister are clever girls and we had a very pleasant day together. I met a lot of nice people and enjoyed my little outing thoroughly.

It seems to me that the summer is simply flying. I am so busy. There is so much to do and I don't get half of it done. I want so much to get the *Story Girl* done by September but I fear it will be impossible.

Sunday, Aug. 14, 1910
Cavendish, P.E.I.

I feel quite "played out." Small wonder! This morning in church I encountered Sophy Simpson. She told me she was coming to see me before she went home on Wednesday and, as I did not want her either Monday or Tuesday, when I expected other company I decided to sacrifice the nice, restful afternoon and evening I had planned for myself and asked her over from church. I put in a quite terrible afternoon. Sophy is more Sophyan than ever. She seems to be the concentrated essence of Simpsonism and nothing else. I had to take her through Lover's Lane—may jackals sit on her grandmother's grave for asking it! It desecrated the place. Faugh! The flavor of Sophy Simpson must hang around it for weeks. She is increasingly difficult to talk with and has lost none of her old aptness for saying the wrong thing at every possible opportunity. I had to go up to the Baptist Church this evening with her but glory be, I got rid of her after the service. And how blissful was my walk home alone in the moonshine of the summer night. Sophy would make anyone in love with solitude.

She remarked condescendingly as we passed through Lover's Lane, "After all, I think there is nothing so pretty as Nature."

How flattered Nature must feel!

Sunday, August 21, 1910
Cavendish, P.E.I.

Frede has been here since Thursday. We enjoyed every minute of the time. She went home today and I miss her terribly. She is going to Macdonald College[1] this fall to take the course in Household Science. I am going to give

---

1. Affiliated with McGill University and situated at Ste-Anne-de-Bellevue, the College was founded and endowed in 1905 by Sir William Macdonald, a Montreal manufacturer born in Prince Edward Island, for the teaching of agriculture, domestic science, and pedagogy.

her the money for it. Frede is too clever a girl to be wasted any longer teaching rural schools in P.E. Island. She must be given a chance to do something with her brains. I wanted her to go to McGill and take an Arts course, telling her I would put her through. But she finally decided against it. I think she feels she is rather too old for that and perhaps she is right. When a girl nears twenty five she does not feel like going into the classes with sixteen year olds. My good fortune came a little too late for Frede, as far as the B.A. is concerned.

Friday, Aug. 26, 1910
Cavendish, P.E.I.

Uncle L.'s went this morning. It is a relief. He is a very unpleasant guest, poor man, and grandmother is always more or less upset during their sojourn. I hope I shall be able to get some work done now. I have accomplished almost nothing these past six weeks. If I had been having a *real* vacation that would not matter. But to be prevented from working merely by constant petty happenings and worries is very unsatisfactory.

Lover's Lane

This afternoon I went to Lover's Lane—that beloved spot which I love better than any other spot in the world and always will. I have got nearer to God there than in any other place.

I was trying today to remember just when I began to call it Lover's Lane. But I could not precisely. It is a long time. I had a passion for naming places in my childhood. All the pretty nooks and corners about the old place I named. In the spruce and maple grove behind the old barn—a very lovely grove then though a forlorn and ragged spot now—were three beautiful spots— "My Grove," "The Fairy

"No Man's Land"   "Birch Palace"

Palace" and "No Man's Land." A grassy round hill beyond Uncle John's barn where violets purpled in spring and strawberries crimsoned in summer was "Fairyland." It was the first place I ever named. There was a big boulder on it which I called "The Fairy Queen's throne." The swamp beyond it was "The Fairy Swamp." An open nook in the grove behind the house was "Golden Rod Palace." There was, I know, a "Silver Palace" and a "Strawberry Palace" but I do not remember where they were. My fancy ran much to "palaces" in those days. "Birch Palace" was at the foot of the "front orchard." The leafy square in the back orchard where the four big sweet apple trees grew, was called "The Bower." I have forgotten the names given

"The Bower"

to other spots—oh yes, there was a "Cherry Palace" in Uncle John's cherry orchard—and it was a divine spot in blossom time—"a lovesome place."

Tuesday, Sept. 6, 1910

Yesterday evening I spent at Alec Macneill's. I came home about ten o'clock and found the following rather disconcerting telegram from Lieutenant Governor Rogers[1] awaiting me.

"His Excellency Earl Grey will be in Ch'town on Sept. 13th and wishes to meet you."

Earl Grey[2] is our present Governor General. This was something of an honor—but rather an unwelcome one and one with which I would rather have dispensed. Not that I had any foolish dread of meeting "lords and ladies of high degree"—who are just human beings who have to wash behind their ears as I do—but because, circumstanced as I am, I foresaw a great deal of preliminary bother and worry over the matter and that, too, when I had a worrisome summer and was hoping for a quiet fall. However, there it was— almost "a royal command"—certainly not to be disregarded if it could be obeyed. There seemed to be no way out of it, short of breaking my leg or taking the smallpox. So I must; but I did not sleep much last night—and it was not gratified vanity that kept me awake either.

---

1. The Hon. Benjamin Rogers (1837–1923) retired from Liberal politics in 1904 and was appointed Lieutenant-Governor of Prince Edward Island, 1910–15.

2. Albert Henry George Grey, fourth earl; as Governor General, the king's representative and statutory head of state in Canada (1904–11), he strengthened imperial ties, supported drama and music festivals, and donated the Grey Cup for national championship in football.

This morning I went to the manse and talked the matter over with Margaret—which cleared my ideas somewhat. I had, like the celebrated "Miss Flora Macflimsy,"[1] nothing to wear—at least nothing suited to any vice-regal function, however informal. And as I did not know just what the function would be I hardly knew what to get.

I decided to go up to Mr. Hillman's forthwith and see if Bertie Hillman[2] could make me a dress before Saturday night. I went and found that she could. Then I had to scurry around arranging for a rig to take me to the station tomorrow and cancelling some engagements I had made for the rest of the week. I feel very tired tonight and not at all in good fettle for what will be certainly a tiresome expedition tomorrow.

Wednesday, Sept. 7, 1910
Cavendish, P.E.I.

This morning it threatened to rain; but rain or not "needs must" etc. I started for the station at eight o'clock, rattling along in Pierce Macneill's[3] old wagon which is decidedly the worse for wear and giggling to myself over what Earl Grey and his staff would think if they could see my equipage and steed! I arrived at Hunter River[4] just in time to escape the rain which began to come down heavily as the train started. I was lucky enough to meet my cousin Will Sutherland and his wife on the train. They are home from British Columbia on a visit and I was very curious to meet her for reasons connected with Frede. Will S. is the man Frede loved and I am inclined to think he cared a good deal for her. But he was engaged to Lilian Donahue and eventually married her, thereby destroying Frede's chance

Will and Lilian

for the highest happiness. Well, there are few who have that, I think, and there are I hope many things in life for Frede besides Will Sutherland's love.

---

1. She "had thousands of dresses but nothing to wear" in a poem from American comic writer William Allen Butler's *Two Millions* (1858).

2. Dressmaker and daughter of John, owner of the forge at the western end of Cavendish.

3. Pierce Macneill's (1861–1929) house at the crossroads was the inspiration for Mrs. Rachel Lynde's home in *AGG*.

4. The nearest railway station was at this village southwest of Rustico.

But, judging from my impressions of Lilian, Will has made a mistake. Lilian seems a pleasant but very "common" person with nothing at all distinctive or charming about her. She was very nice to me—overdid it in fact. But I think if I had not written *Anne* she would not have bothered her head much about me and I am sure I should find a prolonged dose of her society very wearisome.

I dined with them at the Victoria.[1] Then, as it was still raining heavily, I hired a carriage to do my shopping in. I got a piece of pretty brown silk with other necessary accoutrements and managed by dint of "hustling" to finish my shopping before train time. Then I scurried down to the station and had an agitated half hour's chat with Bertie. I reached home at night, dead tired.

Yesterday I had a letter from Dr. MacPhail[2] of Montreal who is in town and who is going to entertain the Earl's party at his old homestead in Orwell.[3] Dr. MacPhail himself is a brilliant man and a noted writer. He wrote that Earl Grey was "an ardent admirer" of my books and wished to meet the author. This is flattering, I suppose. Yet I do not think it is really half as flattering as the opinion of many an obscure individual who may yet be a better literary critic than Earl Grey. Dr. MacPhail's own opinion is probably of more real importance than His Excellency's. Yet it speaks something for "Anne" too, that she should have been sufficiently delightful to a busy statesman to cause him to single her out in his full life and inspire him with a wish to meet her creator.

Saturday, Sept. 10, 1910
Cavendish, P.E.I.

This has certainly been a nerve-racking week, flying about attending to a score of different things, answering letters, and making arrangements. At present the programme stands thus:—I go to town Monday. At eleven o'clock Tuesday morning the Vice-Regal party leave for Orwell on a special train, where a luncheon will be served at the MacPhail place. I am to join the party at the station. This will mean an informal meeting and I am very glad, since it will be much easier.

This afternoon, feeling tired and a little nervous, I went to Lover's Lane. It made me my own woman again. What mattered principalities and powers in

---

1.   A hotel in Charlottetown.

2.   Dr. Andrew Macphail (1864–1938), professor of the history of medicine at McGill, essayist, editor of *The University Magazine*, Prince Edward Islander, and Imperialist. His best-known book is *The Master's Wife* (1939).

3.   This community, east of Charlottetown, has been restored as a National Historic Park and tourist site, with the Macphail home as its centrepiece.

that green sun-flecked seclusion, where the soul of me stood up unafraid and I felt and realized the enfolding presence of God as I have never felt or realized it anywhere else. What did it matter that, on the one hand, a great honor had been done me for my work's sake, or on the other, that I felt shy and timid when I thought of meeting Lord and Lady Grey? It mattered nothing as long as the wild free wind and the sweet autumnal sunshine and the peace of the firs was still my own.

Lover's Lane

Sunday Night, Sept. 11, 1910
Cavendish, P.E.I.

Today was very beautiful. We had service in the morning. Almost everyone has heard of the "Grey affair" and most of the folks in church looked at me as if they found it rather hard to believe. My friends are all pleased—and those who are *not* my friends seem rather uncomfortably speechless. There is nothing for them to say. They cannot deny or belittle it—and they will not admit it. I confess that in regard to them I do feel a little bit of triumph.

Aunt Mary Lawson, who is visiting in Cavendish, came over with me from church. She is far more excited over the matter than I am. She looks upon it as a tremendous honor done to the clan and it warms the cockles of her Macneill heart. I had to show her the telegram and the letters and put on my dress for her. My dress is really quite pretty and I think it is suitable and becoming. I leave tomorrow morning for town. I wish it were all well over.

Aunt Mary Lawson

In dress made for the "Earl Grey Affair"

Friday, Sept. 16, 1910

It is all over—and I'm very thankful—and besottedly glad to get back to my own quiet life again. This does not mean that I have not had a pleasant and interesting time. I had; but there has been a great nervous strain with it all, and I am relieved that this has come to an end and I can return to my books and pen, and homely simple tasks and pleasures.

Monday morning I drove to Hunter River and went to town. It was a very beautiful day of summer air and sunshine mingled with autumnal mellowness and I looked longingly to the purple woods on the western hill where I would much rather have spent the day.

Bertie met me at the train and I went with her to her room at Mrs. Sutherland's,[1] Upper Prince.[2] She gave up housekeeping in the spring—a wise course. I am glad she did, for the double responsibility of teaching and housekeeping was far too heavy for her. But I miss the old home in town very much. Dear Aunt Mary! How proud she would have been over the compliment that has been paid me! How pleased to do anything that might help me!

Mrs. Sutherland's

But Bertie has a very nice room and her kindness and thoughtfulness and general unselfishness were beyond my power to express. I shall never forget it and I don't know how I could have got along in all the consequent worry and fuss without going clean crazy had it not been for her.

When I came in from downtown Monday afternoon I found a note from Mrs. Rogers (Lieutenant Governor's wife) saying that a wireless from Earl Grey had informed her that the *Earl Grey*—the Government steamer, named after him, on which he travelled would not get into town until three o'clock Tuesday afternoon. This, she supposed, would upset Dr. MacPhail's arrangements and the Orwell expedition would not come off until Wednesday.

This upset the arrangement of other people than Dr. MacPhail. My own carefully laid little plans were scattered to the winds. On second thoughts, however, I was well pleased. I was tired and I would have Tuesday to rest in and complete my preparations at leisure. It would involve staying in town

---

1. Isabella Henderson Sutherland, wife of James Sutherland, was an aunt by marriage to LMM's cousins Will and John Sutherland. The original entry in the journal for this date was excised and replaced, perhaps to eliminate some family gossip.

2. A fashionable street in Charlottetown.

another day than I had allowed for but I had got Judy Gallant[1] to stay with grandmother in my absence so I did not have to worry over that.

Therefore, I put off all finishing touches till Tuesday, spent the evening calling on friends and finally went to bed without even putting my hair in "crimpers," as was necessary for the style I wanted to wear. Then, rashly thinking that I would have plenty of time to get my "beauty sleep" for the Orwell Expedition the next night I began reading Dr. MacPhail's new book "Fallacies,"[2] not wishing to encounter him with it unread. I began it as a duty but continued it as a pleasure for it was a very fascinating and stimulating volume, with a good deal of disagreeable truth in it.

x. Bank of Nova Scotia

Tuesday morning I went placidly down town to do some shopping but presently had to come flying up again in anything but a placid fashion—and a long walk it was, too. I had called in at the Bank of Nova Scotia where Cuthbert[3] informed me that Mrs. Sutherland had telephoned to him that there was a letter from Mrs. Rogers at the house for me. When I got back I found to my dismay that we were to leave for Orwell that afternoon as soon as the *Earl Grey* got in.

"Then and there was hurrying to and fro." I had to go down to the Queen's and call on Mrs. Rogers. Then I met Bertie at the Plaza for dinner and then hurriedly added the last touches to my dress. Then I dressed, Bertie patiently playing the part of lady's maid. I was to be at the station at three and the Earl's party was expected to arrive soon after. I was there at three—but I had to wait until four before they came. Mrs. Rogers fished me out of the waiting room and took me over to where the Earl's party stood. I was presented. It was very informal and there was nothing at all terrifying.

Lady Grey and Earl Grey

---

1. Member of a French-speaking community near New Glasgow.

2. Dr. MacPhail's book (1910) is critical of contemporary feminism, education, and theology. Two other books with similar titles appeared in the same year: Yves Guyot's *Socialistic Fallacies* and Guilford Molesworth's *Economic and Facts and Fallacies*.

3. Bertie McIntyre's brother; another first cousin.

Earl Grey shook hands with me and began at once to talk about *Anne* and the pleasure it had given him.

He is a tall genial elderly man, with a frank pleasant face, and a most unaffected "homely" manner. He has bright dark eyes, very prominent teeth and is only passably good looking. I was then presented to "Her Excellency," the Countess, and her daughter, Lady Evelyn. The countess is a big "blowsy" woman, not in the least pretty and possessed of no charm

Her Excellency

whatever of manner or expression. She wasn't in the least "Vere de Vereish"[1] in appearance. Bertie MacIntyre, woman for woman, looks ten times more like the traditional countess.

Lady Evelyn is young and quite pretty, with fresh rosy cheeks and her father's dark eyes. Lady Evelyn was very nice to me and her mother tried to be, but neither of them has his trick of putting you perfectly at your ease. I felt at home with him from the first and could talk to him freely.

The special left at once. In "our" car were also the Governor and Mrs. Rogers, Judge and Mrs. Fitzgerald,[2] Premier and Mrs. Haszard.[3] They were all very nice to me. I liked the Fitzgeralds very much. Did not care much for the Haszards.

When we reached Orwell we were all met by carriages and driven half a mile to the old MacPhail homestead, a quite pretty place. There we had afternoon tea served in the glass veranda built across the front of the house. Then we strolled about in groups and amused ourselves. The evening was delightful. Mrs. MacPhail, the doctor's mother, and his sister Janetta seemed very nice people. The doctor himself is a strange-looking man—looks like a foreigner.

Presently Earl Grey asked me to go for a walk, saying he wanted to hear all about my books etc. We went through the orchard and followed a little winding path past the trees until we came to a small white building. "Let's sit down here," said His Excellency, squatting down on the steps. Accordingly, I "sot," too—since there did not exactly seem to be anything else I could do. I could not say to Earl Grey "This is the MacPhail water closet"—although that is what it was!! I suppose Earl Grey didn't know there were such places

---

1. Ultra-aristocratic; from Tennyson's "Lady Clara Vere de Vere," echoing Walter Scott's "Vere de Vere" in *Anne of Geierstein*.

2. Rowan Fitzgerald (1847–1921), Justice of the Supreme Court of PEI and his wife, Tremain Fitzgerald.

3. The Hon. Francis Long Haszard (1849–1938), lawyer and magistrate, later became premier and Attorney General, 1908–11; his wife was Elizabeth DesBrisay Haszard.

in existence. It was a neat little building, painted white, and even had a lace curtain in the window—likely put on for the occasion. And that is where His Excellency and I sat for half an hour and had our heart to heart talk. He never let the conversation lag, for he could ask a "blue streak" of questions. He asked me to send him an autographed copy of *Kilmeny* and my poems and was altogether delightful to me. But I was suffering so acutely from a suppressed desire to laugh that I hardly knew what I was saying. The Earl thought I was nervous and asked me if I had been rather dismayed at the idea of meeting him and when I said, "Yes, I've been in a blue funk," he laughed and said "But you won't feel that way any more, will you." I said "No," but I really think if we had sat there much longer I would have gone into hysterics—and never been able to explain why. I was mortally afraid that some poor unfortunate was cooped up in the house behind us, not able to get out; and I beheld with fascinated eye straggling twos and threes of women stealing through the orchard in search of the W.C. and slinking hurriedly back when they beheld the Earl and me gallantly holding the fort!

Finally the Earl got up and we went back to the house, I internally thanking my gods. Dinner was served. There were three tables—one in the dining room and two on the veranda. I was at one of the latter. Beside me on the left was Judge Fitzgerald. Opposite us were Mrs. Fitzgerald and a Mr. Armory,[1] Canadian correspondent of *The Times*—a very clever fellow. At one end of the table was a man I did not know and at the other, just at my right hand was a homely, red-haired, insignificant individual who, I had been told by someone, was a human being named Brock,[2] of the Ottawa geological survey. Accordingly, I held him in no awe and talked to him quite "sassily," laying down the law on the politics of Ancient Egypt (the history of which I have been studying lately) and the ultimate fate of the British Empire, contradicting him flatly as to Germany's designs and telling him the story of how I once got "drunk" on a medicinal dose of whisky. Later on I was somewhat horrified to discover that he was really Lord Percy, the A.D.C.-in-waiting of the Earl's suite. Had I known who he was I would have been tongue-tied. Not because he was Lord Percy[3]—after the Earl and the W.C. a mere Lord at a dinner table had no terrors for me—but because I would have supposed he must know vastly more of the subjects we were discussing than I could.

---

1. The Charlottetown paper gives the name as "Amery." The London *Times* ran his story about Lord Grey's Charlottetown visit in its midday edition.

2. Reginald Brock, F.R.C.S., born the same year as LMM (1874), had been director of the Geological Survey in Ottawa since 1907.

3. Alan Ian Percy (1880–1930), later eighth Earl of Northumberland; aide-de-camp to the Governor General, 1910–11, had served with distinction in South Africa and the Sudan. Lord Percy was grandson of the Duke of Argyll, and his father was A.D.C. to King Edward VII.

After dinner we had a pleasant half hour in the parlor and then left. I drove to the station with Lady Evelyn. Her manner is more like her father's than her mother's but she cannot "make talk" as he can. She told me she was "shy" so perhaps she was more ill at ease than I was.

We reached town at 10.30 and I bade them all good-bye and thankfully got into my cab and drove to Prince St. I was very glad it was all over. As I told Bertie I felt as if I had been for a flight in an airship. It was very interesting and delightful, but the best part was in getting back to good firm earth again.

I was so tired I did not sleep well. Next morning I went down town shopping. I made an engagement with my dentist for three and another to take tea with Perle Taylor[1] at six. Then I met Bertie at the Plaza for dinner. After dinner we went up to Prince St. promising ourselves a pleasant two hours of rest and chat. Alas for our delusive hopes! Mrs. Sutherland met us with the information that the Earl of Lanesborough[2] had called when I was out and left a letter. This proved to be an invitation to dine with their Excellencies on board the Earl Grey that evening at 7.30.

I did not want to go—that was all there was to it. I had thought I was through with the whole "Grey" matter. But help there was none. I had to fly to the telephone, cancel my engagements, order a cab, flowers, etc. etc. Then I lay down until five but could not sleep. At five I began to dress, aided by the patient Bertie. At seven my cab came and I went down to the marine wharf, where Lord Lanesborough had said a boat would be waiting for me. It was—at least some boat was, though I discovered later on that it was not the boat which had been sent to meet me. Mr. Armory and Dr. McCrae were in it also and we were rowed out to the *Earl Grey* in a pouring rain. Lord Percy came and took my wraps and Lord Lanesborough and Mr. Brock (the real Brock who *looks* much more like a "lord" than Percy) talked to me until the other members of the party came—Lieutenant Governor Rogers and Mrs. Rogers, Mayor Rogers[3] and his wife, Judge and Mrs. Fitzgerald, Professor and Mrs. McNaughton, Colonel and Mrs. Ogilvie.[4] Then "the Greys" came in, and presently we all went down to dinner. Professor McNaughton[5] took me down. He is Professor of Classics at McGill and the

---

1. A friend from Dalhousie University days.

2. John Brinsley, seventh Earl of Lanesborough (1865–1929), military secretary to the Governor General of Canada, 1909–10, had succeeded to title in 1905.

3. Benjamin Rogers Sr., wholesale retail hardware merchant, was mayor of Charlottetown, 1910–12; his wife was Mary Tremain Rogers.

4. Canadian military aide-de-camp. The viceregal party also included Dr. John McCrae (who was the medical doctor on the trip; he would later write the famous poem about World War I, "In Flanders Fields"), Douglas Sladen, and John Agnew.

5. John MacNaughton (1858–1943), born in Scotland, taught at Queen's University (1908), McGill (1908–19), and the University of Toronto (1919–25).

only man I ever met who talks as people do in books. His conversation was brilliant but somewhat too continuous. I had no time to look about me and not much time to eat. The menu was quite elaborate but none of the food tasted any better than many a dinner I've eaten in old country farmhouses and some of it not nearly as well. The pudding in particular was a vile concoction. We drank the King's health in champagne. It was all interesting but I was really too tired to enjoy it fully. However, the memory will always be a pleasant one. The only disagreeable part was in curtsying ourselves backward out of the Vice-Regal presence. However, I think I managed it as gracefully as the rest, though I narrowly escaped falling over the high doorstep and my train combined. I kept my eye on Mrs. Rogers and did just as she did.

Upstairs we had a rather dull time until the gentlemen rejoined us. Then we had a pleasant half hour. Earl Grey came and chatted to Mrs. McNaughton and me very interestingly, squatted on the floor between our chairs. He asked me all about grandmother and told me to give her his "very special regards." I thought that little act of thoughtfulness betokened the real nobility of the man more than anything else. I do not wonder that he is a popular Governor General.

We left at ten in a pouring rain and were rowed ashore. The *Earl Grey* left for Pictou[1] soon after. Cuthbert met me at the wharf with a carriage and I eventually reached "home" in a rather damp plight, so wretchedly tired that I could not sleep at all well. Next morning I spent shopping and then Bertie and I went to dinner at the Taylors. We had a drive about town afterwards but I did not enjoy it. The Taylors, in spite of their advantages in wealth and social position, are stupid, uninteresting people. Perle has not given any sign of remembering my existence since we sojourned together in Halifax until this Grey affair has given her memory a sudden jog. Perle was always a bit of a snob.

I left town at 5.30. Got to Hunter River at seven and drove home, getting here at nine. Stella Campbell was here. At any other time I would have been glad to see her but now I did not want to see *anyone*. I only wanted to get to bed in silence. This was not possible. I had to recount the details of my trip to Stella and what with laughing and talking got "past my sleep" again and spent a restless night. Stella went home this afternoon—and I am going to bed at six o'clock! I never felt so tired in my life. Physical weariness and nerve fatigue combined have made a wreck of me!!

---

1. A port in Nova Scotia, across the Northumberland Strait from Charlottetown, PEI.

Wednesday, Sept. 22, 1910
Cavendish, P.E.I.

Until yesterday I was very ill ever since Saturday with a bad cold and an attack of cholera morbus.[1] Had grandmother not been sick in just the same way I should have blamed my recent excursion into "high life" for my collapse. And indeed, no doubt the nervous strain of the past three weeks has left me less able to cope with physical ills.

Sunday and Monday grandmother and I were both so ill that we could not do anything, not even wait on each other. I could not lift my head without vomiting painfully. I was so thankful yesterday to feel better and be able to do something. But there is so much to do, for everything has got so behind hand these past three weeks. I certainly ought to keep a servant. To do the housework I do in connection with my increasing literary work is too much for me. But grandmother would never hear of such a thing and would think me crazy if I suggested it.

Sometimes I feel as if I could *not bear* for one day longer this ceaseless tyranny in petty things to which she subjects me. It is a useless waste of time and nerves to make any protest. Nothing has the slightest influence on her. One might as well talk to a pillar of granite. If asked why she does this or behaves thus she simply denies it flatly. If I show any resentment she cries for hours together and—in plain English—sulks. Many times I feel at my wits' end between the chains which bind me on all sides and the numerous calls and claims which my literary success has brought forth. My life was hard enough before I became "a celebrity." My success, instead of making it easier, has made it twice as hard by doubling the worries and mortifications which attend my circumstances here. I am well off and tolerably famous—but the conditions of my life are not even physically comfortable and I am beset with difficulties on every side—and all, or mainly, because I must live in subjection to a woman who, always inclined to be domineering and narrow-minded, has had

Lover's Lane

those qualities intensified by age until life with her means the utter suppression of all individuality in those who live with her.

---

1. Probably influenza, not the epidemic disease, dormant since the 1880s in Canada.

Well—well—well! I went for a walk in Lover's Lane tonight and forgot all these worries for a time in its ideal beauty. It is always lovely but tonight it seemed more beautiful than I had ever known it. The soft, warm rain of the afternoon had extracted all the woodland odors until the air was dripping with fragrance—dying fir, frosted ferns, wet leaves. That walk this evening gave me such exquisite pleasure as is impossible to express in clumsy words and furnished me with a little strength to go on with life and work.

Saturday, Sept. 25, 1910
Cavendish, P.E.I.

Have been very ill again since Thursday morning with a return of cholera. Tonight I feel exhausted and when the choir came here to practice I could hardly sit on the organ stool to play. I had a letter from Earl Grey today—as kind and thoughtful as a letter could be—a thoroughly "nice" letter.

But what avail Vice-Regal compliments when one has no appetite—none whatever? Since Thursday I simply *cannot* eat. I can think of nothing I would like and if I force myself to swallow a mouthful it will not stay swallowed. I never *felt* sicker in my life.

Sunday, Sept. 26, 1910
Cavendish, P.E.I.

I felt a little better today. This evening I spent at the manse. Margaret and I sat before the grate fire in the library and talked. How I do love an open fireplace. I love it so much that I feel sure I shall never have one of my own. No, I shall be doomed to stuffy stoves or—worse still!—a radiator all my life. To sit before an open fire with a "kindred spirit" and talk of "cabbages and kings"[1] is about as good a thing as life can offer.

The Manse

---

1. Quoting Lewis Carroll's *Alice in Wonderland* (1865).

Thursday, Sept. 30, 1910
Cavendish, P.E.I.

Have been gradually improving and am able to eat again. My cold still clings to me however. I cannot shake it off.

Today I received a very bright, amusing, interesting letter from a girl of sixteen in faraway Australia. It was a pleasure to read. I get so many such letters—two or three almost every day. Some of them are lovely, all are kind but some are rather monotonous. So far I have answered all with a note at least but I am finding it a good deal of a tax. In future I must make post-cards do duty instead. But the little Australian must have a real good answer to hers. What a small big world it is! And how far little red-haired Anne has travelled!

Today in reading "Elizabeth and Her German Garden" I found this pertinent paragraph:—

"The passion for being forever with one's fellows and the fear of being left alone is to me wholly incomprehensible. I can entertain myself for weeks together, hardly aware, except for the prevailing peace, that I have been alone at all."

To which I say devoutly, "Them's my sentiments too." But I fancy very few people could say so. To ninety-nine out of a hundred solitude is the worst punishment that could be inflicted on them. They must have "some company"—meaning thereby solely other human beings and barring out books and trees and *thoughts* tee-totally.

Well and good! I don't quarrel with them for this. Human companionship, when it is of the right sort, is a most excellent and delightful thing. But I *do* find fault with them for this—they cannot realize that not *all* people feel so and are never content to leave me alone when I am yearning to be left alone. No, they must "entertain" me. Sometimes, when I go out "to spend the afternoon" I am tempted to wonder if my friends are afraid that I will steal the spoons if they leave me alone for a minute. And when I have talked for an hour or two on trivial subjects in which I haven't any real interest I think, "Oh, if they would only leave me alone for ten minutes to rest!"

But they never do. They are doing as they would be done by. *They* wouldn't want to be left alone so nobody else could.

Tuesday, Nov. 29, 1910
Cavendish, P.E.I.

Two months since my last entry—and it really seems more like ten years. In those two months, or rather in fourteen days of those two months, I have "lived" more than I've done in the past twelve years—lived more, learned more, enjoyed more. For those fourteen days I was re-bathed in youth. And now I must write all about it in this poor old journal which has been blotted with so many dismal entries and now must receive the unaccustomed entry of a joyous one.

It began in an odd fashion on October 13th. Through September and October I had been having a rather agitated correspondence with Mr. Page[1] over some complaints the Musson Book Co.[2] of Toronto had made to me in regard to Mr. Page's business methods. The matter was eventually cleared up—to a certain extent at least—after a vast deal of typewriting and scribbling.

Then on October 13th I received from Mr. Page the final letter on the subject. He said that I should be personally acquainted with my publishers and that this affair which had involved so much correspondence could have been settled in ten minutes' conversation—that it was almost necessary to have a personal interview regarding my new book; and finally that he and Mrs. Page would be delighted if I could go to them for a visit in October or November.

When I read the letter I had not the slightest notion of going. It seemed to me that I might as well try to go to the moon. It would be impossible to get away; my wardrobe was not ready for such a trip and to make it so, especially at this time of year and under existing conditions, was also impossible; and, finally, I did not want to go. I dreaded meeting new people—I dreaded new surroundings—I dreaded what I believed would be the demand for nervous energy and exertion—a demand which I felt I could not meet, so physically miserable had I been ever since September. No, I laughed at the very idea of going to Boston; and I sat me down and wrote a letter to Mr. Page, saying I could not possibly go this fall; but I added that I would try to go up for a brief visit in the spring—for he had concluded his letter by saying that if I did not go up he thought he would have to come down to P.E.I. To have him come *here*, under present conditions was unthinkable. So I flung out the spring suggestion to head him off in that idea, trusting to luck that by the spring he would have forgotten all about the matter.

I sealed the letter and left it in my portfolio for the next day's mail. Then I went to tea at the manse, met "the Greens"—Rev. Mr. Green[3] and his wife,

---

1. Lewis Coues Page (1869–1956), president of L.C. Page, LMM's Boston publisher. In publishing since 1891, he had his own firm since 1897. LMM consistently refers to him as "Louis" Page, perhaps because he had signed his letters "L. Coues Page."

2. Toronto publishers, founded 1894, Canadian agent for L.C. Page, and for the British publisher Hodder and Stoughton. Charles J. Musson had suggested to LMM that Page was not giving accurate accounts of Canadian sales.

3. The Rev. William I. Green of New London was a missionary in Trinidad.

a most uninteresting couple—and afterwards went to prayer-meeting. Then I went home and went to bed.

Now comes an odd little psychological incident. I was almost asleep—in that dreamy state between sleeping and waking, when suddenly a thought flashed vividly into my brain, exactly as if a voice had spoken it to me—"Go to Boston." I sat up, wide-awake, tingling all over with some strange electric inrush of energy and determination. In a few moments the whole plan unrolled itself before me like a scroll or picture. "I *will* go. Stella Campbell is going up to visit Lucy Ritchie.[1] I will go when she goes. Judy Gallant is a steady trusty French girl and is just now out of employment. I'll hire her to stay with grandmother while I'm away. And I'll get what clothes I need after I go up."

There it all was, resolved on. I lay down again and went to sleep. In the morning I tore up the letter to Mr. Page and wrote another accepting his invitation.

Then remained to carry out our plans. I knew that this would mean a good deal of bother and worry but somehow I faced it all undauntedly—nay, with positive enjoyment. I felt strangely blithe and joyous—as I had not felt for years.

I had finished my book "The Story Girl." I was sorry to finish it. Never, not even when I finished with *Anne*, had I laid down my pen and taken farewell of my characters with more regret. I consider "The Story Girl" the best piece of work I have yet done. It may not be as popular as *Anne*—somehow I don't fancy it will. But from a literary point of view it is far ahead of it. It is an idyl of childhood on an old P.E. Island farm during one summer. I have written it from sheer love of it and revised it painstakingly—up there by the window of my dear white room. It may be the last book I shall ever write there.

I wished to get the typewriting done before I left. The first half I had done in town, the second half I did myself. From that time until I left for Boston I was a busy mortal.

Inside of room   Outside

---

1. Another first cousin, now in Boston, daughter of Uncle John and Aunt Emily (Macneill) Montgomery of Malpeque.

As soon as I heard from Stella when she was going (I had offered before this, by the way, to pay the expenses of her trip, because I felt that she was bitterly jealous of Frede's going to Macdonald) I walked back to "Toronto" to see Judy. By the road it would be nearly five miles. But I took a "short cut" back through Lover's Lane and over the fields beyond to "Toronto," as the little French settlement back among the hills is called. I did not know the exact way and several times lengthened the cut by wandering around looking for a path through some thick growing spruce grove. But it was an exquisite day and I enjoyed my walk through those golden fields and green dreaming woods.

Finally I reached Judy's home and secured the promise of her services during my absence. Before arriving there reason told me not to count too surely on getting her. She might be going to another place—she might not be able to come—but nothing worried me. I *felt* that I was to go to Boston. I *knew* that all my plans were going to be carried out. Judy would agree to come. And she did.

I had quite an experience getting back. Judy's mother assured me that the "shortest" cut was a road that led through the woods back of their house. I rashly decided to go that way, found the road—*a* road at all events—and trod it blithely. But alas, it dwindled away and away till it was a mere cow-path—and then, lo, it was not! To turn back would mean loss of time. I plunged blindly on. I knew I would come out in time if I kept on—but such a woeful scramble as it was, through a trackless wilderness of maple scrub and underbrush. I tore my skirt and ruined my rubbers and lost my temper. I was just "plain mad" when I finally did come out and found myself after a full hour's pilgrimage in the very field I could have reached in ten minutes had I gone from Judy's house by the way I came.

But I *was* there—and the air was like golden wine—and the sky blue—and I soon regained my peace of mind and had a walk home that was as sweet a pleasure as anything that came later on.

The next thing was to go to town. I had planned to go by train but, getting a chance in with "Jim Robert" Stewart, took it and we drove in the following Thursday, Oct. 31. It was a beautiful day and with anything of a companion I would have enjoyed the drive enormously. But with "Jim Robert"—well, silence is sometimes more expressive than words!

I had a bad tooth attended to, then met Bertie and did some shopping. The only important purchase I made was a fine set of mink furs. I have always loved good furs but never could afford them before. I got a beautiful collar and muff which were afterwards much admired in "The States."

At five we started home. The day was beautiful no longer. It had turned bitterly cold and a northeast hurricane was blowing in our faces. This was bad enough but might have been endured. What *couldn't* be endured was that four miles out it began to rain heavily and from that to the end of that twenty-four mile drive it *poured*. It was unendurable and we didn't endure it—we just tore through it and cussed—at least J.R.S. "cussed" and my *thoughts* were profane. I had a bad cold and neuralgia in my shoulder. It took us both to hold up one umbrella against the wind, and then our arms ached woefully. I don't think I should have thought it worth while to live through such a nightmare had it not been for the thought of some sausages I was carrying home with me. I have quite a weakness for sausages and the picture of myself at home, eating sausages for supper, gave me enough grit to worry through that fearful drive. I thought it was worth while to keep on living until I had eaten those sausages!

Seriously, we had a dreadful drive and I shall not soon forget the unpleasantness of it. I paid the price of my Boston pleasures in that expedition.

But I finally got home, got dried, and fried my sausages for supper!!

Having made all my arrangements I screwed my courage to the sticking point and told grandmother my plans. I had dreaded to do so, for I did not know how she would take it. Had I been going off on a mere "pleasure exertion" I fear she would not have taken it very well. But the word "business" had a magic sound and reconciled her to a great extent. Moreover, she knew Judy well and liked her.

From that until Nov. 5, the date fixed for going, I was exceedingly busy. But I enjoyed my "busyness" and found myself looking forward to my trip with a zest and keenness of anticipation such as I could not have believed possible a few weeks earlier. Friday, Nov. 4, was damp and foggy with frequent showers of rain. I completed my preparations, put the house in apple pie order, and packed. Then in the evening I borrowed Pierce's antiquated old "rig" and started to get Judy. No short cut was possible this time. I had to go by the road and a vile road it was, mud and water in equal proportions. Besides, it was drizzling and I could not hold up an umbrella and drive. Verily, for the moment my heart failed me and I thought pessimistically, "Is it worth while going through all this for the sake of a brief trip away among people I don't know and scenes I have no love for?"

However, I found Judy's place eventually, got her and started back. It was now dark and raining heavily. Old "Tom" was so slow I thought we'd never get home. But we did, and I went to bed with a conscience void of offence towards all men.

At 4.30 I was up. It was still raining—a nice prospect for an eleven mile ride. Was this to be an omen of my weather while away? I dressed, got breakfast, gave Judy sundry and diverse

Daffy

directions, including what to do in case of fire, and bestowed a farewell hug upon indifferent Daffy. At six Mr. Laird,[1] who had kindly offered to drive me to the station, came. The rain had ceased but it continued foggy and we had several drizzles on the way up. The roads also were very bad. I wondered if Stella were likewise bowling along the Kensington road, and wondered dismally what I should do if anything prevented her coming.

At eight we arrived at Hunter River; and from that moment until I got off the train at Kensington on my return everything was as pleasant, easy, and delightful as it could possibly be. For a whole fortnight I sojourned in Fairyland.

When I reached Kensington I peered eagerly over the crowd and my heart gave a throb of relief when I saw Stella. We laughed almost incessantly from that until we reached Boston. Stella has some failings which render her a not altogether agreeable person to *live* with continually. But for a travelling companion she is almost as good as can be wished—full of fun, resourceful, seeing the humorous side of everything, even of discomforts. As for me, I enjoyed *everything*, as a *child* might. The most trifling thing had pleasure for me. For the first time in twelve years I had left home without having to carry a burden of worry with me. No wonder everything seemed like a dream!

Stella

We had a beautiful crossing from S'side[2] to Pointe du Chene. The strait was as calm as a mill pond but the fog was too thick to see the scenery. Stella and I sat on deck until driven in by the drizzle becoming heavier. Then we went and had dinner. Hitherto, when I travelled I have always had to be as economical as possible and consider ways and means very carefully. This never increased the pleasure at all. I am candidly thankful that the day for this has gone by. Whatever worries life may still hold for me—and I have no hope that it will ever be very free from them—it does not seem likely that lack of money will hereafter be among them.

We had a good dinner on the boat and I ate with an appetite such as I have not known for years. All the time I was away I was wholesomely hungry and everything "tasted good."

When we reached the Pointe it was pouring rain but the train was waiting and we steamed away to St. John.[3] The scenery from the Point to St. John

1. Farmer next door; the father of several of LMM's schoolmates.

2. Summerside, PEI, where the ferryboats leave for Pointe du Chêne, New Brunswick.

3. At this New Brunswick city the Canadian Pacific Railway joined the American line; the train crossed the border at St Croix/Vanceboro.

must be very pretty in summer. Indeed, I know it is from my recollections of it when I went out west. But at this time of year there is little beauty and that little was effectually blotted out by fog and rain. However, Stella and I entertained each other excellently and did not find the journey monotonous. When we reached St. John station at 5.30 it was dark and we had an hour to wait. We put this in getting a dandy supper in a nice little restaurant in the station and writing post cards to friends. I thought of the last time I had been in that St. John station—twenty years ago when I went west with dear old Grandfather Montgomery. Well, I have lived a lifetime since then; but that night I felt as if I were a girl of fifteen again. Life seemed to have suddenly started on from where it stopped with me thirteen years ago. It was all a dream, of course—I expected to waken from it at any moment—but while it lasted I meant to enjoy it to the utmost.

We left St. John at 6.40. Owing to the fact that I had delayed writing to engage a sleeper until too late we could not get one, so had to sit up all night. It was a very wearisome night, spaced by unrefreshing cat-naps, but we did extract a lot of fun out of our tribulations. We could see nothing of the scenery of course until sunrise. Then we rode for two daylight hours through a country which must be very pretty in summer.

When we had left Vanceboro we had put our watches back, thus gaining an hour. Of course when I returned to Vanceboro the process was reversed and the hour was lost again. To me there seemed a symbolism in this. I had found a new hour—and it was a fairy hour which held a lifetime in fairyland—it was *my* hour, which had struck at last, after a lifetime of toil and endeavor and waiting. It was mine and I lived it to the full, draining it like a cup of enchantment—and then I came back and had to yield it up again. But its memory is left to me—and the memory of an hour in fairyland is worth many years on upper earth.

We reached Boston at 8.30 Sunday morning. It was a beautiful morning—as all my mornings were while away. Every day was fine. We expected to be met by Lucy Ritchie—Aunt Emily's second daughter who is married to George Ritchie and lives in Roslindale, one of the Boston suburbs—and also by Mr. Nernay, one of Mr. Page's salesmen. Mr. Page himself, being a suburbanite, could not get in so early but Mr. N. was to wear a white carnation as a means of identification. Accordingly, when we got out in the big North Station I scanned the crowd anxiously and in a moment caught sight of a young man adorned with a white carnation pacing along. We pounced on him at once. Then Lucy Ritchie appeared also.

Stella and I had expected to go out to Roslindale with Lucy R. by the unpretentious and cheap electrics.[1] You pay five cents and take a seat if you can get one or hang on by a strap if you can't—and in due time you get to your destination. But Mr. Nernay had a taxi all ready to take us out to Roslindale and in a few minutes we were all bowling along through beautiful streets to Roslindale. I had never been in an automobile before but I must say it is a very delightful way of getting about. Fifteen cents would have taken us to Roslindale; I suppose it took about fifteen dollars to get us there in a taxi.

Hitherto my literary success has brought me some money, some pleasant letters and an increase of worries and secret mortifications. I had experienced only the seamy side of fame. But now I was to see the other side. I was to find everything made easy and pleasant for me. It was very delightful— but of course it was only a dream!

Reason told me that it was no wonder that my publishers, who have made a fortune out of my books, should take some pains to please me. But my subjective mind, long inured, even from the earliest dawn of memory, to believing that I was an insignificant person, of no importance to anybody, refused to be convinced and went on telling me that the good people who made a fuss over me must be taking me for somebody else—or were making fun of me!

The Ritchies have a cosy little home. I had never met George Ritchie since we were children and then only once for a day. He is a very nice little chap, very intelligent and kind, but afflicted with con-genital hip trouble which makes him very lame. Lucy R. was always a nice sensible girl but a bit of a "stick." They have two children—Kenneth, aged four, and Jean, aged two.

Jean and Kenneth Ritchie

In regard to Kenneth Ritchie I had a rather strange experience. I have never, as to speak frankly, been a lover of children *as* children. I have always felt that if I were married I would strongly desire to have children of my own. If a friend I loved had children I felt interested in and attached to her children for her sake. Occasionally also I have met with children who were so sweet and attractive that I became very fond of them. Little Marian Webb, for example, here in C. is a dear kiddy and has always been a pet of mine. When people ask me that absurd question "Do you like children?" I always feel like

---

1. The Boston subway for electric trams began construction in 1895, connecting with surface and elevated lines; a single fare would take a passenger over 100 miles (161 km).

retorting—and sometimes do, if I think the questioner has brains enough to understand the retort—"Why don't you ask me if I like grown-up people? I like some very much, detest others, and am indifferent to the vast majority."

Hitherto, even with the nicest children it has been a mere matter of *liking*. Never, until I met Kenneth Ritchie, have I seen a child I really *loved*. And I love Kenneth so much that I don't see how I could love him any more if he were my own child. If there was the slightest use in asking his parents to give him to me I would adopt him. I cried with loneliness when I left him and I long for him every day. He is the child of a woman who always bored me and a man who is virtually a stranger to me. I had not expected to care a pin for him—and I loved him. He is a beautiful child with a beautiful disposition. Yet I have seen as beautiful and as good children before and did not love them as I loved Kenneth Ritchie. To me this love is one of the sweetest things that have ever entered my life. If my visit to Boston has held nothing but my discovery of Kenneth I should think it well worth while.

Soon after we arrived at the house, while I was desperately trying to erase the too visible marks of a sleepless night from my face, the bell rang and a boy handed in a box containing a dozen magnificent roses for me, with the Page Co.'s card. They were so lovely that I haven't got over their beauty yet.

Stella and I wanted to go right to bed, but couldn't. Jim Montgomery—a second cousin of mine—and his bride had been invited to dinner to meet me. They came and we put in a dull afternoon. I was too sleepy and stupid to talk. Mrs. Jim was a pretty, sweet-faced, charmingly gowned little doll, and Mr. Jim was a rather patronizing and uninteresting individual. We felt devoutly thankful when they went.

After tea we decided to go into town to Tremont Temple[1] and hear Cortland Myers. But when we got there there was not even standing room and we had to go to Park St. church instead where Dr. Conrad preached a rather prosy sermon. The music was good, however, and I liked the atmosphere of the service.

When I got into bed that night I thought it was the best place in the world!

At nine o'clock Monday morning Mr. Nernay was out with a taxi to take me into town. We first went to the Page Co.'s new office on Beacon St. where I met Mr. Louis C. Page, the head of the firm, and his brother George Page.[2] This is as good a place as any to record my impressions of them.

George Page is a short, stout, round-faced man, quite commonplace in appearance—quite likeable but without any special charm or distinction. He does not resemble his brother in the least. Louis Page is a man about

---

1. A Baptist church in central Boston; Cortland Myers (1865–1941) was its pastor, 1893–1921.
2. Like his brother Lewis, George had been in his stepfather's firm, Estes and Lauriat.

forty and is, to be frank, one of the most fascinating men I have ever met. He is handsome, has a most distinguished appearance and a charming manner—easy, polished, patrician. He has green eyes, long curling lashes and a delightful voice. He belongs to a fine old family and has generations of birth and breeding behind him, combined with all the advantages of wealth. The result is one of those personalities which must be "born" and can never be achieved. He was, in the main, very much like the mental picture I had formed of him from his letters.

Am I then perfectly satisfied with my publisher?

No—o—o!

Why not?

I cannot say definitely. But the fact is that I do not trust him.

Mr. Page was exceedingly kind to me during my visit and left nothing undone that might give me pleasure. This, combined with his personal charm, makes me feel very ungrateful and foolish in mistrusting him. Yet the feeling is instinctive and will not down.

Mr. Page seemed very anxious that I should come up to Boston to clear away the last shreds of misunderstanding *re* the Musson affair. Yet all the time I was there he never referred to it. Nor did I. I was bound I wouldn't until he did, for it was in his place to do so. Yet he never remotely hinted at it. Did he forget it? Or deem it of no importance? Or was he only too glad to steer clear of it since I did not bring it up?

Again, before I went to Boston I wrote Mr. Page that I did not intend to sign any more contracts containing the binding clause.[1] It is not fair that I should be held indefinitely to such poor terms as he gave me for *Green Gables*. The clause was renewed with *Avonlea* and *Kilmeny* but I was resolved it should not be so again.

Mr. Page never referred to this part of my letter in his reply and later on invited me to Boston. I did not expect to receive or sign the contract for the *Story Girl* until I had sent the MS which would not be until my return home. Consequently I was surprised when, on the last morning of my visit, Mr. Page asked me if I would sign it if he brought it home that night. I wondered that he should want to commit himself to the publication of a story he had never seen but I said "yes" and at night took it up to my room. To my disgust, the binding clause was in it.

Now, did Mr. Page forget what I had written him two months before? Or did he reason thus:—"She has been my guest; I have been exceedingly good

---

1. LMM's contract bound her to offer Page first refusal on her subsequent work for five years on terms established at the time of publication of *AGG*: 10 percent royalties on the wholesale price, rather than 15 percent on the retail price (as was usual for successful authors).

and agreeable to her; in my house and as my guest she won't want to start a discussion which might end in a wrangle and stiffness; so she will sign it without question."

If he did I justified his craft for I decided to sign for just those reasons, though I vowed it would be for the last time.

These two little things are slight matters to cause distrust and would not have done so if some instinct in me had not whispered a protest. Anyhow, I can do nothing just now. Even if I had more justification for my distrust I am bound hard and fast to him for five more years and must get on as agreeably as possible during that time.

After my call at the office Lu, Stella and I went shopping. Some of the big dep't stores[1] up there are very fine. At first I found them bewildering places but in a few days I "got the hang" of them and began to feel quite at home in them.

That day I got a brown broadcloth suit and an exquisite afternoon dress of old rose cloth, hand embroidered in pink silk. This last garment cost eighty dollars. My old ingrained, economical instincts gave a wild squawk of protest as I said "I'll take it," but I heeded them not. There was no reason why I should. Yet I don't think I shall ever be able to spend money like this without an effort. I shall always have to remind myself that I can afford it— always have to appease my conscience by telling it that eighty dollars means no more to me now than eight once did. There have been very few years in my life when eighty dollars would not have covered the cost of all the clothes I got in that year.

In the late afternoon we went home and I had just time to dress when the ever useful Mr. Nernay again arrived with the customary taxi to take me out to Brookline. We had a delightful drive there through the crisp autumn dusk gemmed with its countless lights. Brookline is a beautiful suburb and Mr. Page has a beautiful home. I was met at the door by a maid and taken straight to my room. It was a nice one—well-furnished, rather stiff,

Front view Page home   Side view Page home

---

1. Filene's and Jordan Marsh, major department stores in Boston in 1910.

but with every convenience. I think the convenience I found "convenientest" was the mirror door of the closet. It really was scrumptious—to see yourself from top to toe in full regalia—to know just how your skirt hung and how the different parts of you harmonized.

Corner of Page Library

When I had got my wraps off the maid came up with a message from Mrs. Page—would I have some tea in the library. I went down over a polished hardwood staircase, the side of which was lined with a fine collection of prints of Mr. Page's ancestors. The library is the most beautiful room I was ever in. The furnishings were in perfect taste and noth-

Mildred Page

ing made any inharmonious note. Built-in shelves, beautiful windows, splendid books, delightful easy chairs, big fireplace. A large picture of *Anne*—the original painting of the cover design—occupied a prominent position on the wall.

Mrs. Page is a woman of about 35 and fairly good looking but utterly without "charm." She was so very nice to me—instructed to be so by Louis P. no doubt—that I couldn't help liking her; but I found nothing of the race-of-Joseph in her. We do not talk the same language.

I was not the only guest in the Page household. Mr. and Mrs. Paul Marcone of New York were there on their honeymoon. He is an Italian, his father a New York Banker, his grandfather a Sicilian count. Anita Marcone is a niece of the notable Senator Hanna and is a Philadelphian. In evening dress she is the most beautiful girl I ever saw. When she is forty she will not be beautiful—she will be fat and coarse. But just at present, in full toilette, she is something I could not keep my eyes off. She is very nice; well educated, witty, superficially clever. I really liked her. Paul was a nice little boy, likable but not in the least clever or brilliant. I can't just make out why Anita ever married him. I am rather of the opinion that their marriage was something of a runaway, so she must have been in love with him; but he seems like a schoolboy to her woman of the world.

Mrs. Paul Marcone in her wedding dress

After tea I went to my room and dressed for dinner. I like dinner in the evening. I like the soft lights gleaming on pretty faces and white necks and

L.M. Montgomery in fox fur at
L.C. Page home

jewels and beautiful gowns. And I must candidly say that I liked the life of the Page menage and that it fitted me like a glove. I suspect I should grow tired of it in time and long for the old simplicity. But for a change it was very delightful.

Tuesday I spent shopping with Mrs. Page and got several pretty things, including a sweet little hat of black velvet with a pale pink rose at the side. That night there was a notice in the *Herald* that I was in Boston and thenceforth I was besieged with invitations and telephone calls. Wednesday Mrs. Page, the Marcones and I spent the day in the new Museum of Fine Arts. It was a wonderful day—but it should have been a week instead of a day. I had no time to *study* anything—I could only look and pass on. And there was so much to look at—I wanted to stand for an hour before everything and absorb it. The collection of Japanese pottery was marvellous—the amber room was a delight beyond words; the Egyptian department was wonderful and the Greek Statues were—Greek statues. And as for the paintings—but I cannot write about them. I had seen engravings of most of them but to see the pictures themselves was a revelation.

We must have walked unconscious miles in our peregrinations about the Museum. When we got home I was woefully tired but so full of what I had seen that I couldn't remember I was tired. In the evening we all went to see "The Chocolate Soldier."[1] It was a musical farce and I didn't care for it. The whole thing seemed deafening and dazzling—eye, ear, and senses ached. It was considered good of its kind by the others but I didn't enjoy it at all.

Lucy Lincoln Montgomery

The Americans are a noisy nation. I had heard and read this and now I found it out for myself. They do not seem able to enjoy themselves unless there is a tremendous noise going on about them all the time. Even in the restaurants there is such a crash of music that you have to shriek to be heard. No wonder "The American Voice" is notorious. I

---

1. Operetta by Oscar Strauss based on George Bernard Shaw's *Arms and the Man* (1894); the heroine's part was played by Alice Yorke, a Canadian actress.

cannot but think such a constant racket most injurious. One may "get used to it" but the bad effect on nerves must remain.

Thursday morning I went out to Wakefield where I had promised to lunch with Lucy Lincoln Montgomery[1] my unseen literary correspondent. As soon as I left the train I saw her, recognizing her from her photograph. She seems to be a very sweet woman, of about 60 years of age. Her sister and brother-in-law, General and Mrs. Goodale,[2] live with

Glad Hill

her and they have a nice home called "Gladhill." Another sister of hers, Mrs. Slocum,[3] the wife of a college president, was also there. I spent a very delightful day. They were nice, refined, cultured people, not so aggressively "smart" as the Page set and consequently much more restful. In the evening I returned to Brookline. A Mr. and Mrs. Jones dined with the Pages that night and we had a pleasant evening. Friday morning I spent in Mr. Page's office— met all the staff, was shown over the establishment and was interviewed by Mr. Alexander of the *Herald*, a canny delightful old Scotchman. Then I went home and dressed for the luncheon which Mrs. George Page gave for me that afternoon. I wore my old rose dress and carried a big bouquet of double violets which Mrs. George Page had sent. The George Pages have a beautiful home at Chestnut Hill. Mrs. George is a "sweet" little woman—very much sweeter than Mrs. L.C. but not such good company. A number of her friends were at the luncheon. It was the "smartest" function I attended in Boston. The menu was quite elaborate. Here it is—in memory of the first society function at which I was "guest of honor." Oyster cocktail, green turtle consomme, mushrooms under glass, devilled squab on toast, cucumber and tomato salad, with cheese balls, and ice cream.

To tell the dreadful truth the only thing I really liked was the ice-cream. The other courses were very pretty but I wouldn't give a fig for them compared to a good P.E.I. "duck supper" with accoutrements.

---

1. An American verse-writer (a correspondent but not a relation to LMM) living in Wakefield, MA.

2. Greenleaf Goodale (1839–1915) had served in the Civil War and in the Philippines, and retired in 1903.

3. Probably the wife of the author William Frederick Slocum, born in 1851 in Grafton, MA, and president of Colorado College, 1888–1916.

From the luncheon we went into Boston to a reception which the Boston Authors' Club gave me at their rooms in the Kensington. Arriving there I was given another box of roses with Mr. P's card. I had a most enjoyable evening, meeting so many authors whose writings I had read—Nathan Haskell Dole,[1] Charles Follen Adams,[2] J.L. Harbour,[3] Helen Winslow,[4] Abbie Farwell Brown,[5] Ellen Douglas Deland[6] etc. A reporter from the *Post* also came to interview me. In the article which came out next day he described me as wearing a gown which "shimmered and dazzled." And me in that quiet little old-rose frock!!

I was tired when I got home but I sat up to an unholy hour reading the MS of a novel on which Mr. Page wanted me to pass an opinion.

Saturday morning I had to hie me into town to get an evening dress for a big reception at Basil King's,[7] to which I was invited. I got a sweet little dress of apricot chiffon over silk, with all the appurtenances thereof. Then I went to the Hotel Touraine to meet and be interviewed by a *Traveller* reporter—a girlish little creature who looked too young to be a journalist but who was quite an expert in her line, as her consequent write-up showed. When she had finished asking me questions she took me out on the Common and had a photographer "snap" me. In her write-up she said I was "petite, with the fine, delicate features of an imaginative woman."

Anita Marcone then joined me and we went to the matinee to see the "Summer Widowers."[8] It was another musical comedy but I enjoyed it considerably because of some very beautiful scenic effects and dances in it. When it was over Mr. and Mrs. Page, Mrs. Jones, and Paul joined us and we

---

1. Nathan Haskell Dole (1852–1935), author of eleven books, editor of the *Encyclopedia Americana* and of many volumes of poems and letters, translator of Tolstoy and others. LMM owned a copy of his edition of the poems of Robert Burns. Dole wrote an introduction to *Further Chronicles of Avonlea* in 1920.

2. Charles Follen Adams (1832–1918), author of humorous poems in German dialect since 1872; Page had published his *Leedle Jawcob Strauss and Other Poems*.

3. A native of Iowa, author of over seven hundred short stories, and a popular lecturer, J.L. Harbour (1857–1931) had been associate editor of *Youth's Companion*, 1884–1901 (covering the years when LMM's first publications appeared in that journal).

4. Helen Winslow (1851–1938), editor and publisher; connected with women's clubs; author of eleven books, including *Spinster Farm* (1908) and *Woman for Mayor* (1909).

5. Abbie Farwell Brown (1860–1935), editor of *Young Folks' Library* since 1902 and author of many books for children, such as *Friends and Cousins* (1907).

6. Ellen Douglas Deland's (1860–1923) popular girls' books included *Josephine* and *The Friendship of Anne*.

7. Born in Charlottetown, but long a resident of Cambridge, MA, Basil King (1859–1928) was an Anglican priest who wrote popular novels with moral themes, including *The Wild Olive* (1910).

8. "A Musical Panorama in 7 Views" by Glen MacDonough and Baldwin Sloane.

had a table-d'hote dinner in the Rathskellar of the American House where everybody—more or less—was celebrating the big Harvard-Yale football match. I enjoyed this immensely. The bill of fare was delicious, the "sights" most interesting. I revelled in enjoyment of it all. A certain requirement of my nature, which has been starved for years seemed to be having full satisfaction at last. There are things I love better and which are far more essential to me than gay, witty companionship and conversation, delicious food, and dazzling sights—*and Chateau Yquem*.[1] But I *do* like them very well, too, and I believe that it is necessary for my normal well-being that I should have them occasionally.

As for the Chateau Yquem—well, I didn't drink as much of it as the others did. But I had to walk *fearfully straight* when I left the table!

When all was over I was woefully tired. So Sunday morning I went out to Roslindale and just rested and loved Kenneth.

In the evening I went back to Brookline for dinner. After dinner Miss Conway of the *Republic*, called to see me—a most charming woman. I liked her "write-up" better than any of the others. It was written seriously and not in the "smart," flippant style which the younger generation of journalists seem to affect. Some of the paragraphs ran as follows:—

"As the young author entered the Pages' beautiful library one thought came to us, 'It is a repetition of history—Charlotte Brontë coming up to London'—Miss Montgomery is slight and short—indeed of a form almost childishly small, though graceful and symmetrical. She has an oval face, with delicate aquiline features, bluish-gray eyes and an abundance of dark brown hair. Her pretty pink evening gown somewhat accentuated her frail and youthful aspect. It would not be easy to exaggerate the retiring manner and untouched simplicity of this already famous woman—more and more her individuality came out, until we remembered the word of the first eminent literary man of our acquaintance who was wont to declare that the strong original characters usually develop in the small, secluded places till the unconscious shining of their light attracts attention...[2] For all her gentleness and marked femininity of aspect she impressed the writer as of a determined character with positive convictions... we could not imagine her as a 'woman of affairs' or aught but the modest, quiet little gentle woman of the warm heart and vigorous, creative brain that she is. Bostonians are charmed with her unique personality not less than with her books."

Have I really a "unique personality," I wonder!

---

1. Chateau d'Yquem, a classic wine from the Sauternes area in Bordeaux, France.

2. In LMM's handwriting, long dashes appear here to suggest she is leaving material out.

When Miss Conway had gone Mrs. Mountain[1] of the Canadian Club and Mrs. Morrison of the Intercolonial Club[2] came to invite me to a combined reception of the two clubs the next evening. When bedtime came I went to my room and finished reading that MS. If it had been any good, or had shown any sign of promise I wouldn't have grudged the time spent on it. But it was absolute trash. "The Flight of Virginia" received a very unfavorable report from me—a report which, I understand, settled its fate without any further reading.

Monday morning I went into town—by this time I had become quite accustomed to the noise and bustle, to sprinting after cars and hanging to straps—and met Lu Ritchie and Stella and that darling Kenneth. I gave them lunch at the *Exeter* and then I went out to Worcester to attend a reception given me by the Maritime Association of that burg. A deputation of the folks met me at the station and took me for an automobile drive to see the city. Then we went to the parlors of the Presbyterian church where the reception was held. After the reception there was a short program. I had to sit on a chair on the platform while the Rev. MacLeod Harvey[3] sat on the other. Then he made a speech referring to me and my books very nicely. To me, it seemed that my dream was growing so ridiculous that I *must* waken soon. It could not be *I* who was sitting there on that platform, honored by "potent, wise, and reverend seigniors"[4] in that fashion

[The First Presbyterian Church, Main and Hermon Streets, Worchester, Mass.]

while the audience gazed at me as if it did really suppose I was a celebrity! Of course it was not I. I think I really wanted to laugh—it all seemed so absurd that they should think my presence a matter of such moment. I never felt so utterly insignificant in all my life as I did while I was perched there on that platform and be praised!

I left at 5 and got to the Back Bay station at 6.30. Mrs. Morrison met me and whisked me out to Roxbury where the Canadian Club reception was

---

1. Mrs. Benjamin F. Mountain of Roxbury, MA; Mrs. James Kay Morrison of Winthrop, MA.

2. The Canadian Club and the Intercolonial Club are no longer in existence in Boston. Besides the Boston clubs, there was a Canadian Club at Harvard University.

3. Pastor of First Presbyterian Church, Worcester, MA.

4. *Othello* I.iii. (Shakespeare makes them "grave" rather than "wise.")

held at Mrs. Mountain's house. I would have enjoyed it if I hadn't been very tired. But I was "dead" tired. It seemed to me that I must have been shaking hands and smiling and saying, "I'm glad you enjoyed it" for a year. I met a great many Island people there and they were all lovely to me and I did feel pleased and proud. But under it all I was thinking, "Oh, if I could just get to bed!"

I didn't get to bed until twelve, and then I was too tired to sleep. I was taking a cold, too, and altogether I didn't spend a very pleasant night.

Tuesday afternoon I went in to town, met Stella and took her out to Brookline. Then she, the Marcones and I, started out on an expedition which filled in the most delightful day of my whole trip. First we went to Cambridge to the Agassiz Museum to see the "Ware Collection of Glass Flowers." I wasn't feeling very anxious to see them for the sound of "glass flowers" didn't please me. But I am glad I didn't miss that wonderful collection. Yes, they are indeed wonderful—so wonderful that they don't seem wonderful at all—they seem to be absolutely real flowers and you have to keep reminding yourself that they are made of glass—of *glass*—to realize how wonderful they are.

Just after lunch

Then we went to Lexington[1] which of course teems with relics of the war of '76. The most interesting of them was the old Hancocke-Clarke house[2] which is kept just as it was then and contains besides a great number of relics collected from all over New England. We had lunch at the Russell House and then went to Concord.[3] Concord is the only place I saw when I was away where I would like to live. It is a most charming spot and I shall never forget the delightful drive we had around it. We saw the "Old Manse" where Hawthorne lived during his honeymoon and where he wrote "Mosses from an Old Manse," the "Wayside" where he also lived, the "Orchard House" where Louisa Alcott wrote, and Emerson's house. It gave a strange reality to the books of theirs which I have read to see those places where they

---

1. A town 11 miles (29 km) northwest of Boston; site of the first skirmish in the American Revolution, April 1775, moments before the "shot heard round the world" was fired at Concord.

2. A historical museum house in Lexington, where Samuel Adams and John Hancock stayed on the eve of battle with the resident parson Jonas Clarke. LMM misspells as "Hancocke."

3. Nineteen miles (31 km) northwest of Boston, birthplace of revolutionary action; in the 1840s the home of Ralph Waldo Emerson and Henry David Thoreau.

once lived and labored. We were very sorry that we could not go to the Sleepy Hollow cemetery and see their graves but we had not time.

Stella stayed all night with me. Wednesday was the most strenuous day I put in up there. In the forenoon, Mr. Page's mother, Mrs. Dana Estes[1] (she was married twice) called on me—a very stately and imposing old dame. She took me for a pleasant drive around Brookline in her limousine and then drove me to the Hotel Touraine where the three girls from Mr. Page's office, Miss Lacey, Miss Chapman, and Miss Lebert gave me a luncheon. It was very sweet of them, but, beyond the by no means insignificant pleasure of tasting good food, there was no especial enjoyment in it for me. The girls seemed rather in awe of me and I consequently couldn't feel especially at ease with them. Besides, I was really so tired that it was an effort to talk at all. From there Mrs. Page and I went to a celebration of the N.E. Women's Press Association's 25th Anniversary in the Hotel Vendome. This was a big affair and the only thing I didn't enjoy in Boston at all. I was bored. The program didn't interest me at all. Then I had been asked to stand on the receiving line and I stood for two weary hours and shook hands with hundreds of women, who all said pretty much the same thing and had to receive pretty much the same answer. When Mrs. Page and I finally left I told her I was sure a smile must be glued on my face and that I doubted if I could say anything for the rest of my life but the parrot cry of "I'm glad you liked it." Anne, Anne, you little red-headed monkey, you are responsible for much!

In evening dress for the first time!

We got home at half past six. I was dreadfully tired—so tired that I shrank from the thought of going to another reception that night. But a good dinner, a half hour's rest and the excitement of dressing toned me up again. My chiffon dress looked very pretty. It was the first time I had ever worn a low-necked dress and at first I felt as if I wasn't clothed at all. I had had my hair done in town and wore little pink satin roses in it, and I had a lovely white chiffon beaded scarf and the dearest little black velvet slippers. At least, I thought they were dear when I put them on; but there is a sequel to that. When we got out of the cab at the King house I happened to look up, while Mrs. Page was making some arrangements with the chauffeur, and I saw that the moon was in eclipse! Instantly I thought of home—I could see the dark hills, the old fields, the

---

1. Mother of Lewis and George Page. As a widow she had married Dana Estes, the founder of Estes & Lauriat publishing company, bought by L.C. Page after his stepfather died in 1909.

distant woods. If I had been home I would have been watching that eclipse—and it would have given me a keener delight and a more real pleasure than even the Basil King reception.

But the latter was very enjoyable. The Kings have a beautiful home and are very nice people. He is a noted author—a very peculiar-looking man, his peculiarity enhanced by green goggles, but he has a delightful voice and manner. The rooms swarmed with celebrities. One was Colonel Thomas Wentworth Higginson,[1] a very old man, the sole survivor of the Longfellow-Whittier-Emerson set. I, myself, seemed not altogether uncelebrated. When I came away Mrs. King said, "You have been our 'great gun' this evening." Altogether, I had a really lovely time. But still, I did regret missing that eclipse!

I enjoyed that reception; and yet through it all I endured "agony untold." Those wretched slippers! They "drew" my feet until I could have shrieked. The minute I got into our homeward cab I kicked them off, thanking "whatever gods there be" for the relief.

Next morning I had to go into town and be photographed for the Press Bureau. That done I visited the State library—a very beautiful building; but I was too tired to enjoy it. After lunch I packed up; and that evening on the 7.30 train I left Boston. Mr. Page went to the station with me. A deputation from the Canadian and Intercolonial clubs were there to see me off. The ladies of the clubs gave me a bouquet of violets, the gentlemen gave me a box of big yellow chrysanthemums, and Mr. Page had another box of violets sent up. Then the train pulled out and I went to bed. In the morning I reached St. John. Aunt Mary met me and I stayed with them until Saturday. In the afternoon I went to a tea and spent the evening with a Mrs. Smith—a very clever woman, not quite clever enough to conceal her cleverness and consequently something of a bore now and then—but very kind and jolly.

I left next noon and arrived in Kensington at 8.30. I stepped off the train into a black, snowy night. My easy, pleasant times were over.

George Campbell met me but gave his place to Bruce Howatt who was looking for a chance down. We had a horrible drive. The roads were so bad the horse could only walk and the sleet blew in our faces the whole way—quite a change from the drives I had been having. Somehow, the whole thing seemed symbolical. I was going back to the worries and discomforts of my usual life. That drive was typical.

But we got to Park Corner eventually. I stayed there until Monday. It was very lonely without the girls. George brought me home on Monday. I found everything as usual and all well. Since then I have been very busy, trying to

---

1. Dean of American essayists, author of over thirty books, including biographies of Longfellow and Whittier. Page was the publisher of his *The Afternoon Landscape* and *The New World and the New Book*.

catch up with the accumulated work and correspondence. We have had a great deal of rain and it has made things very dull. I have also had a bad cold and am only now getting over it.

Sunday, Dec. 11, 1910
Cavendish, P.E.I.

Lover's Lane

This was a fine day and this evening I had a most beautiful and soul satisfying walk in Lover's Lane. Since coming home I have been so busy and the weather and walking so bad that I had no opportunity to go before.

I have never found the lane so exquisite as it was tonight. It was not the Lover's Lane of June, blossom-misted, tender in young green; nor yet the Lover's Lane of September, splendid in crimson and gold. It was the Lover's Lane of a still, snowy winter twilight—a white, mysterious silent place, full of wizardry. I walked softly through it and, as ever, all things of life fell into their relative places of importance. The pleasures of my Boston trip seemed, after all, quite tawdry and insignificant and unsatisfying compared to the spirit delight of that dream-haunted solitude. That wood lane caters to the highest in my soul. *Its* pleasures never cloy—*its* remote charm never palls. How shall I ever be able to live without it?

Monday, Dec. 26, 1910
Cavendish, P.E.I.

Yesterday was Christmas—a very dreary day. It rained heavily from dawn to dark. This past fortnight has been dreary all through—bad weather, bad walking and a great many worries, especially over Aunt Annie's recent illness, a bad attack of congestion of the lungs. I have felt very dull and dispirited and, worst of all, there has been a return of that terrible feeling of inability and lack of strength to cope with life. Oh, I hope I shall not be as ill this winter as I was last. I shall never forget the horror of it. I would rather die than go through such a time again. But I hope I shall not be so bad. I feel much better physically than I did this time last year. And then I have Margaret near by to go to when I feel a "blue" spell coming on. An hour of cheery chat with her generally averts or at least lessens the nervous attack. So far, too, I am sleeping well.

I have been revelling for a week in Mrs. Gaskell's novels,[1] Mr. Macdonald[2] having given me a complete set of her works at Christmas. They are delightful. And I have read "Romola"[3] again. Oh, truly, there were giants in those days in literature. We haven't a writer today of either sex who can compete with them. While reading those books I felt ashamed to think I had written things I called books at all. Mine seemed so trivial and petty compared to those masterpieces.

Saturday, Dec. 31, 1910
Cavendish, P.E.I.

Have been reading Bliss Carman's "Pipes of Pan."[4] I enjoyed them, too. Carman is the foremost American poet of the present. That, to be sure, is not a dizzy elevation. There are no master singers nowadays. Some of Carman's work is very charming—yes, that's just the word for it—charming. A large dose of it palls. He has only one or two notes and the constant repetition of these becomes monotonous, no matter how much they pleased at first. Then, he deals only with the *joy* of life. And no poet can be great who does not take the *pain* of life also into his poetry.

---

1. Elizabeth Claghorn Gaskell (1810–65), novelist and wife of a minister, raised social issues in *Mary Barton* (1848), *Ruth* (1853), and *North and South* (1855). Her biography of Charlotte Brontë was also a favourite of LMM's.

2. LMM had been secretly engaged to marry the Rev. Ewan Macdonald since 1906. After a period of study in Glasgow and two years in churches in Bloomfield and Bedeque, PEI, Macdonald had been called to a parish in Leaskdale, ON, early in 1910. As a young man he signed his Christian name as Ewen, but she spelled it "Ewan" in her journals (both are Gaelic form of "Hugh"). Both spellings appear on his tombstone.

3. George Eliot's historical romance (1863) about the duty of self-sacrifice.

4. In 1910 this popular New Brunswick poet was settled in Connecticut. *The Pipes of Pan* was published in 1906.

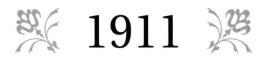

1911

Sunday, Jan. 15, 1911
Cavendish, P.E.I.

It seems hard to believe that it is the middle of January. We have had no snow and wheels have been running right along. For myself, I prefer this. Not to have to wade about in snow or freeze with cold means a good deal to me. I am feeling fairly well so far this winter—much better than for many winters. When I think of my condition this time last year it makes me cringe. The very remembrance is almost more than I can endure. I do not think I shall break down this winter. Yet it is impossible not to feel alarmed lest I may. I do feel so worried and unhappy all the time. I cannot even write my worries out here—they go too deep and cut too keenly. I seem to enjoy *nothing*. Always there is the undercurrent of dread and anxiety and heartsickness. I never know a minute's peace of mind. A hundred different fears distract me. The only hours when I can win a momentary forgetfulness are when I lose myself in a book.

I am very busy. There are a thousand things to do. I work continually, with a gnawing worry at my heart all the time. It is hard to live thus. If I had anyone to share the worry with me—to talk things over with—to assist—to encourage! But I have no one. And everywhere I look I can see nothing but darkness.

> It is very good for strength
> To know that someone needs you to be strong.[1]

So, Elizabeth Barrett Browning. Yes, that is true. But it is hard to make a show of strength when one is really weak and tired and overworn.

But I am writing this at night—and the night of a dull, lifeless, winter day. The world always looks its blackest to me under such conditions. In the mornings it never seems quite so bad. I have not so far had any of the dreadful sleepless nights of last winter. But some of my nights have been broken and disturbed. I have strange dreams—some very depressing ones which leave their impress on me all day, others so bright and beautiful that it is heart-sickening to wake from them. One such I had Thursday night—and all day Friday. I had no heart for anything. I could not bear the contrast between that dream and the succeeding reality.

> There's a lot of things that never go by rule,
> There's an awful lot of knowledge
> That you never get at college,
> There are heaps of things you never learn at school.

---

1. From Elizabeth Barrett Browning's *Aurora Leigh*, book 7.

This old verse is not poetry but it's truth. In fact, very few things "go by rule"—and that is what makes life so perplexing. Two and two always make four in arithmetic. But in "real life" they are just as apt to make five or seven or eight—and where are your calculations then? "Do this, and such and such a result will follow"—but it doesn't. Something quite unexpected and illogical follows. To be sure, I suppose we should only be concerned with doing what is right and leave the results to some Higher Power. But as long as we have to *suffer* from the results it is not an easy thing to ignore them—sometimes we find it impossible.

Tuesday, Jan. 17, 1911
Cavendish, P.E.I.

I am writing in my journal principally because I am so miserable with tooth-ache—or rather with facial neuralgia—that I can't do anything else.

We are having a cold snap—ten below zero and a savage north-west wind blowing. I always dread these cold snaps. Owing to Grandmother's ideas about fires it is impossible to keep the house comfortable and we really suffer keenly. Yesterday was a bad day but as I worked hard all day I did not mind it. But when I went to bed my room was terribly cold. My face began to ache and so disturbed my rest that I have felt miserable all day. The quilts about my face froze with the moisture of my breath. Everything seemed dark and lonely and hopeless. I felt very tired and dispirited. Today I read most of the time as I did not feel well enough to work. I tried to do a little at revising a short story this evening. Mr. Page wants to bring out a volume of short stories sometime and I am re-writing such of them as are worth including in such a volume. I think very few of them are. Most of my short stories were written as "pot-boilers." I should like to write some good short stories. I consider it a very high form of art. It is easier to write a good novel than a good short story.

I dread the night very much. That cold room and my sore face are a bad combination. It seems strange to think there was a time when I liked winter. But so far we have had a very mild, snowless winter and that is much to be thankful for.

Sunday, Jan. 22, 1911
Cavendish, P.E.I.

This has been a hard, hard week. I have suffered from facial neuralgia and ulcerating teeth the whole time, night and day. As a result my nerves are in a bad condition. I cannot eat or sleep. It has been very cold all the week also. However, I am much better today. I am free from pain and had a good sleep last night. This makes a vast difference in my outlook on life.

Yesterday was really a heart-breaking day. I lay on the kitchen sofa, racked with neuralgia, utterly wretched. I would have stayed in bed but could not because, my room being upstairs, grandmother could not do the necessary waiting on me up there. Indeed, poor old soul, it was hard enough for her as it was. I tried to make as little trouble for her as possible but some things were necessary, for I could not lift my head without turning sick.

Russell Macneill brought me up some neuralgia pills in the evening. On principle I disapprove of these things, for I believe their effect is ultimately injurious. But I was ready to grasp at any means of relief and I took them. They certainly did cure the pain as if by magic—and whatever their effects are I doubt if they are worse than the poisoned physical conditions induced by wakeful nights and unceasing pain. I daresay that, if they are taken only occasionally, they are not especially injurious. Probably it is only when used frequently for every trivial pain that they do much harm.

Last night at twilight I heard a sound of something falling upstairs. I dragged myself up to see what it was and could have cried—*did* cry—when I saw a lot of plaster fallen from the ceiling in my room. Plaster has fallen from nearly every ceiling in the house as a result of old leaks and I have had many trying times endeavoring to patch up the breaks with white cotton. But hitherto my own dear little room has escaped. And now such a sight! A great, ugly stretch of bare lathes over my bookcase, all the pretty paper torn

My bookcase

and hanging in shreds. Somehow, it hurt me terribly. It seemed to have an evil symbolism. All my old world is falling into ruins. And oh, what will the new be like, even if I have strength to fashion it? Well, I suppose I can repair the damage in my room in some fashion but it will never look the same again.

I have been re-reading the life of Charlotte Brontë by Mrs. Gaskell this week.[1] It is a wonderful book. It is hard to decide whether its charm is due to Mrs. Gaskell's style or to the real life of Charlotte Brontë—that woman genius whose outward life was so hard and bitter and tragic. It is a dear wish of my heart to make some day a pilgrimage to Haworth and see the old house she lived in and wrote her wonderful books in.

---

1. Gaskell's biography (1857) of Charlotte Brontë deals with Brontë's late marriage to a curate.

Somehow, today my mind seems haunted by an old familiar verse—I think it is in one of Whittier's poems.

> The Beauty which old Greece and Rome
> Sang, painted, taught, lies close at home,
> We need but eye and ear
> In all our daily walks to trace
> The outlines of incarnate grace
> The hymns of gods to hear.[1]

It is as true as beautiful, and oftentimes its truth has come home to me in my own "daily walks" by wood and field and shore. We must have beauty in our souls, or we shall not be able to find it, even in old Greece and Rome; and if we have it, there is satisfying beauty all around us. The "hymns of gods" sound in every sough of fir, in every diapason of sea-wave, in every gurgle of wood stream, in every threnody of raindrops on still meadows. Even in the chill harping of the winter wind beneath the cold stars we can hear it—though too often our own personal pain and weariness dulls our ear to that.

Something I read today set me thinking about trees—especially the old trees that are, or used to be, around this old house. Some of them are very dear to me. I have always loved them; and when I have "lived with" a tree for a long time it seems to me like a beloved human companion.

When I was very small there were two large spruce trees growing in the back yard, one at the northwest corner of the orchard, one at the southwest. I recall sitting on the back steps in the summer evenings and revelling in the color made by the sunset light on their green plumy tops. The southwest one disappeared very early in my life—I do not know whether it was blown or cut down. The other remained until I was eight or nine. The "pigs' boiler" used to be under it, also the wood-pile.
I can yet see the glowing fire under that dark tree on autumn nights, and the circle of fallen cones that was always around it. The tree, I think, blew down in a windstorm.

Behind the "pig-house" was a spruce grove, with an odd maple and birch here and there in it. Only one tree in this grove

x. The one in the south-east corner. xx. "New" barn.

---

1.   From "To – : Lines Written after a Summer Day's Excursion" (1851) by John Greenleaf Whittier. The couplet concludes that beauty "lies close to home."

possessed any individuality for me—the one in the southeast corner on the road to the barns. It stood out from the others like an outpost sentinel. This tree blew down only a year or two ago and my heart ached over it.

Behind the "new" barn was another spruce grove and behind the old barn was a once-very beautiful grove of spruce, maple and birch, with a lovely floor of green things, checkered over with glossy wild lily-of-the-valley leaves or scarlet pigeon-berries. There were some especially beloved trees in this grove. One was a large white birch in a part of the grove I had named "The Fairy Palace." Its roots formed a little hillock open to western suns and covered lavishly with leaves and blossoms and wood-berries in their seasons. Another tree was a freakish maple in the south-west corner, just behind the "old" horsestable. Two maples had apparently sprung from the one root. One grew one way along the ground for a couple of feet, the other, the other way. Then both sprang up into great gray columnar trunks. The result was a beautiful seat, large enough for three or four people. Grandfather cut those trees down when I was about fifteen. I found it a hard thing to forgive.

In the south-east corner was a spot I liked—"No Man's Land"—a comparatively open space with some fine maples and a beautiful birch in it. Close to the fence grew a pair I called "The Lovers"—a spruce and a maple so closely intertwined that the boughs of the maple were literally interlaced with those of the spruce. I remember I wrote a poem about them—"The Tree Lovers." They really did seem fond of each other and they lived in happy union for many years. They are dead now. The little maple died first and the spruce held her dead form in his green faithful arms for two more years. But his heart was broken and he died too. They were beautiful in their lives, and in death not long divided; and they nourished a child's heart with a grace-giving fancy.

Behind the kitchen were several large "Balm of Gileads" or, as we pronounced it "Balmagilias"—a variety of poplar—and a large birch. These trees I loved. Their boughs came out bright against the sunset, or waved darkly across the northern stars on summer nights. The soft "down" of the balms floated down over the roof and lay in the yard. The birch had a peculiarly shaped bough resembling a beautiful, bent white arm.

x. Another mixed grove

Behind these trees was a locality known as "the little bushes"—a place of green nooks tenanted by fairies and pixies and unearthly folk generally and therefore to be avoided after nightfall.

Looking from the front door to the right of the "front garden" was another mixed grove. A beautiful double maple grew here, hanging a banner of crimson in front of the west window of the kitchen in October. And there are several white birches which I always remember as shining like silvery spires among the dark evergreens, when I was coming home up the lane on moonlight nights. On dark nights they caught the lamplight shining on them through the kitchen window with spectral effect. At the foot of the front garden and up its left on the dyke was a row of large white birches—very

"The Lady"

beautiful trees. They are associated in my mind with winter sunsets against which their delicate tracery darkled. Always on coming home from anywhere, west and south, those birches were the first thing to catch my eye in the distance. There used to be two big balsam poplars there also, but grandfather cut them down long ago, because "suckers" from them were ruining the field beyond.

Just inside the south-west corner of the dyke grew a most beautiful little birch tree. I always called it "The Lady" and had a fancy about it to the effect that it was the beloved of all the dark spruces near and that they were all rivals for its love. It was the whitest, straightest thing ever seen. A few years ago Uncle John cut it down. He has been cutting the trees down recklessly for firewood ever since grandfather's death but I notice he never plants any. I notice, too, that it is always some favourite tree of mine that is cut down—a petty spite which is very characteristic of the man. It went to my heart that "The Lady" should be cut down. And yet I think I

would rather that than know it was here after I had gone, neglected and unloved, growing old and ragged and unshapely. In my memory it will live as long as I do, young and fair and maiden like.

Further up the dyke was a "juniper" as we called it. It was not really a juniper at all but a tamarack. It is a very large tree, its top bending to the north as the tops of all good tamaracks should do. It is one of

x. Tamarack. xx. Cherry trees.

the trees I can see from the window of my room and many a twilight I have watched evening star or young moon over its lofty crest.

The curve in the lane

Running up from the juniper is a row of cherry trees—always a drift of snow in early June. Just inside of the dyke were two patriarchal old cherry trees, just the right distance apart for a swing. We had one there on several summers. They are gone now, having grown old and died. At the curve in the lane where the cherry row began grew an aspen poplar with trembling leaves. It died a few years ago. A few yards from my window grew a huge poplar, much beloved by me. How the morning sunshine used to strike on its boughs! and how heartbroken I was, on coming home one vacation to find that my dear poplar had been cut down. Its trunk was decaying and they feared it would blow down on the house. But nothing could reconcile me to its loss. That pang aches yet when I think of it.

Away up on the south hill was a spring with a cluster of spruces around it and one maple. I used to love to go there and lie among the little grassy hillocks to dream. I recall in especial one mild gray autumn evening when I was about ten. I went up to the spring and my two pet kittens "Catkin" and "Pussywillow" went with me. They frisked about my feet, tore madly along the fence rails, chased each other over the fields and played bo-peep among the cradle hills. I can see the cute little gray face and bright eyes of "Pussywillow" peering at me over a hillock yet.

The hill spring

Below the front garden was the "Haunted Wood." It was composed mainly of thick-growing spruce trees, but on its southern side was a magnificent white birch. This was the tree of trees to me. I worshipped it and called it "The Monarch of the Forest." One of my earliest poems was written on it—the third one I ever wrote, I think. Here it is—or at least all of it I can recollect.

> Around the poplar and the spruce
> The fir and maple stood,
> But the old tree that I loved the best
> Grew in the Haunted Wood.

It was a stately tall old birch,
With spreading branches green,
It kept off heat and sun and glare,
'Twas a goodly tree I ween.

Among its leafy boughs entwined
The sunshine lay at rest
Between two noble branches—
May it be forever blest!

'Twas the Monarch of the Forest,
A splendid kingly name,
Oh, it was a beautiful birch tree
A tree that was known to fame.

There were other verses but I have forgotten them. The line that it was "known to fame" was a poetical fiction but all the rest was true. Alas, death spares nor king nor tree. Oliver Wendell Holmes says,

There's nothing that keeps its youth,
So far as I know, but a tree and truth.[1]

But even a tree does not live forever. Grandfather cut the spruce grove down. He left the big birch standing. But, deprived of its accustomed shelter of the thick-growing spruces which had crowded around it, like obsequious courtiers around a veritable king, the birch tree gradually died before the bitter northern blasts. Every spring more of its boughs failed to leaf out. The poor tree stood like a discrowned, forsaken king in ragged cloak. I was not sorry when it was finally cut down. "The land of dreams among" it resumed its empire and reigns in fadeless beauty.

x. The tree I loved best

Of course, the apple trees were dear friends of mine too. The "front" orchard was the oldest one having been planted by grandfather's father, old "Speaker Macneill." We always called it "the front garden," although there was no garden in it. But there had been once and the name clung. The only traces of it left were in a blue-flowered, ivy-like plant, which grew lavishly in all the open spaces, and the caraway that spread wildly. The trees were nearly all "sweet" and we children were about the only ones who cared

---

1.   Couplet concludes, "So far as I know, but a tree and truth." From Oliver Wendell Holmes, "The Deacon's Masterpiece" (1858).

for the apples. The tree I loved best there was a very old one, near the spruce bush, leaning wholly over to the south like a bent broken old crone.

The "back" orchard was the one grandfather and grandmother had planted. Every tree in it had some humble, homely name. Just inside the gate on the left was a square of four large trees—"Uncle John's tree," "Aunt Emily's tree," "Aunt Clara's tree," (my mother's) and "Uncle Leander's tree." "Aunt Annie's tree" and "Uncle Chester's tree" had died. These four trees all bore large sweet apples. I called the space they overshadowed "The Bower." It was fit for a queen's bower in blossom time. Just beyond Aunt Emily's tree was a smaller sweet tree called "Russell's tree" for the excellent reason that every fall we gave the apples to Russell Macneill who came up and picked them. Close to the northern fence stood the "Little Syrup Tree." The tree

The back orchard

was one of the largest in the garden but the apples it bore in great quantities were small, rosy, tart ones which boiled up whole into a very delicious, syrupy, sauce. Not far from it was the "Spotty Tree" bearing apples of a very delicious, nutty flavor, but quite leprous in appearance, their skins being always covered with odd, lichen-like spots and seams.

To the right of the gate were the damson plum trees, which the fatal "black knot" eventually killed. In the southwest corner was the "Spider Tree," so called because of an odd resemblance in its long flexile branches to a many-legged spider. Back of the damsons grew the two "American trees" as we called them, because they had been bought from a Yankee salesman. Their real name was not known to us, but it was supposed they were "Wagoners." They bore very delicious, ruddy apples. Behind them was "Aunt Margaret's tree" grown from a seed from an apple tree belong to Aunt Margaret MacKenzie. These apples were hard and sour beyond belief—literally good for nothing. But next to Aunt Margaret's tree was the "August" tree, whose yellow white-fleshed apples came to their prime in late August and were very delicious. In the South-east corner grew the "Little Red Tree," another big tree named from its little red apples of a peculiarly pleasant flavor and the reddest of satiny skins. Behind it grew a nameless tree, bearing pretty apples of a yellowish green on one side, and a hectic red on the other—"the side that's next the sun." They had an especially glossy skin and a nice acid flavor. Next to this tree grew one, bearing small, whitish-green apples, called "Gavin's tree," so named because a certain small boy named Gavin Jack, who was hired over at Dr. Murray's (the then minister who also farmed) had once been caught stealing them. Why the said Gavin should have lost his reputation and imperilled his soul by electing to steal apples from that particular tree I could never understand for they were bitter, flavorless things, good neither for eating raw or cooking.

Eastward of them grew the only aristocrat in the orchard—the only one with an assured legitimate name, "The Duchess of Oldenburg," bearing palatable summer apples.

"Wild cherries in Lover's Lane"

Since grandfather's death the orchard has been neglected and is a poor place now. It blooms and bears scantly. Today, in the graceless nakedness of a snowless winter, it is a sorry place.

Only sometimes of a summer night in blossom time the moon makes a spell of wizardry, and youth returns for a space to the old orchard.

I have many beloved trees back in the woods—wild cherries in Lover's Lane, a certain maiden-like wild plum half way up it, a wild cherry in the field beyond, a silver maple and a pine by the brook, another pine in the "deep hollow," and a maple growing in the corner of "Pierce's field," not to mention a row of stately white birches in the woods.

God be thanked for trees. I shall always be grateful that my childhood was passed in a spot where there were many trees—"old ancestral trees," planted and tended by hands long dead, bound up with everything of joy and sorrow that visited the lives in their shadow.

Dear old trees! I hope you all have souls and will grow again for me on the hills of heaven. I want, in some future life, to meet the old "Monarch" and the "White Lady" and even poor, dishonest Little Gavin's tree again!

Stately white birches

Friday, Jan. 24, 1911
Cavendish

I had a delightful starry walk tonight. I had been in along the road to see Lizzie Laird and it took me nearly two hours to come home—a distance of nearly half a mile. I loitered. I took three steps and stood still for five minutes. I was tranced in unearthly pleasure. All the world was dark and dim and soft in a southwest wind; but overhead the stars were brilliant and I met all my old star friends of last winter again, hanging in just the same places over the hills and woods and sea. Orion shook his lion's hide and walked with gem-shod feet over the azure southeast, Sirius lorded it dazzlingly over the sidereal hosts, Capella flashed over my head. Cassiopeia sat queenly in her jewelled chair. In the east the great sickle reaped a harvest of heaven and Pegasus coursed along the path of the sunset. Oh, how regretfully I came in and shut them all out—all that "poetry of heaven" writ on the firmament in living light by the fingers of Him who inhabiteth the halls of Eternity. Verily, "the heavens declare the glory of God, the firmament showeth his handiwork."[1] What a magnificent verse that is!

A sentence in one of Barrie's books took my fancy today—"The useless men are those who never change with the years."[2] Indeed, they are worse than useless—they are pernicious. They block progress and bring unhappiness into the lives of those who are intimately connected with them. They are fossils. When a human being ceases to change he is dead. As long as there is life there *must* be growth of some kind and consequent change. Yet some people actually pride themselves on the fact that they "never change their mind." A stunted shrub might as well be proud that it never grows! To change one's mind—for good reason, that is. I am not referring to the fickle mind that flies around like a weather cock—is simply to admit that we are wiser today than we were yesterday—have received new impressions that have revised our old opinions, have climbed to a higher peak and beheld a view we did not know existed.

Friday, Jan. 27, 1911
Cavendish, P.E.I.

Margaret and I had a delightful walk down the road this evening in the twilight. It was a very still, breathless evening—a storm evidently brewing. The world was white and dim and windless.

I cannot get used to the pleasantness of having a congenial friend near me. It seems rather unnatural. I have never had living near me a friend with whom I could talk freely on subjects near to my heart. Even long ago, when I regarded Amanda and Lucy as friends, there was never any real communion of spirit or mind between us. Lucy could talk of nothing but dress and petty

---

1. Psalm 19.

2. Words of a wise old man in *The Little Minister* (1891), by Scottish novelist and playwright J.M. Barrie (1867–1937).

gossip and Amanda was little better. And of late years there has been no one near me with whom I could, or cared to, go any deeper than the surface. But now I have Margaret with whom I can discuss many—not all—subjects, understanding and understood. It means much to me. A little congenial companionship goes a long way to sweeten life.

After Margaret went in I prowled about a bit by myself. There were no stars out but there were shadowy woods and white spaces and dim treelands. I looked on them and loved them. How I love Cavendish! I love it for its beauty—I love it for its old associations, as I will never love any other spot on earth.

Today I was again annoyed and amused—with the annoyance distinctly uppermost—to be asked, as I so constantly am, "Was So-and-So the original of This-or-That in your books"?

This annoys me because I have *never* drawn any of the characters in my books "from life," although I may have taken a quality here and an incident there. I have used real places and speeches freely but I have never put any person I knew into my books. I may do so some day but hitherto I have depended wholly on the creative power of my own imagination for my book folk.

Nevertheless I have woven a good deal of reality into my books. Cavendish is to a large extent *Avonlea. Mrs. Rachel Lynde's* house, with the brook below, was drawn from Pierce Macneill's house. I also gave Mrs. Pierce's name to *Mrs. Lynde* but beyond that there was no connection whatever between them. *Green Gables* was drawn from David Macneill's house, now Mr. Webb's[1]—though not so much the house itself as the situation and scenery, and the truth of my description of it is attested by the fact that everybody has recognized it. Had they stopped there it would be well, but they went further and insist that David and

David Macneill's house from back, showing back yard

Margaret Macneill figure as *Matthew* and *Marilla*. They do not. The *Matthew* and *Marilla* I had in mind were entirely different people from David and Margaret. I suppose the fact that David is a notoriously shy and silent man makes people think I drew Matthew from him. But I made Matthew shy and

---

1. Ernest Webb (1880–1950) had married Myrtle Macneill in 1905. Their house is now the Anne of Green Gables Museum in the National Park at Cavendish.

silent simply because I wished to have all the people around *Anne* as pointedly in contrast with her as possible.

In connection with this there was one odd coincidence which probably helped to establish the conviction that David was *Matthew*. *Green Gables* was illustrated by an artist unknown to me and to whom Cavendish and David were alike unknown. Nevertheless, it cannot be denied that the picture of Matthew when he brings *Anne* home, has a very strong resemblance to David Macneill.

The brook that runs below the *Cuthbert* place and through *Lynde's Hollow* is, of course, my own dear brook of the woods which runs below Webb's and through "Pierce's Hollow."

Although I had the Webb place in mind I did not confine myself to facts at all. There are, I think, willows in the yard but there are no "Lombardies," such as *Anne* heard talking in their sleep. Those were transplanted from the estates of my castle in Spain. And it was by no means as tidy as I pictured *Green Gables*—at least, before the Webbs came there. Quite the reverse in fact, David's yard was notoriously *untidy*. It was a local saying that if you wanted to see what the world looked like on the morning after the flood you should go into David's barnyard on a rainy day!

They had a good cherry orchard but no apple orchard. However, I can easily create an apple orchard when I need one!

Marilla is generally accredited to Margaret. This is absurd. Whatever accidental resemblance there may be between David and *Matthew* there is none whatever between Margaret and *Marilla*. The former is a very intelligent, broad-minded woman, which poor *Marilla* certainly was not. Others imagine *Marilla* was drawn from grandmother. This is also false. There are certain qualities common to Marilla and grandmother—and to many others—but those qualities I put into *Marilla* for the same reason I made *Matthew* silent and shy—to furnish a background for *Anne*.

When I am asked if *Anne* herself is a "real person" I always answer "no" with an odd reluctance and an uncomfortable feeling of not telling the truth. For she is and always has been, from the moment I first thought of her, so real to me that I feel I am doing violence to something when I deny her an existence anywhere save in Dreamland. Does she not stand at my elbow even now—if I turned my head quickly should I not see her—with her eager, starry eyes and her long braids of red hair and her little pointed chin? To tell that haunting elf that she is not *real*, because, forsooth, I never met her in the flesh! No, I cannot do it! She *is* so real that, although I've never met her, I feel quite sure I shall do so some day—perhaps in a stroll through Lover's Lane in the twilight—or in the moonlit Birch Path—I shall lift my eyes and find her, child or maiden, by my side. And I shall not be in the least surprised because I have always known she was *somewhere*.

The idea of getting a child from an orphan asylum was suggested to me years ago as a possible germ for a story by the fact that Pierce Macneill got a little girl from one, and I jotted it down in my note book. There is no resemblance of any kind between *Anne* and Ellen Macneill who is one of the most hopelessly commonplace and uninteresting girls imaginable. But I may mention here another odd co-incidence. Although Ellen Macneill never crossed my mind while I was writing the book, yet a stranger who was in Cavendish two years ago, boarding at Pierce's, told Ellen that her profile was exactly like the *Anne* profile on the cover of *Green Gables*! And when I heard this I agreed that it was, although the profile on the book has distinction while Ellen's is hopelessly common. This picture was also drawn by an artist who had never seen Cavendish or Ellen!

Bright River is Hunter River. *Anne's* dislike of being laughed at because she used big words is a bitter remembrance of my own childhood. *The White Way of Delight* is practically pure imagination. Yet the idea was suggested to me by a short stretch of road between Kensington and Clinton, which I always thought very beautiful. The trees meet overhead for a short distance but they are beech trees, not apple trees.

Corner of "Lake of Shining Waters"

Anne's habit of naming places was an old one of my own. The *Lake of Shining Waters* is generally supposed to be the Cavendish Pond. This is not so. The pond at Park Corner is the one I had in mind. But I suppose that a good many of the effects of light and shadow I have seen on the Cavendish pond figured unconsciously in my descriptions; and certainly the hill from which *Anne* caught her first glimpse of it was "Laird's Hill," where I have often stood at sunset, enraptured with the beautiful view of shining pond and crimson-brimmed harbor and dark blue sea.

White Sands was Rustico and the "shore road" has a real existence, and is a very beautiful drive. I remember one moonlight drive I had around that road. I shall never forget the starry, sparkling, shimmering beauty of sky and sea.

The house in which *Anne* was born was drawn from my own little birthplace at

Entrance to *Anne's* "Haunted Woods"

Clifton. The *Katie Maurice* of Anne was *my* Katie Maurice—that imaginary playmate of the glass bookcase door in our sitting room. The idea of the *Haunted Wood* was of course taken from the old Haunted Wood of the Nelson boys and myself. But the wood I had in mind as far as description went was the spruce-clad hill across the brook hollow from Webb's. The *Dryad's Bubble* was purely imaginary but the "old log bridge" was a real thing. It was formed by a single large tree that had blown down and lay across the brook. As far back as I can remember it lay there and must have served as a bridge for a generation before that for it was hollowed out like a shell from the tread of hundreds of passing feet. Earth had blown into its crevices and ferns and grasses had found root in it and fringed it luxuriantly. Velvet moss covered its sides. Below was a clear, sun-flecked stream.

A year or two ago the old log-bridge became so worn and slender that it was quite unsafe. So Mr. Webb put a little bridge of longers across the brook and we use that now.

Anne's tribulations over puffed sleeves were an echo of my old childish longing after "bangs." "Bangs" came in when I was about ten. In the beginning they figured as a straight, heavy fringe of hair cut squarely across the forehead. A picture of "banged" hair of course looks absurd enough now; but, like all fashions, "bangs" looked all right when they were "in." And to anybody with a high forehead they were very becoming.

Well, bangs were "all the rage." All the girls in school had them. I wanted a "bang" terribly. But grandfather and grandmother would never hear of it. This was unwise and unjust on their part. Whatever the present day taste may think of "bangs" it would not have done me or anyone any harm to have allowed me to have one and it would have saved me many a bitter pang. How I did long for "bangs"! Father wanted me to have them—he always wanted me to have any innocent thing I desired. Oh, how well he understood a child's heart! I often pleaded with him when he came to see me (that was the winter he was home from the west) to cut a "bang" for me, but he never would because he knew it would offend grandmother. I was often tempted to cut one myself but I dreaded their anger too much. I knew that if I did I would be railed at as if I had disgraced myself forever and that I would never set down to the table that grandfather would not sneer at them.

"Bangs" remained in a long time—nearly twenty years. When I was fifteen and went out west I got my long-wished for "bang" at last. Grandfather sneered at it when I went home, of course, but the thing was done and he had to reconcile himself to it. Besides, the "bang" had changed a good deal in that time. The heavy straight bang was gone and the accepted fashion was an upward curling fluff, not unlike the pompadour of today in general effect, with only a loose curl or two downwards. How I did envy girls with naturally curly hair! My hair was very straight. I had to curl my poor fringe constantly and even then the least dampness would reduce it to stringy dismalness. It is only about six years since bangs went hopelessly out. It is not likely they will ever come in again—in my time at least. But I shall never forget them. I longed for them and how humiliated I felt when I could not have them.

I had beautiful hair when I was a child—very long, thick, and a golden brown. It turned very dark when I grew up—much to my disappointment. I love fair hair.

The *Spectator*, in reviewing *Green Gables*—*very* favorably, I might say— said that possibly *Anne's* precocity was slightly overdrawn in the statement that a child of eleven would appreciate the dramatic effect of the lines,

> Quick as the slaughtered squadrons fell
> In Midian's evil day.[1]

But I was only nine years old when those lines thrilled my very soul as I recited them in Sunday School. All through the following sermon I kept repeating them to myself. To this day they give me a mysterious pleasure.

I remember that Maggie Abbott and I swore eternal friendship as *Anne* and *Diana* did. Only we did not do it in a garden but standing on a high loft beam in Uncle John Montgomery's barn at Malpeque. Amanda and I also once wrote out two "Notes of Promise," vowing everlasting faith, had them witnessed by two of the schoolgirls, and finished them up with a red seal. I have mine yet somewhere. I think I was true to *my* vow. But if Amanda thinks she was, her ideal of friendship must be very different from mine. Still, she *was* my friend once in childhood and early girlhood. Perhaps she could not help—or did not know how to help—the strange temperamental change which came over her at the threshold of womanhood. These things are bound up with physiological mysteries beyond our penetration. In early life Amanda was her mother's child. When she grew up her dormant inheritance from her father developed and she changed into an altogether different being. To me, the Amanda who was my girlhood friend is as one dead. I think of her lovingly and regretfully. I can never feel that the Amanda of today is the same person as my friend of long ago.

x. Our playhouse site

---

1. From "The Race that long in darkness pined," a hymn by Rev. John Morison (1781) based on Judges 8 and Isaiah.

The playhouse of *Diana* and *Anne* had many proto-types. I was the greatest little home builder when I was a child. My first playhouse was behind the "new" barn. Lucy shared it with me. It was on the long hillock formed by the roots of a spruce tree. We had a row of stakes and clam-shells all around it and we scooped out "cupboards" between the big roots, lined them with moss and kept our "dishes" therein. Then the Nelson boys came and they and I had our playhouse in the grove to the right of our front orchard. After they went away Lucy and I had another playhouse in the spruce grove down beside Uncle John's cherry trees. This was a really lovely place and for three summers we had delightful times there. At least I had. I don't think Lucy cared much for it, but I had the purest enjoyment fixing up that little "house" and "making believe" in it.

A large square space between four conveniently placed trees was our "kitchen." Off it was a smaller square which was our "parlour." With a hatchet we trimmed off all the dead boughs which interfered with us and railed off our "house" from the big world around us by a row of little sticks driven into the ground. We swept the floor with brooms of spruce boughs until all the deposit of spruce needles was cleared away and the hard, bare, root-veined earth came into view. We put boards on the stubs of branches to serve for shelves, covered them with moss, and arranged our "dishes" on them. We had a very fine collection and were very proud of them—as proud as a real housewife would be of her real china. That long spruce grove running up along the fence from our playhouse was a veritable Golconda of broken bits. Before Uncle John bought the farm it had belonged to Dr. Isaac Murray, who combined preaching and farming. The doctor's family—or his servants—had no mercy on the dishes, and the broken pieces were flung into that grove. Every now and then we went exploring in it with rakes and hoes, and "treasure trove" always rewarded

Dr. Isaac Murray

us. We loved the "spray pieces," as we called them—bits of white china with a feathery, bluish-gray design all over them like fine sprays of moss. The "show" bit of our collection—always kept on the parlor shelf of course—was a piece of the fluted edge of a plate with a spray of red and yellow ivy on it—"The Ivy Piece" we called it. This figures in *Green Gables* as does also the "fairy glass"—an old prism broken from a hanging lamp. What rainbows it made on our shelves! The broken bottom out of an old green glass bottle was quite a pretty thing too—so perfectly round, so seemingly deep, with such mysterious lights and shadows in it. Then we had a great many pieces of the old blue and white striped ware that was once in fashion for bowls. But space and time fail me to catalogue more of our bric-a-brac.

We had big stones, mossed over, for seats. Right in the middle of our "parlor" grew a small cherry tree, just reaching over our heads and in early June it formed a white fragrant ceiling. No cherries every ripened on it, however—it was too shady in the spruce wood.

When I outgrew playhouses I hadn't the heart to throw those beautiful dishes away. There was a big boxful of them. What to do with them I didn't know. So I dug a hole in the "Fairy Palace" and buried them. There they stayed buried for many a year. Then I dug them up, smuggled them upstairs and kept them in a box under the bed in the lookout. There they remained for several years, until they came to be nothing after all but broken dishes— and then I threw them out! But I am sorry now that I didn't keep the "fairy glass" and the "Ivy Piece."

Anne's idea that diamonds looked like amethysts was once mine. I did not know there were such stones as amethysts but I had read of diamonds. I had never seen one nor heard one described, and I pictured to myself a beautiful stone of living purple. When Uncle Chester brought Aunt Hattie to see us after their marriage I saw the little diamond in her ring and I was much disappointed. "It wasn't my idea of a diamond"—well, many things in life and in the world have not been like my idea of them! I love diamonds now—I love their pure, cold, dew like sheen and glitter. But once they were a bitter disillusion to me.

Lover's Lane

Lover's Lane was of course *my* Lover's Lane. *Willowmere* and *Violet Vale* were compact of imagination. But the Birch Path exists somewhere, I know not where. I have a picture of it—the reproduction of a photo which was published in the *Outing* magazine one year. Somewhere in America that lane of birches is. *Avonlea* school was the Cavendish school, but the teachers were mythical. *Miss Stacey* resembled Miss Gordon in some respects but I cannot say she was drawn from her. The episode of the mouse falling into the pudding sauce once happened to a friend of mine—Mrs. George Matheson; old Literary concerts furnished forth the description of the concert in *Avonlea Hall*. The scene where *Anne* and *Diana*, jump into bed on poor *Miss*

The Birch Path

Barry was suggested to me by a story father told me of how he and two other boys had jumped into bed on an old minister in the spare room at Uncle John Montgomery's long ago. I worked it up into a short story, published early in my career in *Golden Days*; then used the idea later on in my book. The old "Mayflower" pic-

Aunt Emily's house

nics of Miss Gordon's devising were used. The affecting farewell speech of James MacLeod was used also although, to do Jim justice, he was not in any respect like *Teddy Phillips*, being a very fair teacher. We used to make balsam Rainbows in the school spring, just as *Anne* and *Diana* made them in *the Dryad's Bubble*.

As for the notable incident of the liniment cake—when I was teaching in Bideford Mrs. Estey flavored a layer cake with anodyne liniment just as it happened in the story. Never shall I forget the taste of that cake. What fun we had over it! A strange minister was there to tea that night—a Mr. Kirby—and *he* ate all his piece of cake. What he thought of it we never knew. Possibly he imagined it was simply some new-fangled kind of flavoring. The dialogues which the girls had in their concerts "The Society for The Suppression of Gossip" and "The Fairy Queen" were old stand-bys of schooldays. We had the former at our first school concert in which I personated the amiable "Miss Wise," and the latter at a school examination. I was the *Fairy Queen*, being thought fitted for the part by reason of my long hair which I wore crimped and floating over my shoulders from a wreath of pink tissue roses. I "appeared" suddenly through the school door, in answer to an incantation, in all the glory of white dress, roses, hair, kid slippers and wand—and I enjoyed my own dramatic appearance quite as much as anybody! That really was one of the most *satisfying* moments of my life.

The Story Club was suggested by a little incident of one summer long ago when Jamie Simpson, Amanda Macneill, and I all wrote a story on the same plot. I furnished the plot and I remembered only that it was a very tragic one and the heroine was drowned. I haven't the stories now—I wish I had—but they were very sad. It was the first, and probably the last, time that Jamie and Amanda attempted fiction but I had already quite a little library of stories— in which almost everybody died! I do wish I had kept them. I burned them in exasperation on the day I realized what trash they were. They *were* trash— but they would have been quite valuable trash to me now, because they were so enormously funny. One was entitled "My Graves" and was a long tale of the various peregrinations of a minister's wife. I made her a Methodist minister's wife so that she would have to peregrinate frequently. She buried a child in every place she lived in! All Canada, from Newfoundland to Vancouver, was peppered with "her" graves. I wrote the story in the first person, described the children, pictured out their death-beds and described their tombstones and epitaphs! That story was never finished. After having killed off about seven children—she was to have thirteen altogether—I wearied of so much infanticide and ceased from my slaughter of the innocents.

Then there was "The History of Flossie Brighteyes"—the autobiography of a doll. I couldn't kill a doll but I dragged her through every other tribulation. However, I allowed her to have a happy end with a good little girl who loved her for the dangers she had passed and did not mind a few legs and eyes missing.

But what dazzlingly lovely heroines I had! And how I dressed them! Silks—satins—velvets—laces—they never wore anything else! And I literally poured diamonds and rubies and pearls over them. But what booted beauty and rich attire? "The paths of glory lead but to the grave."[1] They must either be murdered or die of a broken heart. There was no escape for them.

The incident of *Anne's* dying her hair was purely imaginary. Oddly enough, however, after *Green Gables* was written, but before it was published, Sadie Macneill, a Cavendish girl who had fiery tresses dyed her hair black. I was appalled when I heard of it for I felt sure that everyone, when the book came out, would think that I had made use of this fact. And they did! And probably always will! And her family are furious with me! Yet am I innocent.

The entrance examination of *Queen's* was "drawn from life" as well as the weeks of suspense that followed. *Matthew's* death was not, as some have supposed, suggested by grandfather's. Poor Matthew must die so that there might arise the necessity for self-sacrifice on Anne's part. So he joined the long procession of ghosts that haunt my literary past.

There was less of "real life" in *Avonlea* than in *Green Gables*, and much more of invention. Some of my own experiences in school-teaching were reflected in it, but in the atmosphere only, not in the incidents. I felt exactly as *Anne* felt when she opened school the first day—and I was as woefully tired and discouraged at night. My Bideford pupils used to drive crickets. A Bideford pupil gave the same definition of "freckles" as *Jimmy Andrews* did— "George Howell's face, ma'am," and several other answers were genuine.

The scene of the walk in the *Golden Picnic* was laid through the woods and fields back of Lover's Lane but Hester's garden is purely imaginary. *Davy's* idea that heaven was in "*Simon Fletcher's* garret" was suggested by a belief of

---

1.   From Thomas Gray's "Elegy, Written in a Country Churchyard" (1751), stanza 10.

my own childhood. One Sunday when I was very small—I could not, I think have been more than four—I was with Aunt Emily in Clifton church—the old church with its square box pews. I heard the minister say something about heaven. "Where is heaven?" I whispered to Aunt Emily. She simply pointed upward. With childhood's literal and implicit belief I took it for granted that this meant the attic of Clifton church. For a long time I firmly believed that heaven was there! As mother was "in heaven" she must be there, too. Now, why could we not get up there and see her? There was a square hole in the ceiling. Surely it was quite possible. It was a great puzzle to me that nobody ever seemed to think of doing it. I resolved that when I grew older *I* would find some way of getting to Clifton and getting up into heaven anyhow. Alas! Hood wrote in his delightful "I Remember" that he was further off from heaven then when he was a boy. I can echo that. When I was a child heaven was only seven miles away. But now! Is it not beyond the furthest star?

Kilmeny reflects very little out of my own experience. *Jack Reid's* sentence, "Courting is a very pleasant thing which a great many people go too far with" was the *bona fide* opening sentence Jack Millar wrote in a composition in Bideford school. The view of *Lindsay Harbor* and the gulf, with the revolving light, is drawn from the view I have so often gazed on over New London Harbor. "Old Charlie's" Latin prayer was really delivered by old Professor Macdonald at a Dalhousie convocation. James Laird's place up on the hill was my model of the *Williamson* place—but James and Mrs. Laird are most decidedly *not* the *Williamsons*. The woods through which *Eric* walked to meet his fate are the woods beyond Lover's Lane.

Sunday, Feb. 5, 1911
Cavendish, P.E.I.

This has been a hard week—so stormy and cold—snow to be shovelled in the mornings, bitter nights to be endured. Today is mild and sunny however—such a welcome relief. But I am thankful that my health is so much better than last winter. So long as my "nerve juice" doesn't give out I can endure all else. But there are many times, especially on stormy days and wakeful nights, when that horrible *dread of life* steals over me again—when I feel as if I had no courage to go on facing the difficulties in my way. There seems to be so many of them every way I look—so many things that appear unendurable. I know that when I come to them I shall probably be able to endure them tolerably well—that they are far worse in anticipation than in reality—but this knowledge has little effect on tortured feeling. It seems to me that I cannot *bear* any more pain! I have had to bear so much of it in the past fourteen years that it seems to me I have no longer any power to bear it—that I *cannot* endure any more if it comes. I know that thousands of people have much worse things to bear than I have. But perhaps there are not many who have had absolutely no one to help them bear or share it. This dreadful "aloneness" is what has made it always so hard for me.

I had one of my bad sick headaches yesterday and last night and they always leave me very down-hearted and pessimistic. I have had these headaches ever since I was twenty-one and no medical skill has ever been able to help them. They are very distressing, especially here, where I have no one to do anything for me when the attacks come on.

This week in a book of Barrie's I came across the following pertinent little sentence:—

> "This is indeed a sad truth that we seldom give our love to what is worthiest in its object."[1]

I shut the book and leaned back to think it over. Yes, it *is* a truth—and a sad one. We do not love people for what is worthiest in them. We *admire* them for their good qualities, but we do not *love* them for them. Nay, worse, we often love them for what is positively unworthy. I do not mean "love" as merely between man and woman—I refer to all kinds of love. It is very hard—nay, it is impossible to explain why we love some people and have no love for others. I know many people who, I feel sure, are good and admirable. Yet I find no pleasure in their society and in some cases dislike them. Again, they are people who are far from being perfect whom I do love and in whose society I find delight and satisfaction. Now, why is this? "Oh," says someone, "it is because you are very far from being good yourself that you dislike good people and find your kindred spirits among those not so good."

Well, this would be a very simple explanation if I disliked *all* good people and liked only bad ones! But I do not. There are many good people whom I fondly love and there are many not good whom I cannot tolerate at all. So that can't be how it is. George Eliot says, "In that curious compound, the feminine character, it may easily happen that the flavor is unpleasant in spite of excellent ingredients."[2] Had she said "human" in place of feminine she would have struck the mark even more fairly, for I know many men of whom the same can be said "Excellent ingredients"—yes; but they are not mixed well—baked well—the flavoring is left out—or, as with Mrs. Estey and the anodyne liniment, a distasteful flavor has been chosen. Yes, I believe

---

1. From *The Little Minister* (1891), chapter 18, by J.M. Barrie (1867–1937), a novel about a young minister's obsession with a wayward gypsy-like woman.

2. From *The Mill on the Floss* (1860), chapter 12, by George Eliot.

that is the secret. *Sam Weller*[1] says "It's all in the seasoning"—kitten or veal, it doesn't matter so long as it is properly flavored. Yes, it's "all in the seasoning." But for all that it is, as Barrie says, a sad thing that we do not and cannot love people for their good qualities alone, regardless of what may be lacking.

Tennyson says,

> We needs must love the highest when we see it.[2]

But that is false—utterly false! There is no such compulsion—more's the pity. We must *admire* the highest when we see it—but it does *not* command our *love*. *Guinevere* was right when she said "The low sun makes the color."

I re-read *Adam Bede* this week. It is a great novel in spite of its inartistic ending. I could have pardoned the marriage of *Adam* and *Dinah*, however, if it had not been brought about in such a hurried and artificial manner. *Mrs. Poyser* is a delightful creature in a book. Out of it she might not be so agreeable. The character of *Hetty Sorrel* is wonderfully analyzed. *Dinah* is just a little bit too good for "human nature's daily food." Yet there are such people—and the rest of us are not fit to untie their shoe latchets. Nevertheless, *Dinah* does not enlist our sympathy or interest. We don't care a hoot whether she ever gets a husband or not. But our hearts go out to poor, pretty, vain, sinning, suffering Hetty. After all, it is the sinners we love and pity—perhaps because they are nearer to ourselves and we recognize so many of our own hidden weaknesses in them. So perhaps it is a kind of self-pity or self-excuse which leads us to pity and excuse them. "To understand is to forgive."[3]

February 6, 1911
Cavendish, P.E.I.

Last night, when coming out of church, I saw one of the young bloods of Cavendish step up rather bashfully to a miss of fifteen and ask in the time honored formula "May I see you home?" I do not know if it was the first time she had been thus accosted but, judging from her expression, as they went past the lighted window arm in arm, I am inclined to think it was. Hers was the face of one upon whom the cachet of young ladyhood has been conferred. She was "grown up." She had "an escort home"!!

I smiled—and continued to smile as I took my escortless way across the field home. I thought of olden things and of the wonderful night, so

---

1. Mr. Pickwick's cockney servant in *Pickwick Papers* (1837).

2. From Alfred, Lord Tennyson's "Guinevere" (1859), line 660. LMM rejects this notion: love makes free, irrational choices.

3. Based on *Pensées* 12 (1672) by Blaise Pascal (1623–62).

amazingly long ago, when I, too, had an "escort home" for the first time—
both of us secretly and desperately elated—he, in "seeing home," I, in being
seen home.

When I was a little girl at school I, and all the other little girls thought
it a very wonderful event to have someone to "see you home." We saw the
grown-up girls being walked off every night of public meeting by their
respective swains, some of the bolder sort cutting their beloveds out of the
bevy at the very door of the church or hall, the shyer or less assured waiting
until the girls were going down the road, where the darkness was kind and
there was less of the glare of publicity. We saw all this and wished in our
secret souls that *we* were grown-up enough for someone to say to us, with
an arm stiffly crooked towards us, "May I see you home?" How proud we
should be to walk off with a really truly "beau." Next day in school it was
all talked over at the various desks—who had gone home with whom, and
what this, that, and the other felt and said about it.

Well, "children take long to grow"—or it seems so to them—but in course
of time I became grown-uppish and one night, as aforesaid, a schoolmate
walked home with me. I have never felt so truly "grown-up" as I did that
night. Why, I was so excited I couldn't sleep! Nor was this because I cared
particularly for my escort at all. It would have been the same if any of the
other boys had been in his place. It was just the dazzling, amazing incredible
fact that *I* had had an escort home! I!!

It was not long before the gloss and radiance of novelty vanished from
such an experience. It soon became very commonplace—pleasant enough
with a nice companion but no longer at all wonderful. I am afraid that in
still later years it became an absolute bore. For the past four or five years
I have had no "escorts" home, and had almost forgotten that there were
such things. But that girl's face tonight reminded me that they still existed
and that there were probably just as many little hearts beating with the
hope of having one some day as ever. I wonder if that girl will lie awake
as I did, recalling how his arm trembled as they started off, how he made
jerky remarks about the weather and the roads, how passing, unattached
youths irreverently whistled or jested, and perhaps how at the home gate
his arm was slipped about her and his boyish lips sought hers in a shy
good-night kiss.

It is easy to laugh at the foolishness of youth—but is the wisdom of
maturity half as sweet? I laugh at myself now and at that old memory—but
I am sure I shall never again feel so enormously proud of anything as I did
that night over having "an escort home."

Thursday, Feb. 9, 1911
Cavendish, P.E.I.

Stella came down Tuesday to spend a few days and we have been putting in a jolly time. This morning we went down to Will Houston's and spent the day. As usual there we had a delightful time. And as Stella was with me I could enjoy it without being haunted by the secret fear that I might have to drive home alone with Will!

There are few—if any—things in life without a flaw. The "trail of the serpent" *must* reveal itself—some little mis-weaving or mischance *must* mar the perfect pattern. For several years my friendship with Tillie Houston has been one of the pleasantest things in my life. Yet it has been shadowed for me by my knowledge that her husband was in love with me and made no scruple of avowing it to me.

Mr. and Mrs. Wm. Houston

Tillie Houston was formerly Tillie McKenzie, my mother's first cousin. In her youth she was *not* the charming and lovable woman into which she developed later in life. She was remarkably beautiful and her beauty was not a blessing to her. It attracted around her a crowd of not always worthy admirers and "beaux"; and it seemed, in her own estimation, to absolve her from the necessity of making any effort to please apart from her beauty. In brief, I think, from what I recall hearing others say, that she presumed on her beauty. As a result, she was not well liked by her own sex; and, in spite of her numerous lovers, she did not marry and several broken engagements left her with something of a "shopworn" savor.

When I was a child of ten father was home from the west for a visit. Tillie, then 26 years old and still very pretty, attracted him. She liked him in return and their marriage would probably have been the result if it had not been for grandmother's interference. Somehow or other—I do not rightly know how—she succeeded in turning father against Tillie and the affair was broken off. It was long before Tillie forgave her for that. She and grandma had a bitter quarrel over it and for many years she never spoke to grandma or came here, though she was always friendly to me when we met elsewhere. I do not blame her for her resentment. Grandmother should certainly not have meddled in the matter at all. In view of the fine woman which Tillie eventually became it certainly was a great mistake. Father married a woman whose evil temper and hateful disposition made his life miserable, whereas with Tillie he would have been happy. But, as I have said, Tillie was at this time a rather frivolous beauty and grandmother cannot be altogether blamed for thinking none too highly of her. What *was* blame worthy was her meddling in the matter—and her *motive* which was, not any wish to serve father's interests or promote his happiness but a determination that Tillie McKenzie should not occupy her daughter's vacant place.

Well, father went away again and Tillie drifted more and more into an old maidenhood which I think was especially bitter to her. She had to occupy a home where a married brother and his family lived. She had no recognized place in society. Her beauty faded to a marked degree. She always remained a nice looking woman but nothing compared to what she had been.

Finally, at the age of 39, she married Will Houston of North Rustico.

Will was a remarkably handsome man, with an agreeable personality. He was also very well off. But he did not belong to Tillie's class. He was—a Houston! Moreover, his associates were of an inferior caste and he had a somewhat rank reputation where "wine and women" were concerned.

But Tillie, to use the country phrase, "made a man of him." Too often, when a woman marries beneath her, she sinks to the level of her husband's caste. Tillie was an exception to this rule. She lifted her husband to hers. He went with her into the society of her class; in a few years his old reputation was forgotten and he had acquired a new one, that of being a charming fellow. As for Tillie, she also seemed a changed being. She had a nice home and a certain prestige in society as the result of being the mistress of it. She loved her husband and believed herself loved in return. In this congenial soil of happiness all the better qualities of her character, hitherto shadowed and dwarfed, first by vanity and frivolity, and then by discontent and disappointment, began to grow and flourish. She became a staunch, loyal, sympathetic woman, with enough love of him and mirth to render her a very pleasant comrade and enough tact and tenderness to make her a true friend. In a very few years people had forgotten that she was ever anything else. She became beloved by everyone.

She and Will live in an old-fashioned cosy house in North Rustico. Tillie's taste has made of it a pretty, dainty place. She is a pattern housekeeper and a queen of cooks. Out of doors she has a lovely garden and orchard. Altogether, it is a charming spot. She and Will seem—and indeed are—a very harmonious pair. They entertain their friends royally and they visit a great deal—a smiling, good-looking, prosperous middle-aged couple.

All this would appear happiness. And it *is* happiness for both of them—a very real, substantial, work-a-day happiness, by no means to be despised.

But, on Will's side at least, it is not perfect happiness. The flaw—the fatal flaw—to him is that he does not love Tillie—never has loved her. He liked her and he married her simply because he was badly in need of a housekeeper. He is fond of her and is a good and kind husband to her. But she does not hold his fancy and his heart.

Wm. Houston's house

Up to the time of Tillie's marriage she and I were little more than indifferent, superficial acquaintances. I belonged to the younger generation; and the relations between her and grandma were not at all cordial, although for a few years before her marriage the old bitterness had died away to such an extent that they "spoke" when they met and Tillie occasionally called here for the mail.

Grandfather's death took place soon after Tillie's marriage. I came home to stay and our friendship dated from that. I went often to see her in her new home. She and Will returned my visits; and we grew to be very good friends all round.

It was rather strange that she and grandmother became as fond of each other as they have been for the past ten years. The old quarrel and anger seem utterly blotted out. Grandmother really loves Tillie now more than she loves either of her own daughters; and certainly Tillie is more of a daughter to her than either Aunt Annie or Aunt Emily.

I liked Will Houston very much. For that matter I like him still, just as well as ever, when he behaves himself. I have always been frank and cordial with him. Although I am not a young girl Will Houston is old enough to be my father and it never occurred to me that there was any reason why I should not be as free and friendly with him as with Tillie.

Then, about five years ago, I discovered that he loved me. The knowledge dawned on me rather slowly from various significant speeches and looks on his part. It was long before I could believe it. At first I thought I must be mistaken. Then I thought Will was merely joking. Finally, I was compelled to believe it. He lost his head one night when we were alone in their living room for a few minutes and I realized what I had to combat.

I was appalled. For my own part, I knew there was not the slightest danger. Will Houston has no power whatever over me. He is not of the type that attracts me and I could never care a straw for him in any way, even if he were as free as air. But I was placed in a very difficult position and he knew it and took full advantage of it. I could not withdraw my friendship from him. To have done so would have offended Tillie, if she did not suspect my reason—or, if she did, would have destroyed her happiness. I could not do this and Will knew I would not unless he drove me to extremes. As long as he confined his love-making to words he knew I would be obliged to tolerate him for Tillie's sake. I could laugh at his utterances, snub his presumptuous remarks, and generally keep him in order; and he knew that if he persisted in attempting or asking for caresses, an open rupture would come. So, apart from speech, he has had to behave himself, and this is the basis on which we have been meeting for five years.

During these five years I have enjoyed many pleasant visits at Tillie's home. But over them all was this shadow of his unwelcome love. Sometimes my fears would prove quite groundless. Tillie would come with us when he drove me home—and I always coaxed her to do so most fervently—or Will, perhaps mindful of my previous mockery, would say nothing out of the way. But again an evening would come when nothing availed to keep his tongue in check. I could never understand why he persisted in talking so, when I say such merciless things to him. He knows I care nothing for him and never could care, under any circumstances. But this seems to make no difference. Talk and rave he will. He has a tolerable opinion of his own fascinations, this same W.H., and I really believe he has deluded himself into believing that it is only because he is married that I will have nothing to do with him and that if he were only a free man I would fall promptly into his arms. He thinks, I imagine, that any statements I may make to the contrary are only to save my pride and protect myself from his pursuit, since he *is* married.

I hate to be alone with him. And I always have the feeling that I am walking over a powder-mine. The last night I was down there, when he was driving me home and talking absurdly I said sharply, "You ought to have learned by this time that I don't flirt with married men." He said, *"And what if I am not always married? What then?"* It made my blood run cold. Heaven knows what mad thing that man might do if he fancied it would open a path to me.

The worst of the whole business is that it gives me such a degrading feeling of disloyalty to Tillie, who is a true friend of mine. This feeling is, of course, absurd. I am not disloyal to Tillie. I have never tried to attract, or desired to attract, her husband. I hate his insulting love and I would not even keep on civil terms with him were it not for her. But I suffer from the feeling nevertheless.

Today, however, I had no secret dread of the drive home to cloud my pleasure. We had a lovely day—laughter and jest, a dinner and tea such as only Tillie can set up, and a merry drive home through a clear moonlight night over satin smooth roads.

Wednesday, Feb. 15, 1911
Cavendish, P.E.I.

This has been a very cold day and no foreign mail came. I have felt nervous and dispirited this evening and that horrible dread of living has come over me again. It is such a dreadful feeling. Yet I am really much better this winter than I have been for several years. My nervous attacks are not so frequent or so long continued. Oh, when I recall my condition this time last year I cringe at the recollection. I earnestly hope that I may never again suffer as I did through January, February and March of last winter.

Much of my improvement this winter is, I believe, due to the fact of Margaret's nearness. When I am tired and nervous and blue I hie me to the manse and a half hour's cheerful chat and laughter fixes me up as good as new—rests the fagged brain cells by turning the current of thought from them. How much *one* friend near us means! It is the difference between dark and light.

Friday, February 24, 1911
Cavendish, P.E.I.

Wednesday morning I went to town to get a bad tooth treated. McGuigans' team came down for me and I left at daylight. Just as I was leaving it struck me how very frail and old grandmother looked. She had dressed hurriedly and was consequently rather untidy and her gray hair was hanging in wisps about her face. This always makes an old person look older. But apart from that there was a look in her face that sent a chill to my heart. For a moment I thought I could not go to town and leave her. True, I had Judy to stay with her; she was seemingly as well as usual; and it was really necessary that I should go. Yet I was on the point of sending back the team and staying

Daffy

home. I carried a sad, worried heart to town with me. I went to an afternoon tea at Mrs. Fitzgerald's[1] that day and in the evening the Ch'town Women's Club gave me a reception. I should have enjoyed myself but I didn't. All the time I was haunted by the remembrance of the look on grandmother's face as I had seen it in the gray morning light. I laughed and talked and smiled—but my thoughts were elsewhere all the time. I came home Thursday evening

---

1. Wife of Judge Rowan Fitzgerald of Charlottetown.

over wild, "slewy"[1] roads. As I drove up the old lane I felt a dread of what I might find on getting home. But what I found was a snug kitchen, Daffy purring on his cushion, and grandmother quite well and smiling. I laughed at my fears. But I shall not soon forget those two miserable days of absence.

Saturday, Mar. 4, 1911
Cavendish, P.E.I.

Both grandmother and I have been sick since I wrote last. A week ago I took grippe very badly. There has been an epidemic of it here. Last Saturday, Sunday, and Monday I was as ill as I could be. Since then I have been able to drag around, which was fortunate, since grandma took it on Wednesday and was very sick until yesterday. Since then she has been improving. But she will *not* stay in bed and I feel so worried and anxious about her lest she get more cold. I feel very miserable yet. The worst of grippe is the languor and depression it leaves behind it for so long. I feel good for nothing—and don't want to feel good for anything! I just want to lie still and not talk or be talked to. However, we are both a great deal better tonight and I hope the worst is over.

Will and Tillie were up last night and cheered us up considerably. It's a good thing to have friends!

It is not often that I read a magazine story nowadays which takes any hold on me. Indeed, I read few magazine stories of any sort, for the majority of them are not worth the waste of time involved in reading them. There are a few writers, however, whose name is a tolerable guarantee of something worth while and when I met a story "Man and Dog" by Lawrence Houseman[2] in *Harper's* this week I read it—and re-read it—and read it again—and then cut it out to preserve and read at intervals all my life. I cannot recall reading any other story that gripped me so hard. The only thing I can compare it to is Poe's "Black Cat"[3] and in some respects it is superior to that. It is as strong and vivid and weird as Poe's tale; and it has, besides, a bitter pathos which Poe's does not possess. Last night after I went to bed I cried myself to sleep over it. Of course, I am depressed and sad and sick at heart to an unusual degree, as a result of illness, and so the tale affected me more deeply and haunted me more insistently than it might have done in my normal state. I could not shake off its influence. One sentence in especial clung to my

---

1. Roads where a driver could swing round involuntarily.

2. Laurence Housman, best known as a writer of plays and fairy stories, sold this murderous fantasy to *Harper's*, the most respected American general magazine.

3. A horror tale published in 1843 by Edgar Allan Poe (1809–49), about a murderer whose crime is finally revealed, thanks to a howling cat.

memory, reiterating itself over and over. "At nightfall the tired body and dull brain went back to their rest." I do not know why but the thought of grand-mother seems strangely bound up with those words—perhaps because she has been so weak and feeble this past week and it seems so hard for her to move about as she insists on doing.

Oh, I am very tired and lonely and sad. I feel as if I could hardly drag myself upstairs to bed. But I really am much better than I was the first of the week and so is grandmother. It is just that we are both weak and dull as the grippe always leaves people. I know this; but all the "pep" seems to have gone out of me and I cannot look life in the face at all. How I wish the winter were over!

†January 28, 1912
The Manse,
Leaskdale, Ont.

I look at the above entry rather stupidly, since I have written it down. It seems unreal. I cannot quite believe that it should be so written—that any-thing save "Cavendish" should be the correct heading for any entry in this journal. And when I force myself to realize it there are elements of bitter heartbreak and homesickness in its realization. In one way, I am well con-tent—even glad—that it should be "The Manse, Leaskdale"; but I cannot, *cannot* forget

> that far shore
> Beloved and deplored.[1]

and it seems to me that I never shall be able to forget it, or the secret, ceaseless longing for it.

The Manse, Leaskdale

It is nearly a year since I last wrote in this journal—nearly a year since I laid down my pen that cold, wintry March night, never doubting that I should take it up again shortly to write another entry of my Cavendish life. But almost a year has passed—a year most strangely compounded of bitter heartbreak, of bereavement, of the agony of separation and parting, and of a certain joy and sweetness in the realization of long-cherished dreams. But the pain is more vividly remem-bered, as one day of storm and tempest stands out in memory more insist-ently than many days of quiet sunshine and peace.

---

1. From Lord Byron's "Don Juan," Canto VI.

Can I now, after a season of calm and leisure has again come to me after many months of ceaseless change, write out the story of this past strange year? I shall try. In part I may write it. But the poignancy of it can never be written.

I recall distinctly that night of March 4th—the last night I was ever to sleep in my dear old room! But I did not know that as I went drearily up the stairs to it—and it was well that I did not. I loved that little room more than I ever loved another place on earth—and more than I shall ever love any place. And I had often wondered how, when my last night in it should come, I should ever endure the anguish of it. But the last night came and I knew it

not. Yet I was very sad and sick at heart—weak, ill, dispirited. There was on mind and soul, as well as on body, a weight I could not shake off. I cried myself to sleep in the cold darkness—and thus was passed my last night in that old beloved white room, where I had dreamed my dreams of girlhood and suffered the heart-aches of lonely womanhood, where I had written my best, where I had endured my

My dear old room

defeats, and exulted in my victories. Never again was I to lay my head on its pillow there—never again waken to see the morning sunshine gleaming in at the little, muslin-curtained window where I had knelt so many nights since early childhood to pray beneath the stars. I had looked from it on spring blossom and summer greenness and autumnal harvest fields and winter snows. I had seen starshine and moonrise and sunset from it. I had known

there great happiness and greater sorrow. And now that was all finished and the Angel of the Years turned the page of life whereon it was writ. Thank God, I did not know it!

Sunday, March the 5th came.[1] It was a bitter cold day, with a furious wind blowing and whirling the light snow wildly. There was no service in Cavendish that day and I did not go out and saw no one all day. I still felt

My old window

very weak and languid. Grandmother seemed better than she had been. Her appetite was improved and she ate some dinner. All through the forenoon

---

1. Presented as a flashback in this long entry of January 28, 1912. From this point follows a series of retrospective entries.

and afternoon she seemed fairly well, but she sat in her armchair and did not even read. I lay on the sofa most of the time. It seemed a long day. But it wore to its end, as even the longest day will.

We had our tea at five o'clock. We had sat so together at the old kitchen table for many meals, just the two of us. I did not know that we were sitting so for the last time. After tea grandmother washed the dishes. I had generally done this. But after tea I had gone upstairs for a few minutes and when I came down grandmother had most of the few dishes we had used washed. I let her finish them, as she seemed to wish to do so, and said she felt stronger. The little task done, she sat down in her chair and folded her hands—folded them forever after the work of almost eighty seven years. Her work at last was done.

The old kitchen

The evening closed down—wild, dark, stormy. Just at dark I noticed that grandmother suddenly began to cough quite continuously. She had had a cough earlier in the week but it had almost gone. All at once, however, it returned. It was hard and tight and seemed to distress her. I applied what simple remedies were accessible and suggested to her that, since her room was very cold, she let me make her bed up in the kitchen where it would be warm. Grandmother assented with an indifferent willingness that surprised me. She was usually so strongly averse to making any change in the routine of her life that I had expected that she would refuse or yield very reluctantly. I moved her bed to the kitchen and we spent the night there. I did not sleep. Every little while I got up to replenish the fire, or prepare a hot drink for grandmother, whose cough continued troublesome, preventing her from sleeping. But about five o'clock she fell into a deep slumber, unbroken by any coughing. In my inexperience with illness I took this to be a good sign; but I knew she was feverish, and, thinking she was taking a relapse of grippe, I resolved to send for the doctor as soon as it was possible to venture out. As soon as daylight came I slipped out, leaving grandmother still sleeping, and made my way through the drifts down to Geo. R.'s to ask him to go for the doctor and also to send a telephone message from Stanley to Aunt Annie.

The news soon spread that grandmother was ill and in a short time I had plenty of kind and sympathizing neighbors to help me. We put up a bed in the sitting room and removed grandmother to it. She was very weak when she wakened up but said she felt better and did not like it when she found I had sent for the doctor. But very soon after she drifted into a sort of drowsy stupor from which she seldom again roused. The doctor came.

He said grandmother had pneumonia. When that was said all was said. We knew that at her age such an illness could have but one ending.

I could not believe it. It did not seem credible or possible to me that grandmother should die—grandmother, who had always been there! The rest of that week seemed like a dream through which I moved and worked like an automaton—a dream? Nay, a nightmare, of people coming and going ceaselessly, day and night, of long vigils through the hours of darkness when poor grandmother moaned in distress. She had no pain, but the deadly weakness and difficulty of breathing were even worse. It was terrible to watch her. Tillie Houston came up Monday night and stayed till all was over—poor, poor Tillie, then so strong, cheerful, sympathetic—a tower of strength for us all in our weakness and dismay. The thought of her in that week wrings my heart now. For, strong, brave, cheery as she was, for her, too, the end was near. Before the mayflowers bloomed in the April barrens Tillie was to sleep near grandmother in Cavendish graveyard.

Aunt Annie and Aunt Emily came down Tuesday morning. And, for the first time in five years, Uncle John came over to see his mother. I think his conscience, if he possessed such a thing, must have been wrung as he looked down upon her and remembered how he had used her. I would not like to have had his memories at that moment. Nor did I pity him. Ever since his father's death he had behaved to his mother with the utmost selfishness, greed, and indifference, and for the past five years his conduct towards her had been heartless in the extreme. I watched him as he went away, walking with laggard step and bowed head like an old man. I think in that hour his punishment came upon him.

Dr. Simpson[1] had said on Monday that he hardly thought grandmother would live through the night. Yet she lived until a little after noon on Friday. It was a bitter, anxious time, seeming in retrospection as long as a year. Grandmother suffered much distress part of the time; the rest she lay in a sort of stupor from which she seldom roused. She took no interest in anything; for her, the world and the things of the world had gone by and were as a tale that is told. She never asked after anyone or left any message for anyone, not even her first-born. The only living creature she remembered or spoke of was *Daffy*, the little gray animal she had petted and which had been her constant company when I had to be away. Wednesday evening, as I sat by her bed, holding her poor,

Daffy

---

1.   The nearest medical practitioner lived in Stanley Bridge, 3 miles (4.8 km) southwest of Cavendish.

nerveless old hand, she suddenly opened her eyes and said, clearly and distinctly "Where's Daffy?"

"He is out," I said. "Would you like to see him?"

"Yes, when he comes in," she said.

Room where Grandmother died

The old parlor

I went out, hunted him up, and brought him to her bedside. She put out her hand and feebly stroked his back several times. "Poor little Daffy! Poor little Daffy," she said gently. Not again did she rouse herself, or display interest in anything.

On Friday she died, after an hour of great distress and that moment, in which a lifelong tie was broken, was very dreadful to me.

At dusk grandmother lay in her casket in the same room—the old parlor—where I had seen my mother and grandfather lie. I went in alone to look at her.

Grandmother had always been a pretty woman and she retained much of her beauty to the end of life. She was tall, very slender, delicate featured with large gray eyes and cheeks that were pink to the last. In her coffin she looked so young. All the lines went out of her face and she looked no more than fifty-five or sixty—just as I remember her when I was a little girl. Her hair was quite dark under the little black "net" she had always worn. She was dressed in her black satin dress.

She had that dress made twenty five years ago and wore it always on any special occasion. It always became her and never looked "out of fashion." She always looked stately in it—"like a queen," as poor old Aunt Jane said. And it had never become her better than it did in her coffin, with her black lace scarf over her shoulders and breast.

The most wonderful transformation was in her hands. Grandmother's hands, as long as I can remember, at least, had been her most unbeautiful feature. They were very thin and a lifetime of hard work and some rheumatism in

Grandmother

her later years had twisted and distorted and discoloured them out of all proportion and grace. Yet Death, amid many other miracles, had transfigured them. Folded over her still breast they were waxen white and shapely as in youth. To me, nothing about grandmother was as touching as those hands, made beautiful again in the consecration of death.

Oh, what a wonder worker is that same death! How he blots out, for the time being at least, all remembrance of any human imperfection in our beloved dead! We can think of nothing then but their good and lovable qualities. As I stood there by grandmother's coffin and looked down at her I thought only of her much kindness, her faithfulness, her patience in earlier years, her love—ah, yes, her love! For she loved her own deeply and was very loyal to them. And, as Uncle Leander said to me in his letter later on, we of the younger generation had not known grandmother before age and infirmity had stolen most of the brightness from her life—we could not remember her as young, gay, happy and lovable.

Grandmother's birthplace

I had often read of the "mysteriously wise" smile that is sometimes seen on the faces of the dead. I have looked on many dead faces and on none had I ever beheld it. But I saw it on grandmother's—the strangest little smile—"mysteriously wise" indeed, a smile such as I had never seen on her lips in life and which was quite out of keeping with her simple, non-subtle personality—a smile knowing and remote, with just a tinge of kindly mockery in it, as if she were smiling at our grief and at the importance we were so mistakenly attaching to earthly things. It was the smile of *one who knew* and, so knowing, thought us all little children, chasing bubbles, and grieving and rejoicing over things that mattered not a whit—"even as I myself did before I *knew*," said the smile.

Grandmother's maiden name was Lucy Ann Woolner. Her father was Robert Woolner and her mother's name was Sarah Kemp. Grandmother was born in Dunwich, England, on August 28, 1824. When she was twelve years old her parents emigrated from England and came to Prince Edward Island, where they settled at Rustico. She was married when only nineteen to Alexander Marquis Macneill, then aged twenty-three.

Grandfather

To me, it seems difficult to think of grandfather and grandmother as a young couple of that age—mere boy and girl. They always seemed so icy and austere where youth was concerned. Grandfather's grandfather, John Macneill had come out to Canada somewhere around the year 1780. His family belonged to Argyleshire and had been adherents of the unfortunate Stuarts. Hector Macneill, a minor Scottish poet, mentioned by Byron in his "English Bards and Scotch Reviewers," was a cousin of this John Macneill's. He was the author of several beautiful and classic Scottish lyrics, often falsely attributed to Burns—"Come under my Plaidie," "I lo'e ne'er a laddie but ane" and "Saw ye my wee thing, saw ye my ain thing" being among them. I have a copy of the original volume of his poems. John Macneill married Margaret Simpson, whose family came from Morayshire—this being the first "alliance" of Macneill and Simpson, whose intermarriage later on became a by word. They had a family of twelve children. The oldest was William Macneill who was the first white male English child—and I think the first

white male child of any race—to be born in Charlottetown. A female child had, I believe, been born before him. He became my great grandfather, commonly known as "old Speaker Macneill," because he was Speaker in the Provincial House. He was a very clever man, well educated for those days and exercised a wide influence in colonial affairs. He married Eliza Townsend, whose father, Captain John Townsend, was an officer of the British navy and had received a grant of land in P.E. Island

[Wm. McNeill, Esq. Former Speaker of House of Assembly and Prominent Member of the Society.]

for his services. He died later in Antigua, the West Indies, and was buried there. Grandfather Macneill was one of their numerous family.

For some time after their marriage—I do not know how long but not less than three years or more than four grandfather and grandmother lived on a farm at South Rustico, near the Catholic chapel there. Then they moved up to Cavendish to live with "Speaker Macneill" and his wife in the old Macneill homestead. They had six children—Uncle Leander, Aunt Annie, Uncle John, my mother, Aunt Emily and Uncle Chester. They were very happy together. They suited each other in temperament. Grandfather was

The old Macneill homestead

a man who never interfered in minor household affairs, giving grandmother full liberty there, while she never interfered in his departments.

Grandmother's life up to the time of grandfather's death was a very happy one, I think. The happiness went out of it then, but seventy four happy years are more than fall to the lot of most people. My mother's death was the only bitter sorrow in it and even that, I think, was much blurred by the fact that before it and after it grandmother herself was very ill with a complication of ailments which threatened her life and rendered her so weak that what otherwise might have been keener feelings were blunted and softened. At times her death was hourly expected and one time they thought she *had* died— Mrs. Murray, the minister's wife of the time, always laughingly referred to the date as "the year Aunt Lucy died." But she recovered completely and became a remarkably healthy woman, never having another serious illness until the one that caused her death. Yes, on the whole grandmother had a happy life and at the last she died as she had wished to die—in her own old home, surrounded by familiar and loving faces, tended by affectionate hands, and with as little suffering as is generally found in death.

Saturday was a hard busy day. There was much to be done by way of putting the house in order for the funeral. All through the time I was haunted by a strange feeling of *disloyalty*. So many things had to be done which grandmother would have disapproved of had she been living. To me, it seemed dreadful that we should do them when she could no longer prevent us—as if we were, some how, taking an unfair advantage of her. This feeling was foolish and illogical, to be sure, but it existed and made me most miserable as long as I remained in the old house.

It was particularly strong during the sorting out of the contents of grandmother's room. Aunt Emily, Aunt Annie and I did this ourselves, not choosing that the hands and eyes of any strangers should desecrate her personal belongings. The task was a hard one, indeed—one of heartbreak; and yet mingled with a ludicrous element, too. Many a time we had to laugh while the tears glistened on our faces. For we found the most curious things in that room.

As grandmother grew older she developed a tendency often found in old people. She hated to discard or throw away *anything*, no matter how completely its use was gone or its glory departed. Everything must be kept—"it might come in handy sometime." When I grew up and began to take a hand in housecleaning every room and receptacle in the house was crammed with odds and ends, most of them absolutely useless and serving only to accumulate dust. I soon found it was time and energy wasted trying to induce grandmother to discard any of them. So I said nothing but every spring I contrived to weed out and burn a few without her ever suspecting it. So, at her death, there was hardly anything superfluous in the house—except in her room. With this, and its boxes, drawers and chests, I had never meddled at all, and we had to ransack the hoards of years as we examined the contents thereof. And *such* a mixture! Old rags, cast-off clothing, old letters, boxes, clippings, odds and ends of every conceivable kind were mixed together with nice things, such as scarfs and shawls of lace, silk waists, handkerchiefs, sachets, etc. which had been given to her as Christmas presents by children and grandchildren and never used. Indeed, I think she had quite forgotten that they were there. As I have said, the exploration of that room was a mixture of comedy and pathos. For example:—in her old black trunk we found a pair of very nice new blankets. To them was carefully stitched a bit of paper on which was written, in grandmother's tremulous hand, "For L.M. Montgomery." She was afraid, I suppose, that they might fall into other hands and so safeguarded against it. It seemed as if she had come back from the grave to do me this little material kindness and the tears rushed to my eyes. And yet, when we opened two carefully wrapped up parcels under the blankets I had to laugh. In one, we found a faded, matted "false front" worn by her own mother over fifty years ago; the contents of the other parcel were still more ludicrous. A few years ago I had a small hand mirror with a white celluloid back. An accident happened to it by which the glass of the mirror was broken into fragments and the celluloid frame bent almost double. The thing was of no further conceivable use; and, as I could not burn it, I threw it away out in the underbrush behind the hen house. Grandmother, who often wandered through this brush, looking for hen's nests, must have found it and brought it in; for there it was, carefully wrapped up in that parcel!

The task, for all its pain, was finally finished. All the useless odds and ends were burned and the rest apportioned out among friends who would appreciate them. By night all was in order and a hush fell over the old house. For the first time in a week it was very quiet again; and in the darkening parlor grandmother lay at rest, with that strange little smile on her face, and all about her the whiteness and sweetness of the flowers I had sent for. For grandmother was fond of flowers. She seldom went out in summer without bringing a spray of blossom when she came back; and my culture of flowers was one of the very few of my pursuits with which she sympathized and to which she had

The front orchard

never objected. And so I was determined that she should have them about her in death and that they should be laid close around her face in the grave.

Sunday was a quiet day—the last of many quiet Sundays in the old home. There was a very beautiful sunset that night which made the snowy front orchard a thing of wonder. On Monday afternoon grandmother was buried. There was a large funeral. Before anyone came I went in alone to say good-bye to her. It seemed to me an impossible—an *outrageous* thing that I should never see "Grandma Macneill" again. She had *always* been there. Even all through the preceding week it had seemed to me that she *must* be somewhere about—that at any moment the door might open and she enter, with her accustomed quick, noiseless footstep. But *now* I realized that the door between us would open no more. Grandmother, who for so many years had never left her home, was *gone*. She had fared forth on a long journey.

I said good-bye to her and went out and shut the door—shut it on the old life with all its sweet and all its bitter.

It was all over. Grandmother had been carried to her rest beside the bride-groom of her youth in Cavendish graveyard. To us, in the deserted home, all that remained was to strip and dismantle it—and go.

For my part, I felt that since the time had come to go I must get away as soon as I could. I wished to have the pang of parting over. Stella and Aunt Emily stayed down to help me, and Tillie Houston came up every day. The next morning we began.

It was a heart breaking—a hideous task. Every picture I took down from the walls, every article I packed away, seemed to wrench my very soul. It seemed sinful to *divorce* the old articles of furniture one from the other, to be given to this one or that. They had been together for so long that they seemed to have grown together—to belong to one another. But the work had to be done. We toiled unceasingly and by Wednesday night it was completed. That was the last night in the old home. For years I had slept under its roof—as child, as girl, as woman. And now I had to leave it!

The Manse

Thursday morning the neighbors came with teams and took all that was to go over to Park Corner. Aunt Emily also went home. Stella and I spent the day in the old house, putting it in order and burning everything that was of no value to anyone. To me, the whole thing seemed like a dream—and I, moving in the midst of it, a dream.

When all was done we locked the house and went over to the

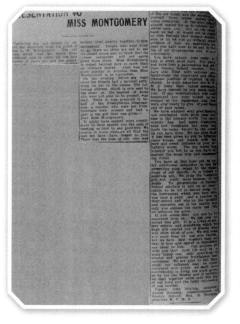

manse. The Cavendish people gave me a farewell reception that night and presented me with an address and a silver tea-service. They were all very nice and I felt that I was leaving many kind and sincere friends behind me. That night I could not sleep. The fine weather had broken and a wild wind howled around the manse. I lay and thought of the old house beyond the spruce grove—stripped, deserted, its homelight quenched forever. For the first time perhaps since it was built, certainly for the first time in my recollection, no light shone out from its windows through the old trees. The soul of the home was gone. It was henceforth to be but an empty shell, the mockery of wind and storm. I knew this—I knew that no living creature was in it, save a little gray cat, crying his heart out with loneliness in one of the upstairs rooms; and yet I was haunted all night by a weird fancy that *grandmother* was there, wandering from room to room with her candle in her hand, muttering to herself over the desecration, complaining of those who had dismantled her home. It was a horrible fancy but I was nervous and worn-out and I could not dispel it. I was thankful when morning came.

It was a very bitter day with a furious west wind blowing. George Campbell and Bruce Howatt came down for us. We went "over home" and got our

The old trees that encircled home   The pond

wraps and valises. Poor Daffy was rescued from his solitary confinement in the "lookout" room and at once condemned to a still more ignominious incarceration in a market basket. Then I went out and closed the door of the old home behind me. Never again would I re-enter it. Whatever feet would cross its threshold in the future mine would not be among them. All the bitterness of death was in that moment—and it was repeated as we drove up through Cavendish and familiar scenes and beloved haunts disappeared one by one from view—the manse, the old trees that encircled home, the graveyard on the hill with its new red mound, the woods in which was Lover's Lane— beautiful, unforgotten, unforgettable Lover's Lane—the sea-shore, the pond, the houses of friends—all drifted finally out of sight. I had left Cavendish forever, save as a fitful visitor; and in leaving it felt that I was leaving the only place on earth my heart would ever truly love. The world might have a home for me somewhere; but the only home my inmost soul would ever acknowledge would be that little country settlement by the gulf shore.

I felt real regret over parting from most of the Cavendish people. I think I shall write a short sketch of them here in my journal—my real reason for doing it, I believe, being that I love to write of anything concerning Cavendish and somehow am loathe to leave the subject.

Will and Tillie Houston lived in Rustico but were so much in Cavendish that they seemed to belong there. Of them, however, I have already written in this book. McLures too are, strictly speaking, Rustico folks, living just across the district line. Henry was the only one of the family I knew very well. Poor Henry died last fall of Bright's Disease. He had been married some two or three years before and, somewhat oddly, his wife and I became very good friends. At least, we found each other's company entertaining. She was Bessie Schurman, rather pretty and quite clever—really superior to Henry with whom, however, she seemed to be genuinely in love. She had no suspicion that Henry had ever cared for me and used to provoke my secret amusement somewhat by telling me that she was the only woman he had ever wanted to marry and similar confidences of the sort. However, I really liked her very much and we had an agreeable surface intimacy. After Henry's death she went away to her brother in one of the States and I missed her quite considerably.

Next to McLure's was the old McKenzie homestead built away down in a little cove by the shore, quite out of sight of the road. Here, when I was a little girl, Uncle John McKenzie and Aunt Margaret lived. Aunt Margaret was grandmother's sister. Of Uncle John McK. I have only a faint recollection. I remember being there once or twice when I was a little girl. Then after the quarrel between Tillie and grandmother I never went there again until within the last fifteen years. By that time Uncle John was dead. Aunt

Margaret is still living and is 89 years old. She is, and always was, a sweet old soul, universally beloved. She was of a more open manner and less reserved temperament than grandmother and in so far was the more popular woman of the two. She had a family of eight children of which the only ones remaining in Cavendish after Tillie's marriage were "Toff," Ewen, and Hammond.

Toff—short for Theophilus, which his parents likely thought a very fine, mouth-filling name—is one of those jovial, jolly folks whom everybody likes well. He has never married but has lived on at the old homestead, never seeming to grow old but always being counted in among the younger set by reason of his mirth and jollity. From a worldly point of view he did not amount to much—more by reason of being a square peg in a round hole I think, than because of anything else. Toff was not meant for a farmer but if he had been a doctor he would, I believe, have been a striking success, for he had every natural qualification for such a profession. As it was he did not amount to much but Cavendish without old Toff would not seem the same place. For twenty years or more he "went with" Mary Laird, but they could not marry because she could not leave her father. After her father died we all looked for the marriage but it never came about—why, nobody can say. Finally, last summer Mary coolly married another man and the old, old question that had been asked so often, "Do you think Toff and Mary will *ever* be married?" was finally answered.

Ewen McKenzie was another failure—partly because of chronic ill-health perhaps. He married young, before he had anything to "keep" a wife and family on. And a family he certainly had to keep! They had twelve children! Of his wife, a silly, loose-tongued woman and his family, scantly more to my taste, I knew little. Ewen, however, was a member of the choir and so I knew him rather better, and liked him, too. He was a fine singer as were all that family. They also belonged to what might be called the "smart set" in Cavendish. They were not at all intellectual, as were the Macneills and Simpsons, but they dressed smartly, drove spanking teams, used the most up-to-date slang, were the first to adopt a new fashion and in general, to use the colloquialism, liked to "cut a dash."

Hammond was the youngest of the family and the least popular. I don't think anybody really likes Hammond McKenzie. Yet he can be very agreeable and pleasant company when he likes. He and I have

Hammond and Emily McKenzie, and family

always got on admirably and have had plenty of fun together at choir practices and social functions. But in any intercourse with Hammond McKenzie, I, and I think most people, had the feeling of walking over a mine which might explode into bad temper or an insulting remark any time. His wife is very well suited to him and they are, I imagine, a very harmonious pair. They take life easy—which is perhaps the best way. They are *not* fond of work—they *are* fond of gossip. You would not be dull in their society, neither certainly would you be much edified!

Angus McKenzie lived on the next farm. He died before I was old enough to remember him very clearly. His wife was a quiet woman who never went anywhere because of her extreme deafness. I knew the family well. Mary Louisa, the oldest, was a delicate girl. She never married and a few years ago died of consumption. She was one of those quiet, busy women who are missed surprisingly when they are gone. "Bob," the oldest boy is a nice fellow whom everyone likes but who will never set the river on fire. After Louisa's death he married Jennie Stevenson of New Glasgow and a new home has been founded on the ruins of the old. Bertha was my particular friend in the family, although she belonged to the "set" just before me in age. Charlie and Clara went to school with me. I must candidly say I always detested Charlie McKenzie. He had the best-developed opinion of himself I ever knew and anybody to have—and very little to justify it. He married and settled elsewhere. Clara I liked but was not intimate with. She was a girl, sweet of voice and manner, with a sufficient number of thorns under her sweetness. She married a Stevenson in New Glasgow. Milton is the youngest of the family. He counts for nothing in any way. He is ignorant, boorish, uncouth, yet thinking himself quite a pretty fellow.

"Old" Ewen McKenzie was a brother of John and Angus and lived down near the shore. I have only the faintest possible recollection of him. But I remember his wife—or his second wife—most distinctly. She was not a person whom, having once seen, you *could* forget. Such a cadaverous, death-in-life countenance I never saw in any other human being. She was in a sort of slow decline for years. After her husband's death the boys used to call her "Mrs. Dead Ewan," to distinguish her from the other lady whose "Ewen" was still alive, and the name had a gruesome appropriateness. She died a few years ago. She had six daughters one of whom, Laura, went to school when I did. She died of typhoid

Alex. Macneill's house

before her mother. After Mrs. Ewen's death the girls all went away and the old house has been closed ever since.

Alec and Albert Macneill's places come next. When I was a little girl they were unmarried boys at home in the old homestead where Russell now lives. That is one of the houses I have never gone past for the last few years without a pang, caused by a sense of the changes that have come about in since my childhood. Charles Macneill and his wife lived there then. It was one of the few places in Cavendish where

1. Lily Macneill. 2. "Mr. Charles." 3. "Mrs. Charles." 4. Minnie Macneill. 5. Albert Macneill. 6. Rob. Macneill. 7. Mrs. Albert Macneill. 8. Mrs. Alec Macneill.

I was allowed to visit, and I was there a great deal, because of my childish intimacy with Pensie. Charles Macneill was a rather intelligent but some-what peculiar man. He had a pet expression—"that way"—which he used continually, often in the most grotesque combinations with other words. "I was going to town the other day that way and I met the peddler that way with a new outfit that way, and I thought to myself that way 'There's a tidy little horse that way,'" etc. etc. Though he himself was quite unconscious of using the expression it is hard to believe anyone who listened to him could be. But May told me after her marriage to Alec that he had never noticed his father's use of it until she called his attention to it. Charles Macneill was not very popular with some of his neighbors and in his old age his aforesaid peculiarities intensified into very marked crankiness. But when I was a child I worshipped "Mr. Charles" because he was so kind to me. Kindness was a distinguishing feature of both him and Mrs. Charles. Mrs. Charles was a little bent slave of a woman, cheery, kind, ignorant and gossipy. She still lives at the old place where she has a rather miserable existence with Madam Russell. Charles died a few years ago.

The family were all hard-working creatures, caring for little save work. Albert and Robert, the two oldest boys were quiet steady plodders. Albert married Bessie Stevenson of New Glasgow—a woman a good deal like his mother—kind, hard-working, gossipy—not of a very exalted type of char-acter or intellect, but a good, decent body of her kind. Rob was the only one who went far afield. He drifted out to the western states and settled and married there. Lily and Minnie came next—two kind, pleasant girls, a good deal older than I, so not very well known to me at that time. They, too, are married and gone. Alec and Pensie were the two members of the family I knew best. Alec used to drive me about a little in our times but he never interested me at all. Later on he married a very nice girl, May Hooper, who was greatly his superior. Alec, however, has improved considerably since his marriage. They have a nice home but are childless and feel it keenly.

Pensie and I were chums because our families were good friends and because we were both fond of fun. There was no other tie and so when we grew up we drifted apart. Pensie was a pretty girl with curly auburn hair, blue eyes and a fair freckled complexion. We had "no end of fun" together in those early days. Pensie was the picture of health then. She married Will Bulman of New Glasgow and died a few years later of consumption—I believe she literally worked herself to death. Russell, the youngest of the family, is not and never was a popular personage. He is certainly very low in the scale of intelligence, if not, as some think, actually defective mentally. At school he was the most absolute dunce imaginable and to this day I don't think he can either read or write. Anecdotes of Russell's speeches are always going the rounds—his "generous purpose" horse, his "information of the lungs," his "I will tell you a little innocent," his "don't mention it as coming from me" are all local jokes. He is a man nobody has any respect for. Although now nearing forty he has no more standing in the community than a schoolboy of ten. Yet Russell contrived to marry a woman of average intelligence. What motive induced her to marry him only she herself can tell. Certainly nobody else can. She is no more popular in Cavendish than her liege lord. Her chief exploit since marrying Russell has been to set mortal enmity between him and everyone of his brothers and sisters and to foster it and intensify it. I have visited there occasionally for grandmother's sake, since she had to get Russell to haul her coal for her, but I have never enjoyed going there since she came. It is not the place it was in olden days and never can be again. For me it is haunted by ghosts that are sorrowful because of their joyousness. Pensie comes back from the grave, laughing-eyed and rosy-cheeked once more and beckons me up the willow-shaded lane, to our old frolics of wood and garden and harvest scented barns. But I know better than to follow that spectral lure. That little beckoning ghost must wait alone among the shadows.

After Albert's farm is passed comes what is now called Arty Macneill's. When I was a child it was "Big George's." Big George Macneill lived there, so called to distinguish him from "Little George" Macneill. He was a big man with a bushy gray beard. I knew him and his wife well by sight, but not otherwise, for they were Baptists and in those days the Jews had no dealings

"Big George" Macneill's house

with the Samaritans. Big George was a deacon and a leading light in the Baptist church. He died about ten years ago and his wife a few years later. They had a large family of whom I knew well only those who went to school with me—Alma, Clemmie, Nellie and Arty. Of these I certainly did not like Clemmie and Nellie. Arty was an insignificant creature of no especial interest to anybody. Alma was the flower of the family and universally popular. She was a very pretty girl, bright, clever, of pleasing manner. She went to Boston when she grew up but came home almost every summer and we always kept up our intimacy. She is in California now. When I was a child that old house sheltered a large family. Now there is no one in it but Arty, keeping a forlorn bachelor's hall.

The next farm belongs to William A. Macneill—"Will Sandy" as he is popularly known—as odd a creature as ever lived, with queer streaks of sentiment and distorted genius pervading his make-up. He writes sarcastic poetry about people who have offended him which he can sometimes be prevailed on to recite when he has partaken of the cup which cheers *and* inebriates. His wife is a kindly, brainless soul, with a reputation for being deceitful which may or may not be deserved. His oldest daughter Sadie is the damsel who dyed her pale red tresses black and so is persistently regarded as the proto-type of "Anne of Green Gables." There is certainly no other resemblance between them!

Adjoining them is John Laird's farm. In my early days it was "Old Sandy Laird's farm." Old Sandy was regarded with just as much respect as might be inferred from his nickname. He had been a loose-liver all his life, drunken and licentious. Yet his days were long in the land. He lived to be very old and for ten years preceding his death was a burden to all around him, especially his daughter Mary, who was a fine creature—patient, mild, steadfast, reliable. Truly "the mother makes us most." "Old Sandy's" wife had been a good woman and Mary was all her mother.

Mary Laird

John Laird was more his father's son, though leavened enough by his maternity to live a more decorous life outwardly. He "had to get married" as the country phrase goes to Ida Stewart. She was a daughter of John Stewart of Bay View. This was another "smart set" family and all the daughters but one achieved matrimony in the same fashion. Ida Stewart was an exceedingly pretty girl but her beauty was all she had to recommend her. John did not wish to marry her and rumor assigns them an unhappy life together.

William Laird, John's older brother, lived on the next farm. He and his wife were always good friends of mine and were very kind to me, especially after Myrtle's illness and death. I waited on her a good deal and they always seemed to remember it gratefully. Last fall they sold out and went to British Columbia. I felt very sorry to think of their leaving Cavendish. Although I have left it myself, I fear forever, I hate to hear of any changes there. Nelson McCoubrey of New Glasgow has bought the farm and moved in.

The next farm was "Old" Henry Robertson's. Old Henry was another Cavendish resident who was but little respected. He was extremely mean, avaricious, ignorant, "small." He lived only to hoard and accumulate money. His son Murray was but small improvement on his father, yet he contrived, like Russell, to marry a woman much his superior—Emily Woolner, a niece of grandmother's. Also, there lived there then Asher Robertson, the illegitimate son of one of old Henry's daughters. Asher was a schoolmate of mine and I rather liked him. He did not amount to much when he grew up. I do not know where he is now, nor what has become of him.

Emily and Murray had no children, so they adopted a nephew, Gordon Robertson, who has grown up to be a rather negligible factor in Cavendish society. Recently he took unto himself a wife who is a fairly nice little soul in her way.

Uncle John's farm came next. Uncle John bought it from Dr. Murray after his marriage to Anne Maria McLeod of Park Corner. From my earliest recollection Uncle John figured in my consciousness as a man to be hated and shunned. His manner to me, and indeed to most children, except those of whose parents he had a salutary awe, was brutal, domineering and insulting. I don't think I was ever in Uncle John's presence that he did not say something unkind to me—and if I were a field's length away he would probably yell it at me. In all the 36 years I lived beside him I cannot recall one kind word or deed from him. And yet I was the child of his dead sister and it was said his favorite sister. I never knew a man so utterly inconsiderate of the feelings and rights of other people—of anyone over whom he dared to tyrannize—and so utterly selfish. He ruled his family with a rod of iron—with the usual result in such cases—they turned out weaklings and failures. He had a remarkably loud harsh voice and on calm summer evenings when he raged at some of his children he could be heard all over the settlement much to the amusement of the dwellers therein. He stormed at his children for every trivial fault as if they were guilty of something atrocious. As a result they had no respect for his opinion and he had no influence over them when they grew up. They, therefore, did just as they pleased once they had outgrown their fear of his bluster.

Yet Uncle John could be agreeable enough when he liked and anyone who never met him save in society might have supposed him to be quite a nice man. He was intelligent, sober, and industrious. But his faults of selfishness, bad temper and tyranny overrode everything else. He lost all control of himself if he could not get his own way in everything.

Had Uncle John married a woman with a bit of temper too I believe he would have been a much better and more agreeable man because he *could* control his temper when he had to. Like all bullies he was a coward at heart and never attempted to domineer over a person who could and did confront him boldly—"give him as good as he sent." But Aunt Anne Maria was a placid, smiling, good tempered *animal*. Nothing ever ruffled her. She fostered all the worst elements in Uncle John's nature by truckling to him to his face and then taking her own way by guile and deceit behind his back and bringing up her family to do the same. She was a pretty woman, kind when kindness cost her nothing, absolutely selfish, smooth, shallow and specious. She had but one ambition, "to make a show," and she constantly "toadied" to people whom she thought wealthy or of social standing. With all her smooth amiability she was not popular in Cavendish. I often wondered why, for in my childhood, I worshipped Aunt Anne Maria. I had not then discovered or suspected the depths of deceit and treachery which underlay her pleasant exterior. While she was so kind to me and apparently so sympathetic outwardly she was in reality doing all she could to prejudice my mother's family against me by falsehood and innuendo. When I grew up I discovered this and my old love for her was changed into contempt. She never succeeded in doing me any real harm for the people I cared for were beyond reach of her influence; but the fact remains that she tried.

Lucy was their oldest daughter, a girl three years younger than I. Through our childhood and young girlhood we were playmates and chums. Lucy had her mother's temperament but not her mother's good looks. She had a good figure but very coarse features. She was a good-natured, fond of dress, fun and pleasure. I loved her and trusted her as a sister. I cannot now understand my blindness in the matter for, looking back, it seems to me that I had plenty of warnings as to her real nature. I always knew that her other friends were never my friends. They all seemed to regard me with dislike and distrust, which I could not think I had given them any reason for. This fact alone should have opened my eyes. But it did not. I kept on believing Lucy to be my true friend until I had unmistakeable evidence of her falseness and deceit. When once my eyes were opened I investigated the matter thoroughly and a sickening tale of underhand malice and envy was revealed. I found that all her life Lucy had been doing her utmost to prejudice against me anyone to whom she dared reveal her real sentiments. She had not stopped with distorting facts and insinuating malicious opinions. She had employed absolute falsehood. What her motive was it would be hard to say. The main factor no doubt was a petty jealousy of certain advantages which I had and which she had not. But Lucy was false to the core. It was the fundamental defect of her character that she could not be true to anyone. She talked to me about her other friends just as I afterwards discovered, she talked to them about me—and all this with the greatest show of sweetness to our faces. In her youth Lucy had three intimate friends—Pensie Macneill, Blanch Howatt, and myself. We all three at different periods turned against her for the same reason—we found her out in deceit and malice.

But even before I discovered this I was beginning to realize how little Lucy and I had in common. Lucy seemed to have but three objects of ambition in life—to be showily dressed, to have a good time, and to get married. Beyond this she had no interest in anything and when I left early youth behind me I found her companionship less and less satisfying as years wore on. When the discovery of her treachery came I was hurt and grieved but I missed her not at all when I put her out of my life. I told her plainly why I did it and she has hated me ever since with the pitiful, impotent hatred of the woman who realizes that she is known for what she is.

Yet I can find it in my heart to pity her for the wreck she has made of her life. She married Ben Simpson, a creature whom nobody respected and who was almost a pauper. Her parents were bitterly opposed to the match but they had no influence over her. She was determined to throw herself away on an ignorant boor whose outstanding attribute was an enormous conceit of himself and who was not fit to be her lackey. Yet she married him and has been a drudge ever since. He took her to a miserable mortgaged farm down at St. Peter's where they lived for two or three years. Ben was too lazy, to work and poor Lucy, eager to "get on" and justify her choice in the eyes of her little world slaved herself almost to death. She looked, as I heard someone say, like a woman with a broken heart; but I think it was rather a broken pride. She realized, I suppose, that she could not lift her husband to her level but must dwell on his. Finally they had to give up the struggle, sell out and go to the States, where Ben got a job as driver of a street car, and there they have been living ever since. Lucy's health is broken and she is the shadow of her former self. Sometimes I forget the way in which she behaved to me and find myself thinking gently and tenderly of her, of our old intimacy, our jokes, our fun, our larks together. Then remembrance rolls back in a flood of bitterness—the bitterness of a heart and trust betrayed.

Uncle John had three sons—Prescott, Frank and Ernest. For none of them did I ever feel any cousinly affection or comradeship. They certainly never displayed any towards me, and they never at any time showed me common neighborly kindness. Prescott was meanness and pettiness incarnate. I can never forget the way he used grandmother and the things he said to her. Poor creature, he need not have been in such a hurry to turn grandmother out of her home. When she told him he might wait until she was dead he told her brutally he could not wait for that—"you may live ten years yet" he said. Well, she outlived him. He died two years ago from tuberculosis of the spine, after a long illness made very bitter to him by the heartless conduct of his mother and sister. They were said to neglect him shamelessly. Uncle John, who had plenty of money, grudged every cent he had to spend on doctors and would not even get poor Prescott a wheelchair to move himself around in and he had to lie in bed because he could not walk.

Frank, the second son, was a good looking, empty headed, conceited youth. His father wished him to take an education and would have sent him to college. But Frank had no ambition or perseverance. He grew tired of school and insisted on going into a store. And in a store he is yet, discontented and repining, but with no chance of being or doing anything else now. He is married and his wife is a nice little girl who has to endure public insults from her husband as her husband's mother before her did. Frank calls her a "fool" before others and apparently thinks it smart.

Poor Kate was the best of them. She was pretty and agreeable. She was very popular. Some thought her deceitful but I think she had less of it than any of the others. But she had the family failing of low ideals and petty aims. When her father sent her to P.W.C. she neglected her studies for a social good time and then in despair of passing her exams threw up her year and went into a store as clerk. Always kept down and tyrannized over at home she had no judgment to regulate her social life when she found herself in comparative freedom. She went to extremes in her love of a good time, became engaged to a very immoral man, got herself talked about—I believe unjustly—and finally wrecked her health by heedlessness. She died of pneumonia, following wilful disregard of her doctor's advice. Her death was a severe blow to Uncle John. None of the rest of the family seemed to feel it keenly. Even her mother very speedily recovered her smiles and good spirits. But Uncle John was never quite the same man again. Kate was the only one of his family of whom he could be at all proud and his pride and his affection both suffered from the blow.

Ernest, the youngest son, is rather like "chips in porridge." He regards himself as quite a lady-killer and is rather good-looking in a commonplace way. There is nothing in him but he is free from most of the unpleasant characteristics of his brothers. Annie, the youngest daughter, is a compound of the worst features of both her parents. She has her mother's good looks, her mother's deceit, shallowness, low ideals and falsity, along with her father's temper and tyrannical bent. She is exceedingly unpopular. I have never heard a person speak well of her. She cannot speak the truth about anything and she behaved preposterously to grandmother. To her dying brother she was notoriously harsh and unkind. I cannot see in her one redeeming feature of disposition or character—unless the ability to meet and cow her father with his own weapons can be accounted unto her for such. Her moral character has been blown upon owing to her indiscreet conduct with various fellows of the baser sort. Lucy and Kate were well-bred girls and always conducted themselves as such in society but "Tot" makes an absolute exhibition of herself upon all public occasions and seems to be growing more notorious in this respect as she grows older instead of improving.

I sometimes wonder, what life would have been like if, say, Uncle John Campbell and Aunt Annie and their family had been living where Uncle John and Aunt Anne Maria lived. I know it would have been much pleasanter for me and for grandmother. It would have made all the difference in the world these last thirteen years!

Between our place and George R.'s farm is the Manse. Mr. Archibald and his family were the first occupants of it and were there all through my childhood and early youth. Mr. Archibald was liked by the older people but not by the younger. He was too reserved and anaemic. His wife was rather nice but commonplace. Only two families have occupied the manse for a brief space since

The Manse

their departure. Now it is occupied again by John and Margaret Stirling.

Across the road from the manse used to be the little low-roofed white house where "Uncle Jimmy" and "Aunt Jane" lived. Uncle Jimmie was an older brother of grandfather's and a most eccentric individual—a curious compound of child and genius. He was a born poet. He composed hundreds of poems and would recite them to favored individuals. They were never written down and not a line of them is now extant. But I have heard grandfather repeat some of them and they were real poetry—most of them being of the satirical and mock-heroic order. They were witty, pointed, dramatic and picturesque. His masterpiece was an account of a local fight which had taken place at New Glasgow. I recall two lines,

> Round Houston's corner now the battle raged
> And every man was busily engaged.

—and I suppose those two lines are all that survive out of the thousands composed by Uncle Jimmie—most of them as he sat boiling potatoes for the pigs in winter time! Uncle Jimmie was something of a "mute inglorious Milton"—or rather Burns. He was a failure as a farmer but had he been an educated man he might have "made his mark" in the world—if his eccentricities had not stood in his way. His wife was as odd as himself without his redeeming qualities of intellect and ideals. He married Jane Harker. She was his inferior; his family considered her so; Jane knew that they considered her so and bitterly resented it. When I was a child I had the most deeply-rooted terror of "Aunt Jane." She had been out of her mind several times and was always of a most ungovernable temper. Sometimes when I went to the house she would shut the door in my face. Again she would receive me civilly but would rail bitterly against everyone in the community—except the dead, who, no matter what their faults in life became canonized in aunt Jane's mind at the moment of death and henceforth were flawless. She had the lunatic's idea that people were continually plotting against her and hers, and always threw out dark hints of something that was terribly wrong but would be made right somewhere. She never in my recollection went out anywhere. She stayed at home and brooded over her fancied wrongs until her judgment and viewpoint, never very accurate, became hopelessly poisoned and perverted. As I grew older I learned how to manage her better and even found a rather wicked amusement in her bitter jeremiads against the Simpsons, her sly "digs" at the Macneills and her persistent melancholy view of everybody and everything. Poor Aunt Jane! Her life has been a misery to herself and to all those who had the misfortune to live with her, and endure her tempers and tantrums.

Evie

They had three living children. Another died when he was about fourteen; and eight more were born dead. No wonder poor Aunt Jane was not normal. The oldest bore the—to her—singularly inappropriate name of Evangeline. She was always called Evie, however. Evie Macneill is one of the most hopelessly plain women I have ever seen—but she possesses a most beautiful disposition and soul, sweet, unselfish, patient loyal uncomplaining, through a life that can have held very little sunshine for her. Evie is one of the best arguments for a future life I know of. There *must* be another existence where all that she missed in this will be made up to her and where the innate, essential beauty of her spirit must be made manifest in outward

Very poor snap of "Geo. R."

loveliness. She has never married and has been a slave to her mother's imperious whims all her life.

Grace, the second daughter, was also a very sweet woman, with a pleasing, Madonna-like type of beauty. She married and went away when I was a child. The only son "George R."—short for George Raglan—was a clever popular fellow. Somehow, he never married. At one time he was engaged to Miss Gordon, but it was eventually broken off, why or how, or by whose fault, was never known. He is today a rather peculiar man of fifty with a keen intelligence and a well-stored mind. But his life has warped him in some ways. I have always liked George very much and found a congenial friend in him. He often came up for the mail and would spend the evening discussing books and world events. "Maud is the only girl in Cavendish who never talks gossip" he said of me once. But I *did*—only I never talked it to him, since he was able to converse of other things, which very few Cavendish men,—none of my generation—could do. He built a new house some years ago and has one of the prettiest, neatest places in Cavendish.

The old "Cavendish Road" branches off at the graveyard corner and runs on to Mayfield. James Laird's house is the first along it now but when I was a child "old Cyrus" lived down in the hollow below the school in a small house which has long ago been demolished. Cyrus was a Macneill and the "black sheep" of the clan. At least, he was incurably lazy and shiftless and had taken unto himself a wife of his bosom who belonged to the same type and was of a caste decidedly inferior to the Macneills, who, as Aunt Mary Lawson says naively, are "inclined to consider themselves above the common." This promising couple, if they could do nothing else, could at least reproduce their kind. They had a large family of boys, real "chips of the old block." The "Cyruses" were a "tough" family. Old Cyrus was generally away in the daytime and it was a local tradition that when he came home in the evening he "belted" the boys all

Geo. R.'s new house

round for the offenses of the day. Certainly the fearful howls and yells which floated up from the hollow on the calm stillness of the summer evening seemed to be born of physical suffering. In spite of this gentle paternal correction the "Cyruses" did not turn out very brilliantly. Cyrus might not have spared the rod but the sons were assuredly spoiled. They are scattered over the world now and the father and mother are dead. Their dwelling place has become heaps and their name is remembered no more.

Up on the hill James Laird lives—or "Jimmy Laird" as he is commonly called. It is a tradition in our family that Jimmy, who was quite a "buck" in his youthful days, was in love with my mother and was told by his father "Old Sandy" that if he got Clara Macneill he should have the Lockerby farm. But Clara Macneill did not see it so and Jimmy never got the Lockerby farm! Certainly mother could never have cared for such a man—but if she could have—and did—what would I be, supposing I existed at all? "Nine tenths another to one tenth me?" Well, I certainly wouldn't wish to be nine tenths or even one tenth Jimmy Laird!

He is a man with one aim and object in life and one only—to make and hoard money. He never spends a cent if he can avoid it. He did nothing for his family and has scrimped his wife all his life. Their domestic infelicity is proverbial but it is not all Jimmy's fault, in spite of his shortcomings. His wife is equally bad tempered and miserly, and devoid of all tact and pliancy. Yet, as a woman, she is superior to Jimmy as a man. Everett, the oldest son, is now almost as odd as his father, but when he went to school he seemed rather a nice fellow, always making dry, comical speeches which kept us laughing. John, the second son, was a nice fellow and quite nice looking. Austin was another oddity. Ellice, the only daughter, was a rather nice little thing.

Farther in along the road is Everett's place. He married Lizzie Stewart two years ago after a long and—seemingly—a by no means ardent courtship. 'Twas a curious match, Lizzie was much older than Everett but far too good for him.

Coming back to the east and west road, Pierce Macneill lives down in the Mill Brook Hollow. Pierce is one of the oddities of Cavendish. His wife is the only woman in the world who would have married him, just as he is the only man who would have married her. She is the homeliest woman in the world. Yet they are perfectly satisfied with each other and are, I believe, far happier than many handsomer couples. Pierce is generally nicknamed "By Creon" because that is his favourite expletive.

"Uncle David"

Next on the left is the farm that once belonged to David Macneill. He and Margaret live there yet. In my childhood "Uncle David"—grandfather's uncle but not very much older than himself—lived there, too. He was a fine-looking, very intelligent and well-read old man, seemingly very agree-

Mr. and Mrs. E. Webb, and the oldest children

able to meet. But I am told he was a tyrant in his family and a very autocratic man. After his death David and Margaret lived alone for some time. They never visited anywhere or had any visitors there. David was a very shy man, and Margaret, though a very clever woman, had no social instincts or aptitudes. About fifteen or sixteen years ago their niece, Ada Macneill, came to live with them, bringing her illegitimate daughter Myrtle with her. Ada had not been rightly used and was not judged harshly for her misfortune. Later on, she married Walter Simpson of Bay View but Myrtle lived on with David and Margaret until her marriage to Ernest Webb of O'Leary. Mr. Webb then bought David's farm. He is a nice young fellow, Myrtle is a nice woman and they have three nice children. I have visited there often of late years and shall miss the Webbs very much. I am glad Mr. Webb owns Lover's Lane. He will appreciate it and care for it, I think. I had always had a dread that David's farm might eventually be sold to someone who would not care for the lane—who might even cut down the trees, or desecrate it in some hideous fashion. But with Mr. Webb as owner it is safe.

Down by the pond is Amanda's old home—one of the prettiest spots in Cavendish, though sadly allowed to run to seed of late years. "Willy Makum"—as people called him behind his back, from his father Malcolm Macneill—lived here. In childhood I was always rather afraid of him. He used to "make faces" when he talked and his grimaces were a local joke. To see old William tiptoeing down the church aisle in

Amanda's old home

squeaky boots, grimacing fearfully at every squeak was unforgettable. He had an ungovernable temper and an overweening sense of his own importance—a sense which nothing in his personality or life justified. Yet he bitterly resented anyone's not realizing this importance. And as nobody *did* realize it, because it did not exist, and as nobody ever paid him the deference he believed his due he was always in a state of impotent annoyance with the world. He was a poor manager, got over ears in debt and finally closed his life's failures by drowning himself in Clark's pond a few years ago. He was, I think, insane when he did. But his insanity was simply the result of bad temper and morbid egotism which had finally gained control of the whole man. His wife I always liked. She was a mild, gentle, delicate woman. William's sister Caroline lived with them—a wrinkled, patient old drudge. The boys were all failures. Tillie was the oldest daughter. She resembled her mother—mild and amiable but rather a nonentity. She had little force of character—was one of those people who "never make mistakes or anything else." She and Hamilton, the youngest son, live there alone now. Amanda lives in at Mayfield and seems to be a most unhappy woman. I fear she will yet go as her father did if she does not learn to control her temper and her egotism.

Next to them live John and Jane Macneill, brother and sister, who being elderly Baptists never entered into my life. The adjoining family was William Simpsons', whose large family all went to school when I did. He is now dead and his wife is in Vancouver. Somehow, that family "petered out." The boys did not amount to much and all were rather delicate. The three girls, Janie, Ella, and Lottie, were all very nice. One of Arthur Simpson's sons owns the place now and keeps bach-

Darnley and Mrs. Clark and boys

elor's hall in the house. Darnley Clark's farm is next. He and his wife were always good friends of mine. Their children were my schoolmates. Chesley is in the west where he is married. Maggie is married to Walter Buntain of Rustico. Fred is married to Hettie Houston of New Glasgow and has built a house across from the hall. Wilbur was married a year ago to Nellie Bullman of New Glasgow and has built a house near the Baptist parsonage.

Tillie, Mary, Maggie and Janie Clark used to live in the old Andrew Clark homestead where I was a girl. They were not very popular with the young set. I liked Janie and Maggie. The latter went insane and drowned herself in their pond. A few years ago "The Clark girls" sold out and moved to Kensington.

Jim Simpson of Hope River bought their place. Across from them lived Alec Stewart—"roaring Ack." He died a few years ago. Fenner Stewart married Laura Wedlock of Stanley and lives on the homestead. Charles Simpson's farm is next. He and his wife and youngest daughter still live there. Mamie and Emma, the two older girls were my schoolmates. Both went to Boston several years ago. Emma married there. Mamie went under. She has trodden ever since the way that takes hold on hell.

Cavendish ends there. The next district is Bay View. Many of its people however, come to Cavendish church and hall. It is the main habitat of the Simpsons.

But Cavendish and all the kindly and beloved friends of youth and maturity must be left behind. For the first time I was leaving Cavendish with no hope of returning, save as a transient visitor. Always before, when I had left it, I left there the old home with some beloved one in it, to which my heart might look back amid strange surroundings, knowing that some day I would or might return to it. But now I had no longer this consolation. The old home was broken up forever, stripped and desolate, its household gods scattered, its homelight and hearthlight quenched.

We arrived at Park Corner after a cold drive. That afternoon, pursued by a spirit of restlessness, I began to unpack my personal belongings. But I was

Uncle John Campbell's house; x. is the window of my room there.

View I of my Park Corner room

View II of my Park Corner room

unequal to the task. Everything I took out of my trunk wrung my heart for I would see, as I touched it, the very spot it had occupied in my old room. I broke down utterly and spent the rest of the day lying on my bed in tears,

aching with bitter homesickness, stripped of all courage for the future.

Next morning, however, I was calmer and though the task was a painful one I got all my things unpacked and arranged in the room I was to occupy while I remained at Park Corner. I do not know what I should have done if I had not had Park Corner to go to in the interval between leaving Cavendish and my marriage. Hard as it was, the wrench was somewhat allevi-ated by going to a place which had always been a second home to me. And though I could not

View from window to right

have stayed there long contentedly, owing to the discord prevailing between the two families, for a short sojourn that did not matter seriously and, save for the many inevitable hours of homesickness and heart hunger, I passed some very pleasant weeks at Park Corner last spring. All were very kind to me and Stella was a jolly companion.

But the first few days were hard—hard. In the day I could bear up but when nightfall came my spirit fainted within me. Few were the nights upon which I did not cry myself to sleep. The only comfort I had was to go to bed, shut my eyes, and imagine myself back in my old

View to left

room at home, with all the old things in their places around me. This was an illusory peace but while it lasted it was very potent.

That little gray creature of a Daff was a real comfort to me. He seemed like a living link between me and the old life. Besides, his antics and our anxiety over them furnished us with a little comedy during those spring weeks. He was bitterly discontented at first and as wild and frightened as a hare. When he disappeared, as he frequently did, we were sure he had started for Cavendish. But he always turned up and eventually became reconciled to his new abode. At least, he loved the big barn with its mousy straw-loft and the woods around. But all the time I was at Park Corner he never became really domesticated in the house. He seldom was willing to stay in it and never seemed to get over his fear of strangers, of whom there were generally some about. The whole household made a pet of him and were as much interested in him as I was myself. Even George seemed to have a warm spot in his heart for "old Daff," and five-year-old Danny,[1] who called him "a Newfoundland cat," because he was so big, was quite jealous of his affection and declared that "Daffy loves me more than he loves Aunt Maud." Daff was really wonderfully tolerant of Danny. He had always been so impatient of any handling save by me that I was seriously afraid

Daffy

Daff   Danny

if Danny began hauling him about as children generally do with cats Daff would injure the child. Instead, he submitted to be lugged around, half the time upside down, without a protest and with the most comically resigned expression on his face which seemed to say, "Danny is only a little boy so I am enduring this patiently, though I would rend in pieces any grown-up person who offered me such indignities."

Now that poor grandmother had gone there was no longer any reason for delaying my already long-deferred marriage and it was arranged that Ewan and I should be married early in July. A little over a year previously he had left P.E. Island and taken a congregation in Leaskdale, Ont. I felt badly over the prospect of leaving the Island. But since I had left Cavendish it did not matter so much.

We also decided to go over to England and Scotland for our wedding trip. I was pleased over this for I have always wished to see those old storied lands. But I was by no means as jubilant over it as people seemed to imagine I would be. When they said to me, "What a perfectly lovely time you will have!" I acquiesced with a smile. But I knew quite well that there would be many drawbacks to the "perfectly lovely time." I have outlived my youthful illusion that travelling is unmixed pleasure. I expected to have a very interesting and pleasurable trip; but I knew quite well that the discomforts and inconveniences of it—the constant moving about from one place to another

---

1. Donald Campbell (1907–71), son of George (1881–1918) and Ella Johnstone Campbell (1876–1955).

and "living in trunks" meanwhile—would, especially to one of my systematic and domestic tastes, discount quite heavily from the real pleasure of the trip.

I had a very busy spring, preparing for my marriage and new home—so busy that most of my ordinary pursuits were dropped for the time being. During my first four weeks at Park Corner I was quite miserable physically. I suppose I felt the effects of the nervous strain and hard work of those last two weeks in Cavendish. I took a second attack of grippe and then had a siege of that most unromantic and painful complaint, *boils*. When this was over, however, I was very well the rest of the spring and, in spite of my frequently recurring agonies of homesick longing, I could not but feel, as well, the relief from those thirteen long years of petty carking worries and anxieties.

I was so busy that I could not keep this journal up in any regular fashion. Besides, I long shrank from the pain I knew would be attendant upon the writing of grandmother's death and leaving Cavendish. But occasionally through the spring, when I had a little spare time, or when pain demanded some outward expression, I wrote some stray entries in a notebook. One of these occurs on Wednesday, April 12, 1911.

++*Wednesday, April 12th, 1911*

Today was cold but fine. The snow is almost all gone and as it froze tonight the walking was good. This evening Stella and I went up to McKays[1] on an errand. Coming back through the clear moonlight night I saw the row of silver birches at the back of the grove behind the house. They recalled the birches around the old "front garden" at home. A very anguish of homesickness overwhelmed my soul. It seemed to me that I must *die* if I could not get back to Cavendish. For the time, I did not believe that I could go on living away from it. Oh, if I could find myself in the cold spring moonshine walking up the old lane at home, seeing the kitchen

The old lane at home

The curve by the cherry trees

---

1. John Mackay of French River was the son of Donald and Matilda (MacNeill) Mackay (Penzie's aunt).

light gleam yellowly through the trees, turning the curve by the cherry trees, opening the old, kitchen door, and finding grandmother reading in her armchair by the fire and Daffy curled up on his prescriptive cushion on the sofa! But around me were alien fields and hills I did not know.

On April 17th, I got a telephone message from William Houston, telling me that Tillie was dead!

When Tillie left our place it was to go to Hammond's to nurse her mother, who was very ill with grippe—so ill, indeed, that it was not thought she could recover. While there Tillie took measles. I had known she was ill and very ill with them; but a letter from Margaret two days before had said she was over the worst and was recovering. Therefore this message was a horrible shock.

To this day I am not any more reconciled to Tillie's death than I was then, and I *cannot* become reconciled to it. Grandmother was very old and life had ceased to hold much happiness for her so that, although the rending of lifelong ties caused anguish at the time, my mind accepted it as what, after all, was best for her and what was inevitable in any case. But Tillie was in the prime of life, happy, useful, beloved by all. Her death has made in my life a blank which can never be filled. She was one of the few Cavendish people who really mattered to me, one of the few people in the world whom I deeply and intimately love. The bitterness in the thought of re-visiting Cavendish after the great change had been alleviated by the thought that Tillie was there, and that in her home I should always be a welcome guest. And now she was gone and when I went back I must always miss her. The pang in that thought, as I write, is just as keen as it was the day I first heard of her death.

The next day George drove me down to Cavendish. It was just when the roads were breaking up and they were in dreadful condition. I had dreaded going back to Cavendish the first time, fearing that it would be all pain. But it was not. Instead, it was a joy to see all the old places again, even though they were in the unbeautiful dinginess of earliest spring. But ah, the pang came when I had to go to the manse—and *not* home! Never before had I returned to Cavendish without a home there to go to.

That evening Mrs. Wm. Laird drove me down to Hammond's and I saw my dear friend—for the first time without

The Manse, Cavendish

a smile or greeting for me. She did not even look very nice—she who was so pretty in life. Her face looked as if she had suffered much.

That night in the manse I suffered from my old obsession that I should be home—that grandmother must be waiting for me in the old house through the spruce wood, and wondering why I did not come. My heart seemed steeped in the misery of it. And when I slept I dreamed I saw her there, sitting a-cold by her fireless hearth, weeping for my not coming.

I have dreamed hundreds of times since I left home, of being back there, and never once has the dream been a pleasant one. The first few months those dreams were absolute torture to me. It was always the same dream— I was back home and grandmother was there, too. But all was confusion and desolation, and grandmother was invariably reproaching me for having destroyed her home and deserted her while she was yet living. What a relief it was to waken from such a dream! Of late, the character of the dream has changed. Home is as it used to be and grandmother is in it; part of the time she is alone, in other dreams grandfather is there also. This is strange, because, in all the years after grandfather's death, I never dreamed, save once, that he was alive again. But now I dream it frequently. When I dream that grandmother is there alone I am in agony as to how I can be married and living far away while she is there, and worried as to how I can leave her and return to my own home. These dreams are distressing. And, much as I have desired to, I have never once dreamed of being in Lover's Lane. Not a day passes that I do not think of it, but never in the land of sleep do I see it. Perhaps it is as well—for it might be with my dreams of it as my dreams of home—changed and desolate, and that I would not wish.

I found Cavendish in a flame of gossip over tales of Will Houston's indifference towards his wife during her illness. Knowing what I did of him, I found it hard *not* to believe them—though I did not say so to the gossipers! And yet, in another way, I found it hard *to* believe them. Will had always been very good to Tillie during her lifetime. He might cherish a crazy passion for me but even he could not have deluded himself into believing that I would ever marry him, even if he were free, and, apart from that, there could be no motive for any secret, horrible wish on his part for Tillie's death. I would hate him if I suspected him of it. But I do not. I believe he simply did not realize that Tillie was dangerously ill until she was gone. Nobody else did, so why should he? Even her own family—nay, her very doctor, had never felt the slightest fear that she might not recover. I saw Will for only a few minutes the day of the funeral but he seemed to me a grief-stricken man. He had lost such a home-maker as he would never find again and I think he had enough sense and perception to realize it, no matter how his inclinations might have wandered during her life.

And yet—it is hard to say what dark thought may have lurked in the recesses of his heart. God help us all. Life is a tangled thing. It is hard to know where truth ends and falsehood begins in a nature where both are entwined as they are in Will Houston's. At all events, he made Tillie happy while she was alive and the rest must be between him and his judge.

Tillie was buried in Cavendish graveyard, not far from where grandmother lay. George and I went back to Park Corner that same evening over dreadful roads, in the teeth of a bitter wind. I was almost played out when I reached there.

Poor Tillie! I think of her every day. It seems to me that I should be getting letters from her. I cannot think of her as dead—I cannot think of the little home, made beautiful by her taste and labor, without her presence.

++*Sunday, May 7th, 1911*

Aunt Emily's house   Aunt Emily's house

Yesterday Stella and I drove up to Malpeque to see Aunt Emily. I had not been there for nearly twelve years. Many memories of old days came back. The first time I ever visited Malpeque—or Princetown, as it is alternately called, one being the Indian, the other the English name—was the summer after Aunt Emily was married. She and one of her sisters-in-law, I think, came down to Cavendish and took me back with them. The drive from Cavendish to Malpeque is one it would be hard to surpass anywhere. On the way we saw a most miserable hovel built on one of the river banks. Upon my exclaiming with horror over its appearance Aunt Emily seriously informed me that it was just the same sort of a place she lived in! I was only seven and I still believed implicitly in everything which was told me by a grown-up. My anguish at this statement was quite indescribable and, as I could not conceal it, furnished much amusement to Aunt Emily and her companion. *Why* is it that the agonies of children generally do furnish amusement for their elders—people who would not wantonly inflict pain on any human creature? I suppose it must be because they do not realize that the child is really suffering. *They* could not feel pain over so small a matter and therefore they cannot understand that a child may. I hope and pray that, if ever I have a child, I may not sin in this, and laugh at its heartbreak because the cause seems trifling to me.

At all events the rest of that drive was spoiled for me. I think my family pride—which was very well developed even at that early age—barbed the suffering most keenly. It seemed a dreadful thing to me that my aunt should be living in a place like that! I couldn't endure the humiliation of it. How great was my relief when we finally reached our journey's end and I found a most respectable and comfortable, though old-fashioned, farmhouse awaiting me! I was so thankful that I forgot to feel rancor towards Aunt Emily for deceiving me so.

Her home was within a stone's throw of the bay shore—Richmond Bay. It was a rarely beautiful place, as far as sea scenery went, though the absence of trees made it seem a little bare. What sunsets I have seen on that bay! And what effects of moonlight on dark cape and islet!

I visited Malpeque quite often in the following years, as long as poor Uncle John was alive. It seems to have changed very little, but few of those I knew in the old days are there now!

Bertie and I take a drive in the Park

On May 8 I went to town to attend to shopping and dressmaking. I stayed in ten days. Bertie and I had never had such a good visit together and we enjoyed it hugely although it was clouded for us both by the shadow of coming change. Bertie and I felt very badly over my leaving the Island and I felt wretched over the thought of being far separated from her and seeing her so seldom. We have been such congenial friends. There seems to be a perfect harmony between us and a perfect understanding. And in the future we may see but little of each other and have to find our associates among people whose companionship cannot give us one tenth the pleasure we can give each other.

I had a busy and fatiguing time in town, for in addition to a great deal of business I was asked out to tea almost every evening. Sometimes I enjoyed myself, but more often I was bored and wished myself in

[View from Victoria Park, Charlottetown, P.E.I.]

Bertie's room discussing "life and literature" with her. In younger days, when I would have enjoyed this social life and the opportunities of improvement it brings, it was not mine. And now that it has come to me I no longer care greatly for it or desire it.

Last spring in Park Corner was pleasant in many ways. I had some nice friends there. Aunt Mary Cuthbert's home was a nice place to visit, and so was Mrs. Ramsay's on the next farm to Uncle John's. Mrs. R. is a jolly, likeable soul, and her adopted daughter, Alice Smallman, a mite of six, is one of the quaintest children who ever lived out of a book. "Aunt Eliza"—Uncle Jim's widow— reigns supreme in the old Montgomery homestead beyond the bridge. I paid her two or three visits of courtesy, but they were far from enjoyable.

Bertie

How changed that place is from what it was in the days of the "old Senator." It is a beautiful house inside but there is no attraction for anyone there now. Aunt Eliza is not liked by anyone. She has two children. Heath, the oldest, is a fine-looking young fellow, but reckless and dissipated. There are gleams of his father in him that warmed my heart to him, for I always loved Uncle Jim who so strongly resembled my father. But there was another strain I did not like. Lula, his sister, is a kind, hard-working creature, but a hopelessly awkward and lumpish girl. I don't think anything can be made of her.

Alice

There is only one of my father's family now living—Aunt Maggie Sutherland. All the rest are gone—most of them in their prime. Uncle Jim and Uncle Cuthbert were comparatively young men when they died. I remember them as kind, handsome merry fellows. I wish Aunt Eliza's children were able and willing to carry on the traditions of their race—but they are not. The old name must decline. It will never again stand for what it once meant.

Grandfather Montgomery's house

When housecleaning time came Stella and I cleaned the big house and enjoyed it, in the long beautiful spring days. In the evenings we beguiled

The Bridge

Housecleaning regalia   Blossom time at Park Corner

dull care away by going down to the pond and trouting over the bridge. We caught plenty of trout and had a great deal of fun. But I found the most pleasure in the charm of water and evening sky and fresh budding woods.

I shall never forget blossom time at Park Corner last spring. The place was like Paradise. Park Corner, taken all over, is not to be compared with Cavendish for beauty. But there is no one place in Cavendish as beautiful as Uncle John Campbell's place. It really is, I believe, the loveliest farmstead I have ever seen, with that magnificent grove of beech and maple behind it and the big orchard before it.

I recall one evening of last spring in especial. I sat at the front door and drank in the beauty of the world until I was drunken with it. The dew was falling, the orchard was literally white with blossom and the lilac trees at the orchard gate were masses of purple bloom in the twilight. My heart ached with the transcendent beauty of it and with the agonizing homesickness which it evoked. For I thought of spring evenings in Cavendish, full of vanished sweetness, and of how white the old orchard at home must be that very evening—and how misty and bridal and sweet the arches of Lover's Lane. And when the night had blotted out, or rather, wrapped

Part of the grove

The lilac trees at the gate

away the beauty of the scene I went upstairs alone and cried my heartache out—and somehow the tears and the pain and the longing and the loveliness of that evening are blended together in a memory that is half a delight and half a torment—and wholly dear.

++*Tuesday, May 23, 1911*
Park Corner, P.E. Island

Today *The Story Girl* came—and with it a heartache. For I thought there were two dear ones who would have read it proudly but could never read it now. When I wrote it they were with me—and now they are gone. I wrote it in my dear old room where I shall never sit and hold pen more.

I have been haunted, ever since leaving home, with a nasty obsession that I can never write again. This I know is foolish, but I cannot shake it off. The very idea of taking up my pen again is distasteful to me. No doubt, when the time comes that I can do so, I will find again the old joy in creation and fancy, but I cannot feel this way now.

The "Carlisle" of *The Story Girl* is practically Cavendish—and the site of the *King* homestead is "Jimmy Laird's place" on the hill above home. But the *King* household is most certainly *not* Jimmy Laird's household, nor their house the Laird abode. But I have always loved that site and woven innumerable dreams around it. I used it in *Kilmeny* as well as in the *Story Girl*.

All the children in the book are purely imaginary, though no doubt there are people who will firmly believe and assert that I myself am the *Story Girl*. The old *King* orchard is in the main imaginary also, though our old orchard at home and the orchard here at Park Corner furnished many descriptive hints for it. *Paddy* is a "composite" cat, with the characteristics of several pets of mine and the physical attributes of "Daffy the Second." *Peg Bowen* was drawn from "crazy Mag Laird," the terror of whom haunted my childhood. We children were always being threatened that if we were not good Mag Laird would catch us. The threat didn't make us good—it only made us miserable. Poor Mag was really harmless enough when she was not teased or annoyed. If she were she could be vicious and revengeful enough. In winter she lived perforce in a miserable little hut in the Rustico woods but as soon as spring came the lure of the open road proved too much for Mag and she started on a tramp that lasted till the return of winter snows. She was known over most of the Island. She went bareheaded and barefooted and her clothing was ragged and dirty beyond description. She smoked a pipe and told extraordinary tales of her adventures in various places. In her earlier years her life was far from being moral, but she could hardly be held responsible for her actions. Her family relations were respectable people but Mag was an Ishmaelite from her cradle. Occasionally she would come to church, stalking unconcernedly up the aisle to a prominent seat. She never put on hat or shoes on such occasions but when she wished to be especially grand she powdered face, arms and legs with flour! Poor old Mag died only a few years ago.

The *Rev. Mr. Scott* was aforetime the Rev. Mr. *Sprott*, an old Scotch minister of Nova Scotia, whose daughter married Dr. Murray, a former minister of Cavendish. He was a very eccentric person. I have heard Grandfather tell many tales of him, not only those I used in the *Story Girl* but many others.

The story of *Nancy* and *Betty* Sherman is an old family yarn of the Montgomery's. The Penmans were a family who lived somewhere near Port Hill in the early days of the Island. I have heard two conflicting stories as to their coming to P.E. Island. As Grandfather Macneill used to tell it they were a family of United Empire Loyalists who came to Canada at the close of the American War of Independence. Having lost all their property they were very poor but the beauty of the Penman girls was so great that they married into the best families of the colony. But George Montgomery told me this spring that George Penman was a paymaster in the British army. Perhaps both accounts are true and George Penman may have acted in that capacity in the States before the war. At all events, the rest of the story is beyond dispute. Nancy and Betsy Penman were very beautiful, especially the former—who, by the way, was buried in Malpeque churchyard, where I saw her grave this spring. *Donald Fraser* was my great-grandfather, Donald Montgomery, and *Neil Campbell* was David Murray of Bedeque. Grandfather Montgomery was the son of Donald and Nancy and inherited his stately presence and handsome face from her. He married his first cousin, Annie Murray of Bedeque, the daughter of David and Betsy. So that Nancy and Betsy were both my great-grandmothers.

In *The Story Girl* I polished up the tale a wee bit—at least to the extent of giving David a horse and sleigh. In reality, what he had was a half-broken steer, hitched to a rude old wood-sled and it was with this equipage that Donald hied him over Richmond Bay to propose to Nancy!

The story of the captain of the *Fanny* is also literally true. The heroine, *Mrs. Boswell*, is still living at Hampton. I heard the story from Grandfather and Aunt Mary Lawson many a time.

The "Blue Chest of Rachel Ward" was another "ower-true tale." *Rachel Ward* was Eliza Montgomery, a cousin of father's and the blue chest was in Uncle John Campbell's kitchen from 1849 until about four or five years ago.

Eliza Montgomery a few years before her death

We children heard its story many a time and wondered furiously what was in it. Eliza Montgomery died about five years ago and left directions to open the famous chest and distribute its contents among the connection—such of them at least as moth and rust had spared. I was not at Park Corner when it was opened, though I would have given much to have been. Its contents were an odd miscellany—wedding clothes, shawls, sheets, pillow cases, dishes etc. etc. etc.—and several bars of home-made soap which had not lost its virtue in all the years! My share of the spoils consisted of a blue china candlestick, a quaintly shaped wine bottle of green glass—there was no wine in it!—a handkerchief trimmed with knitted lace, a knitted lace shawl and 2 small glass plates.

I may add here that *Cecily's* "forget-me-not jug" and "cherry vase" were—and are—treasured possessions of my own. When I was a little girl grandmother went to Charlottetown one fall to nurse Uncle Chester through an attack of typhoid fever. When she came home a little girl, Gertie Farquharson, who lived where he boarded, sent me the forget-me-not jug for a present. Grandmother gave me the cherry vase a year or two later. I loved both these things very much and now they are consecrated for me by old memories.

The *Martin Forbes* who called *Cecily* "Johnny" had his prototype in old Mr. Muirhead of Summerside who visited our place with his wife when I was a tiny tot—five or six, I suppose. He was, I believe, an amiable and respectable old man. But he won my undying hatred by calling me "Johnny" every time he spoke to me! How I raged at him for it. It seemed to me a most deadly and unforgivable insult. My anger amused him hugely and incited him to persist in the objectionable name. I believe I could have torn that man in pieces had I had the power! When he went away I refused to shake hands with him because he had called me by such a nickname. Whereupon he laughed uproariously and said, "Oh, well, I won't call you Johnny anymore. I'll call you Sammy after this"—which was of course adding fuel to the fire. For years I couldn't hear that man's name without a surge of hot anger. Five years afterward, when I was ten years old, I remember writing in my diary "Mr. So-and-So Muirhead is dead. He is the brother of a horrid man in Summerside who called me Johnny."

I never saw poor old Mr. Muirhead again so I never had to endure the indignity of being called "Sammy." He is now dead himself and I daresay the fact that he called me "Johnny" was not brought up in judgment against him. Yet he may have committed what might be considered far greater sins that would not yet inflict on anyone one-tenth of the suffering of humiliation which his teasing inflicted on a child's sensitive mind. I *never* tease a child. I have no inclination to do so, for I could never find any pleasure in the mental suffering of others, any more than I could in physical suffering. But if I were inclined that way I should certainly be prevented from indulging my bent by the keen recollection of what I suffered at Mr. Muirhead's hands. To him, it was merely the "fun" of teasing a "touchy" child. To me, it was the poison of asps.

Old *Mr. Forbes* who did not like *Andrew MacPherson's* bass, was "old McKinstrie," who was one of the ancient landmarks of Cavendish church when I was a child. He lived "in along" the Cavendish Road, as Mayfield was then called, and never missed a Sunday. He sat in a front pew directly under the pulpit and looked as I imagined the Hebrew prophets must look, with his snow-white hair and beard. He talked "broad Scotch" and was a quaint old character. One story we always laughed over was "old McKinstrie" telling grandfather that he always "made his own iodine out of strong tea and baking soda." I have never forgotten his comment on Drummond's *Natural Law In The Spiritual World*, which grandfather had lent him—McKinstrie having a Scotchman's liking for theological works. But *Natural Law* was too much for the little man. "I can read sense and I can read nonsense" he said, when he brought the book back, "but that book's neither the one nor the other."

The "ghostly bell" was an incident of my own childhood. One evening when Wellington Nelson and I came home from somewhere we were met in the front orchard by Dave, his face quite white with terror, who assured us that there was someone in the house ringing a bell. We were horribly scared and did not dare venture into the house until the return of grandfather and grandmother from milking, when we found our mysterious "bell" to be the striking of a newly-cleaned clock.

The "judgment Sunday" chapter was suggested by another bitter experience of childhood. One day I read in a newspaper the prediction that the following Sunday was to be the end of the world. From that time until Sunday was over I lived in an agony of terror and dread. I trod the winepress alone[1] for the grown people laughed at me and I had no childish companions then to share my suffering. What a transformed creature I was on Monday morning when I realized that the end of the world was not coming just then after all. I did not believe everything I read in newspapers after that.

I had a spell of writing down my dreams, too, which suggested the "dream book" chapter. All one winter I wrote them down—the winter when I was

---

1. Suffered, with no one to offer help. Isaiah 63:3.

nine years old and had to stay home from school because of ill health. I had to resort to many ways of amusing myself and this was one of them. I wrote my dreams all down in little yellow-covered notebooks that were sent by the score to post-offices as advertisements of a patent medicine firm. In later years I burned them. I wish I had them now—but I remember all the dreams distinctly still, especially the one of seeing the hideous monster on the roof of the house.

++*Wednesday, May 24, 1911*
Park Corner, P.E.I.

It is not often that one of our day-dreams is literally fulfilled—and it is still less often that such fulfilment is completely satisfying. Yet I had such an experience tonight—for the first time and perhaps the last. I did what I dreamed of doing all through the years of childhood—and I found it quite as wonderful and beautiful and inspiring as I had imagined it might be.

I have written before in this journal of the charm New London Point always had for me, when I looked at it from Cavendish across New London Harbour—in childhood, when it was for me the end of the world and beyond it seas of faery—in youth when it was beautiful as an out-post of sea sunsets—and in later years when the revolving light bejewelled it every evening. It has always been my dream to walk out on it to the very tip and look off from there to the wide, ocean wastes beyond.

A dream fulfilled

Tonight I did it. Bruce Howatt drove Stella and me down to the Point. I climbed down the steep rocks by the aid of a ladder and I walked out to the tip of the headland. On my right lay the harbour and away beyond it the misty Cavendish shore. To my left was a sunset sea, veiling itself in twilight shadows. Before me lay the open ocean, purple, murmurous, wind-visited, where the ships came and went on their blue pathway. Over me were early stars. The poignant beauty of it all cannot be put into words—the thoughts and feelings of my heart then cannot be expressed in symbols of earth. I seemed to be caught up into eternity. But the pang that came when I looked across to the distant homeland shore was of earth; and I was sad when I drove away, although my long dream had come true and brought to me all I had dreamed into it.

++*Friday, May 26, 1911*
Park Corner, P.E.I.

I spent this evening with Aunt Mary Cuthbert and walked home alone. I enjoyed this exceedingly. Since coming to Park Corner I have rarely had a walk alone, as Stella is generally with me. As a rule I like this, for she is a jolly companion, with the same taste in jokes. But I love dearly a solitary walk, with no companions but my own wild unfettered thoughts, and sometimes I feel the need of being alone—absolutely alone—with stars and trees and waters. So I walked home very slowly from Aunt Mary's tasting the sweets of solitude and of the spring night. I sought out and found my old friends the stars; and when I came to the pond I leaned over the bridge for half an hour and was happy. The frogs sang with silvery mournful sweetness in the marsh and along the shadowy shores. The stars were reflected in the still water. The darkness was around

A corner of the pond

me and the night wind whispered to me. Afar out the sea called. Oh, spring dusk, how sweet you are! What balm you brought my spirit tonight! I almost forgot to be homesick.

++*May 27, 1911*
Park Corner, P.E.I.

This evening Stella and I walked down to the old graveyard in Uncle Jim Montgomery's field. I always like to go there. It is over a hundred years old and dates back to a time when there was no graveyard near Park Corner, so the early settlers buried their dead on their own land. Then Uncle Jim's farm and Uncle John's farm were all one property, owned by James Townsend, an emigrant from England. His grand-daughter Eliza, married William Macneill and became the mother of Grandfather Macneill.

The little graveyard is on the bank of the pond, near the shore. I do not know how many people were buried in it but more than there are head-stones to mark. Old James Townsend and his wife lie there and on their stone is carved the following epitaph—one of the diffuse epitaphs of a gen-eration which had time to carve such—and time to read them!

"To the memory of James Townsend of Park Corner, Prince Edward Island. Also of Elizabeth his wife. They emigrated from Berkshire, England, to this Island A.D. 1775, with two sons and three daughters, viz:—John, James, Eliza, Rachel and Mary. Their son John died in Antigua in the lifetime of his parents. His afflicted mother followed him into Eternity with patient resignation on the seventeenth day of April, 1795, in the sixty ninth year of her age. And her disconsolate husband departed this life on the 25th day of December, 1806 in the 67th year of his age."

There is another epitaph in the graveyard which has always had a certain fascination for me. A man named Truegard was buried there. I do not think he was any connection of ours. His widow composed an epitaph for his headstone. At least, she was credited with its composition, but as I have recently discovered that some of the lines were stolen from Pope, I do not feel very certain of the authorship of any of them. But most of them are so bad that it is likely she did write them. She began with rhyme, but the Muse evidently deserted her half way and she had to conclude in prose, save for the aforesaid "lifting" from Pope near the last. The inscription is so worn that it is difficult to decipher it, but it seems to run thus;—

Sweet gentle spirit,[1]
Do receive
The vows a grateful widow pays,
Each coming morn, each parting eve
Shall hear her speak her Truegard's praise.
Though thy much loved form must here
Within the cold dark grave decay
Yet from her mind thy memory dear
No time, no change shall wear away.

Do thou from mansions of eternal bliss remember thy distressed relict. Look on her with an angel's love, soothe her sad life and cheer her way through this world's dangers and its griefs, till sickness, pain or death oppress.

Then from her closing eyes thy form shall part
And the last pangs shall tear thee from her heart
Life's idle business at one gasp when o'er
Meet her with thy well-known smiles and welcome
at the last great day.

One feels tempted to wonder irreverently what the "distressed relict" was "grateful" for in the second line! I don't know whether the disconsolate widow was buried by "her Truegard" or not. There is no mention of her on any of the stones.

---

1. This follows LMM's won original layout.

There is a family tradition regarding Mrs. James Townsend. James Townsend had received a grant of land in P.E. Island from George III, which he called Park Corner, after the name of the old family estate in England. He came out, bringing his wife, to the uncut woods of the Island. Bitterly homesick was she—rebelliously so. For weeks after her arrival she would not take off her bonnet, but walked the floor in it, imperiously demanding to be taken home. I never wearied of speculating, when a child, as to whether she took off her bonnet at night and put it on again in the morning, or whether she slept in it. But back home she could not go, so eventually she took off her bonnet and resigned herself to her fate. I wonder if any homesick dreams haunt Elizabeth Townsend's slumber of over a hundred years.

The graveyard is surrounded by a low, grass-grown dyke and overrun with wild rosebushes. It is not adorned with "storied urn or animated bust." Yet

> Perhaps in this neglected spot is laid
> Some heart once pregnant with celestial fire.

There is also in my family history an amusing account of how the Montgomery's came to P.E.I. Hugh Montgomery came to Canada from Scotland. He sailed on a vessel bound for Quebec; but the fates and a woman's will took a hand in the thing. His wife was desperately sick all the way across the Atlantic—and a voyage over the Atlantic was no five days run then. Off the north shore of Prince Edward Island, then a wild, wooded land, with settlements few and far between, the Captain hove-to in order to replenish his supply of water. He sent a boat ashore and he told poor Mrs. Montgomery that she might go in it for a little change. Mrs. M. did go in it; and when she felt the blessed dry land under her feet once more she told her husband that she meant to stay there. Never again would she set foot in any vessel. Expostulation, entreaty, argument, all availed nothing. There the poor lady was resolved to stay and there, perforce, her husband stayed with her. Their son, Donald, was the hero of the old story of Nancy and Betsy Penman.

++Monday, June 5, 1911
Park Corner, P.E.I.

Will Houston and Rachel Woolner came over today. Rachel is Tillie's sister and has been home since her death. How their coming brought the keen pang of bereavement back! I *cannot* feel reconciled to Tillie's death. Will looks lonely and sad. What changes since this time last year!

++*Park Corner, P.E.I.*
Thursday, June 8, 1911

On Tuesday Stella and I started off on another "calie." We have had several jolly little jaunts this spring. To me it seems a strange thing to go anywhere without carrying with me a feeling of worry and care regarding someone left behind. It is years since I really enjoyed an outing and now it does not seem quite right that I should. It seems somehow unlawful and forbidden not to have something on my mind to temper the pleasure.

W. Houston, Mrs. Woolner, and myself

Our main object was to visit Aunt Mary Lawson, who is at present living with William Macneill in Elmsdale. But on our way west we stopped off at Ellerslie to visit friends of Stella's at East Bideford. It seemed quite in keeping that Lou Dystant should be on the platform when we stepped off the train. And as Stella's friends, through a misunderstanding, did not meet us, Lou got a horse and drove us around to East Bideford. Next day he went up west on the same train we did. He has not changed much but looks a good deal older. He has not married and rumor assigns him a somewhat dissipated life.

We had a pleasant visit in Elmsdale. How glad poor old Aunt was to see us! And yet how sad, too, when she recalled many things. She felt keenly the closing of the old home in Cavendish—her old home as well as mine. Aunt Mary Lawson is the only living member of that once large family on the

Aunt Mary Lawson   Mr. and Mrs. Macneill and Aunt Mary

Island. She has yet one sister in the States—"Aunt Phemie." But as this sister went away half a century ago and has never revisited the Island, she is little more than a name to Aunt Mary. Practically Aunt Mary is alone and her loneliness is especially embittered by her homelessness. She is poor and, having no children, has to live around with nephews and nieces, some of whom are not too thoughtful of her feelings. She is a proud old lady—all "the pride of the Macneill's" is strongly in evidence there—and feels this keenly. But she has kept to a wonderful degree the heart and the sympathies of youth.

Aunt Mary Lawson is really the most wonderful woman of her age I have ever known. In her youth she had no educational advantages save the few weeks each year at the district school. But she had a naturally powerful mind, a keen intelligence, and a remarkable memory, which retains to this day everything she has ever heard and read. She is a splendid conversationalist and it is a treat to get Aunt Mary started on tales and recollections of her youth; and all the vivid doings and sayings of folks in those young years of the colony. She is a stately old lady, with a nice amusing little bit of vanity about her yet—she likes to go nicely clad and didn't altogether like the photo I took of her because "so many wrinkles showed in her face." Dear old lady! I felt very sad when I bade her good-bye. I knew it might be for the last time. She knew it, too, and felt it keenly. Yet surely that brave, strong, eager, interested spirit cannot go out into eternal silence. It *must* go on existing and enjoying somewhere."

Frede came home from Macdonald College on June 17th. Stella and I went as far as St. John to meet her and had a jolly trip. From that out we were intensely busy, planning and working. My trousseau, which I had made mainly in Toronto and Montreal, began to arrive and we were all interested in that. My things were pretty. I had worn black for grandmother all the spring but I laid it aside when I was married. My wedding dress[1] was of white-silk crepe de soie with tunic of chiffon and pearl bead trimming—and of course the tulle veil and orange blossom wreath.

These are snaps the girls took of some of my dresses. My suit was of steel gray cloth, with gray chiffon blouse and gray hat trimmed with a wreath of tiny rosebuds. My long wrap was of gray broadcloth. Besides the dresses "illustrated" I had a linen dress, a pink muslin, one of white embroidery, and several odd waists.

---

1. The dress was preserved and displayed at LMM's birthplace in Clifton (now New London); it is now housed in the Confederation Centre of the Arts, Charlottetown, in winter.

| Suit. [L.M. Montgomery's wedding trousseau pictures.] | Wrap | Black voile dress |

| Brown poplin dress | Gray cashmere dress | Navy blue dress |

On Friday, June 23rd Frede and I drove down to Cavendish and stayed until Saturday evening at the manse. I had been dreading this trip. It seemed to me that going back thus to Cavendish must be acute pain. But it was not. On the contrary it was all a sweet pleasure to be there again in that June beauty. The centre of interest at the manse was Margaret's baby[1]—a little daughter, born in May. I felt a double interest in this little lady, because she was Margaret's child and because I had known of her expected coming almost as soon as Margaret herself and had talked matters over with Margaret all along the mysterious way of approaching motherhood.

Saturday afternoon I slipped away by myself. I went first to the graveyard and saw Tillie's and grandmother's graves. Then I went to Lover's Lane. I had expected to feel sad but I did not. Sorrow seems to have no place in Lover's Lane. Its beauty charmed soul and sense, its fairy voices called to me, its fair memories walked hand in hand with me. It was after I had left it that sadness came. I might never walk there again—and it must certainly be long ere I would. And I love that spot so! I do not believe that a day passes on which I do not think of it and long for it.

We had a long-to-be-remembered drive to Park Corner that evening. We went around by the Campbeltown road—a much longer way but very beautiful. I enjoyed every moment of that drive.

Lover's Lane

On Tuesday, June 27, I went to town to say good-bye to Bertie, who was going west for her vacation. We spent a rather sorrowful night together—the last for a long while of all our many pleasant nights and talks. It seemed to me that I could *not* endure any further rending of old ties. Could all that a new life had to offer me compensate for the things the old life took in its going?

++*Park Corner, P.E.I.*
Sunday, July 2, 1911

This evening Frede and I took a walk to the shore. It was very beautiful there. I looked afar out over the blue gulf and tried to realize that a week from then I would be somewhere out there in the "Megantic"—the old life left behind forever. But I could not realize it—it seemed like a fantastic dream.

Park Corner shore

---

1. The baby was named Doris; the Stirlings would later have a son named Ian.

The last fortnight before my marriage was an intensely busy one. There were a thousand and one things to do and every day seemed hotter than the last.

Ewan came Tuesday night. The marriage was to take place next day, Wednesday, July 5th, at noon. That night I did two things I had never exactly pictured myself as doing the night before my wedding day. I cried for a little while after I went to bed—and then I slept soundly the rest of the night!

I hardly know why I cried. I was not unhappy. I was quite contented. I think I wept a lost dream—a dream that could never be fulfilled—a girl's dream of the lover who should be her perfect mate, to whom she might splendidly give herself with no reservations. We all dream that dream. And when we surrender it unfulfilled we feel that something wild and sweet and unutterable has gone out of life!

As for the sound sleep—well, I once thought I'd never sleep a wink on the night before my wedding day. I expected I would be too tremendously excited—too tremulously happy. But that went with the dream. I was just contented. Contentment doesn't keep you awake—but it isn't such a bad bed fellow! It was much better than the bitter loneliness and unhappiness which had often shared my pillow.

Yes, I was content.

The morning of July 5th was cool and gray, threatening rain. But it did not rain and in the evening it cleared up beautifully. Mr. Stirling came over to marry us. I was very sorry that Margaret could not come also. I had not many guests—just Aunt Emily, her son Jimmy and daughter Charlotte, Aunt Mary Montgomery and Cuthbert, Mr. and Mrs. Wm. Ramsay (Uncle John Campbell's next-door neighbors and great friends), Aunt Margaret Sutherland, Marian and Leigh, Bruce and Vivian Howatt. As I stood dressed in my room and heard the guests arriving I thought sadly of one guest who should have been there—whom I had always dreamed of having with me when I was married—who would have been so glad to be there but who, instead of helping to robe me for my bridal, was sleeping in Cavendish graveyard, her once so-busy,

House where I was married

Room where I was married, standing before the mantel

helpful hands folded on her breast. Poor Tillie! If she could only have been at my wedding.

I wore my white dress and veil and Ewan's present—a necklace of amethysts and pearls. My bouquet was of white roses and lilies of the valley. At twelve Uncle John took me down, while Stella and the Howatts sang "The Voice that Breathed o'er Eden."[1] In a few minutes the ceremony was over and they were calling me "Mrs. Macdonald"—something I haven't quite got used to even yet, by the way. It always gives me an odd feeling to be called "Mrs. Macdonald." I have to remind myself mentally that it is I that is being spoken to. Somehow, I felt sorry at giving up my old name—the name of my father, the name linked with the experiences of a lifetime, the name under which I have won my success. To be sure, I shall always keep it in literature. But there will be a difference.

Montgomery-McDonald

The marriage of Miss Lucy Maud Montgomery to the Rev. Ewen McDonald, pastor of St. Paul's Presbyterian Church, Leaskdale, Ontario, was solemnized at the home of the bride's uncle and aunt Mr. and Mrs. John Campbell, Park Corner, P. E. Island on Wednesday July 5th. At twelve o'clock the bridal party entered the parlor while "the voice that breathed o'er Eden" was being sung. The marriage ceremony was performed by the Rev. John Stirling of Cavendish, P. E. Island. The bride who was unattended was gowned in ivory silk crepe de chene and lace with tunic of chiffon and pearl and crystal furniture. She wore a tulle veil with coronet of orange blossoms, and a pearl and amethyst necklace, the gift of the groom and carried a bouquet of white roses, lilies of the valley and maiden hair fern.

Many beautiful wedding gifts were received among which was a silver tea service presented to Mrs. McDonald by the Cavendish Presbyterian Church in which she had been a worker for many years.

In the afternoon Mr. and Mrs. McDonald left for Montreal whence they will sail on the White Star liner Megantic for a three months tour in England and Scotland. The bride travelled in a suit of steel gray serge with chiffon blouse and hat to match of steel gray braid trimmed with satin rosebuds.

I have always liked the name Montgomery. It has a stately sound which pleases me. The name is French. Originally the Montgomerys came from France, where the old Chateau de Montgommerie still exists. There is a Sir Roger Montgomery on the roll of Battle Abbey. Several Montgommeries came over to Scotland in the train of a French princess who married a Scottish King. They settled there and eventually became so "Scotticized" that they had a tartan of their own. The Earls of Eglinton are Montgomerys and it has always been a tradition in our family that we are descended from a cadet of the house of Eglinton but we have no papers to prove it. When Grandfather Montgomery was a young man and a member of the P.E. Island Legislature the governor of the Island was the Earl of Westmoreland, whose wife fell in love with grandfather and made no bones of showing it. She told him she was attracted to him by his astonishing resemblance to the then Earl of Eglinton, who had been her lover at one time. Something had come between them and she eventually married the Earl of Westmoreland. Also I have heard Aunt Mary McIntyre tell that once in some city Grandfather was greeted by a young man as "Uncle." The young man was a stranger and it turned out that he had taken Grandfather for his uncle, the Earl of Eglinton. So there is likely something in the story of our descent from that house.

---

1. An 1857 hymn by John Keble (1792–1866) about "that primal wedding day."

I was named Lucy after Grandmother and Maud after Queen Victoria's daughter, the Princess of Hesse, who died about that time I think. I never liked Lucy as a name. I always liked Maud—spelled *not* "with an e, if you please"—but I do *not* like it in connection with Montgomery. "Maud Montgomery" has always seemed to me a disagreeable combination—why, I can't explain. I like "Maud Macdonald" much better.

After the ceremony we had dinner. That dinner made history in Park Corner I believe. "Gad, they never had the like of this at Government House," gasped old William Ramsay to Stell. It was certainly a memorable repast. Frede was just home from Household Science at Macdonald and she "did herself proud" to produce a menu that should reflect lustre on her college, and training. Not that the Park Corner *cuisine* could not stand on its own merits. But Frede had all the latest frills of decoration and serving and it was the smartest repast I have seen anywhere.

And I shall always think mournfully of that dinner—for I could not eat a morsel of it. In vain I tried to choke down a few mouthfuls. I could not.

I had been feeling contented all the morning. I had gone through the ceremony and the congratulations unflustered and unregretful. And now, when it was all over and I found myself sitting there by my husband's side—*my husband!*—I felt a sudden horrible inrush of *rebellion* and *despair*. I *wanted to be free!* I felt like a prisoner—a hopeless prisoner. Something in me—something wild and free and untamed—something that Ewan had not tamed—could never tame—something that did not acknowledge him as master—rose up in one frantic protest against the fetters which bound me. At that moment if I could have torn the wedding ring from my finger and so freed myself I would have done it! But it was too late—and the realization that it was too late fell over me like a black cloud of wretchedness. I sat at that gay bridal feast, in my white veil and orange blossoms, beside the man I had married—and I was as unhappy as I had ever been in my life.

Kensington Station

That mood passed. By the time I was ready for going-away it had vanished completely and I was again my contented self. We left at four o'clock for Kensington. The sun came out gloriously and we had a very pleasant drive. Frede, Stella, Mrs. Stirling, Marian and one or two of the others went to Kensington with us. We stayed all night in at the Clifton House in Summerside and crossed on the boat the next morning to Pointe du Chene, where we took the train to Montreal. The day was very hot and fatiguing. By evening I was dreadfully tired—and once again that mood of the dinner table returned. Once again I felt fettered, rebellious, wretched—once again that untamed part of me flamed up in protest—and then subsided—forever. I never had any return of that mood, thank God. If it had lasted I would have killed myself. It was a curious psychological experience which I shudder to recall. Never did I reach a blacker depth of despair and futile rebellion than in those two moods. It was so dreadful that it *could not* last. Either I must conquer it or die. I conquered it—thrust it down—smothered it—buried it. Whether dead or quiescent it has not troubled me since.

We reached Montreal on Friday morning and that evening went on board the *Megantic*—a White Star liner and a very nice boat. When we wakened the next morning we were sailing up the St. Lawrence.

On the deck of the Megantic

I had been dreading sea-sickness but we had a very fine voyage. I was never seasick for a moment and I enjoyed the trip over very much. The novelty of life on a big ocean liner was very pleasant. The scenery up the St. Lawrence is beautiful. We did not get out into the gulf until Sunday. The days were all fine and bright, the sea calm and blue. On Monday we saw several ice bergs but were not near enough to them to get a really good view.

Our table-mates were five gentlemen—four of them being young business men going over to England for their firms. They were all agreeable and we used to have very interesting conversations at dinner.

We expected to get to Liverpool on Saturday afternoon and planned to pack up Saturday morning. But, happening to waken Friday night at about one o'clock and not being able to sleep again, owing to the unholy noise the sailors were making on deck, we decided to get up and pack, so as to have Saturday morning for rest. So it happened that on looking out of the port-hole I saw the first sign of the old

Ewan and our seatmates at table

world—a flashing revolving light on the Irish coast. It gave me a "thrill." It was really worth getting up at midnight for.

Saturday morning we saw and sailed by the "Calf of Man"—at which I gazed with considerable interest because of Caine's "Manxman."[1] From one until three Saturday afternoon we were sailing up the Mersey between the famous Liverpool docks. They were interesting but not at all beautiful. We had hoped to get in in time to catch the train to Glasgow but we could not get through the turmoil of the Customs in time so had to stay until Monday in Liverpool. We went to a hotel and when I got to my room I suddenly realized how tired I was. A very wave of utter weariness submerged me. The preceding sleepless night, the excitement of the day, the worry and confusion of the Custom House, all took effect at once. And I was homesick—suddenly, wretchedly, unmitigatedly homesick!

Up to this time I had not been once homesick since leaving Park Corner. The novelty and excitement of the voyage across had prevented that. Amid a constant series of new impressions there was no time or chance for the old to make themselves felt. But now in my physical collapse, homesickness came. I wanted Cavendish—Lover's Lane—Park Corner—the girls—and I was thousands of miles away from them, with a waste of ocean between us! I would have dissolved into a fit of crying—but one thing saved me. In the hall outside my room I found a pussy cat—a big black pussy cat—a most friendly pussy cat, who allowed me to take her up in my arms and cuddle her. I thought of poor gray Daffy, far, far behind in Canada and I was comforted. I went down to tea and the "crying" feeling passed away. But I was so tired that night I couldn't sleep for a long time. I lay there, a stranger in a strange land,[2] and thought of a thousand things. […]

---

1. In 1898 LMM had first recorded reading this 1894 novel by Hall Caine.

2. Echo of Exodus, 1:22.

Illustrations

Index

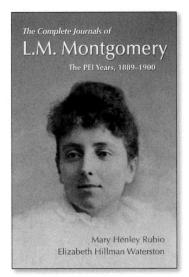

The Complete Journals
of L.M. Montgomery
The PEI Years, 1889–1900

MARY HENLEY RUBIO
ELIZABETH HILLMAN WATERSTON

"Reading these pages and examining the teenaged Montgomery's photographs, we are given a full and intimate look into the development of an astonishingly gifted young writer's life and work." —Jane Urquhart

L.M. Montgomery had begun keeping a private journal before she turned fifteen. In this precursor to *The Complete Journals of L.M. Montgomery: The PEI Years, 1901–1911*, we are introduced to the young Montgomery. The unabridged journals reveal for the first time new sides of this complex and profound personality: a teenage girl becoming aware of her sexuality; a young writer developing as an artist; and a woman suffering from incipient instability, foreshadowing a lifetime of despair.

Hardcover | 496 pages | 6 x 9" | 9780199002108